AIA MONOGRAPH NEW SERIES 2
AND
HESPERIA SUPPLEMENT XXVI

THE SANCTUARY OF ATHENA NIKE IN ATHENS

ARCHITECTURAL STAGES AND CHRONOLOGY

BY

IRA S. MARK

THE ARCHAEOLOGICAL INSTITUTE OF AMERICA
AND
THE AMERICAN SCHOOL OF CLASSICAL STUDIES AT ATHENS

THE AMERICAN SCHOOL OF CLASSICAL STUDIES AT ATHENS
PRINCETON, NEW JERSEY
1993

Library of Congress Cataloguing-in-Publication Data
Mark, Ira S., 1947–
The Sanctuary of Athena Nike in Athens : architectural stages and chronology / by Ira S. Mark
p. cm. — (AIA monograph new series ; 2) (Hesperia. Supplement ; 26)
Includes bibliographical references and index.
ISBN 0-87661-526-4
1. Temple of Athena Nike (Athens, Greece) 2. Athens (Greece)–Buildings, structures, etc. I. Title. II. Series III. Series
Hesperia (Princeton, N.J.). Supplement ; 26.
NA283.T35M37 1993
726′.1208′09385—dc20 93-37431
CIP
r93

TYPOGRAPHY BY THE AMERICAN SCHOOL OF CLASSICAL STUDIES PUBLICATIONS OFFICE
C/O INSTITUTE FOR ADVANCED STUDY, PRINCETON, NEW JERSEY
PLATES BY THE STINEHOUR PRESS, LUNENBURG, VERMONT
PRINTED IN THE UNITED STATES OF AMERICA
BY THE JOHN D. LUCAS PRINTING COMPANY, BALTIMORE, MARYLAND

INTRODUCTORY STATEMENT

In 1988 the Archaeological Institute of America and the American School of Classical Studies at Athens agreed jointly to publish Ira Mark's *The Sanctuary of Athena Nike: Architectural Stages and Chronology*. This coöperation gave both institutions the opportunity to contribute to a monograph that illuminates key aspects of the history of this complex and important Athenian sanctuary. The Institute undertook to edit Dr. Mark's manuscript, and the School assumed responsibility for its production.

With the appearance of the monograph as AIA Monograph New Series 2 and *Hesperia* Supplement XXVI, we bring this project to completion. We hope that this work will add significant new insights and spark renewed debate on the subject.

MACHTELD J. MELLINK
CHAIR, PUBLICATIONS COMMITTEE
Archaeological Institute of America
1987–1990

JAMES R. McCREDIE
CHAIRMAN, MANAGING COMMITTEE
American School of Classical Studies at Athens
1980–1990

PREFACE

My research on the Sanctuary of Athena Nike spans two main periods in my schooling and career. I first became interested in the cult-site as a graduate student at work on my dissertation. My topic was the representation of Nike (Victory) on the Akropolis, a study that encompassed Archaic and Classical votive statuary, bronze vessel attachments, architectural sculptures (particularly, the Parthenon sculptures), and the Nike Parapet. As I pursued my work, I became more and more intrigued by the relation of Nike and Athena Nike, Winged and Wingless Victory, and I made a special attempt to clarify that relation through a closer investigation of the history of the Nike Bastion and the Athena Nike cult. The resulting doctoral study, "Nike and the Cult of Athena Nike on the Athenian Acropolis," was submitted to the Institute of Fine Arts, New York University, in 1979.

Midway in my doctoral research I became aware of a body of notes and plans that to that point had hardly been made use of. These papers, preserved in the archives of the Archaeological Society of Athens, pertain to the major restoration of the Nike Bastion undertaken from 1935 to 1939 by Nikolaos Balanos, then director of the Restoration and Preservation of the Akropolis Monuments. I had at that time neither permission nor, I felt, sufficient background to edit the Nike Bastion papers in full, but their importance was nonetheless unmistakable.

A year's leave from teaching in 1982–1983 allowed me to return to Athens: my aim was to thoroughly examine and publish Balanos' bastion papers and, in the light of these records, to reexamine the remains on the bastion itself. The present study is the result.

I am very mindful of the trust and confidence put in me by my seniors. James R. McCredie was Director of the American School of Classical Studies at Athens when I began this study as a gradudate student. It was he who made me aware of Balanos' papers, and as my teacher, he repeatedly helped sharpen my thinking on the complex problems of archaeological interpretation that their study entailed. Stephen G. Miller, Director of the American School at my return to Athens in 1982, was also highly instrumental in securing me permission to publish the Balanos papers. This study would have been impossible without their support.

As indispensable as the School's support was the sincere and generous cooperation of Greek colleagues. I owe a great debt of gratitude to Anastasios Orlandos and George Mylonas, successive Secretaries General of the Archaeological Society of Athens. They took the unusual and very generous step of opening previously unedited papers to a nonmember of the Society. I am very grateful as well to the successive Ephors of the Akropolis during my period of study, George Dontas and Evi Touloupa. With their permission, I studied and surveyed the remains of the early bastion, first in 1976 and again in 1982.

In an earlier publication I acknowledged the fellowship support that I received as a graduate student. I am grateful for a Fellowship for Independent Study and Research awarded by the National Endowment for the Humanities for 1982–1983. That fellowship allowed me to research and to begin writing this study.

I had the help of a great number of friends and associates at various stages in the preparation of this work. Craig A. Mauzy did the photographs, both of the Balanos drawings and of the early remains from the site. The late William B. Dinsmoor, Jr. and Frederick A. Cooper helped me to take levels on the bastion. I benefited from repeated discussions with Evelyn B. Harrison, who shared with me her then unpublished research on the chronology of Attic sculpture. Gerald Lalonde went with me to the Epigraphical Museum on a number of occasions to look at inscriptions. Balanos' idiosyncratic and nearly illegible handwriting (Appendix A) was transcribed for me by Demetra Photiadis. Anna S. Benjamin prepared an initial translation from Mimi's transcription. Last, I collaborated with Karlene Friedman on the drawings: I prepared the initial drawings in pencil; she prepared the inked version with added labels and numbers.

I know that I must have forgotten many who had a hand in this work. The following come to mind for their unusual kindness or generosity: John McK. Camp II and Susan I. Rotroff, for discussing Agora chronology with me and looking through relevant Agora pottery lots; Manolis Korres, for his attempt, unsuccessful in the end, to find more documentation on the Balanos excavations; Margaret M. Miles, for allowing me to read her then unpublished article on the Temple of Nemesis at Rhamnous; Homer A. Thompson, for reading and commenting on my work in manuscript; and Nancy A. Winter, who repeatedly seemed to think of things that I had not, both scholarly and practical.

There is scaffolding on the Nike Temple as I write this. The third restoration of the site is now under way. I feel it is appropriate that this study, centered on the second restoration of the site, should appear when it does. There is still much to learn about the Nike Bastion. I hope that my review and discussion of the second project may be an aid in work to come.

IRA S. MARK

NEW YORK CITY
August 1992*

* I have attempted to include all relevant bibliography for the study up to 1988, the year the manuscript was accepted for publication. A few more recent titles have been added in the notes.

CONTENTS

ILLUSTRATIONS

Unless otherwise indicated, all drawings were prepared by the author and inked by Karlene Friedman.

FIGURES

Plates

ABBREVIATIONS AND BIBLIOGRAPHY

AA = *Archäologischer Anzeiger*
AAA= *Athens Annals of Archaeology* (Ἀρχαιολογικὰ ἀνάλεκτα ἐξ Ἀθηνῶν)
AcrM = Akropolis Museum, Athens
Agora XIV = H. A. Thompson and R. E. Wycherley, *The Athenian Agora*, XIV, *The Agora of Athens*, Princeton 1972
AJA = *American Journal of Archaeology*
AJAH = *American Journal of Ancient History*
AJP = *American Journal of Philology*
AnnPisa = *Annali della Scuola Normale Superiore di Pisa*
AntK = *Antike Kunst*
AntP = *Antike Plastik*, W.-H. Schuchhardt and F. Eckstein, eds., Berlin, 1962–
ARV^2 = J. D. Beazley, *Attic Red-Figure Vase-Painters*, 2nd ed., Oxford 1963
ΑρχΕφ = Ἀρχαιολογικὴ Ἐφημερίς
AthMitt = *Mitteilungen des deutschen archäologischen Instituts, Athenische Abteilung*
AZ = *Archäologische Zeitung*
BABesch = *Bulletin antieke beschaving*. Annual Papers on Classical Archaeology
Balanos, N. 1956. «Ἡ νέα ἀναστήλωσις τοῦ ναοῦ τῆς Ἀθηνᾶς Νίκης (1935–1939)», ΑρχΕφ 1937, Part 3 [1956], pp. 776–807
Bancroft, S. 1979. "Problems concerning the Archaic Acropolis at Athens" (diss. Princeton University 1979)
Bates, W. N. 1901. "Notes on the Old Temple of Athena on the Acropolis," *HSCP* 12, pp. 319–326
BCH = *Bulletin de correspondance hellénique*
Benndorf, O. 1879. *Über das Cultusbild der Athena Nike*, Vienna
Bennett, F. M. 1917. "A Study of the Word Ξόανον," *AJA* 21, pp. 8–21
Bergquist, B. 1967. *The Archaic Greek Temenos* (*Skrifter Utgivna av Svenska Institutet i Athen*, 4th ser., XIII), Lund
Binnebössel, R. 1932. "Studien zu den attischen Urkundenreliefs" (diss. Leipzig 1932)
Blegen, E. P. 1936. "News Items from Athens," *AJA* 40, pp. 145–153 (especially pp. 145–147), 262–270 (especially p. 262)
———. 1940. "News Items from Athens," *AJA* 44, pp. 537–542 (especially p. 537)
Blümel, C. 1923. *Der Fries des Tempels der Athena Nike*, Berlin
———. 1950–1951. "Der Fries des Tempels der Athena Nike in der attischen Kunst des fünften Jahrhunderts vor Christus," *JdI* 65–66, pp. 135–165
BM = British Museum, London
Bockelberg, S. von. 1979. "Die Friese des Hephaisteion," *AntP* 18, pp. 23–50
Boegehold, A. L. 1969. "The Preamble of the Early Athena Nike Decree," in *Classical Studies Presented to Ben Edwin Perry* (*Illinois Studies in Language and Literature* 58), Urbana, Ill., pp. 175–180
Boersma, J. S. 1970. *Athenian Building Policy from 561/0 to 405/4 B.C.* (*Scripta Archaeologica Groningana* 4), Groningen
Bötticher, K. 1864. "Ergänzungen zu den letzen Untersuchungen auf des Akropolis in Athen. I. Über die Thymele des Niketempels," *Philologus* 21, pp. 41–72
———. 1880. *Thymele der Athena-Nike auf der Akropolis von Athen*, Berlin
Bohn, R. 1880a. "Bericht über die Ausgrabungen auf der Akropolis zu Athen im Frühjahr 1880, I," *AthMitt* 5, pp. 259–267
———. 1880b. "Zum Nike-Pyrgos," *AZ* 38, pp. 85–91
———. 1882. *Die Propylaeen der Akropolis zu Athen*, Berlin
Boulter, P. N. 1969. "The Akroteria of the Nike Temple," *Hesperia* 38, pp. 133–140
———. 1970. "The Frieze of the Erechtheion," *AntP* 10, pp. 7–28

Brommer, F. 1963. *Die Skulpturen der Parthenon-Giebel: Katalog und Untersuchung*, Mainz am Rhein

———. 1977. *Der Parthenonfries: Katalog und Untersuchung*, Mainz am Rhein

———. 1979. *Die Parthenon-Skulpturen: Metopen, Fries, Giebel, Kultbild*, Mainz am Rhein

Brouskari, M. S. 1974. *The Acropolis Museum: A Descriptive Catalogue*, Athens

BSA = *Annual of the British School at Athens*

Büsing, H. 1970. *Die griechische Halbsäule*, Wiesbaden

———. 1990. "Zur Bemalung des Nike-Tempels," *AA* (*JdI* 105), pp. 71–76

Bundgård, J. A. 1957. *Mnesicles*, Copenhagen

———. 1974a. *The Excavation of the Athenian Acropolis, 1882–1890*, Copenhagen

———. 1974b. "Le sujet de *IG* I^2, 24," in *Mélanges helléniques offerts à Georges Daux*, Paris, pp. 43–49

———. 1976. *Parthenon and the Mycenaean City on the Heights*, Copenhagen

Burford, A. 1963. "The Builders of the Parthenon," *Parthenos and Parthenon* (*Greece and Rome* Supplement to vol. 10), Oxford, pp. 23–35

Burkert, W. 1985. *Greek Religion: Archaic and Classical* [Griechische Religion der archaischen und klassischen Epoche], trans. by J. Raffan, Cambridge, Mass.

Buschor, E. 1929–1933. *Die Tondächer der Akropolis*, Berlin

———. 1930. "Heraion von Samos: Frühe Bauten," *AthMitt* 55, pp. 1–99

Carpenter, R. 1929. *The Sculpture of the Nike Temple Parapet*, Cambridge, Mass.

———1970. *The Architects of the Parthenon*, Harmondsworth

Childs, W. A. P. 1985. "In Defense of an Early Date for the Frieze of the Temple on the Ilissos," *AthMitt* 100, pp. 207–251

Clairmont, C. W. 1979. "The Lekythos of Myrrhine," in *Studies in Classical Art and Archaeology: A Tribute to Peter Heinrich von Blanckenhagen*, G. Kopcke and M. Moore, eds., Locust Valley, N.Y., pp. 103–110

Connor, W. R. 1968. *Theopompus and Fifth-Century Athens*, Washington, D.C.

Coulton, J. J. 1977. *Ancient Greek Architects at Work: Problems of Structure and Design*, Ithaca

———1984. "The Parthenon and Periklean Doric," in *Parthenon-Kongress, Basel, Referate und Berichte* I (pp. 40–44), II (pp. 368–369), Mainz

CR = *Classical Review*

Crosby, M. 1949. "The Altar of the Twelve Gods in Athens," in *Commemorative Studies in Honor of Theodore Leslie Shear* (*Hesperia* Supplement 8), Princeton, pp. 82–103

Daly, L. W. 1953. "Nike and Athena Nike," in *Studies Presented to David M. Robinson* II, G. E. Mylonas and D. Raymond, eds., St. Louis, pp. 1124–1128

Delivorrias, A. 1974. *Attische Giebelskulpturen und Akrotere des fünften Jahrhunderts*, Tübingen

Délos XII = F. Courby, *Les temples d'Apollon* (*Exploration archéologique de Délos* XII, i), Paris 1931

Délos XXIV = H. Gallet de Santerre, *La Terrasse des Lions, le Létoon, et le Monument de Granit* (*Exploration archéologique de Délos* XXIV), Paris 1959

Δελτ = Ἀρχαιολογικὸν Δελτίον

Despinis, G. I. 1971. Συμβολὴ στὴ μελέτη τοῦ ἔργου τοῦ Ἀγορακρίτου, Athens

———. 1974. «Τὰ γλυπτὰ τῶν ἀετωμάτων τοῦ ναοῦ τῆς Ἀθηνᾶς Νίκης», Δελτ 29, 1974, Α′ [1977], pp. 8–24

Dinsmoor, W. B. 1913. "Studies of the Delphian Treasuries II: The Four Ionic Treasuries," *BCH* 37, pp. 5–83

———. 1921. "Attic Building Accounts, V," *AJA* 25, pp. 233–247

———. 1923. "The Inscriptions of Athena Nike," *AJA* 27, pp. 318–321

———. 1926. "The Sculptured Parapet of Athena Nike," *AJA* 30, pp. 1–31

———. 1930. "The Nike Parapet Once More," *AJA* 34, pp. 281–295

———. 1939. "Archaeology and Astronomy," *ProcAmPhilSoc* 80, pp. 95–173

———. 1941. *Observations on the Hephaisteion* (*Hesperia* Supplement 5), Princeton

———. 1950. *The Architecture of Ancient Greece*, 3rd ed., London

Dinsmoor, W. B., Jr. 1971. *Sounion*, Athens

———. 1980. *The Propylaia to the Athenian Akropolis*, I, *The Predecessors*, Princeton

———. 1982. "The Asymmetry of the Pinakotheke–For the Last Time?" in *Studies in Athenian Architecture, Sculpture, and Topography Presented to Homer A. Thompson* (*Hesperia* Supplement 20), Princeton, pp. 18–33

Dörpfeld, W. 1885. "Die Propyläen der Akropolis von Athen. I: Das ursprüngliche Project des Mnesikles," *AthMitt* 10, pp. 38–56
———. 1902. "Die Zeit des älteren Parthenon," *AthMitt* 27, pp. 379–416
———. 1919. "Das Hekatompedon in Athen," *JdI* 34, pp. 9–25
Dohrn, T. 1957. *Attische Plastik vom Tode des Phidias bis zum Wirken der grossen Meister des IV. Jahrhunderts v. Chr.*, Krefeld
Donohue, A. A. 1988. *Xoana and the Origins of Greek Sculpture*, Atlanta
Ebert, F. 1910. *Fachausdrücke des griechischen Bauhandwerks*, I, *Der Tempel*, Würzburg
EM = Epigraphical Museum, Athens
Ἔργον = Τὸ Ἔργον τῆς ἐν Ἀθήναις Ἀρχαιολογικῆς Ἑταιρείας
Farnell, L. R. 1896–1909. *The Cults of the Greek States*, Oxford
Feaver, D. D. 1957. "The Historical Development of the Priesthoods of Athens," *YCS* 15, pp. 121–158
Felten, F. 1984. *Griechische tektonische Friese archaischer und klassischer Zeit*, Waldsassen
Floren, J. 1987. *Die griechische Plastik*, I, *Die geometrische und archaische Plastik* (*Handbuch der Archäologie*), Munich
Frazer, J. G. 1898. *Pausanias's Description of Greece*, trans. with commentary by J. G. Frazer, New York
French, E. 1971. "The Development of Mycenaean Terracotta Figurines," *BSA* 66, pp. 101–187
Fuchs, W. 1983. *Die Skulptur der Griechen*, 3rd ed., Munich
Furtwängler, A. 1893. *Meisterwerke der griechischen Plastik*, Leipzig
———. 1898. "Zu den Tempeln der Akropolis von Athen," *Sitzungsberichte der philosophische-philologischen und der historischen Classe der k. b. Akademie der Wissenschaften zu München* I, Munich, pp. 349–390
———. 1906. *Aegina: Das Heiligtum der Aphaia*, Munich
Gallet de Santerre, H., and J. Tréheux. 1947–1948. "Rapport sur le dépôt égéen et géométrique de l'Artémision à Délos," *BCH* 71–72, pp. 148–254
Garland, R. S. J. 1984. "Religious Authority in Archaic and Classical Athens," *BSA* 79, pp. 75–123
Giuliano, A. 1982. "Politische Tendenzen und Arbeitseinsatz bei der Errichtung öffentlicher Gebäude in Athen in der 2. Hälfte des 5. Jhs. v. Chr.," in *Palast und Hütte*, D. Papenfuss and V. Strocka, eds., Mainz am Rhein, pp. 325–332
Gomme, A. W. 1945. *A Historical Commentary on Thucydides* I, Oxford
———. 1956. *A Historical Commentary on Thucydides* II, Oxford
Goulaki, A. 1981. "Klassische und klassizistische Nikedarstellungen" (diss. University of Bonn 1981)
GRBS = *Greek, Roman and Byzantine Studies*
Gruben, G. 1976. *Die Tempel der Griechen*, 2nd ed., Munich
Habicht, C. 1985. *Pausanias' Guide to Ancient Greece*, Berkeley
Hamdorf, F. W. 1964. *Griechische Kultpersonifikationen der vorhellenistischen Zeit*, Mainz
Harrison, E. B. 1970. "Notes on the Nike Temple Frieze," *AJA* 74, pp. 317–323
———. 1972a. "A New Fragment from the North Frieze of the Nike Temple," *AJA* 76, pp. 195–197
———. 1972b. "The South Frieze of the Nike Temple and the Marathon Painting in the Painted Stoa," *AJA* 76, pp. 353–378
———. 1977. "Alkamenes' Sculptures from the Hephaisteion," *AJA* 81, "Part I: The Cult Statue," pp. 137–178; "Part II: The Base," pp. 265–287; "Part III: Iconography and Style," pp. 411–428
———. 1982. "A Classical Maiden from the Athenian Agora,"in *Studies in Athenian Architecture, Sculpture, and Topography Presented to Homer A. Thompson* (*Hesperia* Supplement 20), Princeton, pp. 40–53
———. 1988. "Style Phases in Greek Sculpture from 450 to 370 B.C.," Πρακτικὰ τοῦ XII Διεθνοῦς Συνεδρίου Κλασικῆς Ἀρχαιολογίας III, Athens, pp. 99–105
Heberdey, R. 1919. *Altattische Porosskulptur*, Vienna
Herz, N. 1954–1955. "Geology of the Building Stones of Ancient Greece," *Transactions of the New York Academy of Sciences*, ser. 2, 17, pp. 499–505
Hicks, E. L., and G. F. Hill, 1901. *A Manual of Greek Historical Inscriptions*, 2nd ed., Oxford
Higgins, R. A. 1967. *Greek Terracottas*, London
Hiller, F. 1971. *Formgeschichtliche Untersuchungen zur griechischen Statue des späten 5. Jahrhunderts v. Chr.*, Mainz am Rhein
Hock, G. 1905. *Griechische Weihegebräuche*, Würzburg

Hogarth, D. 1908. *Excavations at Ephesus*, London

Holland, L. B. 1924. "Erechtheum Papers, I," *AJA* 28, pp. 1–23

HSCP = *Harvard Studies in Classical Philology*

Iakovidis, S. E. 1962. Ἡ Μυκηναϊκὴ ἀκρόπολις τῶν Ἀθηνῶν, Athens

———. 1983. *Late Helladic Citadels on Mainland Greece* (*Monumenta Graeca et Romana* 4), Leiden

IG I² = *Inscriptiones Graecae*, I, *Inscriptiones Atticae Euclidis anno anteriores*, 2nd ed., ed. F. Hiller von Gaertringen, Berlin 1924

IG I³ = *Inscriptiones Graecae*, I, i, *Inscriptiones Atticae Euclidis anno anteriores*, 3rd ed., ed. D. M. Lewis, Berlin 1981

IG II² = *Inscriptiones Graecae*, II/III, *Inscriptiones Atticae Euclidis anno posteriores*, 2nd ed., ed. J. Kirchner, Berlin 1913–1940

IG IV² = *Inscriptiones Graecae*, IV, i, *Inscriptiones Epidauri*, 2nd ed., Berlin 1929

IG XI = *Inscriptiones Graecae*, XI, ii, iv, *Inscriptiones Deli*, Berlin 1912–1914

IG XII = *Inscriptiones Graecae*, XII, *Inscriptiones maris Aegeai praeter Delum*, Berlin 1895–

IstForsch = *Istanbuler Forschungen*

IstMitt = *Mitteilungen des deutschen archäologischen Instituts, Abteilung Istanbul*

Jacob-Felsch, M. 1969. *Die Entwicklung griechischer Statuenbasen und die Aufstellung der Statuen*, Waldsassen/Bayern

Jacoby, *FGrHist* = F. Jacoby, *Die Fragmente der griechischen Historiker*, Berlin 1926–1958

JdI = *Jahrbuch des deutschen archäologischen Instituts*

Jeffery, L. 1980. "Some Nike-Statues at Olympia in the Late Fifth Century B.C." in Φιλίας Χάριν (Festschrift E. Manni) IV, Rome, pp. 1237–1238

JHS = *Journal of Hellenic Studies*

JOAI = *Jahreshefte der österreichischen archäologischen Instituts in Wien*

Judeich, W. 1931. *Topographie von Athen*, 2nd ed. (*Handbuch der Altertumswissenschaft* 3.2.2), Munich

Julius, L. 1876. "Über den Südflügel der Propyläen und den Tempel der Athena Nike zu Athen," *AthMitt* 1, pp. 216–228

Jung, H. 1982. *Thronende und sitzende Götter*, Bonn

Kakridis, I. T. 1952–1953. «Παρατηρήσεις σὲ ἀρχαῖα ἐπιγράμματα», Ἑλληνικά 12, pp. 143–145

Kalpaxis, T. E. 1986. *Hemiteles: Akzidentelle Unfertigkeit und 'Bossen-Stil' in der griechischen Baukunst*, Mainz am Rhein

Kardara, C. 1964. «Γλαυκῶπις—Ὁ Ἀρχαῖος Ναὸς καὶ τὸ θέμα τῆς ζῳφόρου τοῦ Παρθενῶνος», ΑρχΕφ 1961 [1964], pp. 61–158

———1965. «Πυκινὸς δόμος καὶ παναθηναϊκὸς πέπλος», ΑρχΕφ 1960 [1965], pp. 165–202

Karo, G. 1936. "Archäologische Funde vom Sommer 1935 bis Sommer 1936," *AA* (*JdI* 51), cols. 94–181

Kavvadias, P. 1897. «Περὶ τοῦ ναοῦ τῆς Ἀπτέρου Νίκης κατ' ἐπιγραφὴν ἐκ τῆς Ἀκροπόλεως», ΑρχΕφ, cols. 173–194

Kavvadias, P., and G. Kawerau. 1906. *Die Ausgrabung der Akropolis vom Jahre 1885 bis zum Jahre 1890*, Athens

Kirchner, J. 1901–1903. *Prosopographica attica* I (1901), II (1903), Berlin

Knell, H. 1979. *Perikleische Baukunst*, Darmstadt

Körte, A. 1910. "Zur Athena-Nike Inschrift," *Hermes* 45, pp. 623–627

Köster, A. 1906. "Das Alter des Athena-Niketempels," *JdI* 21, pp. 129–147

Kroll, J. H. 1982. "The Ancient Image of Athena Polias," in *Studies in Athenian Architecture, Sculpture, and Topography Presented to Homer A. Thompson* (*Hesperia* Supplement 20), Princeton, pp. 65–76

Lawton, C. 1984. "Attic Document Reliefs of the Classical and Hellenistic Periods" (diss. Princeton University 1984)

Leake, W. 1821. *The Topography of Athens*, London

Lemerle, P. 1936. "Chronique des fouilles et découvertes archéologiques en Grèce," *BCH* 60, pp. 452–489 (especially pp. 455–459)

———. 1937. "Chronique des fouilles et découvertes archéologiques en Grèce en 1937," *BCH* 61, pp. 441–476 (especially pp. 443–449)

———. 1938. "Chronique des fouilles et découvertes archéologiques en Grèce en 1938," *BCH* 62, pp. 443–483 (especially pp. 448–457)

———. 1939. "Chronique des fouilles et découvertes archéologiques en Grèce en 1939," *BCH* 63, pp. 285–324 (especially pp. 289–294)

Lewis, D. M. 1955. "Notes on Attic Inscriptions (II)," *BSA* 50, pp. 1–36

LIMC = *Lexicon Iconographicum Mythologiae Classicae*, Zurich 1981–

Linfert, A. 1968. "Vier klassische Akrotere," *AA* (*JdI* 83), pp. 427–434

Lippold, G. 1950. *Die griechische Plastik* (*Handbuch der Altertumswissenschaft* 6.3.1), Munich

McCredie, J. R. 1979. "The Architects of the Parthenon," in *Studies in Classical Art and Archaeology: A Tribute to Peter Heinrich von Blanckenhagen*, G. Kopcke and M. Moore, eds., Locust Valley, N.Y., pp. 69–73

Maier, F. G. 1959–1961. *Griechische Mauerbauinschriften*, Heidelberg

Martin, R. 1944–1945. "Chapiteaux ioniques de l'Asclépieion d'Athènes," *BCH* 68–69, pp. 340–374

———. 1965. *Manuel d'architecture grecque*, I, *Matériaux et techniques*, Paris

———. 1976. "L'atelier Ictinos-Callicratès au temple de Bassae," *BCH* 100, pp. 427–442

Mattingly, H. B. 1961. "The Athenian Coinage Decree," *Historia* 10, pp. 148–188

———. 1965. "The Peace of Kallias," *Historia* 14, pp. 273–281

———. 1982. "The Athena Nike Temple Reconsidered," *AJA* 86, pp. 381–385

Meiggs, R. 1966. "The Dating of Fifth-Century Attic Inscriptions," *JHS* 86, pp. 86–98

———. 1972. *The Athenian Empire*, Oxford

Meiggs, R., and D. Lewis. 1969. *A Selection of Greek Historical Inscriptions to the End of the Fifth Century B.C.*, Oxford

Meritt, B. D. 1941. "Notes on Attic Decrees," *Hesperia* 10, pp. 301–337

Meritt, B. D., and G. Davidson. 1935. "The Treaty between Athens and Haliai," *AJP* 56, pp. 65–71

Meritt, B. D., and H. T. Wade-Gery. 1962. "The Dating of Documents to the Mid-Fifth Century, I," *JHS* 82, pp. 100–117

———. 1963. "The Dating of Documents to the Mid-Fifth Century, II," *JHS* 83, pp. 67–74

Meritt, B. D., H. T. Wade-Gery, and M. McGregor. 1949–1953. *Athenian Tribute Lists*, 4 vols., Princeton

MetMusSt = *Metropolitan Museum Studies*

Meyer, M. 1989. *Die griechischen Urkundenreliefs* (*AthMitt* Beiheft 13), Berlin

Middleton, J. H. 1900. *Plans and Drawings of Athenian Buildings* (*JHS Supplementary Papers* 3), London

Miles, M. 1980. "The Date of the Temple on the Ilissos River," *Hesperia* 49, pp. 309–325

———. 1989. "A Reconstruction of the Temple of Nemesis at Rhamnous," *Hesperia* 58, pp. 131–249

MonAnt = *Monumenti antichi*

Mussche, H. 1961. "La forteresse maritime de Thorikos," *BCH* 85, pp. 176–205

———. 1964. "Note sur les fortifications de Sounion," *BCH* 88, pp. 423–432

Mylonas, G. 1966. *Mycenae and the Mycenaean Age*, Princeton

NatM = National Archaeological Museum, Athens

NC = *Numismatic Chronicle*

Nilsson, M. P. 1952. "Kultische Personifikationen," *Eranos* 50, pp. 31–40

———. 1967. *Geschichte der griechischen Religion* I, 3rd ed., Munich

Noack, F. 1927. *Eleusis*, Berlin

Oikonomos, G. P. 1948. «Ἡ ἐπὶ τῆς Ἀκροπόλεως λατρεία τῆς Ἀθηνᾶς Νίκης», ΑρχΕφ 1939–1941 [1948], pp. 97–110

Orlandos, A. K. 1915. "Zum Tempel der Athena Nike," *AthMitt* 40, pp. 27–44

———. 1947–1948. "Nouvelles observations sur la construction du temple d'Athena Nike," *BCH* 71–72, pp. 1–38

———. 1966–1968. *Les matériaux de construction et la technique architecturale des anciens grecs*, Paris

Orlandos, A. K., and J. Travlos. 1986. Λεξικὸν ἀρχαίων ἀρχιτεκτονικῶν ὅρων (Βιβλιοθήκη τῆς ἐν Ἀθήναις Ἀρχαιολογικῆς Ἑταιρείας 94), Athens

Papademetriou, I. 1951. «Αττικά Ι», ΑρχΕφ 1948–1949 [1951], pp. 146–153

Papadopoulos, J. 1980. *Xoana e Sphyrelata: Testimonianza delle fonti scritte*, Rome

Paton, J. M., ed. 1927. *The Erechtheum.* Text by L. D. Caskey, H. N. Fowler, J. M. Paton, and G. P. Stevens, Cambridge, Mass.

Pemberton, E. G. 1972. "The East and West Friezes of the Temple of Athena Nike," *AJA* 76, pp. 303–310

Petrakos, V. 1986. «Προβλήματα της βάσης του αγάλματος της Νεμέσεως», in *Archaische und klassische griechische Plastik* II, H. Kyrieleis, ed., Mainz am Rhein, pp. 89–107

Picard, C. N.d. *L'Acropole: L'enceinte, l'entrée, le bastion d'Athéna Nike, les propylées*, Paris [1929]

Picón, C. A. 1978. "The Ilissos Temple Reconsidered," *AJA* 82, pp. 47–81

Pogorelski, A. 1923. "The New Athenian Stele with Decree and Accounts," *AJA* 27, pp. 314–317

Pogorelski, A., and F. Hiller von Gaertringen. 1922. "Athenische Inschriftstele mit Volksbeschluss und Baurechnung," *Sitzungsberichte der preussischen Akademie der Wissenschaften zu Berlin, Philosophisch-Historische Klasse*, pp. 187–192
Pouilloux, J. 1954. *La forteresse de Rhamnonte*, Paris
Πρακτικά = Πρακτικὰ τῆς ἐν Ἀθήναις Ἀρχαιλογικῆς Ἑταιρείας
ProcAmPhilSoc = *Proceedings of the American Philosophical Society*
Prott, H. von, and L. Ziehen. 1896–1906. *Leges graecorum sacrae e titulis collectae*, Leipzig
Puchstein, O. 1887. *Das ionische Capitell* (*Programm zum Winckelmannsfeste der Archäologischen Gesellschaft zu Berlin* 47), Berlin
RA = *Revue archéologique*
Rahn, P. 1986. "Funeral Memorials of the First Priestess of Athena Nike," *BSA* 81, pp. 195–207
Raubitschek, A. E. 1949. *Dedications from the Athenian Akropolis: A Catalogue of the Inscriptions of the Sixth and Fifth Centuries B.C.*, ed. with the collaboration of L. H. Jeffery, Cambridge, Mass.
RE = *Pauly-Wissowa, Real-Encyclopädie der classischen Altertumswissenschaft*
REG = *Revue des études grecques*
Rhodes, P. J. 1981. *A Commentary on the Aristotelian* Athenaion Politeia, Oxford
Richter, G. M. A. 1968. *Korai: Archaic Greek Maidens*, London
Ridgway, B. S. 1981. *Fifth Century Styles in Greek Sculpture*, Princeton
Riemann, H. 1937. "Archäologische Funde vom Sommer 1936 bis Sommer 1937: Griechenland," *AA* (*JdI* 52), cols. 86–184 (especially col. 92)
Robertson, C. M. 1939. "Archaeology in Greece, 1938-39," *JHS* 59, pp. 189–209 (especially pp. 189–191)
RömMitt = *Mitteilungen des deutschen archäologischen Instituts, Römische Abteilung*
Romano, I. B. 1980. "Early Greek Cult Images" (diss. University of Pennsylvania 1980)
Ross, L. 1855–1856. *Archäologische Aufsätze*, Leipzig
Ross, L., E. Schaubert, and C. Hansen. 1839. *Die Akropolis von Athen nach den neuesten Ausgrabungen*, I, *Der Tempel der Nike Apteros*, Berlin
Schlaifer, R. 1940. "Notes on Athenian Public Cults," *HSCP* 51, pp. 233–260
Schleif, H. 1933. "Der Nikepyrgos und Mnesikles," *JdI* 48, pp. 177–184
Schlörb, B. 1964. *Untersuchungen zur Bildhauergeneration nach Phidias*, Waldsassen
Schrader, H., ed. 1939. *Archaischen Marmorbildwerke der Akropolis*, Frankfurt
Schuchhardt, W.-H. 1963. "Archaische Bauten auf der Akropolis von Athen," *AA* (*JdI* 78), cols. 797–824
Schweitzer, B. 1950. "Mnesikles und die perikleische Planung des Westaufganges zur Akropolis," in *Aus Antike und Orient: Festschrift Wilhelm Schubart zum 75. Geburtstag*, Leipzig, pp. 116–125
Scranton, R. L. 1941. *Greek Walls*, Cambridge, Mass.
SEG = *Supplementum Epigraphicum Graecum*
Shapiro, H. A. 1989. *Art and Cult under the Tyrants in Athens*, Mainz am Rhein
Shear, I. M. 1963. "Kallikrates," *Hesperia* 32, pp. 375–424
Shoe, L. T. 1936. *Profiles of Greek Mouldings*, Cambridge, Mass.
Siewert, P. 1972. *Der Eid von Plataiai* (*Vestigia* 16), Munich
Sikes, E. E. 1895. "Nike and Athena Nike," *CR* 9, pp. 280–283
Simon, E. 1983. *Festivals of Attica*, Madison, Wis.
———. 1988. "Zur Sandalenlöserin der Nikebalustrade," *Kanon* (*Festschrift Ernst Berger, AntK* Beiheft 5), Basel, pp. 69–73
Smith, A. H. 1916. "Lord Elgin and His Collection," *JHS* 36, pp. 163–372
Sokolowski, F. 1969. *Lois sacrées des cités grecques* (*École française d'Athènes. Travaux et mémoires* 11), Paris
Spon, J., and G. Wheler. 1678. *Voyage d'Italie, de Dalmatie, de Grèce, et du Levant fait aux anneés 1675 and 1676*, Amsterdam
Stevens, G. P. 1908. "The Cornice of the Temple of Athena Nike," *AJA* 12, pp. 398–405
———. 1946. "Architectural Studies concerning the Acropolis of Athens," *Hesperia* 15, pp. 73–106
Stewart, A. F. 1986. "History, Myth, and Allegory in the Program of the Temple of Athena Nike, Athens," *Studies in the History of Art* 16, pp. 53–73

Stuart and Revett = James Stuart and Nicholas Revett, *The Antiquities of Athens*, London 1762–1830
Studniczka, F. 1916. "Zu den Friesplatten vom ionischen Tempel am Ilissos," *JdI* 31, pp. 169–230
*Syll.*³ = W. Dittenberger, *Sylloge inscriptionum graecarum*, 3rd ed., Leipzig 1915–1924
Tanoulas, T. 1987. "The Propylaea of the Acropolis at Athens since the Seventeenth Century: Their Decay and Restoration," *JdI* 102, pp. 413–483
TAPA = *Transactions of the American Philological Association*
Tod, M. 1933–1948. *A Selection of Greek Historical Inscriptions*, 2nd ed., Oxford
Travlos, J. 1960. Πολεοδομικὴ ἐξέλιξις τῶν ᾽Αθηνῶν ἀπὸ τῶν προϊστορικῶν χρόνων μέχρι τῶν ἀρχῶν τοῦ 19ου ᾽Αιῶνος, Athens
———. 1971. *Pictorial Dictionary of Ancient Athens*, New York
Vanderpool, E. 1974. "The Date of the Pre-Persian City-Wall of Athens," in Φόρος: *Tribute to Benjamin Dean Meritt*, D. W. Bradeen and F. McGregor, eds., Locust Valley, N.Y., pp. 156–160
Wade-Gery, H. T. 1940. "The Peace of Kallias" (*HSCP* Supplement 1, *Athenian Studies Presented to William Scott Ferguson*), Cambridge, Mass., pp. 121–156 (= H. T. Wade-Gery, *Essays in Greek History*, Oxford 1958, pp. 201–232)
Waldstein, C. 1902. *Argive Heraeum* I, Boston
Walsh, J. 1981. "The Authenticity and the Date of the Peace of Callias and the Congress Decree," *Chiron* 11, pp. 31–63
Walter, O. 1923. *Beschreibung der Reliefs im Kleinen Akropolismuseum in Athen*, Vienna
———. 1940. "Archäologische Funde in Griechenland von Frühjahr 1939 bis Frühjahr 1940," *AA* (*JdI* 55), cols. 121–308 (especially cols. 143–155)
Washington, H. S. 1895. *A Petrographical Sketch of Aegina and Methana*, Chicago
Welter, G. 1923. "Vom Nikepygros," *AthMitt* 48, pp. 190–201
———. 1939. "Vom Nikepyrgos," *AA* (*JdI* 54), cols. 1–22
Wesenberg, B. 1981. "Zur Baugeschichte des Niketempels," *JdI* 96, pp. 28–54
Wheler, G. 1682. *A Journey into Greece*, London
Wiegand, T. 1904. *Die archaische Poros-Architektur der Akropolis zu Athen*, Cassel
Willemsen, F. 1939. *Frühe griechische Kultbilder* (diss. University of Munich), Würzburg
Winter, Franz. 1903. *Die Typen der figürlichen Terrakotten*, Berlin
Winter, Frederick. 1971. *Greek Fortifications*, Toronto
Wolters, P. 1890. "Zum Alter des Niketempels," in *Bonner Studien: Aufsätze aus der Altertumswissenschaft Reinhard Kekule gewidmet*, Berlin, pp. 92–101
Wrede, W. 1932. "Mnesikles und der Nikepyrgos," *AthMitt* 57, pp. 74–91
———. 1933. *Attische Mauern*, Athens
Wyatt, W. F., Jr., and C. N. Edmonson. 1984. "The Ceiling of the Hephaisteion," *AJA* 88, pp. 135–167
Yavis, C. G. 1949. *Greek Altars*, St. Louis
YCS = *Yale Classical Studies*

THE SANCTUARY OF ATHENA NIKE IN ATHENS
ARCHITECTURAL STAGES AND CHRONOLOGY

I
INTRODUCTION

In January 1934 the Greek Council of Ministers formed a commission to examine the bastion and sanctuary of Athena Nike. The temple had been gradually settling for several years, a cumulative drop of up to a fifth of a meter on the west and south, and the crumbling stonework of the bastion had begun to shift and bow. The commission counseled a thorough restoration, and Nikolaos Balanos, director of the Restoration and Preservation of the Akropolis Monuments, was soon empowered to begin. From October 1935 to his retirement in March 1939, Balanos supervised the dismantling of the temple and of much of the bastion, the replacement of the temple foundations, and the initial stages of rebuilding. The temple had been reerected to orthostate level when Balanos' health began to fail, and he was forced to retire. His successor, Anastasios Orlandos, brought the project to completion in September 1940.

Although the bastion project was planned as a work of restoration only, early on it came upon major archaeological finds. In January 1936, four months underway, the work crew uncovered a naïskos, a small-scale temple of simple ⊓-shaped plan, immured in the foundations of the later temple. Clearing a corner of the naïskos a few days later, they came on a deposit of terracotta figurines set in a stone repository. Further work showed the repository and naïskos to rest on a massive Mycenaean terrace. On the west, a huge corbeled niche at the base of this terrace was immediately seen to relate to the distinctive bipartite niche of the Classical bastion: the latter was a regularized, ashlar copy of this major Bronze Age feature. Finally, work the next season toward the north side of the sanctuary revealed a block inscribed "Altar of Athena Nike," its technique and lettering roughly indicating a mid-6th-century date.

Balanos replaced the crumbling foundations for the Nike Temple with a massive concrete podium reaching fully to bedrock, an installation that required the removal of the naïskos, repository, and adjacent stretches of Mycenaean stonework. Intent on preserving as much of the context of these finds as possible, Balanos later restored them to their original place in a specially built crypt. To enter, one descends a stair southeast of the temple (E on Plan A) and proceeds along the Bronze Age bastion, down the length of the southern crown, and around the west face. A short flight of steps on the south (F on Plan A) leads up to two low rooms enclosing the early remains of the cult: the naïskos, repository, inscribed altar, and other finds at their level.

THE EXCAVATOR'S REPORT AND OTHER ACCOUNTS

Balanos completed a final report on the bastion project in 1940, the year after he retired.[1] This lengthy article is noteworthy, first, for the very year of its publication. Then bracing for war, Greece saw few other projects so brought to a close. However fortunate we are in the fact of publication, the report itself has proved a difficult and discouraging guide.

[1] Balanos 1956. The pre-print is dated 1940.

It is quite summary, describing and interpreting the early bastion in some twelve pages of text and photographs with one overall plan. The difficulties go beyond brevity, however. Balanos rarely discusses chronology. The naïskos is called simply "the earlier structure" (τὸ ἀρχαιότερον κτίσμα), with no indication of absolute date,[2] and the bastion is labeled "Pelasgian", that is, prehistoric, but its place in the Bronze Age is nowhere closely treated.[3] This evident reluctance to date the bastion remains appears itself symptomatic of two other failings. The report makes no reference to stratigraphy and, with one exception, none to pottery. The one mention of ceramics, the finds in the repository, refers simply to "fragments of small vessels" (θραυσμάτων μικρῶν ἀγγείων), with no indication of fabric, technique, or date.[4]

A civil engineer, expert in architectural restoration, not excavation *per se*, Balanos must surely have felt uneasy with the archaeological dimensions of the bastion project. It is notable, at any rate, that he encouraged the unofficial collaboration of Gabriel Welter, a seasoned field archaeologist who had himself excavated on the bastion in 1923. When Balanos retired, Welter published an overview of his colleague's work, bolstering his treatment with observations made firsthand on the site.[5] Important for its independent witness, this report adds substantially to the official account. Welter notes two finds omitted by Balanos and includes several observations on the architecture of the bastion, on the pottery, and on the stratigraphy of the bastion core. He closes with several new proposals for the history of the cult. Citing ceramic evidence, Welter suggests that Athena Nike was not a war goddess, as commonly believed, but a goddess of agonistic competition. He thus ties the Nike cult to the Panathenaic Games. The foundation of the cult, and with it the inscribed altar, date in his view to 566, as part in a major expansion of the Panathenaia attested in that year.[6]

Independent witness may of course cut two ways. Largely content to build on and complete Balanos' findings, Welter at times contradicts the official account. He interprets the "naïskos" as an unroofed, four-sided enclosure, an *abaton*, and dates the structure in two phases: the euthynteria and foundations to the late 6th century, the walls to a post-Persian rebuilding.[7] He further suggests that the repository and its deposit are contemporary with his putative second stage of the *abaton*.[8] Balanos had dated the finds earlier than the naïskos.[9]

In addition to Balanos' and Welter's accounts, there is a third set of sources of evidence on the project, the various annual summaries of archaeology in Greece compiled in the *Bulletin de correspondance hellénique*, the *American Journal of Archaeology*, the *Archäologische Anzeiger*,

[2] *Ibid.*, pp. 784, 787, 795, 797–798, 807. On page 801 of the report, however, the naïskos is once referred to as τὸ ἀρχαῖκὸν κτίσμα, "the Archaic structure", seemingly a slip, for the term is never repeated and the dating nowhere discussed.

[3] *Ibid.*, pp. 787–791, 793, 795, 796, 800–801, 807.

[4] *Ibid.*, p. 785.

[5] Welter 1939.

[6] Finds omitted by Balanos: irregular trapezoidal block on the west crown of the bastion, Welter 1939, col. 10; remains of a mud-brick enlargement of the altar for the naïskos, col. 11; the Nike cult and the Panathenaic Games, cols. 13, 14.

[7] Welter 1939, cols. 11, 12.

[8] *Ibid.*, col. 12.

[9] Balanos 1956, pp. 785, 795.

and the *Journal of Hellenic Studies*.[10] The more detailed of these summaries are several long paragraphs, generously illustrated with photographs and rich in observations and detail, much of it unreported elsewhere. They are an invaluable record both of the organization and methodology of the project and of the context of the finds. At the same time they reveal how clouded was the process of interpretation from the start. A summary in the *American Journal of Archaeology* for 1936 calls the naïskos "probably post-Persian."[11] The *Bulletin de correspondance hellénique* for the same year dates it Peisistratid.[12] The *Bulletin* also labels the terracotta figurines Archaic.[13] The *Bulletin* for 1938 calls them Mycenaean,[14] the *Bulletin* for 1939, sub-Mycenaean.[15]

THE BASTION FINDS IN LATER SCHOLARSHIP

The record on the bastion excavations, spare, scattered, and variously reported, has proved yet more problematic for its partial, uneven attention to written sources. Nowhere are the literary and epigraphical testimonia on the cult systematically compiled. Key passages of Heliodoros and Pausanias on the cult statue of Athena Nike are nowhere cited. The substantial set of inscriptions on the cult is at most alluded to and nowhere examined in full. The legacy of this fragmented record could hardly be otherwise: data worked and reworked, theories argued and opposed, with little agreement on the most basic of findings, and little sense of real progress.[16]

A close discussion of the inscribed altar by Antony Raubitschek, soon after the war, launched the first of a string of penetrating, if in the end flawed, attempts at interpreting the remains.[17] Drawing on Welter's thesis that the Nike cult was founded at the time of the expansion of the Panathenaia in 566, Raubitschek argued that the striding Athena on Panathenaic amphoras depicts a statue on the Nike Bastion, not in the Sanctuary of Athena Polias as generally believed. I will be returning to this thesis in more detail. Here it is sufficient to note the long shadow of the excavation accounts: focused on the archaeology of the find, Raubitschek largely ignored the written sources on the cult, most glaringly the sources on the cult image. Scholars were receptive to his thesis for a time but came gradually to realize its gaps.

[10] Lemerle 1936, p. 455, pl. 51:B; 1937, p. 443, figs. 4–7; 1938, pp. 448–450, figs. 5–7, pl. 50; 1939, p. 289, fig. 3; and Blegen 1936, p. 145, figs. 1–4; 1940, p. 537, fig. 1. Work in 1939 and 1940 is summarized by Walter 1940, cols. 144–152, figs. 18–23; see also Karo 1936, cols. 94–99; Riemann 1937, col. 92; and Robertson 1939, p. 191. The results of the project are summarized by C. Picard, "L'anastylose du temple de la Victoire aptère," *RA* 15, 1940, pp. 256–258.

[11] Blegen 1936, p. 145.

[12] Lemerle 1936, p. 455.

[13] *Loc. cit.*

[14] Lemerle 1938, caption to pl. 50.

[15] Lemerle 1939, p. 289.

[16] For a brief review of scholarship on the bastion, Boersma 1970, no. XV, p. 132; also Travlos 1971, p. 148.

[17] Raubitschek 1949, no. 329, pp. 359–364.

The excavations are treated at greater length in a study of Athena Nike by George Oikonomos, «Ἡ ἐπὶ τῆς Ἀκροπόλεως λατρεία τῆς Ἀθηνᾶς Νίκης».[18] This scholar's treatment is notable for its independence from the excavator's account. Oikonomos considered the terracotta figurines to be prehistoric, reinforcing the sub-Mycenaean date given in the *Bulletin de correspondence hellénique* for 1939. He reinterpreted the repository as a ground altar, an *eschara*, and, reasoning from the terracottas, set the find at the very dawn of the cult (χθονίαν λατρεία παναρχαίας περιόδου).[19] Balanos' report nowhere mentioned a fact that is key to this thesis: the rim of the repository is heavily burned and calcined. Oikonomos appears to have seen these traces himself at first hand. The present study will show the burning to be not Archaic or prehistoric but Turkish, from the period when the repository lay exposed in the floor of a powder crypt directly beneath the temple. Further, the "prehistoric" date of the figurines has become untenable. It is contradicted by two decades of research on the history of Mycenaean and sub-Mycenaean figurines.

Oikonomos' *eschara* and the early dating of the figurines have figured prominently in several more recent studies. A major firsthand survey of the Mycenaean Akropolis by Spiros Iakovidis integrated Oikonomos' theory with the finding that the Nike Bastion suffered a major collapse in the Dark Ages. Thinking that the figurines antedated the collapse, Iakovidis suggested that they came originally from the corbeled niche in the west bastion face and that sometime after the collapse, they were carried atop the bastion to the *eschara*.[20]

A study on the ritual of the Akropolis by Chrysoula Kardara carried the work of Iakovidis a step farther.[21] She located the terracottas in the bastion niche during the Dark Ages, like Iakovidis, but sited there as well the *eschara* and the cult image of the goddess, in her view a Bronze Age work. She posited that the *eschara*, terracottas, and cult statue were first brought atop the bastion in the Archaic period. We have seen the starting point for this line of scholarship, the supposed Dark Age date of the terracottas, to be in error. My other findings obviate other elements in Kardara's thesis: importantly, my discovery that the repository, the so-called *eschara*, was originally a part of the base for the cult statue. The base serves to date the image at earliest to the early 6th century.

The early bastion has been further investigated by J. A. Bundgård, though on lines largely independent of Oikonomos. A study of 1957 on the Mnesiklean Propylaia attempted to correlate the stages of the Nike Sanctuary with stages of the gate area of the Akropolis, directly to the east. Bundgård posited that the stepped forecourt of the Old Propylon, the apparent predecessor of the Southwest Wing of the Propylaia, is contemporary with the naïskos, the predecessor of the Nike Temple. This pre-Mnesiklean stage, judged Archaic

[18] Oikonomos 1948.

[19] *Ibid.*, p. 105.

[20] Iakovidis 1962, pp. 106–112, 166–170, 186–187; for a partial summary of this research, *idem* 1983, pp. 79–80.

[21] Kardara 1965, pp. 169–171, 182–183; *eadem* 1964, pp. 68–71, 79. Kardara's thesis ranges well beyond the early bastion. For broader discussion, see Brommer 1977, p. 149; Simon 1983, p. 58. A major premise of Kardara's studies is that the cult images of Athena Nike and Athena Polias are one and the same, a view patently inconsistent with literary and epigraphical sources, and also with evidence to be discussed below on the cult-statue base of Athena Nike. Compare now C. Kardara, «Ἡ ζωφόρος τοῦ Παρθενῶνος: ὁ κύριος μυθικὸς τῆς πυρὴν καὶ τὸ πανελλήνιον πρόγραμμα τοῦ Περικλέους», ΑρχΕφ 1982 [1984], pp. 1–60.

by Bundgård, was thought to have reflected, in turn, the form of the Bronze Age bastion. Bundgård restored a high Mycenaean terrace over the eastern two-thirds of the bastion, a putative predecessor of the stepped forecourt, and located a Mycenaean forerunner to the Nike cult on the remaining bastion to the west.[22] This scholar's later study on the history and archaeology of the citadel, *Parthenon and the Mycenaean City on the Heights*, laid yet more stress on the Bronze Age cult. He suggested that the natural outcropping of the bastion was itself sacred in the Bronze Age: the niche at the foot of the west face was constructed to allow worship at the base of the outcropping, while a polygonal gap in the ashlar sheathing on the north reveals a second sacred stone part way up the bastion face.[23]

The pitfalls of the excavation record are nowhere more evident than in Bundgård's work. His treatment of the early bastion in *Parthenon and the Mycenaean City on the Heights* follows the lines of his earlier Propylaia study, with one significant exception. The later work considers the naïskos to be mid-5th century, not Archaic,[24] a view firmly supported by the present study. Far from a simple revision, the new dating casts doubt on the very foundation of Bundgård's thesis, that the Nike Sanctuary and gate area evolved in tandem. The stepped forecourt, firmly anchored in the Late Archaic period, has no equivalent on the bastion. We may see the link of the two areas to be illusory also in the Bronze Age. The present study documents two distinct periods of bastion stonework, the Cyclopean bastion proper and a lighter rubble repair of Archaic date. Bundgård founded his upper terrace, forerunner to the stepped court, on Cyclopean stonework at the west and on rubble almost certainly of Archaic date at the east. Finally, this scholar's theories on the sanctity of the rock outcropping of the bastion may be seen to arise in a simple misunderstanding: misreading a pair of labels on a published plan from the excavations, a photocopy reproduced in halftone at greatly reduced scale,[25] Bundgård concluded that the bastion was built around a tall core of living rock, reasoning in turn that the niche and northern opening were contrived to leave especially sacred areas of the rock accessible.[26] The bastion core is in fact a fill of earth and stones, as seen in several excavation photographs and indeed as explicitly described by Balanos and Welter.[27]

Concerned to show the difficulties of the record on the 1930's excavations, I risk painting some two generations of scholarship a flat dark gray. Theory upon theory has indeed given way, but there remains from this research a depth of observation and expertise, be it on epigraphy or Bronze Age architecture, without which the present study would have been everywhere weaker. Having challenged the theories of Bundgård in particular detail above, I

[22] Bundgård 1957, pp. 69–71.

[23] Bundgård 1976, pp. 43–44.

[24] Bundgård 1976, pp. 48–53; first argued in Bundgård 1974b, for which see below, p. 5.

[25] Welter 1939, cols. 5–6, fig. 3.

[26] The level of the natural rock is entered twice on this plan, once behind the northwest corner of the Mycenaean bastion and again south of the Nike Temple. Similar versions in the Balanos archives (cf. Pl. 7) show the first line of the entry to read in each case "ΦΥΣΙΚΟΣ ΒΡΑΧΟΣ" with the level centered below in parentheses: −6.63 at the northwest corner (= +135.58); and −5.20 south of the temple (= +137.01). Bundgård appears to have made out only the first line of the label, concluding that the natural rock was directly behind the bastion façades (1976, p. 178, note 107). In fact the level given by Balanos at the northwest is 1.60 m. below the northern opening.

[27] Balanos 1956, p. 788; Welter 1939, col. 6. Photographs: Lemerle 1937, p. 444, fig. 6 (= Pl. 3:b); Balanos 1956, p. 785, fig. 13 (= Pl. 3:a).

take care to point to one study that, although it too is hindered by the excavation record, yet rises spectacularly above it. "Le sujet de *IG* I^2, 24," a brief article of 1974, argues that the Nike Temple Decree, a mid-5th-century inscription commissioning a temple of Athena Nike, refers not to the Nike Temple proper, as commonly believed, but to its predecessor, the naïskos.[28] The present study develops a body of new evidence that strongly confirms this view.

THE PRESENT PROJECT

To review the last forty years' scholarship on the Nike Bastion is to become aware, perhaps above all, of how intractable are the problems and questions of the site in the absence of a full account of the 1930's project. It is the first aim of my study to correct this loss. It examines the early finds from the bastion in detail and documents them in drawing, in photograph, and through comprehensive description. It is the first such record ever. I gathered the data and prepared the field drawings for the project in two months' work on site in the fall of 1982. With the exceptions of remains now disturbed or inaccessible, all instances of which I have noted case by case in the text, my observations are throughout firsthand.[29]

I owe to the late Anastasios Orlandos the knowledge of several letter boxes of documents on the Balanos project, a collection formed largely of excavation drawings, with an added assortment of ledgers and accounts, and a small sheaf of the excavator's working notes. Originally in the care of the Greek Archaeological Service, the materials were passed to the archives of the Archaeological Society of Athens in 1966 at Orlandos' request. A review of these archives in 1977 and again in 1982 revealed a core of materials that merits publication: a body of drawings, including plans, elevations, and sections of the bastion (Pls. 7–17); and several pages of the excavator's notes (Appendix A). These records can never compensate for the failure to record pottery and stratigraphy. They do help, however, to reconstruct the progress of the excavations, and in documenting such now destroyed remains as the foundations for the Nike Temple and the Turkish powder crypt, they clarify the context and interrelation of the finds as a whole.

The excavations throw light as much on the history and chronology of the ashlar bastion and Classical temple as on the excavated finds themselves. The disassociation of the temple from the Nike Temple Decree, in particular, gives new meaning to a range of other sources on the 5th-century cult. In pursuit of these implications, I review and reexamine the full body of evidence on the architectural history of the site, from such traditional questions as the

[28] Bundgård 1974b, pp. 43–49. He reworks and expands his thesis in *Parthenon and the Mycenaean City on the Heights* (1976), pp. 48–53, 168–169.

[29] The present position of the naïskos, repository, and rectangular altar agrees closely with that recorded by Balanos; these finds were carefully and accurately restored to place. For inaccuracies in the restoration of foundations and rubble remains, see note 2 below, p. 12; note 5, p. 13; note 3, p. 36; note 9, p. 39; and note 10, p. 40. As a point of methodology, I have used Balanos' figures rather than my own for all measurements affected by the restoration, notably elevations and the position of finds. I have taken care to confirm, however, the general accuracy of these earlier measurements with my own. When I have used Balanos' or others' measurements, this is noted in the text.

relative dating of the Nike Bastion and the Propylaia to topics that our research has now radically reshaped, notably, the politics of the Akropolis building program and the career of Kallikrates, the architect, it now turns out, of the naïskos.

The issues at stake draw on such a range of evidence and are at points so potentially controversial that I have thought it best to build my argument by stages. I begin with the material remains of the Nike cult. In Chapters II and III, I examine two finds whose history can be traced through several stages of the cult: the Cyclopean bastion itself, its crown twice rebuilt; and the repository, formed of blocks reused from the base for the cult statue. In Chapters IV–VII, I proceed through the full range of finds from the site, documenting, interpreting, and dating the stages of the sanctuary level by level. In Chapter VIII, I assemble the literary and epigraphical sources on the sanctuary. In Chapter IX, I review the long history of scholarship tying the Nike Temple Decree to the Stage IV (amphiprostyle) Nike Temple and discuss the merits of the alternative association with the Stage III naïskos. And in Chapter X, I present my conclusions, bringing together the material remains and the literary and epigraphical evidence on the sanctuary stage by stage.

The excavations of the 1930's mark, of course, but one stage in a long history of exploration on the Nike Bastion. Balanos came to a temple that had already been once rebuilt. Dismantled by the Turks in the 17th century, it was restored to place by Ludwig Ross in 1836. And toward the end of the 19th century and in the beginning of the 20th there had been limited excavation beneath the sanctuary paving. I conclude this first chapter with a brief history of the site from the close of antiquity to the start of the Balanos project in 1936.

THE NIKE BASTION IN THE MIDDLE AGES

The Emperor Theodosios decreed an end to pagan ritual in A.D. 392. The cult of Nike lay idle from that time on. Through fourteen centuries, under Byzantine sway to 1204, held by Frankish dukes to 1456 and by the Ottoman Turks to 1833, the Nike Sanctuary was by stages altered and reused. The earliest appreciable damage dates from a Frankish refortification of the citadel, completed gradually from the 13th to the 15th centuries.[30]

The Franks walled shut the two main portals of the western ascent, the Late Roman Beulé Gate and the Propylaia, and drew a new line of fortification from the Nike Bastion to the Monument of Agrippa (cf. Fig. 1). One traversed the new line through a passage just inside the Agrippa Monument and continued up a ramp along the front of the Propylaia, across the Nike Bastion, and around the Southwest Wing.

The monumental altar of Athena Nike lay directly across the new approach and was likely razed at this time. Only its prothysis and foundations survive. In contrast, the temple remained largely unharmed. Its roof had likely fallen in, to judge at least from how little survives of the tympana, sima, and tiles, but from the frieze down it was fully intact. The Nike Parapet, the sculptured barrier that edged the bastion on the north, south, and west, also appears to have stood largely unharmed.

[30] Ross, Schaubert, and Hansen 1839, pp. 2–3; Ross 1855–1856, pp. 74–77, 94, 97–98, 99–102, 108, 112–113, 115–116; Bohn 1882, pp. 5–7; Travlos 1960, pp. 164–166; Tanoulas 1987, p. 431.

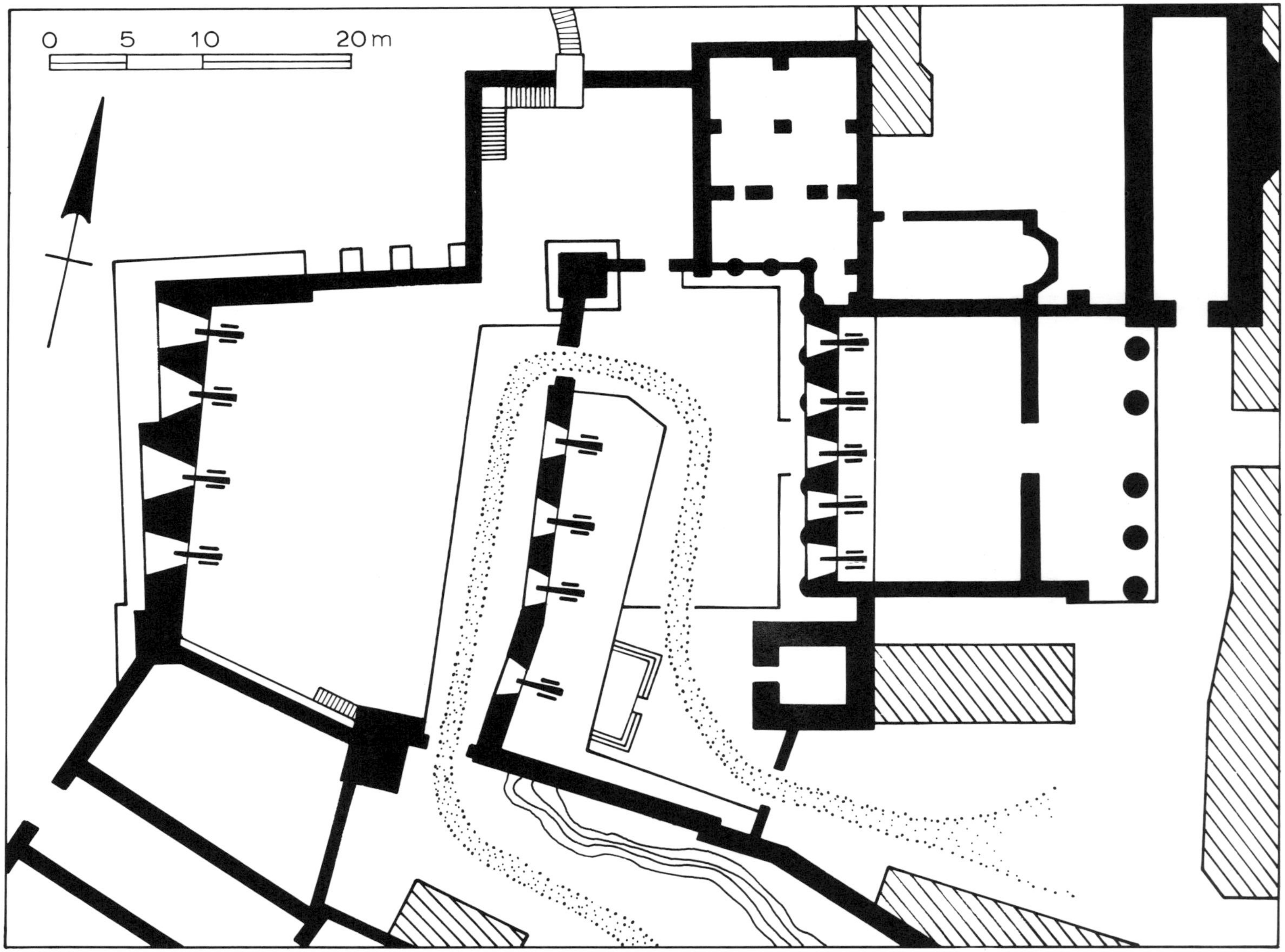

Fig. 1. The western Akropolis before the Venetian siege of 1687

With the installation of cannon on the Akropolis sometime around the 16th century, the Nike Temple was remade into a powder magazine. The Turks pulled up the four paving slabs of the cella and excavated the area inside the cella foundations, partially cutting through the remains of the naïskos. They covered the chamber with a rubble-and-mortar barrel vault, its apex coming to the level of the former paving, and cut a low entrance through the temple krepidoma from the east.[31]

Jacob Spon and George Wheler, visiting Athens in 1671, are the only early travelers to have seen the Nike Temple intact. Ascending the medieval ramp, they linger over the view from the bastion, admire the columns and finely carved frieze of the temple, and note the powder store below.[32] A decade later the temple was gone. Under attack by the Venetians, the Turks razed it to the krepidoma and overbuilt the bastion with a major battery (Fig. 1). The line of wall from the bastion to the Agrippa Monument was strengthened inward and heightened as an emplacement for four cannon. The epistyle, geison, and wall blocks of the temple and four blocks of the figured frieze were built into the inner face of these fortifications, with the remaining frieze slabs, column drums and capitals, and several fragmentary slabs of the Nike Parapet set in as packing behind.[33] The powder magazine survived intact within the temple krepidoma, its roof now protected by the battery, the inner face of which crossed just in front of its main chamber. It appears to have been at this time that several meters of foundations for the temple were torn out, from the northern pier of the doorwall to the northeast anta, and the crypt enlarged to the east.[34]

Antiquarians of the 18th and early 19th centuries found the partially exposed steps of the Nike Temple and its immured wall and frieze blocks an enigmatic challenge. James Stuart and Nicholas Revett include the krepidoma on a plan of the Propylaia and reproduce three of the four visible blocks of the figured frieze. The remains are in their view a temple of Aglauros.[35] A generation later William Leake reexamined the site and reargued its identification as the sanctuary of Athena Nike. He completed his study with a restored plan and elevation of the temple, wildly incorrect (distyle in antis facing north) but of interest for its use of drawings made soon before on site by C. R. Cockerell.[36]

The immured blocks of the figured frieze, close at hand along the ramp, were repeatedly prey to vandals; the drawings of Stuart and Revett, in documenting their condition in the

[31] Ross, Schaubert, and Hansen 1839, p. 3; Balanos 1956, p. 778, fig. 4; p. 782. The crypt is recorded on several drawings in the Balanos archives. A longitudinal section establishes its length and depth (Pl. 13:b). Block drawings of courses 1 and 2 of the temple foundations (Pls. 14, 15) record the base of the rubble vault and, cut through course 1, the entryway. A section across the eastern foundations of the temple includes the south wall of the entryway and, in dotted line, the inner curve of the vault (Pl. 12).

[32] Spon and Wheler 1678, II, pp. 105–106; Wheler 1682, p. 358.

[33] Ross, Schaubert, and Hansen 1839, pp. 3, 17; Bohn 1882, p. 8; Travlos 1960, pp. 190–192.

[34] The general limits of this enlargement are given by the two westernmost blocks of the naïskos euthynteria on the south (E 1, E 2), covered with medieval mortar to within 0.50 m. of their eastern end, and the euthynteria opposite (E 5), crudely reworked and burned along its full length. The temple stylobate was left in place, apparently carried on wooden beams.

[35] Stuart and Revett, II, chap. V, pp. 39–40, pls. II, XII, XIII.

[36] Leake 1821, pp. 191–205.

mid-18th century, indeed establish how rapid and pervasive was the loss. In 1802, Lord Elgin pried the slabs free and shipped them to England, a part of the famed Elgin marbles.[37]

THE HISTORY OF EXCAVATION ON THE NIKE BASTION TO 1935

On its liberation in 1830, Greece immediately formed plans to free its antiquities of medieval accretions, beginning prominently with the Athenian Akropolis. In 1835 Ludwig Ross and the architects Eduard Schaubert and Christian Hansen supervised the demolition of the battery across the Nike Bastion and the Frankish fortifications and ramp beneath. The battery proved to contain nearly all the blocks of the Nike Temple, largely intact and unreworked, and the temple krepidoma was largely intact as well, if badly sunken on the east and south.[38] Ross replaced the section of foundations removed by the Turks, pieced in the steps and stylobate, and restored the superstructure of the building to place.[39] A book on the temple appeared three years later, the text by Ross, the drawings by Schaubert and Hansen, an early landmark in scholarship on the site.[40]

Growing knowledge of the Propylaia following the demolition of a large Frankish tower on the site of the Southwest Wing brought new interest to the archaeology of the adjacent Nike Bastion. In 1880 Richard Bohn partially excavated the interior of the bastion in order to establish the relative dates of the Propylaia and the Nike Sanctuary.[41] He began in medieval contexts south of the Nike Temple, extracting inscriptions, remains of statuary, and large fragments of the Nike Parapet, and continued on the east and north, confining himself to areas where the paving slabs were missing. The earth within these gaps was still largely

[37] London, BM 421–424. On the consignment of the slabs to London, see Smith 1916, p. 215.

[38] Ross, Schaubert, and Hansen 1839, p. 3; Ross 1855–1856, I, p. 100.

[39] The work on the foundations appears to have been done late in June or early in July 1835 soon after clearing the krepidoma, for in a progress report dated July 18, 1935 Ross (1855–1856, I, p. 100) states that he would begin to reerect the temple after replacing a few missing blocks of the stylobate with newly made ones: "Was die Wiederaufrichtung des Tempelchens betrifft, so haben wir noch nicht dazu schreiten können, weil von der obersten Stufe, auf welcher die Säulen stehen, ein Paar Platten fehlen, die neu gemacht werden mussten."

The restored foundations, not distinguished from the ancient on Balanos' plans, form a rectangle roughly 2.2×1.8 m. covering the eastern end of the naïskos. The rectangle is formed of six blocks in foundation course 2 (Pl. 15) and again six in course 1 (Pl. 14). In course 1 the rectangle is truncated on the south to form the passageway for the crypt. The modern date of the repair is established from its relation to Turkish remains. Large patches of medieval mortar cover the south euthynteria of the naïskos, an area overbuilt by the southernmost blocks of the repair, and similarly there is late recutting and several patches of burning on the euthynteria opposite, covered by the repair on the north. The sharp difference between the two flank walls of the crypt passageway is indicative as well. The south wall was roughly hacked out by the Turks and faced with rubble and mortar. The north is trimmed straight and even (Pl. 14). Finally, there are cuttings made for the original temple foundations, distinct in orientation and setting from the blocks put in by Ross. An ashlar-sized rectangular cutting on the inner face of the naïskos north wall is for a block set on the axis of the later temple, not aligned with the naïskos as is the repair (Fig. 7); a pair of ledges along the south euthynteria are for blocks that slightly overlap the euthynteria from the sides, not fully cover it as in the rebuilding.

[40] Ross, Schaubert, and Hansen 1839.

[41] Bohn 1880a, pp. 259–267; *idem* 1882, pp. 15–17. The area west of the Southwest Wing appears to have been reexplored by A. Köster in 1905. See Köster 1906, p. 141, note 35.

undisturbed, revealing an intact stratum of bastion fill and the remains of two walls, one northeast of the temple, the other alongside the Mycenaean circuit wall to the east.

The areas where the paving was intact, untouched by Bohn, were finally excavated by Gabriel Welter in 1923.[42] Constrained to leave the paving in place, Welter cut several narrow tunnels beneath it from the side. East of the temple he came on an intact altar about a meter below the Classical level, the first evidence of earlier cult. To the north he found a square block, a second altar as we shall see, and to the east, a continuation of the wall northeast of the temple first uncovered by Bohn.

The first of the two altars, the predecessor of the monumental marble altar of the sanctuary, points, as no other find does, to the dramatic discoveries of Balanos a decade later. The naïskos, Balanos' major find, is on its axis, at the same level, and of the same stone and workmanship. The two were immediately seen to belong together.

[42] Welter 1923, pp. 190–201.

II

THE MYCENAEAN BASTION: BRONZE AGE STONEWORK AND REPAIRS

A review of the early remains from the Nike Bastion may appropriately begin with the Mycenaean bastion itself, the oldest feature of the site and the very setting of the cult. The partial dismantling of the Classical bastion in 1936 and 1937 left its Mycenaean predecessor fully exposed on the south and along most of the west. Only the first few courses of sheathing were removed on the north and at the northwest corner, to a point sufficient to reveal the early remains in plan.[1] Further work, most important, the repair of the Nike Temple foundations, required the dismantling of at least one Mycenaean wall and the clearing of much of the earth and boulder fill of the bastion down to bedrock.[2]

With the reerection of the Classical sheathing, which began in 1937, much of the early bastion was again rendered inaccessible. A number of drawings from the Balanos archives are thus of special interest: (1) an elevation of the bastion from the south as exposed in 1937 (Pl. 9); my Figure 15 completes this drawing with the inclusion of stonework later exposed to the east, still visible in the modern crypt; (2) an elevation of the bastion from the west, the basis for my Figure 16; (3) a partial elevation from the west, showing the foundations for the Nike Temple in cross-section (Pl. 10); (4) one transverse and two longitudinal sections of the bastion (Pls. 11–13:a), the last recording the large Mycenaean niche at the base of the west face; (5) a horizontal section of the west face, showing the Mycenaean niche in plan (Pl. 8); and (6) a set of plans recording the successive courses of the Nike Temple foundations (Pls. 14–17), plans that include earlier stonework at a number of key points.

As revealed from Balanos' work, the site in the Bronze Age formed a monumental bastion or terrace in Cyclopean technique (Figs. 15, 16; Pls. 7, 9, 10; Plan A).[3] Directly above the bastion to the east there ran the circuit wall of the citadel, a substantial stretch of which survives behind the Southwest Wing of the Propylaia. The bastion was built out from the foot

[1] Balanos 1956, pp. 787–795.

[2] On the dismantled wall, the crosswall of the bastion, see Balanos 1956, p. 796, and further p. 40 below. Photographs and plans make clear that stonework was also removed along the upper edge of the western crown of the bastion and at the eastern end of the southern crown. On the west this stonework was partly replaced, not stone for stone, but in keeping with the general character of the original.

[3] On the date of the bastion, see Welter 1939, col. 6. Welter describes pottery found in the bastion fill as containing Aiginetan Middle Helladic and "a few late Mycenaean (LH III) sherds." On the pottery, compare O. Broneer, "Athens in the Late Bronze Age," *Antiquity* 30, 1956 (pp. 9–18), p. 13. Cyclopean walls elsewhere on the Akropolis have been dated stratigraphically to the 13th century B.C., LH IIIB, roughly contemporary with the major campaigns of fortification at Mycenae and Tiryns. For the Akropolis walls, Iakovidis 1983, p. 86; in more detail, *idem* 1962, pp. 205–206; Mycenae, Mylonas 1966, pp. 19–33; Tiryns, P. Grossman and J. Schäfer, "Tiryns: Unterburg, Grabungen 1965," in *Tiryns: Forschungen und Berichte* V, U. Jantzen, ed., Mainz am Rhein 1971, pp. 72–75; *eidem*, "Tiryns: Unterburg 1968. Grabungen im Bereich der Bauten 3 und '4'," in *Tiryns: Forschungen und Berichte* VIII, Mainz am Rhein 1975, pp. 58–60; K. Kilian, "Ausgrabungen in Tiryns, 1977," *AA* (*JdI* 94) 1979 (pp. 379–411), p. 409.

of this circuit around the three sides of a short east–west spur of rock. Its west face measures 9.7 m. across. The south flank, set at an acute angle to the west flank, has a preserved length of 16.0 m. The north flank, only partially revealed in excavation, starts back from the west at an oblique angle for 3.8 m. and then turns in, assuming a near parallel to the south.[4] The north and south flanks are linked by a crosswall on a line 4.5 m. behind the west face. Its remains, completely dismantled and rebuilt by Balanos, have been partially immured in the modern crypt.[5] As entered on plans, it is 1.45 m. wide and is described by the excavator as having been seated in the fill of the bastion, bonded in its lower courses to the north bastion face.

The elevation of the preserved crown of the bastion ranges from +140.86 on the north, measured east of the square altar of Phase III, to +137.87 on the south, measured 4 m. from the southwest corner. The east end of the south face stands at +140.67, the middle of the west face at +140.40. The northwest and southwest corners stand at +139.03 and +139.18 respectively (Fig. 15).[6]

Among the prominent features of the bastion is a monumental niche formed within the lowest courses of the west bastion face. Exposed temporarily in the course of restoration, it was left largely inaccessible behind the rebuilt sheathing.[7] Measured from archival drawings it is 1.85 m. wide, 1.25 m. high, and 0.50–1.50 m. deep (Pls. 8, 13:a). A poros pier, 0.60 × 0.35 m., stood within the niche, directly at the meeting of the two main boulders of its vault. As suggested by Balanos, the pier dates from the sealing of the niche at the construction of the Classical sheathing. It was seated over a circular rock-cut bedding, seemingly for a predecessor in columnar form.

Balanos presents a somewhat confusing report on this niche, which his archival drawings only partly clarify. The horizontal cross-section Plate 8 shows two niches, one on the right (the sole niche Balanos refers to outright in his report) and a second, smaller niche on the left. The right-hand niche is clear in a pencil drawing of the west face in the archives, the line of its vault set off by a Classical packing of small stones, as Balanos describes (1956, p. 790). The left-hand niche is far less clear. The boulders in that area form no coherent vault, and there is no observable distinction between bastion face and packing, the stonework being of large scale throughout.

4 For the form and dimensions of the bastion on the south and west, Balanos 1956, pl. I. On the line of the north face, Balanos 1956, p. 788. A stretch of wall in irregular trapezoidal masonry gives the line of the north face beyond its bend (D on Plan A). The foundations for the western anta of the Propylaia's Southwest Wing are laid directly against the trapezoidal wall, and the plan of the Southwest Wing itself appears adapted to its line. On the relation of the Mycenaean bastion and the Propylaia, particularly Wrede 1932, pp. 74–91; Bundgård 1957, pp. 70–71.

5 Balanos 1956, pp. 788, 796, cf. note 2 above, p. 12. The wall was mistakenly reinstalled 0.21 m. above its original level. For the partitioning of fills in Mycenaean terrace construction, see J. Wright, "Mycenaean Palatial Terraces," *AthMitt* 95, 1980 (pp. 59–86), p. 61.

6 Elevations are given in meters above sea level. Balanos' general plan, a detail of which is shown in Plate 7, gives the level of the northwest and southwest corners of the bastion as respectively −3.18 and −3.03 m. relative to the northeast corner of the euthynteria of the Nike Temple. Cf. Plate 8: southwest corner of the bastion +139.171; Plate 9: +139.179. The highest and lowest figures are around a centimeter apart. Balanos gives the level of the northeast corner of the Nike Temple as +142.213 on Plate 7, and I have cast the remaining levels for the bastion from this reference. Cf. Dinsmoor, Jr. 1980, plan A, northeast corner = +142.223.

7 Balanos 1956, pp. 790–791.

Describing the clearing of the niches, Balanos (1956, p. 790) mentions a collapse of rock: «'Ατυχῶς δὲν ἦτο δυνατὸν νὰ καθορισθῇ τὸ βάθος τῆς ἀρχαιοτέρας ταύτης κόγχης ἕνεκα ἐσωτερικῶν καταπτώσεων, ἐν πάσῃ ὅμως περιπτώσει ἦτο ἀρκετὰ ἀνώμαλον, ὡς ἐξηκριβώθη τοῦτο κατὰ γενομένην ἀνασκαφὴν ἐν αὐτῇ».

If, as the context suggests, this statement refers to the right-hand niche, then it stands in contradiction to the plan, Plate 8. To judge from the contour line there, the back of the right-hand niche was fully revealed. The contour of the left-hand niche, however, has a softer, less defined appearance, as might be expected were it never fully cleared. We may suggest, thus, that it was in the second niche that the collapse occurred.

Balanos not only omits explicit reference to the left-hand niche, he fails to publish photographs (his report includes two views of the right-hand niche) and failed to leave the area of the left-hand niche accessible in the reconstruction. We need to consider whether a second niche ever existed at all.

It is beyond doubt that some amount of stonework was removed from the bastion face in the area of the "second niche," for Plate 8 and other archival drawings record the contour of the floor of the "niche". Rather, we may suggest that the "left-hand niche" is a modern creation, cleared in a misguided search for a niche corresponding to the left-hand niche of the Classical sheathing. The workmen would have left off this attempt on realizing that both niches of the Classical sheathing refer to the right-hand niche, with the right-hand niche and the Classical niche both marked by a central pier.

Should this explanation be correct, there remains a final enigma. Balanos states (1956, pp. 790–791): «Τὸ ὁλικὸν μῆκος τῆς ἀρχαιοτέρας ταύτης κόγχης εἶναι 5 μ. περίπου, ἐνῷ τὸ τῆς τοῦ περιβλήματος εἶναι 3.135 μ.». The meaning of ὁλικὸν μῆκος is ambiguous here but is most plausibly taken as the width of the niche and its boulder surround together. Niche and surround are *ca.* 5 m.; the surround alone equals 3.135 m.; the resulting width of the niche is thus *ca.* 1.865 m. This is, in fact, the width of the right-hand niche, attested in cross-section (Pl. 8) and elevation (Fig. 16). With the addition of its flanking boulders, however, its width comes to only 3.5 m., not "*ca.* 5 m." Since the niches were inaccessible after 1938, that is, from well before Balanos submitted his report, it is just possible that this section of his text depends on misread or erroneous measurements. The width of both niches with their flanking surround, measured off the cross-section, Plate 8, at any rate, is just 5 meters.[8]

[8] For an earlier discussion of this section of Balanos' text, see Iakovidis 1962, pp. 109–111.

In the lowest course of the Mycenaean face directly north of the left-hand "niche", an area of the face accessible in the modern crypt, Balanos notes a shallow, rounded cutting (Balanos 1956, p. 791; here, Fig. 16, Pl. 11). The bedrock directly below the cutting is carved into steps intended for the backers to the Classical sheathing. In the uppermost of these steps Balanos found a second, rectangular cutting, length 0.30, width 0.22, average depth 0.15 m., apparently a small sacrificial pit. Balanos notes nothing in the pit, but to one side on the rock-cut step were traces of burning and a burned sherd.

An archival drawing of the 15th course of the Classical sheathing shows that the rock step in question was filled with backers up to, but not over, the rectangular cutting: the rear 0.25 m. of the step was left unfilled. The hollow thus created was sealed over by the 14th course (Pl. 8).

Rock cuttings are notoriously difficult to date. By context, however, the rectangular cutting ought not to be earlier than the Classical sheathing; the traces of cult nearby are, of course, contemporary with or later than

THE FORM OF THE BASTION IN THE BRONZE AGE

In the view of major Bronze Age scholars, the bastion formed a key part in a line of fortifications across the western Akropolis.[9] The Lion Gate and Postern Gate bastions at Mycenae are its closest parallels,[10] and on their model the Nike Bastion has been restored as having flanked a major entrance to the Bronze Age citadel of the Akropolis, a distant predecessor to the Propylaia.

A close reconstruction of the Bronze Age entrance lies beyond the needs of our study. In the face of recent research that has challenged a number of long-held assumptions on the bastion, however, some comments are in order.[11] If the arguments set out by Bundgård and Dinsmoor are correct in placing the western Mycenaean circuit not on the ruins of a wall discovered by Stevens below the Propylaia but under the Propylaia on the natural ridge, it follows that the Nike Bastion did not originally protect a gatewall to the circuit.[12] Rather, the circuit would have been too far behind and above it. Granted that the bastion and circuit were independent, the former still ought to have formed part of a consistent line of defense, since a terrace undefended is an invitation to siege and a staging post for the enemy. A ready solution is to restore the bastion as part of a *proteichisma*, a short, preliminary line of defense, that would have followed the western slope of the Akropolis a short way down from the circuit. Stevens' wall would mark the continuation of this line to the north.[13]

The gateway to the *proteichisma*, directly left of and behind the bastion, need not have been as monumental as the citadel gate proper. But even if it was less than half the scale of the Lion Gate, to protect it the Nike Bastion must still have reached several meters higher than it is now preserved. If we place the *proteichisma* gate at *ca.* +139.0, following on this point the general lines of a restoration by Travlos,[14] and restore a gatewall of moderate height, say five meters, then the crown of the bastion, as set by the gatewall, will be at around +144.0.

FIRST REBUILDING OF THE BASTION CROWN

Observations on site, supported by plans from the Balanos archives, establish that the "Mycenaean" stonework of the bastion in fact falls in two periods.[15] The inner face of

the cutting of the step (they lie on it), and the rectangular cutting itself appears carved down from the level of the step. The remains are seemingly those of a propitiatory offering made when the Mycenaean face was sealed.

[9] Welter 1939, fig. 4; Travlos 1960, fig. 7; Iakovidis 1962, pp. 166–170; Mylonas 1966, pp. 37–39, fig. 9; Travlos 1971, fig. 67.

[10] Mylonas 1966, pp. 17–18.

[11] James Wright presented aspects of his work on the bastion in a paper before the general meeting of the Archaeological Institute of America, Atlanta, 1978, "The Mycenaean Entrance System to the Akropolis of Athens."

[12] Bundgård 1957, pp. 48–50; Dinsmoor, Jr. 1980, pp. 1–4. On Stevens' wall, Stevens 1946, pp. 73–77.

[13] For the Pelargikon, which seemingly formed a second *proteichisma* further down the slope, see Judeich 1931, pp. 113–120; Gomme 1956, pp. 63–65; Travlos 1971, fig. 67. Compare the discussion of the Pelargikon by Iakovidis 1962, pp. 179–199.

[14] 1971, fig. 67.

[15] Hitherto, the stonework has been treated as of a piece; so Balanos 1956, p. 787, cf. caption to p. 788, fig. 17; Welter 1939, col. 9.

the bastion on the north provides the initial indications. The boulders forming the lowest fully exposed course on the inner face (seen lower right in Pl. 6:b) are set in a mortar of gray clayey earth and small pebbles. In contrast, the wall above, from *ca.* +140.10 to the crown, is set dry, its interstices filled with a loose reddish earth. This upper stonework is of moderate rather than monumental scale, formed of blocks 0.20–0.40 m. in height.

Stonework similar to the upper courses on the north, dry rubble packed with reddish earth, remains exposed at the eastern end of the south face, beginning roughly from level +139.7.[16] As shown in Figure 15, its rubble is of notably smaller scale than the stonework of the bastion proper. The lower bastion is formed largely of boulders 0.50–1.00 m. in height, true Cyclopean masonry. The stones of the crown, as on the north, average well under 0.40 m. in height. Retained along the inside edge of the crown on the south are remains of an earth fill similar in color and character to the earth packed within the stonework of the crown.[17] Seemingly, the crown and fill are contemporary, the earth having washed into the stonework from behind.

The crown of the western bastion was sealed in cement by the 1930's restoration, obscuring any trace of the ancient mortar. A glance at the scale of this upper stonework, however, makes it evident, as on the north and south, that the crown and lower face belong to different stages.[18] As attested in Figure 16, the west face up to *ca.* +139.10 is built largely of boulders 0.60–1.00 m. in height. The stonework from +139.10 to the crown is less massive, formed of blocks from 0.30 to 0.50 m. in height.

As entered on late 19th-century plans by Bohn and Kawerau, a stretch of rubble wall traversed the eastern end of the sanctuary on a near parallel to the Mycenaean circuit (Plan A).[19] The wall is now sealed beneath modern paving; as recorded, however, it began from a point within three meters of the preserved eastern end of the southern crown and had stonework generally comparable in scale to the crown. It appears to have been part of the upper stonework of the bastion, perhaps having marked the limit of the sanctuary across the closed side of the bastion.

We concluded above that the Bronze Age bastion once stood to at least +144.0, over three meters above its highest preserved level. At some point a major collapse occurred. The rubble crown of the bastion serves to confirm this view. As a direct extension of the original stonework on the north, west, and south, it is clearly a repair or rebuilding. Its evident

16 The earth fill is evident in the excavation photograph, Lemerle 1938, p. 449, fig. 5.

17 Compare again Lemerle 1938, p. 449, fig. 5.

18 Compare a passage from Balanos' preliminary notes (p. 16, Appendix A, p. 147 below): "Behind Course 4 [of the west face of the bastion sheathing] (formed of headers) we found, not the face of the Pelasgian Wall as we expected, but a course of large blocks [backers] similar to the other, badly shattered blocks of the later temple. Behind [this full] fourth course was the face of an older wall of small stones, see photograph, which constitutes, it appears, a continuation of the boulders visible to the inside." Cf. Welter (1939, col. 7), who notes the absence of clay mortar in the upper wall: "In den oberen Lagen waren die Zwischenräume zwischen den Blöcken mit Steinschlag gefüllt."

19 Bohn 1880a, pl. XI; Kavvadias and Kawerau 1906, pl. H′ (marked in light green, «Οἰκήματα καὶ τείχη κυκλώπεια καὶ πολυγωνικά»); Bundgård 1974a, pl. 203. The sole description of the wall is Kavvadias and Kawerau 1906, col. 140: "Südlich von der Merkzahl 89 befindet sich als erwähnenswerter Baurest noch ein kurzes Stück einer Kalksteinmauer, die nur in einer Schicht über dem Felsen erhalten ist, aber doch deutlich eine Fassade nach Osten hin zeigt. Für die Bedeutung dieses Mauerstücks liegen keine Anhaltspunkte vor." Although no date is suggested there, later studies, all after the remains were no longer visible, have considered the wall Bronze Age; see first Welter 1939, col. 7, fig. 4.

purpose, whether the rebuilding was initiated soon or at some interval after the collapse, was to restore the bastion to an even terrace at the lower level.

The first rebuilding may be roughly dated by its masonry. The absence of mortar speaks for a date in or after the Geometric period. Late Helladic walls are all but invariably set in clay.[20] The scale of the rubble in the crown serves as a second, narrower criterion. The blocks are massive by early Greek standards, suggesting a date at earliest in Middle, more likely in Late Geometric times.[21] An upper limit is indicated by the simple rubble technique of the crown itself: starting in the Middle Archaic period, more narrowly from the second quarter of the 6th century on, walls of importance at Athens are in decidedly more developed styles.[22] Among well-published Attic walls, the closest parallel to the crown is the first retaining wall for the Archaic sanctuary of Demeter at Eleusis, comparable for both the scale of its masonry and the manner of laying the blocks.[23] That phase at Eleusis has been variously dated to the 8th or 7th century, depending on differing interpretations of stratigraphy.[24] Although the absolute date is uncertain, there appears no question that the Eleusis walls precede the mid-Archaic walls of the Akropolis.[25] On their example, we may provisionally place the bastion crown in the Early Archaic period, up to, but not later than, the second quarter of the 6th century.

SECOND REBUILDING OF THE CROWN

Remains from a second rebuilding of the bastion survive in a stretch of wall 4.35 m. long along the northern edge of the sanctuary (Plan A). Its face, now obscured by modern fill, was carefully recorded by Welter in his excavations of 1923. It was revealed there roughly to a level of +140.10, to the beginning of the third course (Pl. 6:c); its crown comes to an even horizontal at +140.98.[26] Over part of its length, this northern stretch stands back to back with the inner face of the preceding crown, which stands almost to its level, +140.86 versus

[20] For dry setting in the Geometric period, H. Drerup, *Archaeologia Homerica*, II, O, *Griechische Baukunst in geometrischer Zeit*, Göttingen 1969, p. 107. On Mycenaean mortar, e.g., A. J. B. Wace, *Mycenae*, Princeton 1949, p. 49 *et passim*.

[21] On Geometric stonework, Drerup, *op. cit.*, p. 106. Greek stonework remains characteristically of small scale into the Late Geometric period, built typically of fist- to skull-sized rubble; more substantial blocks, if present, remain largely at foundation level.

[22] Compare the retaining wall for the Archaic approach to the Akropolis, Wrede 1933, no. 20; Vanderpool 1974, pp. 156–160, pick-dressed face and joints, later second quarter of the 6th century; Archaic cistern on the Akropolis south slope, Wrede 1933, nos. 14, 15, tightly jointed polygonal, pick dressed.

[23] Noack 1927, pp. 9–10, pls. 13, 20:b (walls labeled E2 and Θ); Wrede 1933, no. 3; G. Mylonas, *Eleusis and the Eleusinian Mysteries*, Princeton 1961, figs. 6, 12, 14, 15 (walls labeled E1, E5).

[24] Noack 1927, pp. 9–14, esp. p. 13, Archaic or at earliest Late Geometric; Mylonas, *op. cit.*, pp. 56–57, mid-8th century.

[25] We can note that Eleusis wall Noack (1927) B 2, pl. 14 (= Wrede 1933, no. 4), the immediate successor to E2 and Θ, is in a technique rather comparable to the Archaic retaining wall of the Akropolis approach. Together with other walls at Eleusis from the same stage of the sanctuary, it forms the earliest, or at least one of the earliest, examples of Attic polygonal masonry. This early polygonal, however, is dated neither by stratigraphy nor by other firm criteria at Eleusis.

[26] Welter 1923, p. 193, pls. IV; V:1, 7, 9. For earlier reference to this wall, then only partially exposed, Bohn 1880a, p. 267; *idem* 1882, p. 15; Kavvadias and Kawerau 1906, cols. 130, 138. My levels are derived from Balanos, who records the top of the wall as −1.237 relative to the Nike Temple euthynteria (e.g., Pl. 7).

+140.98. The masonry of the second rebuilding is in so-called irregular trapezoidal, that is, the blocks are trapezoids with the horizontal joints parallel and the vertical joints oblique, laid in courses of slightly varying and irregular height.[27] The blocks are for the most part Akropolis limestone, with some Kará, and are trimmed on the front and along their joints only.

A further trapezoidal block was uncovered by Balanos along the west face of the bastion.[28] It is seated on the rubble of the preceding crown at +140.37, standing thus roughly even with the second trapezoidal course on the north.

Inasmuch as the first and second rebuildings form respectively the inner and outer faces of the crown on the north, it is likely that the two stages had a similar purpose. Like the first rebuilding, the second appears intended to repair and level the bastion crown. The portions of the rubble crown that it replaced may have been dismantled or, what is more likely, may have collapsed or been destroyed. The loss of stonework on the north, attested by the difference between the preserved height of the first rebuilding, +140.86, and the lowest recorded level of the second, *ca.* +140.10, was in the range of two or three rubble courses.

In Chapter VI we will be associating the second rebuilding of the crown with our sanctuary Stage III. We may restrict ourselves for the moment to the dating of its masonry. The second crown, although passed over in the standard treatises on Greek building, claims a definite place in the history of Greek walls.[29] With its firm *terminus post quem non* of the mid-430's, given by the Southwest Wing of the Propylaia, it is the first attested example of trapezoidal masonry at Athens. The style recurs in a series of Attic coastal fortifications from the second phase of the Peloponnesian War, beginning with Sounion in 412[30] and including Thorikos and Rhamnous.[31] The 4th century sees it develop, finally, to a virtual *koine* in military engineering.[32]

27 For the definition of the style, Scranton 1941, pp. 70–79.

28 Akropolis limestone, length 0.51 m., width 0.35 m., height 0.22 m. The block is mentioned by Welter 1939, cols. 9–10. It appears in our Plate 4 toward the upper right, held together with rope. In the course of excavation Welter noted that traces of the bedding for further blocks are preserved elsewhere along the crown on the west. The walls and floor of the modern crypt now overlie much of the western crown, but there does remain at least one portion of this bedding exposed just south of the block.

29 On the history of masonry styles, Wrede 1933; Scranton 1941; Maier 1959–1961; Orlandos 1966–1968, II, pp. 129–184.

30 Mussche 1964, pp. 423–432; the date is based on Thucydides 8.4.

31 Thorikos: Mussche 1961, pp. 176–205. The late 5th-century date, given by Xenophon, *Hell.* 1.2.1, is supported by excavation. The dating of the outer circuit at Rhamnous is less well established, cf. Pouilloux 1954, pp. 67–92; a date in the late 5th century is tentatively suggested by Winter 1971, p. 161, note 41. On the north extension of the terrace for the Temple of Nemesis at Rhamnous, see Wrede 1933, no. 81 (late 5th century); this wall has traditionally been thought to follow the building of the Temple of Nemesis, although its chronology may need reexamination in light of recent excavations on the site. See V. Petrakos, «᾿Ανασκαφὴ ῾Ραμνοῦντος», Πρακτικά 1983 [1986], Α′ (pp. 109–130), p. 120. The trapezoidal fortification walls at Phyle likely date from the late 5th century as well: Winter 1971, pp. 138–139. It is generally agreed that irregular and isodomic trapezoidal were in use simultaneously over this period. I have attempted no chronological distinction between the two. Scranton (1941, pp. 80–81) tentatively dates two irregular trapezoidal stretches of fortification wall at Messene from *ca.* 470, associating them with the Third Messenian Wars. The walls would be at that date the earliest known examples of trapezoidal. They remain unexcavated, however, while more recent bibliography continues to regard the 4th- or 3rd-century circuit as the first fortification of the site; so E. Kirsten, "Die Entstehung der griechischen Stadt," *AA* (*JdI* 79) 1964 (cols. 892–910), col. 907, Winter 1971, pp. 111–112, note 23.

32 Maier 1961, II, pp. 109–110.

A date for the genesis of the trapezoidal style is hardly evident on this testimony. If we consider that, our wall aside, trapezoidal masonry is first known from the penultimate decade of the 5th century and becomes increasingly common from that point on, a date for the second crown at or approaching its 430's limit appears most probable.

III
THE BASE FOR THE CULT STATUE AND THE REPOSITORY

I begin with a description of this base as it was found reused.[1] It is fashioned of two rectangular, gray-brown poros blocks carefully fitted with anathyrosis. Together they form roughly a square: length on the front (east side) 1.08 m.; width on the left side 0.96 m.; height 0.28–0.41 m. (Fig. 2, Pls. 1–2:a, A on Plan A). Its back and right sides are broken away and have been partially reworked to a rough plane at the right rear and to a shallow curve at the back left. At the center there is a three-level cavity. Surrounding the cavity there is a raised, framelike band of stone (we will call it a collar) set several centimeters in from the sides of the square. The uppermost of the three levels, formed with three sides straight and the back wall gently curved, measures 0.54 m. in width, 0.53 m. front to back, and 0.095 m. in depth. The third (lowest) level is equal to the second front to back but is slightly narrower: they measure 0.38 × 0.335 m. and 0.33 × 0.335 m.; their depths are 0.08 and 0.09 m. respectively. The collar has a different width on each of its three well-preserved sides, front 0.17, left 0.15, and right 0.105–0.12 m. Traces of an incised line, partially effaced by weathering, can be seen on the upper surface of the collar along the right side at the rear, 0.025 m. in from the right edge.

The outer margin of stone surrounding the raised collar measures 0.105–0.12 m. in width on the front and left. On the damaged right side it survives only in a narrow ledge of stone at the base of the collar on the rear block. Assuming that the collar originally extended to the right edge of the block, we may establish its minimum width from the maximum preserved width of the stone on that side: 0.17 m.

The under edge of the blocks, seen front and left, betrays a number of anomalies. On the left, the forward and rear blocks are trimmed below to different levels. The height of the forward block, measured front and rear respectively, is 0.295 and 0.32 m. The rear block measured front and rear is 0.255 and 0.205 m. The resting surface across the front has been carved back in a series of scalloped depressions, most prominently at the front left corner.

The base has suffered extensive damage. In addition to the breaks along the right and rear, noted above, the front block is split away at the upper left corner at the joint, and the collar at the rear is badly cracked and partly broken away. A further crack runs from front to back across both blocks. The collar shows extensive wear at the rear left, along the left side, and across the greater part of the front. The wear in front ends abruptly at a well-defined line 0.10 m. from the right corner. There are clear, if less pronounced, signs of wear on the surround, both front and left. The left front corner of the collar has partially calcined, attesting exposure to intense heat. Traces of mortar adhere to the collar at the front and right and to the surround along the front. Finally, a dark gray plaster covers the front side of the base, as well as portions of the collar at front and right.

[1] Balanos 1956, p. 785; Welter 1939, col. 11.

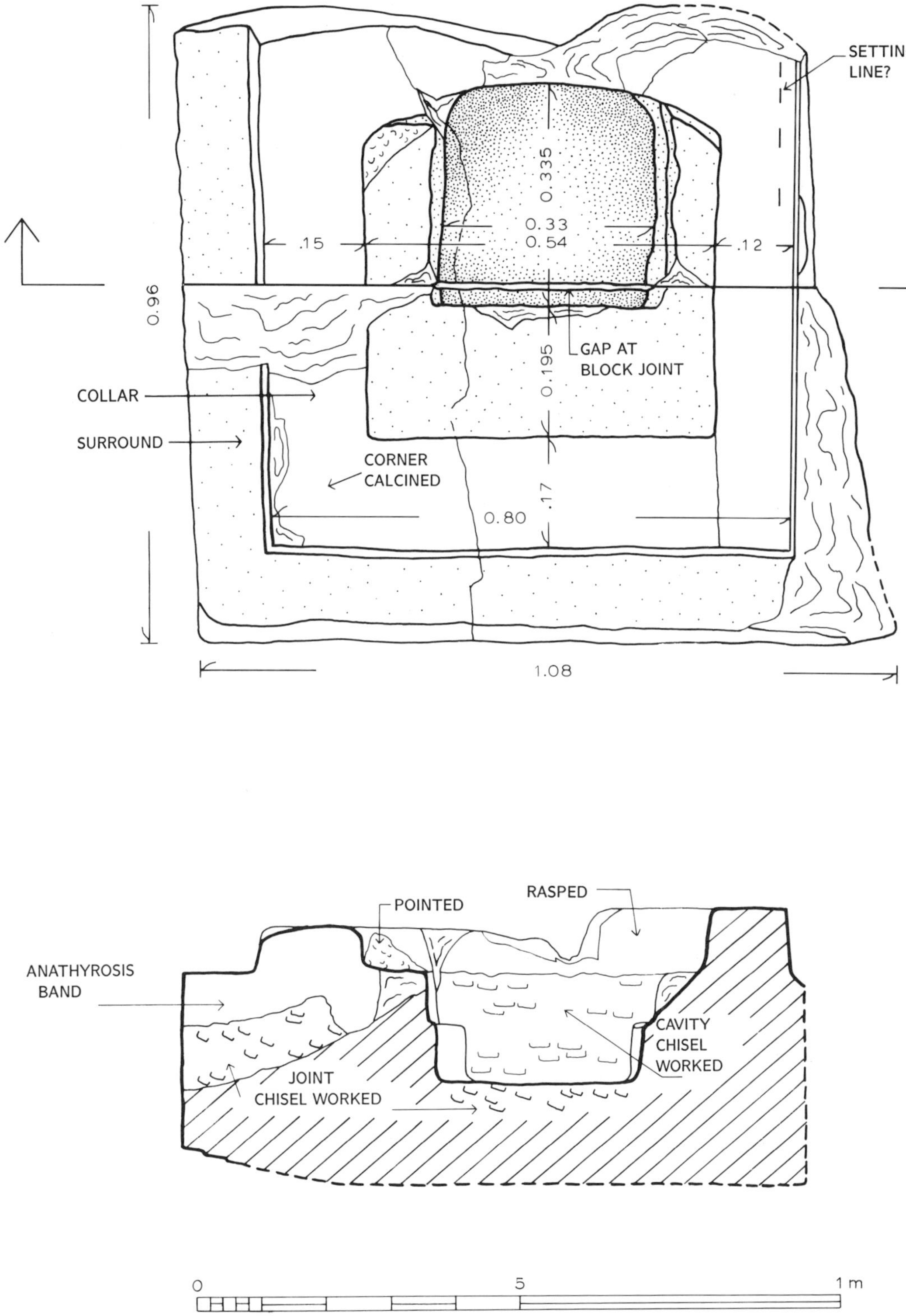

Fig. 2. Plan and cross-section of the repository (base for the cult statue)

TERRACOTTA FIGURINES

Balanos' often discussed find of terracotta figurines came from the bottom level of the base cavity, mixed in with fragments of small vases and a few very small bones.[2] These finds are now lost; an excavation photograph, however, here reproduced as Plate 2:b, conveys at least the general form of the terracottas. They are of a crude, seemingly hand-formed type, from 4 to 10 cm. tall. The body is a thin cylinder flared below to form a base, the arms are rough triangles, and the head is pinched and has a flaring headdress.

THE PHASES OF THE BASE

From the form of the base as detailed above we may distinguish five periods in its history: Stage 1; 1a, minor reworkings; 2, a period of damage; 3, a major reworking; and last, the period of the Turkish crypt.

The form of the base in Stages 1 and 3 can be deduced mainly from the form of the anathyrosis between the blocks, exposed where the front block has split away at upper left (Fig. 2) and from the anathyrosis preserved along the joint between the two blocks within the lowest level of the cavity. As seen at the joint at upper left, the contact band of the anathyrosis follows the upper contour of the base: its lower edge heads up behind the wall of the top level, curves left beneath the collar, and heads down slightly from the collar to the surround. In contrast, no contact band seals the joint down the left side of the base; the slightly recessed, more roughly worked interior of the anathyrosis continues fully to the left edge. The joint across the lowest level bears close analogy to the joint at left. From roughly the floor of the second level down, the joint surfaces pull away from each other slightly, leaving a gap up to 5 mm. in width. The inner faces of the joint thus revealed bear the same rough finish as the interior of the joint at left.

On this evidence we conclude that two areas of the base have been reworked: the left face was cut back sufficiently to remove the border of anathyrosis on that side; and the two lowest levels of the cavity were cut through the anathyrosis from above. In contrast, the features respected by the anathyrosis (the outer margin, collar, and first level) may be safely attributed to Stage 1.

The two areas of Stage 3 reworking (the left side of the base and the two lowest levels of the cavity) are distinctively tooled, showing deep, biting strokes of a flat chisel. The same tooling is evident on the right rear of the base, in the recutting of the break, and on the resting surface of the rear block at left: those areas ought also to date from Stage 3. Finally, the recutting of the base at the back left seems to belong to Stage 3 as well, since it is a curved, irregular reworking roughly analogous to that at the right rear; it is tooled with a point rather than a flat chisel, but the work is in an equally rough hand.

The broken right and rear sides of the base, partially retrimmed in Stage 3, attest a period of damage or destruction, Stage 2. Other parts of the base may also have suffered damage at

[2] In addition to the references in note 1 above (p. 20), see Balanos' excavation notes, p. 10, Appendix A, p. 145 below.

this time, including the left face and the resting surface of the rear block at left. Such damage, at any rate, offers a ready explanation for the Stage 3 retrimming of these areas.

The minor reworking of the base, Stage 1a, is attested by the finish on the right outer face of the collar. The execution of the right collar is exacting: the plane of the face is precise and even, tipped uniformly 3 degrees from the vertical, and the surface of the stone is carefully smoothed with abrasives. In contrast, the remaining sides of the collar, the outer face front and left and the inner wall all around, are coarsely finished with a rasp and are freely drawn. A straightedge placed against the front of the collar touches at two points, right and middle left, standing away from the face elsewhere as much as 3 mm.; the collar at the left rear follows a gentle curve. The verticals show similar variation. The left face at the rear flares 17 degrees from the vertical, the collar at the front right, 8 degrees.

Since of the inner and outer faces of the collar only one, the outer right, is precisely tooled, and since the collar is narrowest on that side, 0.12 m., against 0.17 m. on the front and 0.15 m. on the left, it seems clear that the precise tooling is later than the rough. That the breaks along the side of the base extend fully to the right face of the collar establishes in turn that the precise tooling precedes the Stage 2 destruction. We may suggest that the reworking, Stage 1a, served to dress the right collar for the setting of an additional block. The incised line on the right upper surface of the collar may therefore be understood as a setting line, the new block having been bedded level with the surround and rabbeted over the collar.[3]

To the period of the Turkish crypt belong the extensive wear on the front and left sides of the collar, the calcination of the collar at the left front corner, and the lesser traces of wear on the surround. As recorded by Balanos, the right rear corner of the base was overlaid by an ashlar of the amphiprostyle temple foundations, height *ca.* 0.24 m., on which in turn was founded the north wall of the Turkish crypt (Pl. 15; cf. Pl. 14). Directly west of the ashlar, the crypt wall rested on the rear euthynteria of the naïskos and beyond this to the west, on a row of further ashlars of roughly the height of the euthynteria. The cross-section, Plate 13:b, records the floor of the crypt at +140.59. It lay, that is, not even with the bottom of the crypt wall, at *ca.* +140.87, but rather concealed the ashlars west of the naïskos to only some half their height, while completely exposing the block over the northwest corner of our base. While the northern half of the base remained sealed by that block, its southern half lay exposed, projecting up through the floor of the crypt: the southern collar is worn down to +140.675, to within nine centimeters of the crypt floor.

The abrupt change in the condition of the collar, from relatively fresh and undamaged at the rear right where protected by the Nike Temple foundations to severely worn at the rear left where exposed in the crypt, establishes *prima facie* that the wear is Turkish. The lines of the crypt over the eastern half of the base can no longer be recovered directly, for Ross dismantled the Turkish remains in that area. If we extend the inner line of the north wall of the crypt eastward, however, we may note that it crosses the front of the base 0.10 m. from the right edge of the collar, just where the stone changes from worn to well preserved. The crypt must have widened just east of the collar, reaching fully to the north wall of the

[3] This form of rabbet is a common expedient in Greek masonry. Compare the joints between the courses of the original podium of the Parthenon and the Periclean extension, Bundgård 1976, p. 10, fig. 2.

naïskos, for the front margin of the base is worn across its full width, and from that point on the euthynteria and wall of the naïskos show traces of burning.

Having reviewed the evidence for the periods of the base, we need to consider more carefully its form and use, specifically in Stages 1, 1a, and 3.

STAGE 1

To this stage pertain the collar, preserved to its original width on the front and left; the margin of stone around the collar, minimum estimated width 0.17 m. at the right front; and the uppermost level of the cavity, straight on three sides, curved at the back, depth 0.095 m. We earlier described the tooling on the walls of the collar. The upper surface of the collar, well preserved on the right side, and the margin of stone around it, best seen at the left rear, show a careful finish with abrasives. The floor of the Stage 1 level is worked with a drove, save along its left and front edges and at the extreme left rear corner, where the floor slopes up and shows rougher working with a point, as if the carving had not been fully finished in those areas. The anathyrosis bands of the joint are finely worked with a drove, the interior of the joint more roughly with a drove and narrower flat chisel.

The Stage 1 cavity provides the single major clue to the function of these blocks. Of shallow depth, roughly tooled to an essentially level floor, it has the characteristic form of a plinth cutting for a marble statue; indeed it resembles this and nothing else. Its proportions, roughly square with three sides straight, the fourth curved, belong to a prominent Archaic statuary type, the seated or enthroned figure.[4] We may be confident in view of these criteria that the blocks originally formed a statue base.[5] From the dimensions of the plinth, the height of the image was around 1.0 m. (seated), roughly four-fifths lifesize.

Given that we have correctly established the general class of this monument, we may note two peculiarities that set it apart from conventional bases for votive statuary. The first is

[4] Compare the plinths of the Branchidai, K. Tuchelt, *Archaischen Skulpturen von Didyma* (*IstForsch* 27), Berlin 1970, K 45 (BM B 272), K 47 (BM B 278), K 48 (BM B 275), K 49 (Izmir, Basmane Storeroom 519), K 51 (BM B 274), K 52 (BM B 276), K 55 (Istanbul, Arch. Mus. 1945), K 57 (BM B 277), K 59 (BM B 279). From Attica (Rhamnous), Athens, NatM 2569, H. Möbius, "Über Form und Bedeutung der sitzenden Gestalt in der Kunst des Orients und der Griechen," *AthMitt* 41, 1916 (pp. 119–219), p. 176, pl. 13.

In the case of enthroned figures, the plinth most usually curves around the garment and feet of the figure and is straight to each side, in front of the legs of the throne. The cutting on the Nike base is inset on one side, the southwest corner, in a close parallel to the enthroned type, but it continues in an uninterrupted curve on the opposite side. There are analogous uninterrupted curves attested for seated figures, for example, Tuchelt, K 55, cited above; to my knowledge, however, the disparate treatment of the opposite ends of the curve on the Nike base is unique. Possibly the asymmetry was intended to accommodate an attribute set to the left of the figure. More likely, however, it is simply a small irregularity: plinths, particularly of Early Archaic figures, not uncommonly betray such variations. The rough tooling of the plinth cutting along its edges and at the left rear corner seems best understood as an early feature as well. Compare the Ionic column dedication, Athens, NatM 4797, from roughly the mid-6th century; Jacob-Felsch 1969, pp. 33–35, for the column type. On early seated statuary, Jung 1982, pp. 30–68; Floren 1987, pp. 96–97.

[5] Once the phases of the base are understood, its interpretation as an *eschara*, a ground altar, can be firmly excluded (Oikonomos 1948, p. 105). The deep central cavity, a frequent feature of *escharai*, dates from Stage 3, while the calcination of the collar is Turkish. For the identification of the blocks as a statue base, cf. Romano 1980, pp. 60–61. Romano suggests that the three levels of the central cavity together formed the socket for a wooden image.

the margin of stone around the collar. There survives, to my knowledge, not a single Archaic parallel to this surround,[6] while I can cite but one distant comparison from the Classical period, itself an unusual base.[7] The second peculiarity, also uncommon but with at least one Archaic parallel, is the fashioning of the plinth cutting from more than one block, with the statue thus set over a block joint.[8]

The base cannot be complete as it stands. To have formed a secure setting for a plinth, its two blocks would have needed either to have been clamped or to have formed part of a larger setting that itself held them in place.[9] Either way, our reconstruction of the base will remain largely the same. If the blocks were clamped, then the surrounding margin must originally have been wider than now preserved, for no clamp cuttings survive. If the blocks were held together by additional blocks, again the dimensions of the base would have been appreciably larger. Whichever reconstruction is adopted, we find that the base was of larger proportions than strictly required by the image for support.

The step on this monument from the "surround" to the "collar", as we have called these two elements, and the scale of the whole relative to the image it supported invite comparison with the so-called stepped base.[10] A common support for grave statuary, the stepped form consists essentially of a traditional base, the top step raised to monumentality by the setting of

[6] Although not cut to receive statuary directly, a series of blocks set east of the altar in the sanctuary of Aphaia on Aigina deserves mention. The blocks have each a large rectangular cutting for a second block above and are thus restored by the excavator as the lower step of a two-stepped base. For stepped bases with successive courses inset, compare Waldstein 1902, p. 112, pls. XII, XXIX:B, H. A number of the Aigina blocks have a ledge along one or more sides, cut to support the slabs of a poros pavement that surrounded the altar. See Furtwängler 1906, pp. 71–73, figs. 17–19; D. Ohly, *Tempel und Heiligtum der Aphaia auf Aegina*, 3rd ed., Munich 1981, figs. 15, 18. The ledges, roughly cut with a drove, are an interesting, though distant analogy to the finished surround on the Nike base, but note the theory by Frederick Cooper presented at the annual meeting of the Archaeological Institute of America, New York, in 1987 (abstract published as "The Tetrastylon in Greek Architecture," *AJA* 92, 1988, p. 280). Cooper argues that the Nike Sanctuary base was taken by the Athenians as booty from Aigina and was originally from the same monument as the Aigina bases, namely a tetrastylon.

[7] Quadriga base at Corinth: C. K. Williams II, "Corinth, 1969: Forum Area," *Hesperia* 39, 1970 (pp. 1–39), pp. 6–9, fig. 2.

[8] Compare the cult-statue base in the smaller temple of Athena at Sounion, V. Staïs, Σούνιον, Athens 1920, p. 42, pl. E′; Jacob-Felsch 1969, pp. 24–25; Dinsmoor, Jr. 1971, pp. 50–51. The Archaic dating is based on excavations by Staïs. Note, however, that Dinsmoor has suggested a Classical date for the Small Temple and proposes several phases for the base, of which the earliest ought not to antedate the late 6th century. In contrast to Archaic bases, those of Late Classical and Hellenistic date, particularly podia for large group monuments, not infrequently show plinth cuttings set across two blocks. So, for example, the Daochos Monument, J. Pouilloux, *Topographie et architecture: La région nord du sanctuaire* (*Fouilles de Delphes* II, ix), Paris 1960, pp. 67–80, plan 11, pls. 33–37; cf. the group monument, pp. 80–87, plan 13, pls. 38–42.

[9] For the use of clamps compare the Sounion base, Staïs, *op. cit.*, pl. E′; double-T clamps join the front and back blocks, one to each side of the plinth. For blocks held in a larger setting: base for the cult statue of Nemesis at Rhamnous, B. Petrakos, «᾿Ανασκαφὴ ῾Ραμνοῦντος», Πρακτικά 1979 (pp. 1–25), pp. 8–12, fig. 3; *idem*, "La base de la Némésis d'Agoracrite," *BCH* 105, 1981, pp. 227–253; *idem* 1986, pp. 89–107. The four blocks encompassing the plinth cutting are held within the clamped frame of the dado. Note also bases that secure the top step to the second step with dowels, for example the base of the Early Classical bronze bull dedicated by Eretria at Olympia, F. Eckstein, ᾿Αναθήματα: *Studien zu den Weihgeschenken strengen Stils im Heiligtum von Olympia*, Berlin 1969, pp. 50–53.

[10] Jacob-Felsch 1969, pp. 27–32.

additional, progressively wider courses beneath it. We may infer from the small step on the Nike base, in contrast, that there the upper course itself was enlarged. Either the preserved step continued down in a series of further small steps or, more likely, the surround continued out on a level, the base forming a table or podium above which the image was slightly raised.

Bases larger than strictly called for by the statuary they support occur in two basic forms in the Archaic period, as the stepped base, reviewed above, and as one among the established support types for cult statuary. While the former is attested in a number of well-preserved examples, instances of oversize cult-statue bases, specifically those cases where one can document a discrepancy in scale from image to support, remain far more rare. Their survivals are typically fragmentary, often preserved to the lowest courses only, or merely in foundations. The setting for the cult statue of Leto on Delos is a telling instance. As established in literary and epigraphical sources, the *xoanon* of Leto was a primitive image, was worked separately from its seat, and was dressed in real garments and sandals.[11] It belongs by these traits to one of the earliest stages in the development of Greek statuary and as such was almost certainly under lifesize.[12] By contrast, its base survives in rectangular foundations measuring 2.20 × 2.90 m., occupying most of the temple cella.[13] Evidence from the Argive Heraion is roughly comparable. As described by Pausanias, the ancient image of Hera was a small seated *xoanon*;[14] its rubble podium, so identified from its central position within the 7th-century cella, was imposing by comparison, measuring 1.80 m. on a side.[15] We may note

[11] *Délos* XXIV, pp. 118–120; also F. Courby, "Notes topographiques et chronologiques sur le sanctuaire d'Apollon délien," *BCH* 45, 1921 (pp. 174–241), pp. 230–232. Among literary sources, in particular Semos, cited in Athenaios 14.614b; Jacoby, *FGrHist* III B, no. 396 F 10, p. 287: Καὶ πάντα τὰ κατὰ τὴν νῆσον θαυμάζων ἦλθεν [ὁ Παρμενίσκος] καὶ εἰς τὸ Λητῷον, νομίζων τῆς Ἀπόλλωνος μητρὸς ἄγαλμά τι θεωρήσειν ἀξιόλογον· ἰδὼν δ' αὐτὸ ξύλον ὂν ἄμορφον παραδόξως ἐγέλασεν. . . .

Among Delian inscriptions, in particular *Inscriptions de Délos*, no. 1417, A I, lines 100–102: ΕΝ ΤΩΙ ΛΗΤΩΙΩΙ· τὸ ἄγαλμα τῆς θεοῦ ξύλινον, | δεδυκὸς χιτῶν [ᾶ] λινοῦν καὶ ἠμφιεσμένον | λινωι· ὑποδημάτων κοίλων ζεῦγος· θρόνον | ἐφ' οὗ κάθηται ξύλινον.

[12] On the primitive appearance of early images, Kallimachos, fr. 100 (R. Pfeiffer, Oxford 1949): οὔπω Σκέλμιον ἔργον ἐύξοον, ἀλλ' ἐπὶ τεθμόν | δηναιὸν γλυφάνων ἄξοος ἦσθα σανίς· | ὧδε γὰρ ἱδρύοντο θεοὺς τότε· καὶ γὰρ Ἀθήνης | ἐν Λίνδῳ Δαναὸς λιτὸν ἔθηκεν ἕδος.

See further, Buschor 1930, pp. 4–5, and the lengthier but more problematic treatments of S. Casson, *Technique of Early Greek Sculpture*, Oxford 1933, pp. 55–65, and H. L. Lorimer, *Homer and the Monuments*, London 1950, pp. 443–444; also more recently Kroll 1982, pp. 72–73. On the ritual dressing of early nude statuary, particularly Willemsen 1939, pp. 1–17.

It has occasionally been argued that large-scale statuary existed already in the Late Geometric period; so, for example, V. Müller, "The Beginnings of Monumental Sculpture in Greece," *MetMusSt* 5, 2, 1933, pp. 157–169; H.-V. Herrmann, "Zum Problem der Entstehung der griechischen Grossplastik," *Wandlungen* (*Festschrift E. Homann-Wedeking*), Waldsassen 1975, pp. 35–48; Jung 1982, pp. 176–178 (specifically with regard to Crete). Where the scale of early works is indicated in literary sources, however, it is all but invariably small. The one possible exception is the columnar, 30-cubit-high Apollo Hyakinthios, included by Philostratos (*VA* 3.14) among the earliest Greek images. Even should we admit the existence of isolated large-scale statuary before the kouros and kore types of the mid-7th century, the very ritual that surrounds the early nude cult images (bathing, perfuming, dressing) remains natural and practical only at small scale. See here Willemsen 1939, pp. 5, 14–15.

[13] *Délos* XXIV, pp. 44, 68–69, pl. IV, *ca.* 540 B.C.

[14] Pausanias 2.17.5.

[15] Waldstein 1902, p. 111.

finally the cult statue of Hera on Delos, an image clothed in real garments and anointed in a ceremony of *kosmesis* involving sponges and perfume.[16] Two successive bases for the image are preserved, the first from the 7th-century temple, measuring 2.40 × 0.91 m., the second, from the 6th-century cella, measuring 3.70 × 2.70 m. The former survives in foundations only, the latter to the orthostates of the dado.[17]

Neither these podia nor any other yet more fragmentary survivals of the type aid in interpreting the details of the Nike blocks. None stands to the crowning course, nor is any other fragment of such a crowning course known. Specific parallels apart, however, the class of monument here attested, the large base supporting a small image, suits these blocks well.

Given how battered and reworked the remains of the Nike base are, there can be no secure recovery of its Stage 1 form. Specifically, we remain ignorant of its exterior dimensions and of the form of the base and crown. These uncertainties understood, a tentative restoration of the base is still of aid in interpreting the remains (Fig. 3).[18] Primarily, the restoration clarifies the function of the two unique features on these blocks, the collar and the margin of stone around it. The collar of the base is bordered on the inside by the plinth cutting for the statue, as we have seen. Figure 3 shows that the outer face of the collar, the step up from the surround, creates a low rise at the center of the base right beneath the image. The length and width of this low platform (we will call it the inner podium) are about the same as those of a simple one-step base. It appears to preserve the memory of the more common base type set within the grander but less familiar form of the cult base proper.

Dating

Masonry technique provides perhaps the most important dating criterion for our base, in particular the uneven workmanship seen on the lateral faces of the inner podium (the outer faces of the collar). A careful survey of Attic bases reveals that lateral planes with this form and degree of unevenness are narrowly characteristic of the earliest attested bases for marble statuary. We may compare the dressing and finish on the bases for the Sounion kouroi, the Moschophoros base, and analogous work on other, fragmentary bases from the early Akropolis.[19] By 560, seemingly without exception, standards of workmanship have become

16 A. Plassart, *Les sanctuaires et les cultes du Mont Cynthe* (*Explorations archéologique de Délos* XIX), Paris 1928, p. 212.

17 *Ibid.*, pp. 153–154, 204–205. Plassart (p. 205) notes that a block with a corner cut away in a shallow parabolic curve was found in the general vicinity of the base. He tentatively identifies the curve as the wall of a plinth cutting for the 6th-century base. If correct, the curvature and height of the cutting could only be for a monumental image. The robes and ceremony of adornment attested in the temple accounts and the 7th-century date of the first temple, however, render a large-scale image unlikely. The association of the block with the base has little to recommend it.

We may note, finally, two additional Archaic bases of truly monumental scale but imperfectly preserved and of uncertain restoration: the "Central Basis" beneath the 6th-century temple of Artemis at Ephesos, Hogarth 1908, pp. 53–65, 69–72; and the podium for the third temple of Hera on Samos, Buschor 1930, pp. 76–77; D. Ohly, "Die Göttin und ihre Basis," *AthMitt* 68, 1953 (pp. 24–50), pp. 31, 45.

18 For the *xoanon* of Athena Nike, here restored atop the base, see pp. 93–98 below.

19 Sounion bases, Athens, NatM 2720, 3645 a, 3939, K. Rhomaios, *Antike Denkmäler* IV, v, Berlin 1931, p. 91, figs. 15–19; Jacob-Felsch 1969, pp. 107–109. Moschophoros, Schrader 1939, p. 278, fig. 324; Jacob-Felsch 1969, pp. 6–7. Fragmentary poros bases from the Akropolis: Athens, EM 6222, Raubitschek 1949, no. 317, from a column support for a metal bowl; EM 6213, Raubitschek 1949, no. 318, from a column or pier support

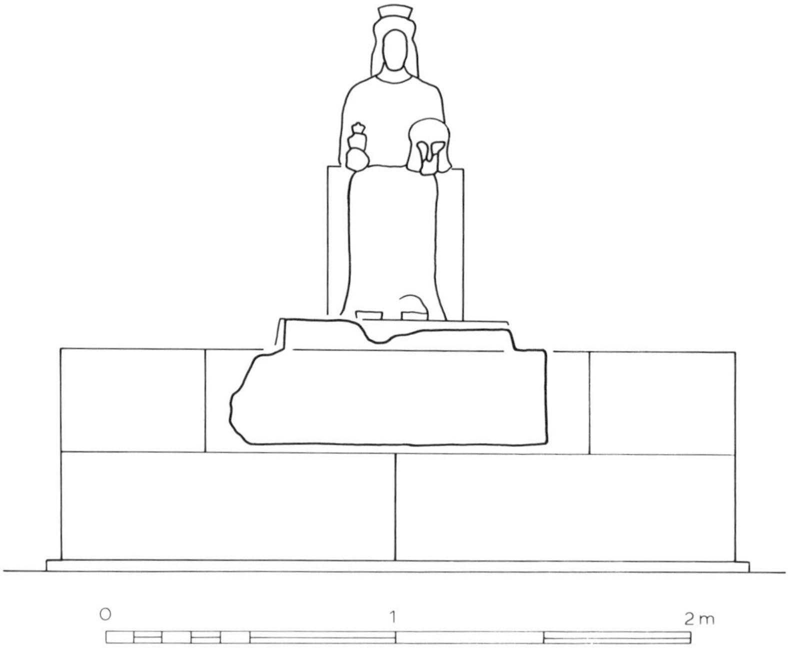

FIG. 3. Reconstruction of the base for the cult statue of Athena Nike

more rigorous, with consistent use of the plumb and straight rule.[20] The tooling establishes 560 as the *terminus ante quem* of the Nike base. A *terminus post* is given by the introduction of marble statuary to Athens around 600 B.C.[21] The material of the base (poros rather than marble), the depth of the plinth cutting, and further details of tooling, while not as close dating criteria, go well with this early date.[22]

for a metal bowl; EM 6216, Raubitschek 1949, no. 1, from the capital of a column dedication. The three bases are dated by Raubitschek to the second quarter of the 6th century. Compare as well the stele base from the Kerameikos, G. Richter, *Archaic Gravestones of Attica*, London 1961, no. 10, p. 14, fig. 28, dated by archaeological context to the late 7th or early 6th century. Among these, the general standards of masonry on the Nike base are closest to EM 6222 and 6213. The dressed faces on the three monuments deviate from a strict plane to a comparable degree, and their standards of finish are roughly equivalent.

On the evolution of early statue bases, see E. Walter-Karydi, "Die Entstehung der griechischen Statuenbasis," *AntK* 23, 1980, pp. 3–12.

[20] The new, stricter standards are exemplified by the following early bases: Athens, Kerameikos Mus., P 1001, F. Willemsen, "Archaische Grabmalbasen aus der Athener Stadtmauer," *AthMitt* 78, 1963 (pp. 104–153), pp. 105–109, Beil. 57–59 (*ca.* 560); I 332, *ibid.*, pp. 110–117, fig. 1, Beil. 60 (*ca.* 550); Athens, NatM, Phrasikleia, L. Jeffery, "The Inscribed Gravestones of Archaic Attica," *BSA* 57, 1962 (pp. 115–153), no. 46, pp. 138–139, pl. 39:a; E. Mastrokostas, *AAA* 5, 1972, pp. 298–324, ill. 1, figs. 17, 18.

[21] E. B. Harrison, *Archaic and Archaistic Sculpture* (*The Athenian Agora* XI), Princeton 1965, p. 3.

[22] Concerning poros used for early bases, see Raubitschek 1949, pp. 434–435. On the height of the plinth cutting, compare Athens, NatM 2, Richter 1968, no. 2, pp. 26–27, figs. 29, 30; J. Ducat, *Les Kouroi du Ptoion*, Paris 1971, no. 46, pp. 77–83, pl. 18 (plinth H. 0.10 m., 640–620 B.C.); Berlin Kore, Richter 1968, no. 42, pp. 39–40, figs. 139–146, C. Blümel, *Die archaisch griechischen Skulpturen der Staatlichen Museen zu Berlin*, Berlin

Stage 1a

As suggested above, the recutting that marks Stage 1a likely readied the base for a block that was rabbeted over the north face of the inner podium. The purpose of the addition remains unknown, but we offer two possibilities: it may have formed either part of an offering table or the base for a subsidiary image.[23]

Stage 3

Stage 3 comes in the aftermath of a destruction that razed the Stage 1 base and left its two extant blocks damaged, the front block on the right, the rear block at the right, back, and underside at left. If the two blocks were separated at that time, as would seem likely given the apparent force of the destruction, then Stage 3 involved their reassociation and realignment, as well as their reworking: the breaks at the right rear and rear left were recut; the left face was trimmed back;[24] a two-stepped cavity was carved down through the floor of the plinth cutting; and the underside of the base at the left rear corner was cut back. The irregular resting surface seen along the front edge of the block ought logically to date from this time as well, for it ill accords with Stage 1, when the blocks served as a crowning course.

We will argue later that the cult statue survived the destruction, to be set upon a new base in Stage 3. There can be no question that the surviving blocks of the old base were put to new use: the votive character of the finds from the lowest level as well as the form of the cavity itself establish that they served as a repository in Stage 3. An early 5th-century repository from the Athenian Agora provides a useful analogy.[25] Its receptacle is two-stepped. The upper stage of the cavity is square, a little over a meter on a side and 0.19 m. deep; the lower is circular, diameter 0.60 m., depth 0.50 m. Of equal interest is the partially preserved lid of the Agora example. It corresponds to the receptacle in its two-stepped form: the upper step of the lid filled the upper level of the receptacle, coming flush with the collar; the second step projected partway into the lower level.

The repository from the Nike Sanctuary, while roughly half the size of the Agora example, has essentially the same form. Its mason used the Stage 1 plinth cutting ready made to form

---

1963, no. 1, pp. 7–10, figs. 1–8 (plinth H. 0.10–0.105 m., *ca.* 580); Cheramyes Kore, Paris, Louvre, Richter 1968, no. 55, p. 46, figs. 183–185 (*ca.* 570–560); kore fragment, Samos, storeroom, E. Buschor, *Altsamische Standbilder* II, Berlin 1935, p. 26, fig. 85; Richter 1968, no. 61, p. 48, figs. 202, 203 (mislabeled no. 60, plinth H. 0.10 m.); fragment of kouros, Athens, NatM 2325, Ducat, no. 149, pp. 278–279, pl. 81 (plinth H. 0.115 m., *ca.* 560). We may note, however, that plinths equal to or approaching this height are attested through the Late Archaic period: e.g., kouros fragment, Athens, NatM, Ducat, no. 72, pp. 141–142, pl. 38 (plinth H. 0.10 m., *ca.* 550); kore by Phaidimos, Athens, NatM 81, Richter 1968, no. 91, pp. 58–59, figs. 284, 285 (plinth H. 0.07 m., *ca.* 540); kore fragment, Athens, AcrM 696, Schrader 1939, no. 20, pp. 61–62, figs. 22–25, pl. 29; Richter 1968, no. 126, p. 81, figs. 405, 406 (*ca.* 500). On early drove work, Heberdey 1919, p. 186; G. Richter, "Drove," *AJA* 47, 1943, pp. 188–193.

[23] On the location of offering tables within the temple cella, see G. Bakalakis, «῾Ελληνικὰ τραπεζοφόρα» (*University of Mississippi and Johns Hopkins Studies in Archaeology* 39), Thessalonike 1948, p. 18. For a cult-statue base and votive table in close conjunction, see Emporio, Athena Temple, see J. Boardman, *Excavations in Chios, 1952–1955: Greek Emporio*, Oxford 1967, pp. 8–9, 13.

[24] Possibly, the front side of the base was also trimmed at this time. It lies under a thick coat of Turkish plaster, making inspection impossible.

[25] H. A. Thompson, "Activities in the Athenian Agora: 1957," *Hesperia* 27, 1958 (pp. 145–160), pp. 148–153.

the ledge and collar for the upper stage of the lid and carved through the floor of the plinth cutting to form the container proper. The middle level, unique to the Nike Sanctuary example, seemingly formed a cradle for the bottom edge of the lid.

We suggest that the lid of the receptacle was broken up and removed either in the laying of the amphiprostyle-temple foundations or in the construction of the Turkish crypt. The deposit found within should be considered disturbed in either event. Its rather modest contents (terracottas, sherds, and bones) may conceivably be the leavings of a more valuable offering stripped at its discovery.[26]

[26] Cf. Balanos' excavation notes, p. 13 (Appendix A, pp. 144–145 below) and Balanos 1956, p. 785.

IV

THE SANCTUARY OF ATHENA NIKE, STAGE I

The first rebuilding of the bastion crown, dating, as we have seen, between the later Geometric and middle Archaic periods,[1] constitutes the earliest post-Mycenaean remains from the bastion preserved *in situ*. To judge from a passing observation by Orlandos, the bastion also preserved pottery and small finds from this earliest Greek phase. Orlandos reports that earth removed in laying the concrete base for the rectangular altar of the Stage III sanctuary (Pl. 5) contained Archaic sherds and figurines similar to those found several years earlier by Balanos in the repository: "Bei der Entfernung der Erdmassen anlässlich der Sicherung des Altars II kamen wieder einige archaische Idole und Vasenscherben zum Vorschein."[2] A contemporary archaeological summary more closely describes the pottery sherds as "des fragments de vases à figures noires."[3] We may better judge the import of these finds against Balanos' earlier comments in discussing the contents of the repository. The excavator notes that terracottas similar to those in the repository lay scattered in the surrounding earth, but that (to the limits he had then excavated) there were no similar finds elsewhere: «᾿Ελάχιστα εἰδώλια εὑρέθησαν πέριξ τῶν λίθων τούτων, ἐξαχθέντα πιθανώτατα κατὰ τὴν ἐκσκαφὴν τῆς κρύπτης, δι᾿ ὃ εἰς τὰς ὑπολοίπους ἐπιχώσιες δὲν ἀνευρέθησαν τοιαῦτα».[4] The earth surrounding the repository was disturbed in the excavation of the Turkish crypt, and, as Balanos observes, the terracottas were most likely scattered from the container at that time. In any event, we will later find evidence that the repository and surrounding fill are contemporary with the naïskos, Stage III:[5] the figurines are from a Stage III context at the earliest. The earth removed in reseating the Stage III altar, in contrast, ought to date from Stage I. The concrete podium for the altar, the trenching for which cut through the terracotta-laden stratum, stands to +140.765, nearly 0.10 m. below the crown of the Stage I bastion on the north. Thus by level, if unconfirmed by stratigraphy, the stratum appears to go with rather than to postdate Stage I.[6] It is unlikely that this earth formed part of a larger fill behind the Stage I crown, for there were no similar finds behind the crown elsewhere. Rather its context suggests that it accumulated in the course of ritual at the Stage I altar, the site of the Stage I altar having presumably lain directly under that of Stage III. In all probability, it relates to the founding of Stage I as a *terminus ante* rather than a *terminus ad quem*.

[1] See p. 17 above.

[2] As reported in Walter 1940, col. 152.

[3] Lemerle 1939, p. 289.

[4] Balanos 1956, p. 785.

[5] Pp. 38–39 below.

[6] Note that in Stage III the ground level at the northern edge of the bastion was around 0.17 m. higher than in the area of the altar. If there was an equivalent grade in Stage I, the terracottas may conceivably have been from above the Stage I ground. The general probability of an attribution to Stage I, however, remains; and we will in fact be able to strengthen it later in our argument with the finding that Stage II follows the Persian Destruction (p. 128). With the chronology of the stages thus narrowed, the Archaic stratum admits of an association only with Stage I.

To judge from the isolated dating criteria furnished in the excavation reports, the stratum with terracottas was laid down not before the late 7th century nor after the early 5th. The pottery is once referred to as Archaic, on another occasion as black-figured, a style well established at Athens by 610 B.C., while the figurines are described as equivalent to those found in the repository (Pl. 2:b), a common Attic type in use from roughly 650 to 480.[7]

In addition to the early bastion remains *in situ*, the rubble crown and the stratum with terracottas, two further objects were recovered from later contexts: the base of the cult image, discussed above, and an inscribed block from an Archaic altar.

ARCHAIC ALTAR

This single survival from an early altar of the sanctuary was found underpinning the southeast corner of the Stage III square altar (Fig. 4, Pl. 6:a; see Plan A).[8] The stone is gray-brown

[7] Higgins 1967, p. 42, Type 1. Large numbers were found in the late 19th-century excavations of the Akropolis at Athens, at Eleusis, and in lesser quantities on the north Akropolis slope at Athens, the Pnyx, the Athena Sanctuary at Sounion, and the Sanctuary of Artemis at Brauron. Akropolis excavations, Franz Winter, "Übersicht über die auf der athenische Akropolis gemachten Funde vom Terrakotten," *AA* (*JdI* 8) 1893 (pp. 140–147), pp. 140–141, fig. 2; *idem* 1903, I, p. 24, no. 2. Eleusis, Noack 1927, pp. 11–13, fig. 3. North slope, C. Morgan, "The Terracotta Figurines from the North Slope of the Akropolis," *Hesperia* 4, 1935 (pp. 189–213), pp. 193–195, fig. 4:b–f; O. Broneer, "Excavations on the North Slope of the Akropolis, 1937," *Hesperia* 7, 1938 (pp. 161–263), pp. 200–201, fig. 35 (AF 624, 653); R. Young, "Pottery from a Seventh Century Well," *Hesperia* 7, 1938 (pp. 412–428), pp. 420–421, fig. 10 (D 30, 32). Munychia, Sanctuary of Artemis, L. Palaiokrassa, "Neue Befunde aus dem Heiligtum der Artemis Munichia," *AthMitt* 104, 1989 (pp. 1–40), nos. 13–21, pp. 10, 21, pl. 3:3. Pnyx, G. Davidson and D. B. Thompson, *Small Objects from the Pnyx I* (*Hesperia* Supplement 7), Princeton 1943, pp. 113–114, fig. 52, no. 1 (from an early 4th-century context but considered a survival). From Sounion, Athens, NatM, lot inv. 14, 934. The figurines from Sounion and Brauron remain unpublished.

These simple, handmade terracottas bear a general relation to figurines of the Late Bronze Age, and one may plausibly suggest that they were inspired by chance finds from that earlier era. Bronze Age examples, however, differ from the Archaic in proportions, details, and technique. On the Bronze Age series, French 1971, pp. 101–187. On Archaic technique, Noack 1927, p. 12; Young, *op. cit.*, p. 420; and Higgins 1967, p. 42, Type 1. Unlike the hard-fired, pink fabric of the Mycenaean figurines, the Archaic examples are pale brown to salmon, equivalent in fabric to contemporary vases. In Mycenaean examples and the earliest of the Archaic series, the decoration is applied in glaze. Through the 6th century the figurines come to be decorated in matt paint, often over a white slip. Among criteria relevant to our Plate 2:b, the most important are the horizontal disposition and triangular shape of the arms of the figurines. The arms distinguish the type from the common Tau, Phi, and Psi classes of the Bronze Age. There survive at least a few Mycenaean figurines with horizontal arms, constituting in French's typology Group D of the Late Psi-type. The group, however, is a rare variant, confined to LH IIIC and is known only from three sites, Asine, Mycenae, and Amyklai. See O. Frödin and A. Persson, *Asine*, Stockholm 1938, figs. 206, 212; French 1971, p. 139, pls. 20:d (Mycenae), 22:a, no. 27 (Amyklai).

As reported by Iakovidis (1962, p. 186, note 361), the Nike figurines were once inspected by Spyridon Marinatos, who judged them Mycenaean on parallel with the IIIC finds from Asine cited above. The Asine examples do appear to be the closest Mycenaean parallel to the Nike figurines, but the latter are more elongated and more regularly formed and wear different headdress. The parallel is not that close. However experienced and distinguished this excavator, he was more familiar with pre-Greek than Greek comparanda. The lack of any finds of Group D at Athens or elsewhere in Attica on the one hand, and the pottery found with the Nike figurines (described as black-figured, Archaic) on the other, put the Archaic dating of the Nike examples beyond reasonable question.

[8] Balanos 1956, p. 786; Welter 1939, col. 12. For the inscription, Raubitschek 1949, no. 329.

poros, length 0.465, preserved width 0.365, height 0.528 m. The right side and the upper right corner are recut, and a ledge is cut into the back above, preserved length 0.15, depth 0.11 m. The sides of the block are slightly oblique to one another: the top and left sides meet at an 89-degree angle; the bottom and left, at 93 degrees. There is anathyrosis on the left, top, and bottom faces. The left face has a contact band at the right (W. 0.05 m.) and across the top (W. 0.06 m.). The top and bottom of the block preserve a band along the front edge only: band above, width 0.03 m.; below, width 0.02 m. There would originally have been corresponding bands at the top and bottom rear; the band above was apparently cut through by the ledge; the rear of the block below is broken away.[9]

The inscription is in five lines, an identification of the altar followed by a dedication, the two divided by a horizontal chiseled line:

τε̃ς 'Αθε[ναίας]
τε̃ς Νίκες̣
βομός

Πατροκ<λ>ε̃ς
ἐποίεσεν̣

Altar of Athena Nike. Erected by Patrokles.[10]

The last two lines of the inscription are less carefully and evenly lettered and less deeply cut.

The block is dressed with a drove throughout, the front face with the tool marks closely aligned across the block, giving a uniform textured background to the inscription. The face of the block is lightly weathered.

As established by the anathyrosis above, below, and to the side, this block formed part of the dado of a built altar.[11] The letter forms of the inscription belong roughly to the middle decades of the 6th century, in the opinion of an expert likely not before 580 or after 530.[12]

[9] For anathyrosis on bearing surfaces, compare the following: geison on the temple of Artemis, Corfu, G. Rodenwaldt, *Korkyra* I, Berlin 1940, p. 21; poros buildings, Athenian Akropolis, Heberdey 1919, p. 147, figs. 157, 162; geison on the West Building, Argive Heraion, P. Amandry, "Observations sur les monuments de l'Héraion d'Argos," *Hesperia* 21, 1952 (pp. 222–274), p. 246, fig. 10, pl. 65:a; Treasury of Byzantion, Olympia, *Die Baudenkmäler von Olympia* (*Olympia* II), E. Curtius and R. Adler, eds., Berlin 1892, p. 47. For the shallow curve of the joint within the contact bands, Martin 1965, pp. 195–196, fig. 81 left.

[10] The name of the donor as inscribed, Patrokes– (*sic*), has no ancient parallel. For the emendation, Raubitschek 1949, p. 359. Testimony for the name Patrokles at Athens, *RE* XVIII, ii, part iii, 1949, cols. 2262–2263, *s.v.* Patrokles (1), (3), and (4); Kirchner (II), 1903, nos. 11,688–11,699, the earliest from the late 5th century.

On the meaning of ποιεῖν, see Welter 1939, col. 12, Raubitschek 1949, p. 359. Cf. *IG* II^2 6636, IV 1580, Raubitschek 1949, nos. 326–328; and see further W. Peek, "Attische Inschriften: Nachträge und Verbesserungen zu IG I^2, II^2," *AthMitt* 67, 1942 (pp. 1–217), pp. 86–87. It refers not to the literal building of the altar but to its commission, carrying a sense akin to ἵστημι or ἀνατίθημι.

[11] The following inscribed, built altars from Athens may serve as comparanda: Pythian Apollo, Meiggs and Lewis 1969, no. 11, pp. 19–20; from the Akropolis, Raubitschek 1949, nos. 330, 331; peribolos of the Twelve Gods, Crosby 1949, pp. 93–94; on the inscription, Thucydides 6.54.6.

[12] Meiggs 1972, p. 498.

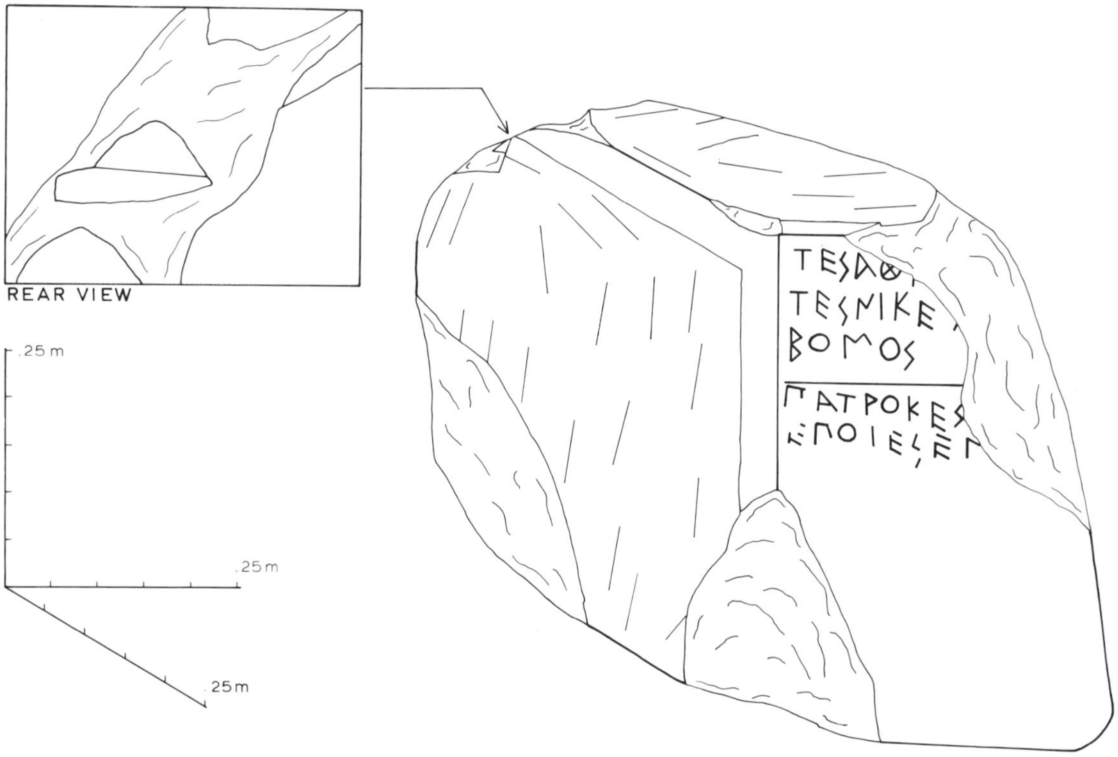

FIG. 4. Block from the Stage I altar

The masonry technique of the block, if less closely datable, gives general confirmation. Its anathyrosis bears comparison with that on the poros architecture of the Akropolis.[13]

A-ARCHITECTURE

The knowledge that Stage I included a statue set monumentally on a broad base, a setting specific to cult statuary, suggests in turn that there was a Stage I temple.[14] The bastion preserves no trace of early architecture; if such a temple indeed existed, however, no matter how thoroughly uprooted from the site, it is unlikely to have disappeared without a trace. We may expect its remains to be somewhere discussed in the body of research on "floating

[13] For the narrow contact bands, compare Wiegand 1904, p. 45, figs. 62, 63; for the use of the drove, Heberdey 1919, p. 186.

[14] It is clear from archaeological and literary evidence that Greek cult statuary was on occasion set in the open air. So, for example, the image of Apollo Hyakinthios at Amyklai: Pausanias 3.18.9–19.5; R. Martin, "Bathyclès de Magnésie et le «thrône» d'Apollon à Amyklae," *RA* 1976, pp. 205–218. The instances of open-air placement, however, remain very few, and we may note that the attested parallels to the Nike base, monumental podia supporting under-lifesize images, are all of them set within the cella of a temple.

temples" from the Akropolis, isolated finds of fictile revetment and poros blocks for which no foundations are known.[15] Among these "floating" remains, two structures, known collectively as the A-architecture, are appropriate to the dimensions of the bastion and to the date and scale of the base. They date roughly from 580 to 550 and in simple distyle-in-antis arrangement were about 5 m. across.[16]

DATING OF STAGE I

We have to this point assumed that the early finds from the bastion, recovered part *in situ*, part reused, belong to one and only one stage of the sanctuary. The chronology of the finds permits their attribution to a single stage, and this is encouraging of itself. The dating limits for the bastion crown are 800–560 B.C.; for the statue base, 600–560; for the inscribed altar, 580–530; and for the A-architecture, 580–550. The four span in common the years 580–560.

To assume a major refashioning of the Nike Sanctuary in the years 580–560 fits closely with the history of cult elsewhere on the Akropolis. The citadel was thoroughly transformed in the second quarter of the 6th century, as attested by architectural remains: the so-called H-architecture, the Red, Herakles, and Olive Tree Pediments, and the rebuilding of the Akropolis approach; and on the evidence of major changes in public and private ritual and devotional practice: the reorganization of the Panathenaia, including the fashioning of a major new image of Athena, and the beginning of private dedications of large-scale statuary.[17] The dating criteria for the early finds from the Nike Sanctuary span just this period of general cultic renewal, and although circumstantial, this is strongly suggestive. The weight of evidence points to a single, comprehensive rebuilding of the bastion between 580 and 560, a program that encompassed a restoration of the bastion crown, the construction of a temple and altar, and the fashioning of a cult image set monumentally on a broad base.

STAGE IA

Stage Ia represents a minor addition to the sanctuary, attested by a recutting along the side of the inner podium of the cult-statue base. As discussed above (p. 29), the recutting possibly accommodated a votive table or the base for a subsidiary image.

15 Wiegand 1904; Heberdey 1919; Buschor 1929–1933; Schuchhardt 1963, cols. 797–824.

16 Most recently, Bancroft 1979, pp. 46–57. For the distyle-in-antis reconstruction, Wiegand 1904, pp. 148–155, and Schuchhardt 1963, cols. 809–810. See further on the A-architecture, Heberdey 1919, pp. 143–156; Dinsmoor 1950, p. 71; I. Beyer, "Die Reliefgiebel des alten Athena-Tempels der Akropolis," *AA* (*JdI* 89) 1974, pp. 639–651.

17 For an overview of building projects on the Akropolis in this period, see Boersma 1970, pp. 11–12. On the rebuilding of the Akropolis approach, see Vanderpool 1974, pp. 156–160. On the Panathenaia, see J. A. Davison, "Notes on the Panathenaea," *JHS* 78, 1958 (pp. 23–42), pp. 26–29; H. W. Parke, *Festivals of the Athenians*, Ithaca 1977, pp. 33–50; Simon 1983, pp. 55–72. On the earliest preserved dedications of statuary, see H. Payne, *Archaic Marble Sculpture from the Acropolis*, 2nd ed., London 1950, pp. 1–13. For a critical overview, see Shapiro 1989, pp. 21–24.

V
THE SANCTUARY OF ATHENA NIKE, STAGE II

The one most valuable source of evidence on the second stage of the sanctuary is a photograph of the excavations in progress published in a French annual report of 1937 (Pl. 3:b).[1]

The view, diagonally across the bastion from the southwest, documents a vertical scarp cut directly below and on a line with the north euthynteria of the Stage III naïskos. The upper edge of the scarp appears on the photograph as a thin whitish line: beginning just below the crown of the Mycenaean crosswall, approximately at level +140.35, it falls gradually to the west (left), passing from view at a point just short of the west euthynteria of the naïskos at *ca.* +140.25. In contrast to the earth revealed in the face of the scarp, a loose and stony fill,[2] the upper edge of the scarp appears packed and firm. The well-defined contour of this upper edge seems to mark the surface of an archaeological stratum.

Just atop the scarp, apparently set directly on the stratum, are two foundation blocks for the north euthynteria of the naïskos, one centered on the middle joint of the euthynteria, the other beside it to the west, half a meter in from the northwest corner of the euthynteria. The northwest corner itself is supported on a third, significantly larger block measuring 0.93 m. square, height 0.45 m. Gauged from the elevation of the scarp in the photograph, the resting surface of the block, at +140.10, penetrated some 15 cm. into the stratum.[3]

Considered simply on its face, the photograph, Plate 3:b, admits of three readings:

(a) The packed stratum may be the ground of Stage II, the sanctuary that directly preceded the naïskos. Its level relative to the naïskos underpinnings would attest in that case that the Stage III builders laid the naïskos foundations in part directly on the Stage II ground (the two blocks along the north euthynteria) and in part in shallow footing trenches (the northwest corner block).

(b) The packed stratum may be the floor of a foundation ditch for the north wall of the naïskos. As viewed in the photograph, the upper contour of the scarp fulfills the two requirements of such a trench: it follows along the full length of the north euthynteria and supports the north wall foundations.

(c) The "stratum" may be modern. The photograph may simply record a stage in the excavations at which, by chance or design, the northern half of the bastion fill was cleared to a level even with the lower edge of the naïskos foundations.

These three readings each has its own bearing on the reconstruction of the level of the Stage II sanctuary. Interpretation *a* yields the narrowest conclusion: that the stratum and the ground level of the Stage II sanctuary are identical. If the packed stratum is the floor of a foundation ditch, case *b*, then the Stage II ground level will have been some distance above it.

[1] Lemerle 1937, p. 444, fig. 6; for the importance of the photograph, first Bundgård 1974b, caption to p. 44, p. 46.

[2] Cf. Balanos 1956, p. 788, ῥιπτῶν χωμάτων μετὰ λιθαρίων.

[3] This third block is the only one of the three preserved and accessible on the site. The second is hidden from view by the repository. The first was removed in the course of restoration and not replaced; it would appear to be entered on the transverse cross-section, Plate 12, but is omitted from the longitudinal section, Plate 11.

One cannot determine exactly how far above. But unless there was a collapse of the bastion at the close of Stage II or a major leveling of the bastion fill by the Stage III builders, then Stage II and Stage III ought to be close in level. The upper limit for Stage II is the ground level of the Stage III naïskos. Finally, interpretation *c*, that the stratum is modern, yields conclusions related to interpretation *b*. For interpretation *c*, as also *b*, the Stage II level is best gauged from its relation to the succeeding sanctuary. Regardless of the packed surface in the photograph, we can assume that Stage III was founded on or cut into the ruins of its predecessor; that is to say, the level of the ground at the close of Stage II lay at or above the resting edge of the Stage III foundations. The converse, that Stage II lay below the resting edge of the foundations for Stage III, would require that the Stage III builders spread down a layer of fill to raise the previous ground level and then set their walls, a dubious manner of construction, given the tendency of fresh fill to shift and settle.

Two closely related chains of inference, the first concerned with the remaining foundations or resting surfaces of Stage III, the second with the relation of these elements to the preserved level of the Mycenaean bastion, reveal in fact that interpretation *a*, not *b* or *c*, is correct.

Most of the foundations for Stage III have uneven resting surfaces. As seen along the exposed edge of the undersurfaces, the underside on these blocks is dressed to a scalloped or undulating contour, an uneven succession of minor hollows and projections. On some parts of the foundations this undersurface, though uneven, remains roughly horizontal across the length of the block; on other blocks it falls or rises on a strong oblique. The block underpinning the south euthynteria of the naïskos at the east has an uneven resting surface roughly on a horizontal: height 0.20–0.215 m. west to east. Its underside is carved in a series of concavities, some rounded and shallow, some abrupt, the largest approaching 3 cm. in depth (Fig. 8, F 1). Oblique undersurfaces, their contours equally curved and varied, are prominent on two blocks, the underpinning to the euthynteria at center west, height 0.215–0.29 m. north to south (Fig. 6, F 3), and the base slab for the rectangular altar, height 0.255–0.37 m. west to east (Fig. 11).

The foundations for Stage III are also notable in that they vary sharply in height from one block to the next. The underpinning for the northwest corner of the naïskos has a height of 0.45 m. (Fig. 7, F 4); the adjacent blocks to the south and east have heights of 0.215 (measured at the northwest) and 0.30 m. respectively (Fig. 6, F 3; Pl. 3:b). Similarly, the block supporting the southwest corner of the naïskos has a height of 0.565 m.; the block directly to the east, 0.20 m. (Fig. 8, F 1, F 2).

If the stratum in Plate 3:b marks the ground level for the stage of the sanctuary that directly preceded the naïskos, our interpretation *a*, then the oblique and contoured resting surfaces and the varied heights of the naïskos foundations are at once intelligible. The taller, more massive foundations for Stage III, specifically the two blocks underpinning the northwest and southwest corners of the naïskos, were bedded in shallow footing trenches, while the remainder of the foundations were set directly on the stony, uneven Stage II ground, their resting surfaces trimmed each to conform to its site. In contrast, the anomalies of the Stage III foundations remain unaccounted for under interpretations *b* and *c*, both of which posit the use of footing trenches throughout.[4]

[4] We may note one seeming exception under interpretation *c* where trenches would not have been used, namely, where the resting edge of III lay at rather than below II. In that instance, however, interpretation *c*

We have now to examine the level and context of the poros repository in the light of interpretation *a.* As explicated above, the repository represents Stage 3 of the Archaic base for the cult statue. The Archaic base (Stage 1) was razed in a violent destruction (Stage 2), with the repository then fashioned from two joining blocks of the crowning course of the earlier monument. The resting surface of the repository, irregularly contoured at the left front corner and across the front, and cut to an oblique at the left rear, surely dates from Stage 3; the blocks will have been bedded on a level as a crowning course, while Stage 3 remains their single major recutting. This stands confirmed by an observation made earlier on the tooling of the repository. The drove work on the resting surface of the repository at the left rear relates closely to three areas of tooling on the upper container: the left side, the right rear, and the middle and lower stages of the central cavity, all areas of Stage 3 recutting.[5]

We earlier assembled fragmentary evidence that Stage 1 of the base and the three remaining finds from the early bastion, the rubble bastion crown, the inscribed altar, and the stratum with terracottas, formed together a single phase of the cult, Stage I.[6] Far more conclusive evidence associates the third stage of the base (the repository) with Stage III of the sanctuary. The resting surface of the repository, contoured and irregular, is broadly analogous to the undersurfaces on the Stage III foundations and lies just at their level. As given by the excavation photograph, Plate 3:b, the block underpinning the north euthynteria just in from the northwest corner was bedded at +140.25, directly on the Stage II stratum. The north side of the repository, close inside it, rested at +140.26.[7] The levels strongly imply that the stratum supported the naïskos and repository alike.

This conclusion is bolstered by two further excavation photographs, Plates 3:a and 4. The two show that the south side of the repository was underpinned by two blocks, one obliquely placed, supporting the length of the south side, the other projecting from under the southwest corner; the latter is tipped downward slightly in the photographs, apparently dislodged in the course of excavation. We may gauge from these views that the oblique block had horizontal dimensions of at least 0.50 × 0.30 m. and was rather thin, for two fieldstones project from under its southern edge at a depth hardly greater than 0.10 m. The block behind it was at least 0.40 m. in length and *ca.* 0.15 m. in height.[8]

The irregular placement of the underpinnings for the repository, one block laid on an oblique, the other projecting close to a half a meter beyond the southwest corner of the repository, all but excludes their having been set in a footing trench. In any event, one would not have expected the builders to dig a trench along the south side of the repository only; we saw the north to have been set directly on the earth. Rather the asymmetrical bedding of the repository points to it having been set on a slope, with the underpinnings raising its south

---

amounts to a restatement of *a*: that the Stage III foundations rest directly on the Stage II ground. Interpretation *a* remains the one appropriate explanation.

[5] See p. 22 above.

[6] See p. 35 above.

[7] Balanos gives the level of the repository as +140.673 measured at the northwest corner of the collar (Pl. 7). The height of the base on the north is 0.41 m.

[8] These blocks were removed in the course of restoration and were not replaced. They are omitted from Balanos' plans.

side to an appropriate level. As true of the foundations for Stage III in general, the repository and its underpinnings were set onto, rather than cut into, the existing ground.

We can check and refine our conclusions on the repository by reference to the naïskos foundations, whose oblique, contoured resting surfaces provide welcome points of reference on the level and contour of Stage II. That the Stage II stratum does indeed fall off to the south is confirmed by the block underpinning the middle of the west euthynteria, height 0.215 m. at the northwest, 0.29 m. at the southwest (Fig. 6, F 3). The naïskos foundations provide equal testimony on the east–west contour of Stage II. The underpinning for the west euthynteria just noted, 0.29 m. at the southwest corner, measures 0.32 m. at the southeast, evidence that Stage II fell gently eastward. To the far side of the repository the ground rose again, as given by the block underpinning the south euthynteria at the east, height 0.20 m. The shallow depression east–west and slight grade north–south of the stratum have together the form of a sloping channel, perhaps best interpreted as a run-off or rill. We may note in confirmation that the lowest preserved stretch of the bastion face, the natural collecting point for such run-off, lay directly below the naïskos to the south.

The attested bedding for the repository and the rill-like contours of Stage II in the western area of the naïskos agree closely. We may picture the north side of the repository as having rested where the ground was relatively flat at the head of the rill, thus the lack of any underpinning on that side. The southeast corner, carved back to an uneven contour, appears to have rested against the east shoulder of the rill, while the south side lay across the channel, thus requiring more extensive support. As indicated by Plates 3:a and 4, the workmen underpinned the south with a thin slab (we may think perhaps of a reused metope) and laid a taller block to the west, to support the more extensively recut southwest corner of the repository.[9] What we initially inferred from the relative level of the naïskos foundations and the repository on the north is strongly supported by these additional observations. The repository is bedded at the same level as the naïskos foundations on its west as on the north, and its undersurface and the naïskos underpinnings accord fully with the apparent contour of Stage II. The repository and the naïskos underpinnings ought to date from the same time.

In addition to the close correlation in levels between the Stage II stratum and the foundations for Stage III, we may observe that the two together correlate with the level of the bastion as preserved from Stage I. The excavation photograph, Plate 3:b, establishes the close relationship between the slope of the Stage II stratum and the level of the west bastion face. Where last visible under the northwest corner of the naïskos, the stratum is seen to be just beginning a gentle incline to the west from +140.25. The west face of the bastion, 3.60 m. distant, stands to +140.40 (Fig. 16, Pl. 5). The stratum thus appears to have

[9] This reconstruction of the bedding receives valuable support from Balanos' transverse section, Plate 12, which shows the repository obliquely trimmed to rest on a stony stratum, by my reconstruction the eastern shoulder of the rill. Observe that the drawing is at odds with what I have concluded about the area to the right of the repository, where the stones of the stratum are shown as having stepped up to the level of the naïskos euthynteria. Having been able to rule out alternative explanations for the stratum in the photograph Plate 3:b, however, we may be certain that on this latter point the cross-section is in error.

The "stratigraphy" on a second drawing, Balanos' longitudinal section, Plate 11, refers not to the sanctuary as excavated but to its restoration in the modern crypt. The drawing includes the modern rubble base for the repository (cf. Pl. 1:b) and records a horizontal "stratum" at +139.96, the level of the concrete floor of the crypt.

come just to the bastion crown. As seen center right in Plate 9, the stratum rose eastward to approach the level of the Mycenaean crosswall: the crosswall is at +140.545; the stratum touched just below at +140.35.

There are equally significant correlations between the preserved level of the bastion and the foundations for Stage III. The block underpinning the south euthynteria of the naïskos at the east rested directly on the bastion crosswall, as may be inferred from the level and slope of the crosswall recorded just north of the euthynteria in Plate 3:b, and on the explicit testimony of a cross-section and a plan of Balanos, Plates 11 and 16.[10] There is less extensive evidence on the relative level of the north euthynteria and the bastion, but judged from Plate 3:b and the elevations on Balanos' plan, Plate 7, the crown of the crosswall and the resting edge of the euthynteria were at most a few centimeters apart. As given by the plan, the crosswall stood at +140.545 measured 0.20 m. south of the euthynteria. The resting edge of the euthynteria lay at +140.55.[11] The relation of the Stage III foundations and the bastion is equally close in the northern area of the sanctuary: the square altar is partially bedded on the northern crown, and the base slab for the rectangular altar, positioned roughly 2 m. in from the crown and 2.5 m. from the crosswall, is bedded at a level intermediate between the two. The north face is preserved to +140.86, the crosswall to +140.545. The base slab rests at +140.765.[12]

That the preserved levels of the Stage I bastion correlate equally with the Stage II stratum and the foundations for Stage III is of twofold importance. The agreement of levels confirms that Stage III was founded with the greater number of its underpinnings laid directly on the Stage II ground. Beyond this, however, it reveals a tie between Stage II and Stage I: the fact that the contours of Stage II accord with the preserved levels of the Archaic crown and Mycenaean crosswall can only mean that Stage II lay behind and was retained by this earlier stonework; the ground level of Stage II was governed by the bastion as it stood at the close of Stage I.

The stonework of Stage I retained Stage II at a level nearly half a meter higher at the north than at the west, at +140.86 in the area of the square altar against +140.40 at the western crown. And we have seen how sloped and stony was the surface of Stage II between these points. The Stage II stratum attests, not a building phase, but the bastion in ruins, the aftermath of a destruction or collapse that brought down broad stretches of the Stage I crown.

As we have seen in Chapter IV, the idea that Stage I closed in a catastrophic destruction finds support in the extremely fragmentary preservation of the early bastion. There were found *in situ* only the few stretches of the bastion crown noted above and the limited stratum

[10] The bastion crosswall was dismantled and a new wall erected in its place in the course of the project. As restored, the wall supports not the underpinning for the south euthynteria, whose resting edge is at +140.33, but the euthynteria itself, at +140.55. (Levels cast from Balanos' reference: naïskos euthynteria = +140.916–.918.) That the restoration falsely raised the wall is as apparent on site as from drawings and photographs. The block underpinning the south euthynteria is properly positioned in the restoration, notwithstanding the higher level of the crosswall, with the result that the rubble crown of the crosswall immures its eastern end.

[11] From Plate 7 I calculate the level of the euthynteria of the naïskos at the northeast as +140.916. The height of the euthynteria on the north is 0.370 m.

[12] Balanos (1956, p. 787) gives the level of the top of the base slab as +0.10 relative to the euthynteria of the naïskos: +140.916–.918 + 0.10 = +141.016–.018. Compare Plate 11, which records the base slab as 1.195 below the euthynteria of the Nike Temple: +142.213 − 1.195 = +141.018. The height of the base plate is 0.255 m. at the northwest corner.

with terracottas from the area of the rectangular altar.[13] The few other early finds from the bastion survived through reuse: the two blocks of the statue base and the inscribed block of the Stage I altar were recovered from Stage III, the blocks of the base recut to form a repository, the block of the altar employed as underpinning for its Stage III successor.

The Stage I sanctuary may have been partially uprooted in laying the foundations for the amphiprostyle Nike Temple, bedded up to a meter and a half below the Archaic level. The north, south, and east foundations of the Stage I temple, in particular, may have been destroyed at that time. With that possible exception, however, it is most reasonable to view the all but total extirpation of Stage I and the bastion collapse that preceded Stage II as one and the same event: Stage I closed in destruction that leveled the temple and altar of the sanctuary and threw down much of the bastion crown. Stage II saw the bastion in the wake of that event left a stony, rutted mound.

It remains to bring the stages of the cult-statue base in relation to Stage II. We have seen that Stage III of the sanctuary is contemporary with Stage 3 of the base (the repository). Both their foundations lay directly on the Stage II ground. To equate the leveling of the sanctuary between Stages I and II and Stage 2 of the base, an episode of destruction follows naturally.

[13] See p. 31 above.

VI
THE SANCTUARY OF ATHENA NIKE, STAGE III

To this stage belong the naïskos, a rectangular altar to its east, a square altar northeast of the naïskos, the poros repository, and a stretch of retaining wall in irregular trapezoidal masonry at the bastion edge on the north.

NAÏSKOS

The remains of the naïskos (Figs. 5–8, Pl. 1),[1] largely overbuilt in Stage IV by the foundations for the amphiprostyle Nike Temple, were first brought to light by Balanos with the dismantling of the later stonework. It is a small cella of simple Π-shaped plan, walled on three sides, fully open at the east: estimated length 3.65 m., width 2.47 m.[2] The stone is Aiginetan poros.[3]

Five blocks of the euthynteria were found *in situ*. Two adjoin on the south: E 1 (to the east), length 0.729 m.; and E 2, preserved length 0.92 m. A third is on the west at the northwest corner, E 3, length 1.35 m.; and two form the return of that corner on the north,

[1] Balanos 1956, pp. 784–785; Welter 1939, cols. 11–12; Travlos 1971, fig. 202:A.

[2] Compare the following structures from the vicinity of the Akropolis, analogous in scale and plan: (1) south of the Areopagus, 6th century, Middleton 1900, pl. 20, no. XXVII; Judeich 1931, p. 299; Travlos 1971, p. 151, fig. 202:C, naïskos length 2.27, width 2.08 m., wall thickness 0.35 m.; (2) near the Theater of Dionysos, P. Kalligas, «᾿Εργασίαι ταχτοποιήσεως καὶ διαμορφώσεως Διονύσου ῾Ιεροῦ ᾿Ελευθερέως τῆς Νοτίου κλιτύος ᾿Ακροπόλεως», Δελτ 18, 1963 [1965], Β′ 1 (pp. 12–18), p. 16; Travlos 1971, p. 151, fig. 202:B, length 2.26, width 2.26 m., wall width 0.405 m.; (3) east of the Church of St. Demetrios Loumbardiaris, S. Charitonidis, «᾿Ανασκαφὴ παρὰ τὸν ῞Αγιον Δημήτριον τὸν Λουμπαρδιάρην ἐν ᾿Αθήναις», ΑρχΕφ 1979, p. 164, fig. 1; Travlos 1971, p. 151, fig. 202:D, length 2.23, width 2.19 m. (measured on the euthynteria) and wall width, 0.46 m.

[3] Buff (cream brown), slightly porous, fossiliferous marl limestone incorporating very small pelecypod (clam) and turreted gastropod shells (typical sizes 0.004–0.006 m.) and oolites. The bedding of the stone is only rarely evident on fresh surfaces. Jointing, in contrast, is very well defined, consisting of cracks and narrow ribbonlike fissures, characteristically on a plane *ca.* 50° to the bedding. The stone is soft and friable, but occasional blocks show thin, significantly harder veins on the plane of the jointing.

The Late Archaic Temple of Aphaia on Aigina is of a poros identical to that of the naïskos in color and fabric and very similar in jointing. By contrast, its fossils are a step removed: pelecypod and gastropod shells tend to be larger and oolites more abundant. Poros at Kolonna shows similar strong ties, attended likewise by slight differences. All things considered, however, the near identity of our Stage III stone with the poros from these two Aiginetan sites in composition, bedding, jointing, and color and the general similarity of the three stones in fossils puts the attribution of the naïskos stone to Aiginetan Tertiary beds beyond reasonable question.

On Aiginetan poros, Washington 1895, pp. 6–7; Furtwängler 1906, p. 21; Paton 1927, p. 181, p. 350, note 2; Herz 1954–1955, pp. 499–505; W. Wurster, *Alt-Ägina*, I, i, *Apollontempel*, Mainz am Rhein 1974, pp. 18–19. The stone is attested in Attic building inscriptions from roughly the mid-5th century, beginning with *IG* I[3] 395, line 7.

E 4 (at the corner), length 1.043 m., and E 5, length 1.078 m. The blocks vary in height from 0.365 to 0.38 m., in width from 0.47 to 0.48 m. Their upper surface is at +140.92.[4]

E 1 and E 2 are joined by an unusual form of clamp, "gamma" on one side, "T" on the other (└─┤). The cutting at the exposed eastern joint of E 1 is T-formed, thus possibly from a similar clamp.[5] There is a pry hole 0.345 m. from the eastern joint of E 1.[6]

There remain two short strips of light brown lime plaster along the inner edge of the upper surface on E 2. The first, at a clear distance of 0.07 m. from the eastern joint of the block, measures 0.12 × 0.04 m. The second, 0.24 m. from the eastern joint, measures 0.13 × 0.03 m. The inner edges of the two strips are straight, aligned on the orientation of the euthynteria, 0.065 m. from its inner edge. Given this alignment, the patches are most reasonably assigned to Stage III, apparently the remains from a plaster floor of the naïskos. There is no trace of similar plaster elsewhere. The floor thus appears to have been laid even with the euthynteria; in the area of the patches it crept a few millimeters higher, spreading over the euthynteria to the base of the wall.

The euthynteria bears evidence of reworking in two periods: the construction of the amphiprostyle temple (Stage IV) and the period of the Turkish crypt. To Stage IV belong two ledges cut along the inner and outer edges of the south euthynteria at its eastern end. The outer ledge (pres. L. 1.07, W. 0.07–0.085, depth, 0.14–0.17 m.) was carved to accommodate three blocks from the second course of the Stage IV temple foundations, as made clear from Balanos' drawings. The second foundation course was bedded at *ca.* +140.75, *ca.* 0.17 m. below the level of the naïskos euthynteria (Pl. 12), and it overlapped the euthynteria by several centimeters (Pl. 15). The foundations recorded by Balanos within the interior of the naïskos are modern, laid by Ross in the early 19th century;[7] Plate 15 shows their jointing to be unrelated to the inner ledge. The technique and dimensions of this inner cutting (L. 0.78, W. 0.055–0.06, depth 0.05–0.06 m.), however, correspond so closely to the outer that the

[4] As entered on Balanos' cross-section, Plate 11, the naïskos euthynteria lies 1.295 m. below the euthynteria of the amphiprostyle temple (E −1.295 = +140.918). Plate 7 records two absolute levels for the euthynteria: +140.916 at the east end of E 5, and +140.918 toward the north end of E 3. Compare the relative level on the same plan: −1.305 m. (= +140.908). Note that Dinsmoor, Jr. (1980, plan A) misrecords the level on E 5 as E −1.346 m. (= +142.223 − 140.877): 5 cm. too low.

[5] T-cutting, L. 0.125, W. 0.09 m. For the "gamma-T" cutting, now only partially visible through a break in anta A 1, see Balanos' plan, Plate 7. The clamp and leading were pried free, apparently in Turkish times, splitting off much of the surrounding stone. Balanos omits reference to the gamma-T in his text; it would appear on Welter's testimony (1939, col. 11) that it was used not only to join E 1 and E 2, but throughout the euthynteria. The upper bed of the euthynteria was fully exposed in the course of dismantling and reinstalling the naïskos, and Welter may have noted its clamps at that time. It is conceivable, however, that he based his report solely on Balanos' general plan, a version of which he reproduces with his text. The rarity of the clamp type is not of itself grounds to doubt Balanos' rendering. All the same, until the south euthynteria can be more closely examined, we should keep open the possibility that the cutting is in fact a double-T with the cross of one of the T's split away.

The following are parallels to the euthynteria clamp as drawn: Delphi, Daochos Monument, euthynteria for the surrounding niche, J. Pouilloux, *Topographie et architecture: La région nord du sanctuaire* (*Fouilles de Delphes* II, ix), Paris 1960, p. 71 (two gamma-T's; remaining clamps double-T); Athens, Erechtheion, securing an exterior course of orthostates to an interior wall course half its height, Paton 1927, p. 48.

[6] Visible through a break at the base of anta A 1, length 0.08, width 0.02 m.

[7] See note 39 above, p. 10.

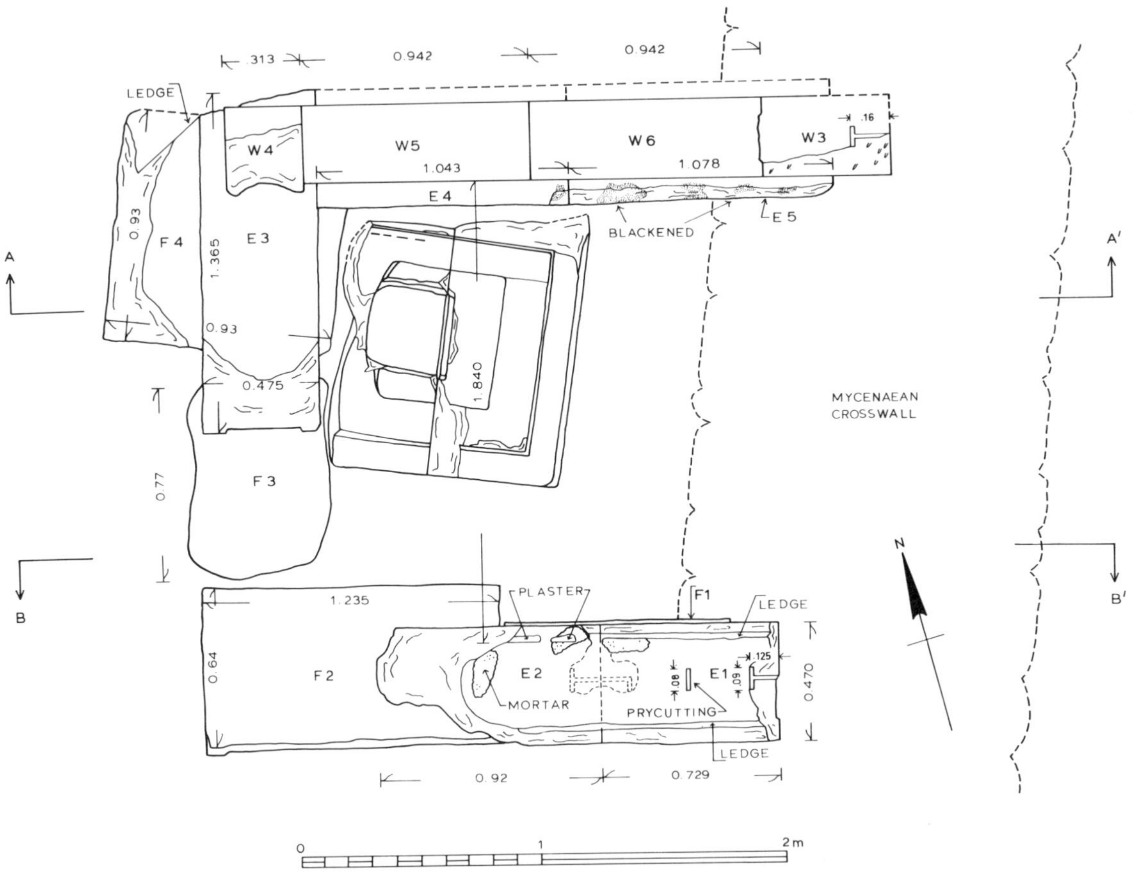

FIG. 5. Plan of the naïskos and repository (base for the cult statue)

two ought surely to have served a similar function. We may conclude that the Stage IV foundations overlapped the south euthynteria from the north as from the south. The distance between the inner and outer ledges across the euthynteria is 0.325 m., around a centimeter greater than the width of the naïskos wall, while the setback of the south wall from the inner edge of the euthynteria (0.065 m. as given by the plaster patches of the floor) and the width of the inner ledge (0.06 m.) are in close accord. It follows that at least the base of the south wall was *in situ* when the Stage IV foundations were laid, with the foundations set against the wall from both sides.[8]

The euthynteria shows two additional areas of Stage IV reworking, two roughly rectangular patches of claw work, one on the inner face of the north euthynteria at its eastern end, the other opposite it on the south. The patch on the south is 0.28 m. long and extends from the Stage IV ledge at the upper edge of the euthynteria to +140.70 (Fig. 8); that on the north is 0.47 m. in length and reaches from the preserved upper edge of the euthynteria to

[8] Compare the evidence of wall block W 7, from a portion of the naïskos wall left standing in Stage IV and dismantled by the Turks.

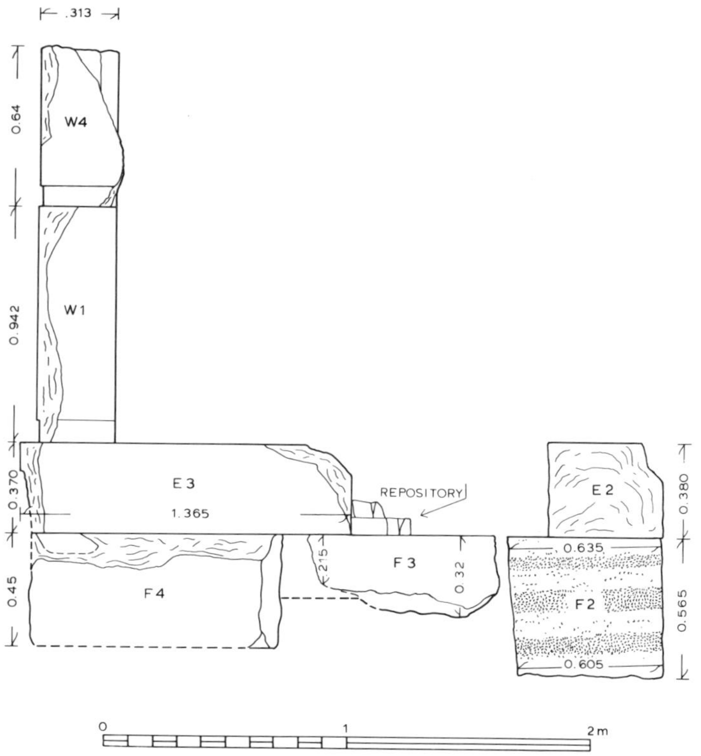

FIG. 6. The naïskos in elevation from the west

+140.695 (Fig. 7). As indicated by their general size, simple rectangular shape, and close correspondence in level, the two accommodated blocks from the third course of the amphiprostyle temple foundations. The condition of the euthynteria on the north makes clear that the stretch of the third foundation course in question was ripped out by the Turks: the inner edge of the north euthynteria has been crudely bashed away and partially blackened by fire. The damage continues across the upper limits of the dressing for course three. The traces of fire date with certainty to the period of the Turkish crypt, while the damaged stretch of the euthynteria, extending 1.15 m. from the east end of E 5, aligns closely with the Turkish wear observed along the east side of the repository.

Besides the hacked-away stretch on the north, two further areas of the euthynteria were crudely worked away by the Turks: the west end of the south euthynteria, E 2, and the upper edge of E 3 at the west. The damage to E 3 is on a line with the base course for the north wall of the Turkish crypt (Pl. 15), while the breaks across E 2 correspond to a step down in the level of the crypt as recorded in Balanos' cross-section, Plate 13:b. Finally, extensive remains from the floor of the crypt, a brownish pink lime plaster mixed with sand and small pebbles, cover much of E 2 and the western end of E 1.

The walls of the naïskos are formed of superimposed orthostatic courses, each marked on the exterior by a continuous drafted lower margin: wall width 0.311–0.313 m. with no apparent batter; height, first course, 0.942 m.; drafts, height 0.082–0.083, depth 0.001–

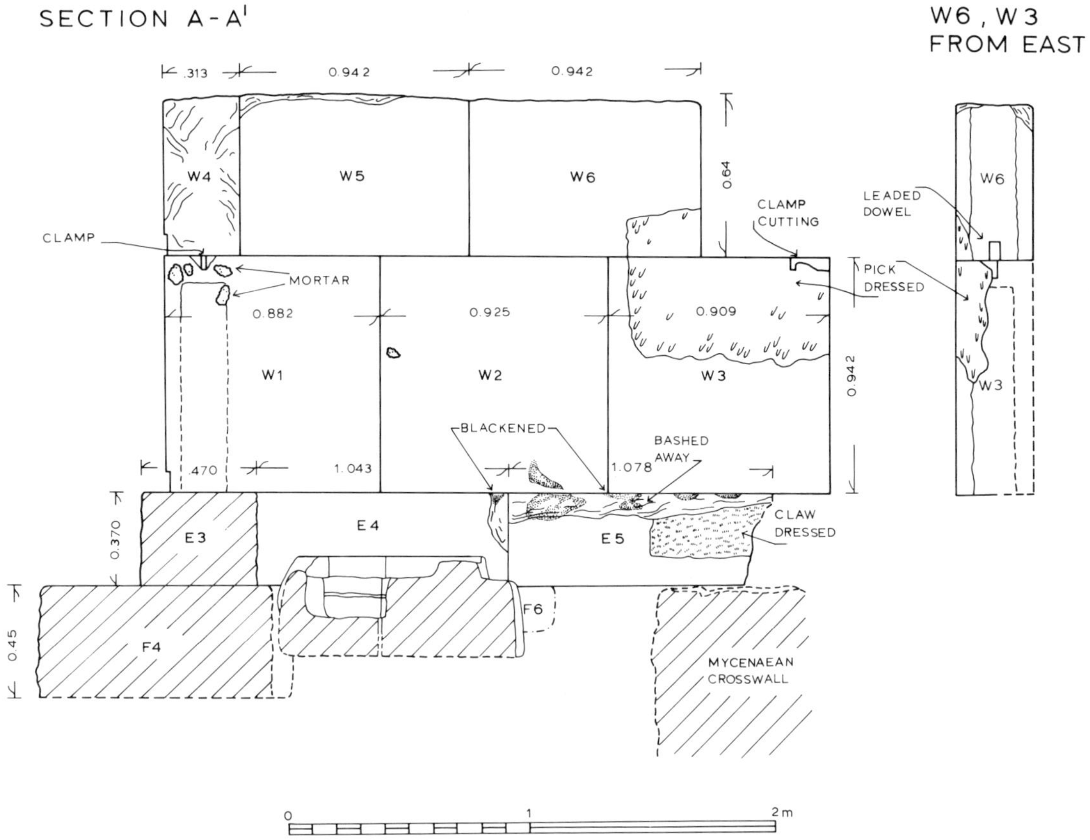

FIG. 7. North side of the naïskos: cross-section A-A′ and east view of blocks W 3 and W 6

0.004 m. The excavations uncovered two courses of the north wall *in situ*, extending 2.72 m. from the rear corner of the naïskos (Fig. 7). The first course is formed of three blocks: lengths west to east, (W 1) 0.882, (W 2) 0.925, (W 3) 0.909 m. The second consists of a return and two blocks: preserved height 0.605–0.64; preserved length of the return (W 4), 0.355 m.; lengths, (W 5) 0.942, (W 6) 0.942 m. Double-T clamps secure the first course;[9] a leaded dowel is visible in the exposed joint of W 6.

Like the euthynteria, the north wall was twice reworked, in the construction of the amphiprostyle temple (Stage IV) and in the Turkish period. Stage IV saw the second wall course of the naïskos trimmed to a level even with the first step of the krepidoma for the amphiprostyle temple (Pls. 11, 12); the backers for the middle step of the krepidoma rested directly atop it. A large, roughly rectangular area of point work on the inner face of the north wall appears to have accommodated an ashlar from the first course of the Stage IV

[9] Plate 7; Balanos 1956, p. 784; Welter 1939, col. 11, fig. 14. The T-cutting at the east end of W 3 measures length 0.16, preserved width 0.08 m. A set of drawings in the archives records the cutting between W 2 and W 3 as length 0.31, width 0.09 m.

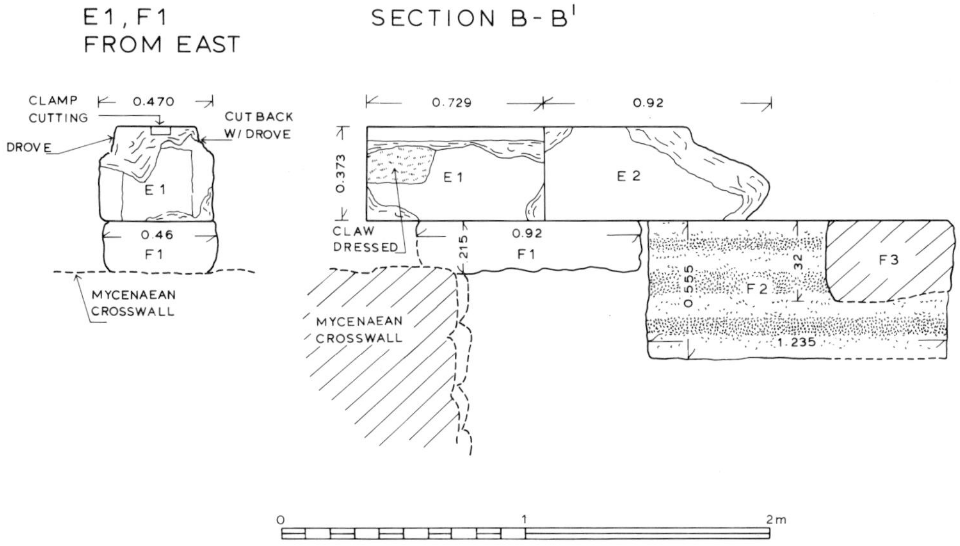

FIG. 8. South side of the naïskos: cross-section B-B′ and east view of blocks E 1 and F 1

foundations.[10] Of Turkish date, apparently, is the crude hacking off of the second course return, W 4, worked away to make room for the north wall of the Turkish crypt.

There remain traces of mortar, a white lime plaster mixed with sand and small pebbles, on the inner face of the north wall at the west: several patches are clustered in the upper left corner of W 1, while a further patch lies near the left joint of W 2. They date from the construction of the Turkish crypt, whose rubble-and-mortar vault overlapped the rear of the north wall by roughly a meter (Pl. 15). Finally, a small area along the base of W 2 is blackened by fire, a continuation of the fire damage on the euthynteria directly below.

Four additional blocks of the naïskos were recovered from the krepidoma of the amphiprostyle temple and from the walls of the Turkish crypt.[11] One, a wall block (W 7), now rests on the west euthynteria of the naïskos, length 0.928, width 0.311, preserved height 0.63 m. (Pl. 1). The block is recut above and across much of the exposed joint. It has the same preserved height as the second course of the north wall, suggesting that it too is from the second course. There was evidently an additional stretch of the naïskos wall trimmed to clear the krepidoma of the amphiprostyle temple. That stretch of wall was dismantled in the construction of the Turkish crypt, with the block W 7 coming finally to be immured in the crypt walls.[12]

A second wall block (W 8) has been set against the side of the modern crypt southwest of the naïskos, preserved length 0.80, preserved width 0.255, preserved height 0.54 m. It

[10] The back wall of the cutting aligns with the jointing on the first course of the Stage IV foundations directly east of the naïskos (Pl. 14). Note that the block recorded by Balanos alongside the cutting was set in by Ross. See note 39 above, p. 10.

[11] Balanos 1956, pp. 784–785; see also Balanos' excavation notes, p. 10, Appendix A, p. 143 below.

[12] So Balanos 1956, p. 784.

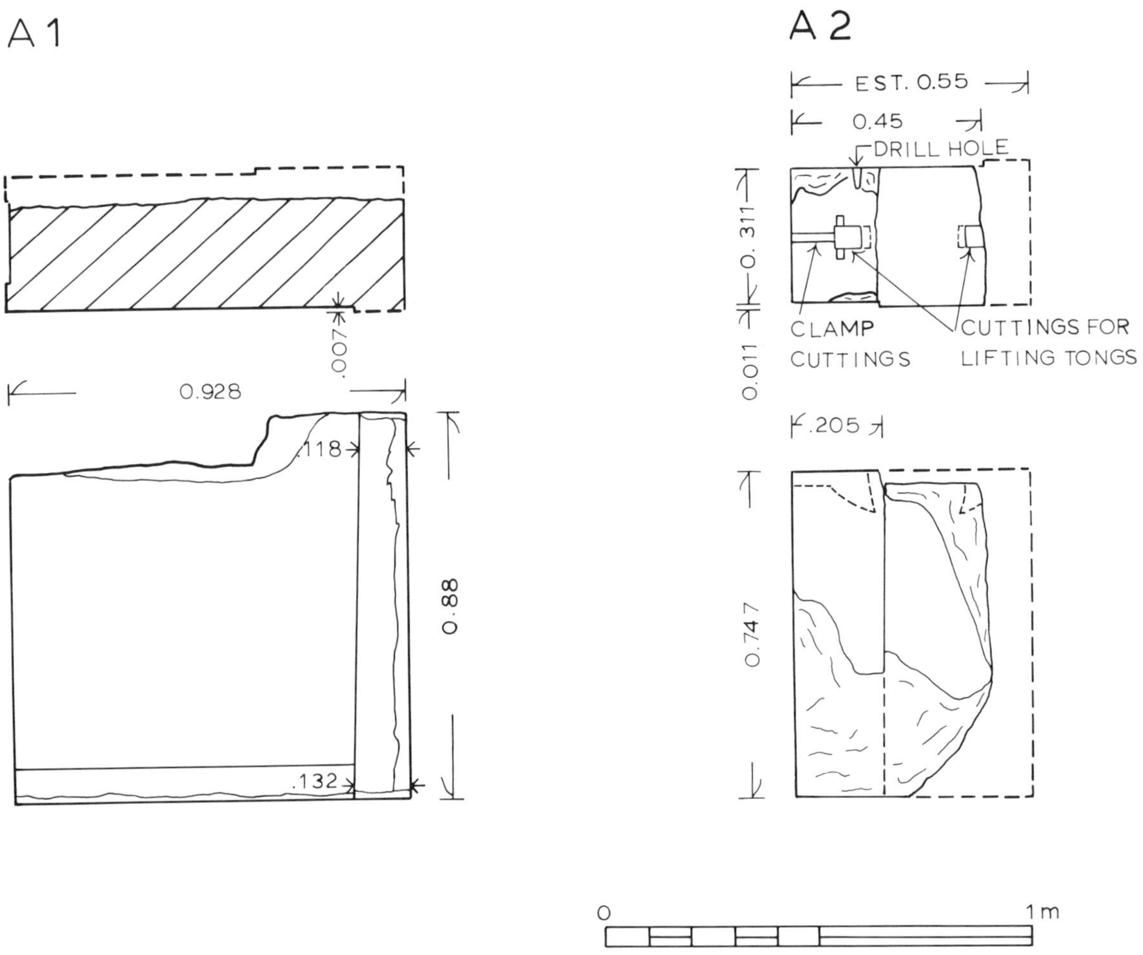

FIG. 9. Blocks A 1 and A 2

is recut above, on the inner face, and at both ends. Its preserved width suggests reuse as a step backer in the krepidoma of the amphiprostyle temple.

A third block (A 1), set on the south euthynteria, preserves part of an anta, length 0.928, preserved width 0.225, preserved height 0.88 m.; outer face of the anta, width 0.132 (base)–0.118 m., projection 0.007 m. (Fig. 9). The block is recut above, on its inner face, and across roughly half the outer fillet of the anta.[13] Several areas on the inner face of the block are reddened and blackened by fire, and there is a calcined area of more intense burning above. Block A 1 is from the south anta of the naïskos, as established by the draft on its outer face. Its preserved width points to reuse as a step backer in the krepidoma of the Stage IV temple, while the remains of fire attest subsequent reuse in the Turkish crypt: apparently

[13] Balanos (1956) would appear to be referring to this stone on his p. 785, note 1: «Εἰς ἕνα ἐκ τῶν λίθων τούτων φαίνεται ὅτι ἀπεκόπη προεξέχον κυμάτιον πλάτους 12–13 ἑκατοστῶν». Compare the excavator's notes, p. 10, Appendix A, p. 143 below.

it was from the narrow strip of the Stage IV krepidoma cut through by the entry passage to the crypt (cf. Pl. 14).

A second anta block (A 2) lies on the floor of the modern crypt south of the naïskos, preserved length 0.45, wall width 0.311, height 0.747 m.; inner face of the anta, preserved width 0.245, projection 0.011 m. (Fig. 9). The principal face of the anta is cut away, and the upper side and inner and outer faces of the block are partially cut back. The upper side preserves the cutting for a T-clamp, sockets for lifting tongs, and a horizontal drill hole sunk from the outer face of the block, diam. 0.009 m. The lifting sockets, carved through the clamp cutting, date from Stage IV.

The original length of block A 2 may be gauged from the lifting sockets. The center point between the two sockets is 0.275 m. from the preserved end of the block, indicating a block length of *ca.* 0.55 m. This in turn yields the restored width for the preserved lateral thickening of the anta, *ca.* 0.35 m. The thickening belongs to the inner face of the block; it is significantly wider and several millimeters more salient than the exterior thickening on A 1. Block A 2 is thus from the north wall. Judged by its height, the block belongs to course two or above. The drill hole suggests a peg or bracket fixed to the outside of the structure.

Four blocks of the naïskos foundations are preserved and visible on the site. Three are of the same Aiginetan poros as the superstructure of the building: F 1, supporting the south euthynteria at the east, length 0.92, width 0.46, height 0.20–0.215 m. (Figs. 5, 8); F 3, at the center rear of the naïskos, length 0.77, width 0.57, height 0.215–0.32 m. (Figs. 5, 6); and F 4, at the northwest corner, 0.93 m. square, height 0.45 m. (Figs. 5, 6). The fourth block, F 2, at the southwest corner, is of Peiraeus limestone,[14] length 1.235, width 0.61–0.64, height 0.555–0.565 m. (Figs. 5, 6, 8).

I dealt earlier with the anomalous undersurfaces on blocks F 1 and F 3, beddings that allowed the blocks to rest directly on the uneven Stage II ground.[15] Of further note is the oblique orientation of the northwest corner block (F 4), shifted off the axis of the naïskos seemingly to accommodate better the oblique western face of the poros repository. A ledge cut across the outer corner of F 4 dates from Stage IV.[16]

The underpinning of Peiraeus limestone, block F 2, merits more detailed comment. The south, east, and west faces of this block cut the natural bedding of the stone on a strict perpendicular, indicating that the block was quarried, as is customary, with its horizontal axes parallel to the quarry bed. The large scale of F 2 would appear to have made it difficult to position on the site: although it was set in a footing trench, the exposed edge of its undersurface is irregularly trimmed back at several points, suggesting that the block

[14] Hard shell limestone. Fossils consist largely of small pelecypod shells (0.004–0.006 m. across) laid in thick, well-defined, highly porous beds. Bedding strata vary in color from gray brown to light gray. On Peiraeus limestone, see G. Lepsius, *Griechische Marmorstudien*, Berlin 1890, pp. 117–118; Heberdey 1919, pp. 182–184; Judeich 1931, p. 2.

[15] See p. 37 above.

[16] The ledge cannot be plausibly attributed to any stage but IV. Its floor, at +140.475, matches the resting level for course 3 of the amphiprostyle-temple foundations as recorded east of the naïskos (Pl. 11, *ca.* +140.46), and the wall of the ledge is parallel to the north face of the Stage IV sheathing. If cut for course 3, however, it was never used. Whereas the foundations on a level with F 4 (course 4, Pl. 17) have the same orientation as the ledge, course 3 overlies the cutting obliquely on the orientation of the temple (Pl. 16).

rested partly on boulders uncovered in the fill. Seemingly as a result, F 2 was left tipped, its bedding plane rising a few centimeters to the south, while the top was redressed to a level in compensation. It is of note finally that, unlike the east, south, and west faces of the block, the north crosses the natural bedding on a slight oblique. There would be no reason for the Stage III builders to have recut the north, and indeed its tooling and finish are indistinguishable from the three other vertical faces. We are left to conclude that block F 2 came to the site with one face, its present north face, dressed to a batter. Its dimensions on delivery will have been length 1.235, width (measured perpendicular to the south face) 0.61–0.635, estimated height 0.58 m.

The photograph, Plate 3:b, records two further foundation blocks: F 5 on the north, close beside F 4 (est. L. 0.50, est. H. 0.30 m.); and F 6, at the joint between E 4 and E 5 (est. L. 0.30, est. H. 0.15–0.20 m.). The former is hidden from view in the modern crypt. The latter was removed in the course of restoration and not replaced.

Masonry Technique and Condition

The tooling of the naïskos, skilled work of high standard, is unconventional in several respects. Wall faces are claw dressed rather than polished,[17] with the drafts more smoothly finished with a drove.[18] The euthynteria is coarsely trimmed top to bottom, with no indication of ground level. Of note are the distinctive marks of a large, blunt, four-pronged claw, used to carve a number of the joints on the euthynteria and wall.[19] Save where damaged in the Turkish period, the surfaces of the naïskos are fresh, seemingly unweathered.

Restored Plan and Elevation (Fig. 10)

The width of the naïskos is given by the patches of floor plaster on E 2, remains whose straight inner border mark the line of the south wall: clear width, 1.840 m.; width across the walls, 2.47 m.[20] The south anta block A 1 from the first course of the wall and the pry hole on the south euthynteria together allow a close estimate of the length of the naïskos. The pry hole establishes that the block joints for course one on the south fell roughly opposite those of the first course on the north, the blocks for both flanks having thus conformed to a standard length of *ca.* 0.94 m. An anta block of this first-course standard added to the north, on the example of block A 1, yields a restored length for the naïskos of *ca.* 3.65 m. The north anta block A 2, short of this standard by roughly a wall width, belongs thus to

[17] On the rarity of the claw finish, see Martin 1965, pp. 182, 414–415.

[18] The contrast of a textured, tooled wall face with smoother drafts, although singular for temple architecture, is common in retaining walls and fortifications. Compare the Periclean circuit wall at Eleusis, Wrede 1933, figs. 37–39, pick-dressed face, claw-tooled drafts; retaining wall for the Grave of the Lakedaimonians, Athens, Wrede 1933, fig. 49, face dressed with point and flat chisel, claw-tooled drafts.

[19] Orlandos 1966–1968 II, p. 52, fig. 42 (detail of the joint on anta block A 1; the captions for figures 42 and 43 are reversed). The masons used several claw chisels, all four-pronged and closely similar. One tool, distinctive for its slightly wider second prong, carved the joints on anta A 1 and euthynteria block E 1: its prongs measure respectively 0.0055, 0.007, 0.0055, and 0.0055 m.

[20] My figures are derived from Balanos, who records the clear width between the north wall and the south euthynteria as 1.775 m., the width between the walls as 1.84 m. (Pl. 12).

a.

b.

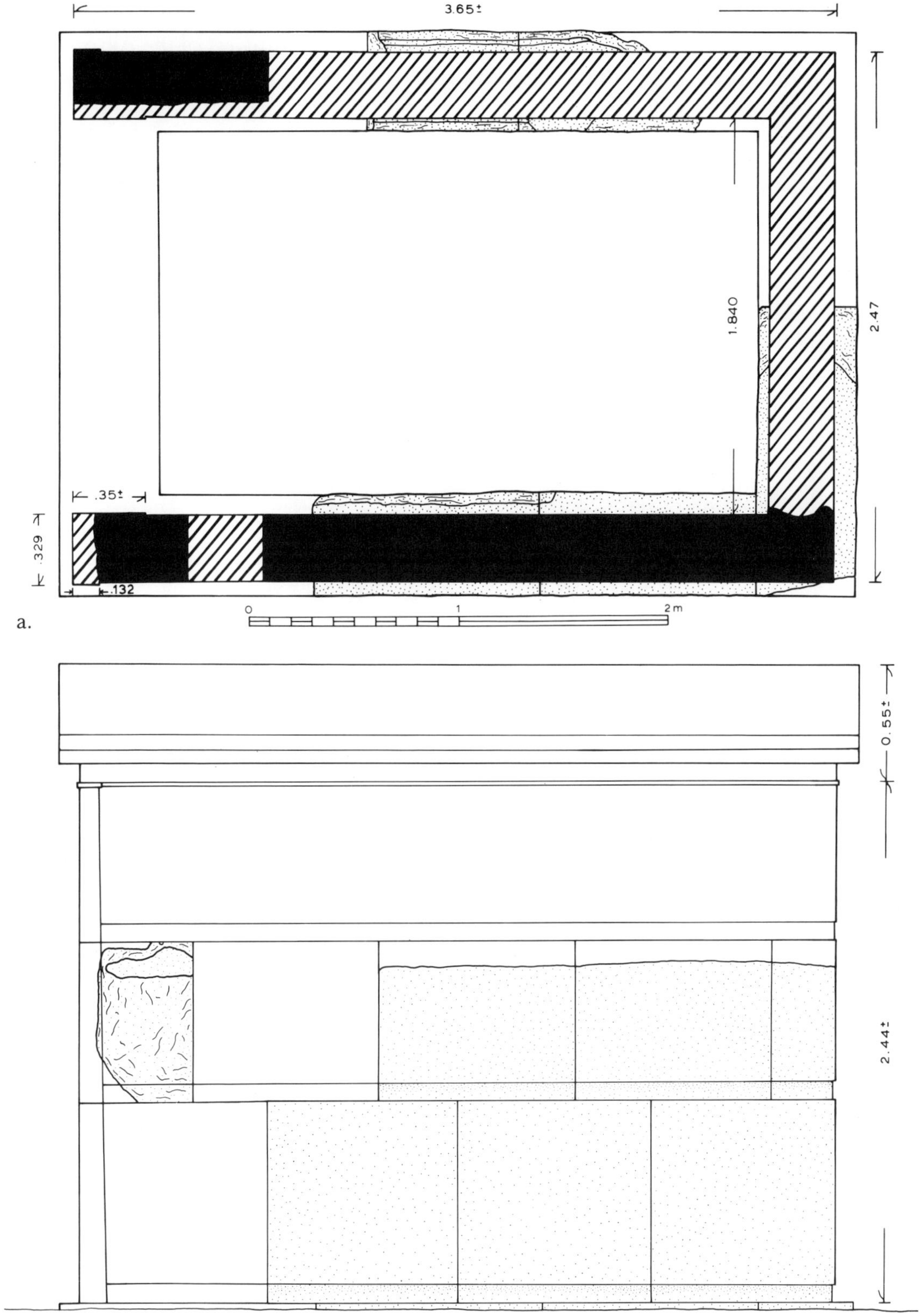

FIG. 10. Restoration of the naïskos: (a) Plan and (b) elevation from the north

the second course.[21] The side walls would have finished in a third course, in all likelihood the same height as course two. Finally, on analogy with a naïskos southwest of the Akropolis near the Pnyx, we may restore an entablature and gabled roof of poros. The structure near the Pnyx has an entablature and gable in one piece, the roof having been formed of several such triangular slabs set one behind the other across the cella walls.[22]

POROS REPOSITORY

The repository, fashioned of two blocks from the Stage I cult-statue base as explained above,[23] was found set within the northwest corner of the naïskos, abutting foundation blocks F 4 and F 5. Its rim stands at +140.67 on the north, 0.25 m. below the level of the naïskos floor.[24] For the deposit that partly filled the lowest level of its cavity, terracotta figurines mixed with a few sherds and bones, see p. 22 above. The asymmetrical underpinnings and irregular undersurface of the repository make clear that it is contemporary with the naïskos; both sat directly on the Stage II ground.

It was common to inaugurate a Greek temple with sacrifices and propitiation at its associated altar.[25] In contrast, the practice attested by the repository, the burying of votives against the fabric of a structure, remains rare.[26] Native to Egypt and the Near East, such foundation deposits have been uncovered through excavation in Greece on the order of a half

[21] One cannot positively rule out a doorwall at the east, but the restoration appears highly unlikely. There is no trace of a return on W 3 or A 2. One would have to restore the doorwall in the gap of *ca.* 0.38 m. between these two; that would place it at most 0.26–0.27 m. behind the inner thickening of the antae, implausibly close to the front of the naïskos.

[22] Charitonidis 1979 (note 2 above, p. 42), p. 164, fig. 1. Compare also the following 4th-century grave naïskoi with cover slabs of roughly similar design: Stele of Aristonautes, H. Diepolder, *Die attischen Grabreliefs*, Berlin 1931, pl. 50; Stele of Alexos, S. Karouzou, "Der Grabnaiskos des Alexos," *AthMitt* 96, 1981, pp. 179–200.

[23] Pp. 29–30.

[24] The level is entered on Balanos' plan, Pl. 7: +140.673. Distance beneath the naïskos floor: +140.918 – 140.673 = 0.245 m. Plate 12 gives the distance as 0.24 m.

[25] Hock 1905, pp. 73–83. Among the major testimonia, Photios, *Lex*: Ὄμπην· Ἀθηναῖοι ὅτ' ἂν τὸν νεὼν ἱδρύωνται πυροὺς μέλιτι δεύσαντες, ἐμβαλόντες εἰς καδίσκον, εἶθ´ οὕτως ἐπιθέντες τὸ ἱερεῖον, συντελοῦσι τὰ ἑξῆς· χρῶνται δὲ τούτῳ καὶ πρὸς ἄλλας ἱδρύσεις καὶ θυσίας, προσαγορεύοντες ὄμπην, εὐθένειαν οἰωνιζόμενοι· ὅθεν καὶ ἡ Δημήτηρ Ὄμπνια. Aeschines, *In Ctes.* 116: ἐξήγγελλετο δ' ἡμῖν παρὰ τῶν βουλομένων εὔνοιαν ἐνδείκνυσθαι τῇ πόλει, ὅτι οἱ Ἀμφισσεῖς ὑποπεπτωκότες τότε καὶ δεινῶς θεραπεύοντες τοὺς Θηβαίους εἰσέφερον δόγμα κατὰ τῆς ὑμετέρας πόλεως, πεντήκοντα ταλάντοις ζημιῶσαι τὸν δῆμον τὸν Ἀθηναίων, ὅτι χρυσᾶς ἀσπίδας ἀνέθεμεν πρὸς τὸν καινὸν νεὼν πρὶν ἐξαρέσασθαι[mss. ἐξειργάσθαι] καὶ ἐπέγραψεν τὸ προσῆκον ἐπίγραμμα «Ἀθηναῖοι ἀπὸ Μήδων καὶ Θηβαίων ὅτε τἀναντία τοῖς Ἕλλησιν ἐμάχοντο». Scholion (ed. Dindorf): ἐξειργάσθαι] γρ. ἐξαρᾶσθαι, τουτέστι πρὶν τὰς ἀρὰς ἐπιτελέσαι, ἃς ἐν ταῖς ἱδρύσεσι τῶν νεῶν εἰώθεσαν ποιήσασθαι.

On the inauguration of altars and statuary, scholion to Aristophanes, *Pax* 923 (ed. D. Holwerda): χύτραις ἱδρυτέον: ὁπότε μέλλοιεν βωμοὺς ἀφιδρύειν ἢ ἀγάλματα θεοῦ, ἕψοντες ὄσπρια ἀπήρχοντο τούτων τοῖς ἀφιδρυμένοις, χαριστήρια ἀπονέμοντες τῆς πρώτης διαίτης ὡς αὐτὸς εἶπεν ἐν Δαναΐσιν· «μαρτύρομαι δὲ Ζηνὸς ἑρκείου χύτρας / μεθ' ὧν ὁ βωμὸς οὗτος ἱδρύθη ποτέ». ποτὲ δὲ καὶ πολυτελεστέρῳ ἱερείῳ ἀφιδρύοντο. . . .

[26] For the terracottas as a Stage III votive deposit, already Welter 1939, col. 12.

dozen times.[27] Among these scattered Greek examples, one appears particularly close in form to the Nike remains, the foundation deposit for the Hellenistic temple of Artemis on Delos. The deposit lay against the foundations of that structure close to an interior corner and, like the Nike deposit, incorporated together with the votives some few bones and sherds.[28]

RECTANGULAR ALTAR

A small rectangular altar[29] (L. 1.245, W. 0.782, pres. H. 0.500 m., Fig. 11, Pl. 5, C at Plan A) lies on the axis of the naïskos to its east, a clear distance of 5.54 m. from the line of the naïskos west wall.[30] Monolithic, fashioned of the same Aiginetan poros as the naïskos, it has a projecting base and crown, cyma-reversa base and crowning moldings and volute barriers, the last largely worked away.[31] It is seated at +141.02 on a base slab,[32] a low block evenly dressed where it emerged above ground level (L. 1.425, W. 0.966 m.) and left rough below. As seen at its edge, the undersurface of the base slab is irregularly contoured and oblique, height 0.255–0.265 at the west, 0.37 m. at the east: like the contoured underpinnings of the naïskos, blocks F 1 and F 3, it was trimmed to lie directly on the Stage II ground. The roughly dressed lower margin of the base slab establishes ground level at the altar as not less than +140.855.

[27] Nilsson 1967, p. 404, note 10; Burkert 1985, p. 89; U. Sinn, "Der sog. Tempel D im Heraion von Samos II: Ein archäologischer Befund aus der nachpolykratischen Zeit mit einem Exkurs zum griechischen Bauopfer," *AthMitt* 100, 1985, pp. 129–158. To the instances listed there add the foundation deposit for the Heroon in the Sanctuary of Zeus at Nemea (S. Miller, "Excavation at Nemea, 1980," *Hesperia* 50, 1981 [pp. 46–67], p. 63) and the coin offering in the recently excavated Altar of Aphrodite Ourania in the Athenian Agora (T. L. Shear, Jr., "The Athenian Agora, Excavations of 1980–1982," *Hesperia* 53, 1984 [pp. 1–57], p. 31).

[28] Gallet de Santerre and Tréheux 1947–1948, pp. 148–254. The excavators associate the deposit with Temple E, which they date to the Early Archaic period, rather than with the Hellenistic Temple (Temple D) built directly around it. In preferring Temple D, I follow "Chroniques des fouilles et découvertes archéologiques," *BCH* 47, 1923 (pp. 498–544), p. 527 and C. Picard and J. Replat, "Recherches sur la topographie du hiéron Délien," *BCH* 48, 1924 (pp. 217–263), pp. 250–251, 261–262. The finds are unquestionably a foundation deposit; at issue is their date of burial. Among the excavators' observations I would give particular weight to the following: a moldmade-bowl fragment was found "dans une couche profonde du *bothros*, mais près des fondations du temple D" (Gallet de Santerre and Tréheux 1947–1948, p. 247). Although the excavators attribute the find to the foundation trench for Temple D, which they consider to have cut into the deposit, they later state (p. 249) that "des objets précieux se trouvaient enfouis tout contre les blocs de cette fondation, très profonde, au contact de laquelle le sol et sa stratigraphie précise n'apparaissent nullement bouleversés, comme si les architectes hellénistiques encore avaient cherché à creuser leurs tranchées et à mettre en place leurs matériaux sans troubler l'ordre du vieux dépôt sacré" (p. 249). This description, though offered by the excavators in support of their thesis, suggests to this reader that the foundations for "D" preceded the deposit.

[29] Welter 1923, pp. 193–194; Balanos 1956, pp. 786–787; Welter 1939, cols. 10–11.

[30] Compare Balanos 1956, p. 787, where the measurement is from the outer face of the west wall.

[31] For the altar type, Yavis 1949, pp. 131–136, 160–165; compare the altar of Aphrodite Hegemone found on the north slope of the Kolonos Agoraios, Travlos 1971, figs. 103, 104; altar found east of the Beulé Gate, Crosby 1949, p. 94, pl. 14:4.

[32] Plate 11 gives the level of the base slab as −1.195 m. relative to the Nike Temple euthynteria (+142.213 − 1.195 = +141.018). Balanos (1956, p. 787) gives the base slab as +0.10 m. relative to the naïskos euthynteria; this is confirmed by Plate 11, which enters the naïskos euthynteria as −1.295 m. relative to the Nike Temple euthynteria.

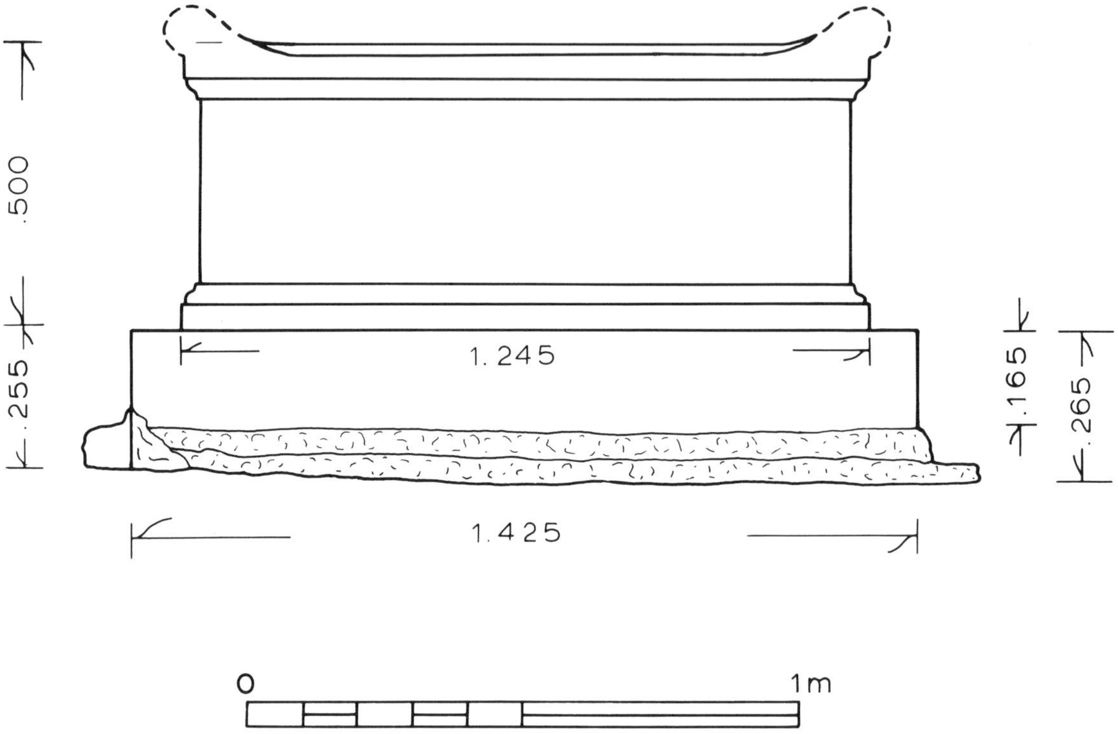

FIG. 11. Rectangular altar from the west

Naïskos and altar thus appear to have been approximately on a level: the euthynteria of the naïskos, a course traditionally left to emerge a few centimeters above ground level, stands to +140.92.

One reworking of the altar, the crude hacking away of its volute barriers, occurred in seating the poros foundations for the Stage IV altar, its monumental successor.[33] Beyond this, the rectangular altar has suffered from extensive water wear, apparently of Frankish and Turkish date: with the dismantling of the Stage IV altar by the Franks, rain water appears to have seeped through the loosely jointed underpinnings of the altar to its Stage III predecessor below. The few areas of the Stage III altar untouched by this run-off are fresh, seemingly unweathered.

The masonry of the rectangular altar bears close comparison to that of the naïskos. The former is dressed partly with a claw (the table of the altar, upper portion of the base slab) and partly with a drove (dado, projecting base and crown, and moldings), in a manner comparable to the wall face and drafts of the naïskos respectively.

[33] Balanos 1956, fig. 16; Welter 1939, fig. 5.

SQUARE ALTAR

A square block of Aiginetan poros (0.935 × 0.94, pres. H. 0.47 m., Pl. 6:b, B on Plan A) is seated toward the northern edge of the bastion on the orientation of the irregular trapezoidal wall.[34] It is bedded at +141.025.[35] The top of the block is recut, trimmed down to seat one of the rails for the Stage IV paving of the sanctuary, under whose pressure the stone has split north to south into two roughly equal parts.[36]

The sides of the block are plain, save for two narrow raised panels, one across the bottom edge of the north face, the other across the bottom edge of the south: height 0.165, projection 0.01 m. The northern panel extends the full width of the block; the southern ends 0.06 m. short of the southwest corner. The treatment of the block is noteworthy in that different sides of the square are brought to different states of finish. The east is coarsely worked with a drove. The north and south are evenly dressed using wide claw chisels with moderately spaced teeth, and the west is more finely worked with narrower, fine-toothed chisels. Balanos reports traces of burning on the surface of the stone.[37] The stone is otherwise fresh, seemingly unweathered.

As recorded in Balanos' published plan of the sanctuary (1956, pl. I) and in numerous archival drawings, the square block was positioned with its southwest corner on a salient boulder of the Mycenaean bastion. The northeast corner rested on the Stage I crown, and the remaining two corners were underpinned with poros: two blocks at the northwest, one at the southeast.[38] The underpinning at the southeast, an inscribed block from the Stage I altar, has been treated in detail above.[39]

Nowhere does Balanos explicitly interpret the square block. In a photo caption,[40] however, as well as on a number of the archival plans (e.g., Pl. 7), it is labeled a βομός, "altar". Altars are far more often rectangular or circular than square.[41] Proportions aside, however, there is much to support Balanos' identification: the more careful finish given the

[34] Welter 1923, p. 193; Balanos 1956, p. 786.

[35] Plate 7 gives the level of the top of the block as −0.718 m. relative to the amphiprostyle-temple euthynteria (= +141.495). Subtracting the height of the block, 0.47 m., gives +141.025.

[36] The paving over the square altar appears to have been destroyed in the Middle Ages. Welter records an intact rail farther to the east as having rested at *ca.* +141.50; see the cross-section in Welter 1923, pl. V:7.

[37] P. 786, 'Επὶ τῆς ἐπιφανείας τοῦ λίθου τούτου ἐμφαίνοντα ἐγκαύματα.

[38] When partially excavated in 1923, the square block appeared to have been seated on a base slab: Welter 1923, pl. V:1–3. The excavation photograph, Balanos 1956, p. 786, fig. 14, confirms Balanos' rendering.

[39] Pp. 32–34.

[40] Balanos 1956, p. 786, fig. 14.

[41] For the rarity of square altars, Yavis 1949, p. 96; D. W. Rupp, "Greek Altars of the Northeastern Peloponnese" (diss. Bryn Mawr College 1974), p. 317. Compare the following domestic altars from Olynthos, D. M. Robinson, *Olynthus* XII, Baltimore 1946, p. 191, pls. 168, 169; 172:2 (marble with overpainting on the dado, 0.21 m. square, H. *ca.* 0.35 m., projecting base and crown with ovolo moldings); p. 191, pls. 170, 171, 172:3 (similar to the above, 0.21 × 0.195, H. 0.34 m.); p. 212, pls. 172:1, 182 (limestone, 0.248 × 0.194, H. 0.303 m., projecting base and crown molded with cyma reversa and hawk's beak respectively); p. 215, pl. 183:1 (limestone, 0.163 m. square, pres. H. 0.10 m., crowning molding ovolo over astragal); p. 247 (marble, 0.186 × 0.175, H. 0.24 m., projecting base and crown, crowning molding). The base slab for an altar 0.75 m. square is preserved in the Chthonic Shrine in the forum at Corinth, C. H. Morgan, "Excavations at Corinth, 1936–37," *AJA* 41, 1937 (pp. 539–552), p. 545, pls. 13, 14.

western face of the block, the canonical side from which sacrifices were made; the traces of burning; and the reuse of the Stage I altar as underpinning.

The last of these points, if circumstantial, remains perhaps the strongest indication that the block was an altar. Possibly the Stage III builders never read the inscription on the block. When we consider how limited a number of reused blocks were employed in Stage III, however, and that the two identifiable Stage I survivals (the blocks from the cult-statue base and the inscribed altar block) are both in the nature of religious relics, truly central to the earlier cult, the possibility of chance reuse appears remote. The Stage I cult-statue base underlay and supported its Stage III successor.[42] It is natural to view the square block analogously, as successor to the altar of Patrokles.[43]

IRREGULAR TRAPEZOIDAL RETAINING WALL

As established in our earlier discussion (pp. 17–19), the crown of the bastion was twice rebuilt, the second rebuilding having survived in a short stretch of irregular trapezoidal retaining wall along the northern edge of the sanctuary. Having paired the first rebuilding of the crown with Stage I of the sanctuary,[44] the tie of the second to the next attested building phase, Stage III, follows naturally.

As given by the resting level of the square altar, the ground level in the northern area of the sanctuary was at least 0.05 m. above the crown of the trapezoidal retaining wall: the resting edge of the altar is at +141.025; the trapezoidal wall comes to +140.98. It follows that the trapezoidal wall continued in a further course: we may imagine a low course that formed a coping on the exterior and, emerging partly above ground on the interior, functioned equally as the euthynteria for a freestanding parapet or temenos wall.[45]

Northeast of the Nike Sanctuary is a small stepped forecourt, seemingly a theatral area, built in the Late Archaic period and in use until the construction of the Mnesiklean Propylaia.[46] One likely entered the Nike Sanctuary from the lowest level or "stage" of the court (Fig. 12). That lowest rock-cut step is at +140.91, as established in excavations beneath the floor of the Southwest Wing.[47] Ground level in the sanctuary is *ca.* +140.86.

[42] Although no trace of the Stage III base for the cult statue survives, by custom it would have stood at the center rear of the naïskos, thus broadly overlapping the repository.

[43] The altar of Patrokles may or may not have been the main altar of the sanctuary in Stage I. If it was the main altar, then the inscribed block had to have been moved. Might it have been thrown from the site of the Stage I altar in the thorough destruction that ended that stage and perhaps have drawn informal, popular offerings where it lay? By the time Stage III was constructed, the new site may have been too holy to abandon.

[44] See p. 35 above.

[45] For the trapezoidal wall as the footing for a temenos wall, Welter 1923, p. 193; Wrede 1932, p. 81, fig. 3; Stevens 1946, p. 84, fig. 6.

[46] Dinsmoor, Jr. 1980, pp. 17–31.

[47] Elevations in the area of the Propylaia are taken from Dinsmoor, Jr. 1980, plan A, adjusted +0.07 m. to conform with Balanos' reference. Note that Dinsmoor, Jr.'s levels vary against those given by Balanos: +0.010 m. at the northeast corner of the euthynteria of the Nike Temple; −0.041 m. at the euthynteria of the naïskos; −0.069 at the base slab for the rectangular altar. My adjustment is at best an estimate.

Fig. 12. Restored plan of the Akropolis entrance in the mid-5th century: Stage III of the Nike Sanctuary, the stepped forecourt, and Stage 3 of the Old Propylon

DATING OF STAGE III

A range of architectural criteria, among them technical details and masonry closely tied to other projects on the Akropolis, establishes a date for Stage III in the middle decades of the 5th century (Fig. 12). The block underpinning the southwest corner of the naïskos euthynteria, F 2 (Figs. 5, 6, 8), provides the project with a firm *terminus post quem*. Of a different stone than the rest of Stage III (Peiraeus limestone rather than Aiginetan poros), of massive scale, and with a batter to one face, it appears to have been quarried for a different project. A thorough survey of possible projects in fact confirms this. Its dimensions, 1.235 × 0.635 × 0.58 m., recur repeatedly in the new-quarried sections of the South Akropolis Wall.[48] Its batter and the exposed sections of that wall agree closely.[49] Also its stone and the characteristic shell limestone of the South Wall appear identical.

Although Aktite stone of this variety is frequent in foundations and fortifications from the mid-5th century on, it is far less common earlier. We may cite four other pre-Periclean projects at Athens that employed it in ashlars of large scale: the inner foundations for the Olympieion; the podium of the Older Parthenon; the Northwest Building on the Akropolis; and the North Akropolis Wall.[50] Of these, only the North Akropolis Wall utilized blocks of the same dimensions as block F 2, and they occur infrequently in that project. The North Wall is formed of ashlars of widely varying sizes, with course heights from *ca.* 0.28 to *ca.* 0.65 m. and block lengths from *ca.* 0.75 to *ca.* 2.65 m. Of the sixty-odd courses recorded in published elevations, eight are 0.58 m. in height. These eight incorporate, in all, fourteen stretchers *ca.* 1.24 m. long. Extrapolating from the elevations, we may estimate that perhaps one of fifty blocks used for the project had the requisite height and width. An attribution of block F 2

[48] See particularly two measured elevations of the South Wall by Georg Kawerau: Bundgård 1974a, pls. 172, 173. The drawings record two stretches along the inner face of the wall, the first beneath the Parthenon *ergasterion*, the other slightly to its west. The upper two-thirds of the wall in both sections is built of courses most usually between 0.55 and 0.59 m. in height. The drawing for the section beneath the *ergasterion* (Bundgård 1974a, pl. 172) records the cumulative height of seven courses as 4.0 m., yielding an average course height of 0.571 m. Compare the following block dimensions measured off the drawings: plate 172 (1st course = 1.0 m. below ground level measured at left), in the 7th course (stretchers) 5 out of 14 blocks measure *ca.* 1.24 m.; plate 173 (1st course = 3.0 m. below the breastwork of the wall), 3rd course (stretchers), 5 out of 10 blocks measure *ca.* 1.24 m.; 5th course (stretchers), 3 out of 12 blocks measure *ca.* 1.24 m. Plate 173, 2nd course (headers), 8 out of 15 blocks measure *ca.* 0.64 m.; 4th course (headers), 13 out of 23 blocks measure *ca.* 0.64 m.; 9th course (headers), 8 out of 22 blocks measure *ca.* 0.64 m. A stretch of the South Wall backing the Chalkotheke remains partially exposed, open to direct measurement. The blocks there are uniformly 1.235 × 0.635 × 0.45 m. The course height is less than our block, as occurs again in a stretch of wall drawn by Kawerau further to the west (Bundgård 1974a, pl. 194). Length and width, however, match exactly.

[49] The face of the South Akropolis Wall is largely covered by medieval stonework, with only one major expanse of new-quarried blocks now exposed, from the southeast corner of the Akropolis to roughly the west end of the Akropolis Museum. As observed there, the batter of the wall has two constituents: the wall blocks are themselves battered, and every second or third course is set back slightly. The following records the batter of individual blocks at the base of the wall: *ca.* 10 m. from the southeast corner, 2nd course up, height 0.52, batter 0.033 m. (0.063: 1); 18 m. from the southeast corner, 2nd course up, height 0.445, batter 0.026 m. (0.058: 1); 3rd course up, height 0.48, batter 0.030 m. (0.062: 1). F 2 batters 0.030 in 0.50 m. (0.060: 1).

[50] Olympieion, G. Welter, "Das Olympieion in Athen," *AthMitt* 47, 1922 (pp. 61–71), pp. 62–63, pls. 7, 10; Parthenon podium, Bundgård 1974a, pl. 227; Northwest Building and North Wall, Kavvadias and Kawerau 1906, pls. I′, K′.

to the North Wall, improbable on the basis of dimensions, is entirely ruled out by batter: for nearly its full length the north circuit is set with a vertical face, while the one exception, a 200-m. stretch of wall at the west, inclines at less than half the angle of our block.[51] In sum, the dimensions and batter of block F 2 accord with the South Wall and that project alone.

The stretches of the South Wall built of newly quarried stone, including those portions of the wall where the dimensions of the blocks are analogous to block F 2, were constructed over a period of decades. They do not date from the beginning of the project, for they partly overlie sections built of reused materials. Ancient testimony ties the South Wall to Kimon, stating that it was funded by spoils from the battle at Eurymedon (*ca.* 467).[52] Counting from the early 460's, we may conservatively set the start of work on the quarried sections of the South Wall, the *terminus post quem* for the naïskos foundations, at around 465.

A lower limit for Stage III is given by the Mnesiklean Propylaia (437–432). The isolated pier, traditionally called a double anta, that terminates the north colonnade of the Southwest Wing and the low Z-shaped wall to the west of this are supported on a single large substructure that is cut to fit against the irregular trapezoidal wall (Plan A). These foundations, laid of a piece with the northern flank of the podium for the wing, almost certainly date from early in the Propylaia project. They establish a date for Stage III at or before *ca.* 435.[53]

Three further criteria, if less strict than the *terminus ante* and *terminus post* reviewed above, offer general corroboration for a mid-5th-century date: the profiles of the cyma-reversa moldings on the Stage III rectangular altar; the masonry technique on the poros structures of the sanctuary, foremost the naïskos; and the masonry of the irregular trapezoidal wall.

As established in the work of Lucy Shoe Meritt, there are broad, easily observable changes in the curvature of cyma-reversa moldings from the 6th to the 5th century.[54] The Archaic cyma reversa tends to have little depth in relation to height and is typified by a short, shallow reverse (concave) curve: the ratio of depth to height falls characteristically between 1:4 and 1:2,[55] and the reverse curve tends to lie close to the diagonal of the molding, the imaginary line that joins the springing of the projecting curve to the base of the return. Reverse curves become larger and deeper through the 5th century, with the cyma reversa thus increasing in relative depth. The ratio of depth to height in the Classical period falls most usually between 1:2 and 1:1. Judged from their proportions and the form of their reverse

[51] Middleton 1900, pl. 4, no. V, recording a batter of *ca.* 0.025:1 at the Northwest Building, *ca.* 0.014:1 beyond the Northwest Building to the west. A survey of the North Wall undertaken in 1980, still largely unpublished, promises to further substantially our knowledge of these remains. See *Acropolis at Athens: Conservation, Restoration and Research, 1975–1983*, Athens 1985, p. 39, fig. III:26a.

[52] Plutarch, *Cim.* 13.6, *Cim. et Luc.* 1.5, *De glor. Ath.* 7; Nepos, *Cim.* 2.5; Pausanias 1.28.3; Judeich 1931, p. 74. On the chronology of the South Wall, Dörpfeld 1902, p. 389; Kavvadias and Kawerau 1906, cols. 113–120; cf. also Bundgård 1974a, pp. 26–27. The South Akropolis Wall continued in construction as late as the 440's. We may note in particular that the upper half of the South Wall east of the Chalkotheke is procedurally later than a temporary retaining wall for the Parthenon (see Kavvadias and Kawerau 1906, col. 120; Bundgård 1974a, pls. 174, 175).

[53] On the chronology of the Southwest Wing, see Wrede 1932, pp. 86–87.

[54] Shoe 1936, pp. 54–57; see more recently, L. S. Meritt, "The Stoa Poikile," *Hesperia* 39, 1970 (pp. 233–264), p. 253.

[55] Shoe 1936, p. 54, note 2; p. 57.

curves, the moldings on the Stage III altar belong rather to the 5th than to the 6th century. Depth to height on the base molding is 1:1.57, on the crown 1:1.54, while the reverse curves on both are broadly concave and well developed (Fig. 13).

If less readily quantified than depth and height, the curvature on a cyma reversa remains an important adjunct for dating. On the altar moldings both projecting and reverse curves approach arcs of a circle, the radius being a step greater in the return. Eastern Greece develops this form by the second decade of the 5th century, as attested by the base molding on a Late Archaic statue base from Paros (Fig. 13, no. 1).[56] The type is known in Attica from the Periclean period, two early examples being the molded toichobate on the Temple of Poseidon at Sounion (Fig. 13, no. 2), 450–440 B.C., and the sills for the pronaos and opisthodomos grilles of the Parthenon, dating from the 430's (Fig. 13, no. 3).[57]

As a foil to the developed Periclean form, we may compare the cyma reversa on four Late Archaic bases from the Athenian Akropolis: EM 6425 (Fig. 13, no. 4);[58] EM 6279 (Fig. 13, no. 5);[59] AcrM 3827 (Fig. 13, no. 6);[60] and AcrM 3821 (Fig. 13, no. 7).[61] The most conservative of this group is EM 6425, both for its slight depth (depth to height = 1:3.51) and shallow reverse curve. The ratios of depth to height for the remaining three are somewhat larger (EM 6279 = 1:2.54; AcrM 3827 = 1:2.25; AcrM 3821 = 1:2.27), but they still fall well below those for the Stage III altar. The curvatures on these Archaic examples are equally indicative. Projecting and reverse curves are of less regular curvature than on the altar. Where the curves do approach conic sections, they tend not to a circle but to a parabola in the projecting curve, an hyperbola in the reverse. The sum of these comparisons, establishing the relation of the altar moldings to Periclean moldings of the third quarter of the 5th century on the one hand, and their evident distance from early 5th-century Attic examples on the other, lends strong support to the Stage III limits discussed above.

The distinctive masonry of the naïskos provides additional dating criteria: The drafted lower margin on the wall courses and the tooled finish on the face of the wall bear comparison

[56] A. Kostoglou-Despini, Προβλήματα τῆς παριανῆς πλαστικῆς, Thessalonike 1979, fig. 4, depth to height, 1:1.70.

[57] The relevant sections of Shoe's (1936) compendium are XIV, "Balustrade, Orthostate, Podium and Altar Crowns," pp. 84–85, and XVII, "Toechobate, Anta Base, Grille, and Threshold Bases," pp. 87–89. Toichobate molding, Temple of Poseidon at Sounion, Shoe, pl. XXXVII:3, depth to height, 1:1.24. Parthenon grilles, G. Stevens, *The Setting of the Periclean Parthenon* (*Hesperia* Supplement 3), Cambridge, Mass. 1940, pp. 67–79; *idem*, "The Sills of the Grilles of the Pronaos and Opisthodomos of the Parthenon," *Hesperia* 11, 1942 (pp. 354–364), pp. 354–364; Shoe, pl. XXXVII:1, depth to height, 1:1.28. The following are slightly more distant comparisons: Sanctuary of Athena Nike, bastion crown, Shoe, pl. XXXVI:2 (420's B.C.); Delphi tholos, toichobate, Shoe, pl. XXXVII:4 (early 4th century). Although its dating has yet to be nailed down, the base molding on the recently excavated Altar of Aphrodite Ourania in the Athenian Agora offers a further important parallel. See Shear (note 27 above, p. 53), pp. 24–33, figs. 13, 16.

[58] For its dedicatory inscription, Raubitschek 1949, no. 296. The letter cutter uses both cartwheel and dotted theta, suggesting a date around 480; see Meiggs 1966, pp. 90–91. The profile of this base and the following, EM 6279, were taken with a template directly from the stone. Remaining comparisons are from Shoe.

[59] Raubitschek 1949, no. 149. Letter forms suggest a date in the late 6th or early 5th century.

[60] Shoe 1936, p. 56, pl. XXV:21. Rectangular base, length 0.44, width 0.195 m.; traces of paint on the molding. Its state of preservation and condition strongly suggest it is from the Persian debris.

[61] Shoe 1936, p. 56, pl. XXV:22.

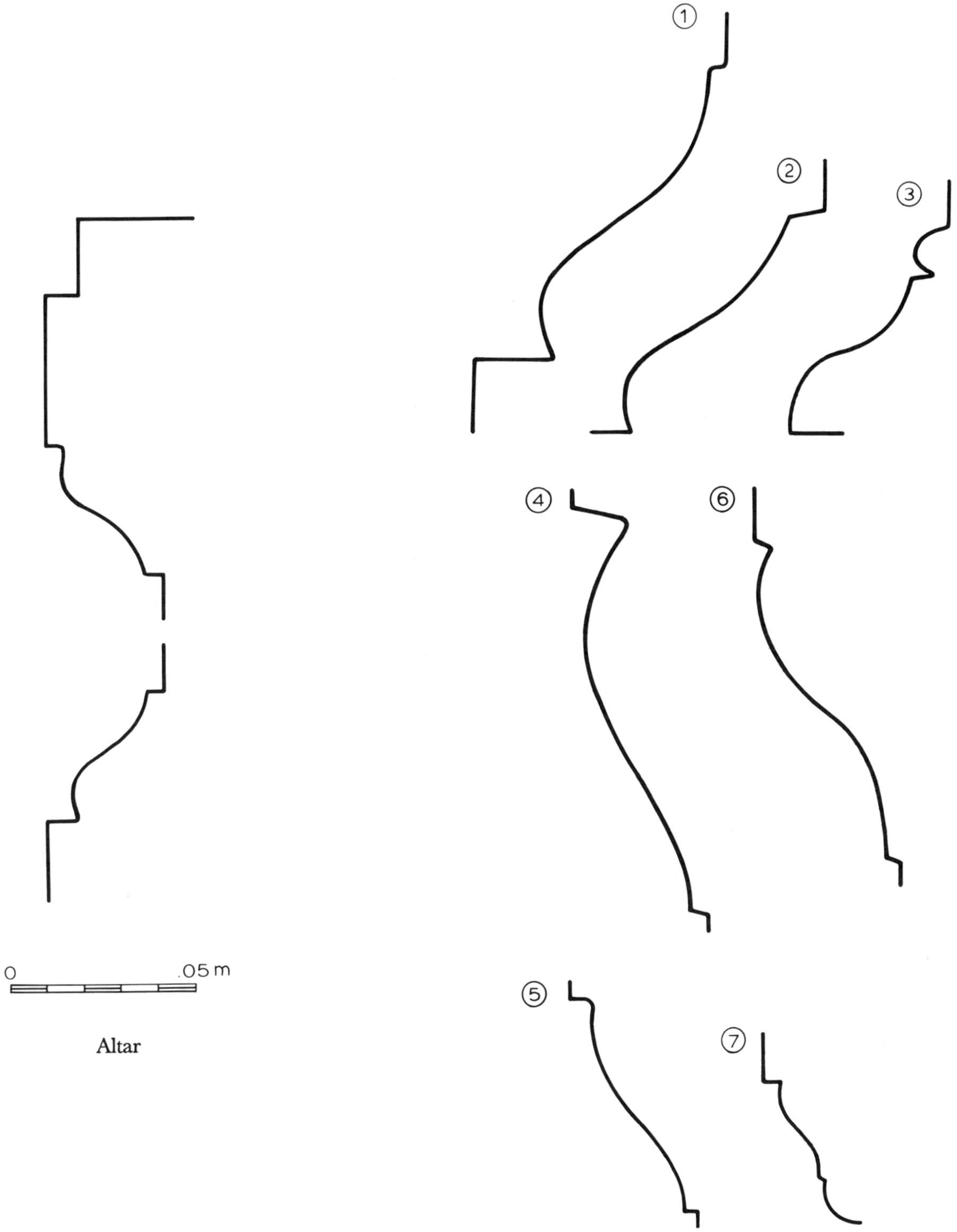

FIG. 13. Profiles of the moldings on the rectangular altar. Cyma-reversa moldings of developed form: (1) base molding on a Late Archaic statue base from Paros; (2) toichobate of the Temple of Poseidon at Sounion; (3) molded sill for the pronaos and opisthodomos grilles of the Parthenon. Cyma-reversa crowns on Late Archaic bases from the Akropolis: (4) EM 6425; (5) EM 6279; (6) AcrM 3827; (7) AcrM 3821

to two other building projects on the Akropolis, the Old Propylon Stage 3, and the upper, freestanding courses of the North Akropolis Wall.[62]

The tie to the upper courses of the North Wall is particularly close. The North Wall is built of a stone scarcely distinguishable from that of the naïskos, an Aiginetan poros bearing comparable fossils and seemingly identical in its fabric, color, and jointing. The drafting of the lower margins of the blocks on the North Wall has the precise form of the drafting on the naïskos. Also, the two projects are tooled in a similar manner, wall faces dressed with a claw chisel and the drafting with a drove.

The anta wall for Stage 3 of the Old Propylon is a slightly less close comparison. The anta wall is of Aktite rather than Aiginetan poros,[63] with the lower margin of the courses drafted on both the front and rear faces of the wall. The wall surface is dressed with a claw chisel, as on the naïskos and North Wall, but only a portion of the drafting is cut with a drove, the remainder with a claw.

We may note, finally, a point of similarity between the North Wall and the anta wall: their drafts are of the same dimensions, height 0.040–0.043, depth 0.003 m.[64]

The drafting on the North Wall, the anta wall, and the naïskos is of a rare form. Wall blocks are normally drafted not only at the lower edge but up the sides or around all four sides.[65] The naïskos and its related Akropolis projects are the first known departures from this standard form.[66] The tooling on the three is no less distinctive. Normal building practice called for a wall face to be smoothed with abrasives, not left with a claw-chisel finish, while drafts were commonly worked with a claw, not a drove.[67] These shared peculiarities, as well as the closely similar poros used in the North Wall and the naïskos and the identically cut rebates on the North Wall and anta wall, suggest that the three

[62] Old Propylon Stage 3, Dinsmoor, Jr. 1980, pp. 56–62, pl. 21; Travlos 1971, fig. 610. North Wall, Kavvadias and Kawerau 1906, pls. I′, K′; Wrede 1933, figs. 32, 33; Bundgård 1976, figs. 77–81.

[63] The poros of the anta wall stands apart from that of the naïskos and North Wall for its gray color and lack of jointing. Aiginetan and Aktite stones are at times so similar as to be hardly distinguishable. Certain beds of Peiraeus have the same marly quality as Aiginetan and are similarly fossiliferous. On the whole, however, Peiraeus tends to greater concentrations of fossils, having thus a more porous, more clearly defined bedding. These latter characteristics are well illustrated in the anta wall. On the relationship of Aiginetan and Peiraeus stones, see Herz 1954–1955, pp. 501–502; Paton 1927, p. 350, note 2.

[64] Dinsmoor, Jr. 1980, p. 63.

[65] On the history of drafted-margin masonry, Scranton 1941, pp. 129–130; Martin 1965, pp. 416–420. Early examples include the Altar of Poseidon, Cape Monodendri, A. von Gerkan, *Der Poseidonaltar bei Kap Monodendri* (*Milet* I, iv), Berlin 1915, p. 10, fig. 10, pls. V:1, XI:3–5, XII:1–4 (mid-6th century); peribolos of Temple D, Selinus, E. Gabrici, "Studi archeologici Selinunti," *Monumenti Antichi* 43, 1956 (cols. 205–408), cols. 226–230, fig. 6 (third quarter of 6th century); Treasuries A and C, Delphi, F. Courby, *Topographie et architecture: La terrasse du temple* (*Fouilles de Delphes* II, i), Paris 1915, pp. 185–188, figs. 141, 143, 145 (before 518 B.C.).

[66] The polished lower border on the orthostates of the Letoon on Delos, while not a rebate *per se*, offers a distant precedent for continuous drafting. See *Délos* XXIV, pp. 37–38, pls. V, XLIX:47, 48.

[67] Compare the following Attic walls with claw-dressed drafts: Eleusis, Periclean retaining wall, Wrede 1933, p. 16, figs. 37–39; retaining wall for the Grave of the Lakedaimonians, Wrede 1933, p. 19, fig. 49; retaining wall for the Theater of Dionysos, Wrede 1933, p. 21, fig. 52; tower at the Sacred Gate, Kerameikos, Wrede 1933, pp. 20–21, fig. 51; Asklepieion, Wrede 1933, p. 23, fig. 55.

projects are close in date, executed by a single crew of masons perhaps, or under the eye of a single architect.[68]

Neither the North Wall nor the Old Propylon Stage 3 is firmly dated. What little evidence remains, however, suggests a date for both toward the middle of the 5th century. The drafted courses of the North Wall overlie the foundations for a large, uncompleted structure northeast of the Propylaia, the so-called Northwest Building.[69] The massive substructure of this building was built largely of newly quarried material and is in part bonded to, in part set against the North Akropolis Wall. The Northwest Building was abandoned half finished, preference having apparently been given to the Mnesiklean Propylaia. As initially planned, the northeast wing of this monumental gateway would have cut straight across it.[70] The fact that the Northwest Building is built largely of newly quarried blocks suggests a date in the 460's at the earliest. In the years immediately following the Persian Destruction, Athens appears to have undertaken only essential building projects and to have employed materials close at hand: the stone from damaged monuments, mud brick, and/or terracotta.[71] The apparent link, in turn, between the abandonment of the Northwest Building and plans for the Propylaia implies that construction on the earlier project continued into the 440's. The crowning courses of the North Wall, built across the foundations for the Northwest Building, appear thus to date from the 440's at the earliest.[72]

68 On the close relation of the anta wall and the North Wall, already Dinsmoor, Jr. 1980, pp. 63–64. The different stones used for the two projects (see note 63 above, p. 62) rule out their blocks having a common source (Dinsmoor, Jr. 1980, p. 63). I would further question whether either set of poros ashlars is reused (cf. Bundgård 1976, pp. 120; 189, note 293; Dinsmoor, Jr. 1980, pp. 61, 63). The North Wall turns at an oblique angle opposite the rear wall of the eastern cella of the Erechtheion and is surely formed there of blocks cut individually to the requirements of the site (Bundgård 1976, fig. 80). These oblique-angled blocks are indistinguishable from the remaining ashlars of the wall in their variety of poros, in drafting and in tooling. The whole appears of a piece.

The Aktite poros of the anta wall, unsightly against the Pentelic marble anta and flank wall of the gatehouse, required stucco, and indeed early scholars noted patches of red plaster still adhering to its face (e.g., Ross 1855–1856, pp. 79, 82; Bohn 1882, p. 16; Dörpfeld 1902, p. 406; *idem*, "Gesimse unter Wandmalereien," *AthMitt* 36, 1911 [pp. 87–96], pp. 93–94; for full references, Dinsmoor, Jr. 1980, p. 61). I am skeptical, however, of the suggestion that stucco filled in the drafts, leaving the wall face smooth (first Bohn 1882, p. 16).

69 On the Northwest Building, see Kavvadias and Kawerau 1906, pp. 64, 70; Bundgård 1957, p. 80; *idem* 1976, pp. 39–40.

70 For the chronology of the Northwest Building, see Bundgård 1976, pp. 39–40, who proposes that remains from the unfinished superstructure of the building are built into the Propylaia foundations. On the northeast wing of the Propylaia, Bohn 1882, p. 31; W. Dörpfeld, "Die Propyläen der Akropolis von Athen I: Das ursprüngliche Project des Mnesikles," *AthMitt* 10, 1885, pp. 47–53; Dinsmoor 1950, p. 204; Bundgård 1957, pp. 77–92.

71 Boersma 1970, pp. 43–46; for evidence from the Athenian Agora, H. A. Thompson, "Athens Faces Adversity," *Hesperia* 50, 1981 (pp. 341–355), pp. 345–346.

72 For the late dating of the upper North Wall, cf. Bundgård 1976, pp. 121–133 (after 434 B.C.). Earlier scholarship has dated the upper North Wall without regard to the Northwest Building: W. Dörpfeld, "Über die Ausgrabungen auf der Akropolis," *AthMitt* 11, 1886 (pp. 162–169), p. 166 (not immediately post-Persian); *idem* 1902, p. 412 (reversing himself, Themistoklean); *idem*, "Das Hekatompedon in Athen," *JdI* 34, 1919 (pp. 1–40), p. 10 ("sicher bald nach den Perserkriegen"); L. B. Holland, "Erechtheum Papers III: The Post-Persian

Dinsmoor, Jr. offers a valuable point of departure for dating Stage 3 of the Old Propylon. We may begin from his conclusion that Stage 3 is the sole restoration of the old gatehouse after the Persian Wars.[73] Stage 3 and *IG* I^3 45, a minor Periclean building decree (*ca.* 450–445),[74] ought in that case to be close in date.

IG I^3 45 decrees that a stretch of the Akropolis walls is to be made secure against thieves and runaways. Kallikrates is to draw up specifications for the project, with construction to be finished within sixty days. Three archers are to stand guard in the interim:

– – – – – – – – – – – – – – –
[. . .]ιε[. . .6. . . κατὰ]
[τ]ὲν πόλιν [τ]α ὀχ̣[υρὰ]
οἰκο[δ]ομε͂σαι : *hό*π̣ [ο]-
[ς] ἂν : δραπέτες μὲ ἐ[σ]-
[ἰ]ει : μεδὲ λοποδύτ[ε]-
[ς] : ταῦτα δὲ χσυνγρά̣-
φ̣σα[ι] μὲν Καλλικρά̣-
[τ]ε : *hό*πος ἄριστα κα-
ὶ εὐτελέστατα σκε̣-
υάσαι. ἀπ̣ομισθο͂σα-
[ι] δὲ τὸ[ς] πολετ[ὰ]ς : *hό*-
[π]ος ἂν : ἐντὸς *h*εχσέ-
[χ]οντα : ἑμερο͂ν : ἐπισχ-
[ε]υασθεῖ : φύλακας δὲ
[ε͂]ναι τρε͂ς μὲν τοχσό-
[τ]ας : ἐχ τε͂ς φυλε͂ς τε͂ς
[π]ρυτανευόσες[75]

The Akropolis was open and free of access in the wake of the Persian Destruction, the invader having razed its gatehouse (Stage 2 of the Propylon) and perhaps stretches of the Mycenaean circuit as well. By the start of the Parthenon in the early 440's, massive retaining

Revision," *AJA* 28, 1924 (pp. 402–425), p. 405 (likely Kimonian); A. Tschira, "Die unfertigen Säulentrommeln auf der Akropolis von Athen," *JdI* 55, 1940 (pp. 242–261), p. 261 (Periclean).

73 Dinsmoor, Jr. 1980, pp. 52–54, 63. Dinsmoor Jr.'s arguments have been questioned more recently by Kalpaxis 1986, pp. 102–108. Dinsmoor's Stage 2 shows damage by fire, which encourages its placement before the Persian Wars. Kalpaxis dates Stage 2 to the early Periclean period, *ca.* 460–450, but it is difficult to see why Stage 2 would have needed to be replaced by a provisional building (Stage 3 is built of poros and reused blocks), and this only a decade later.

74 Dated on letter forms. Diagnostic are sloping nu and V-shaped upsilon, both of which go out of use in the 440's; sigmas are four-barred, a form first attested in the Athenian tribute list of 453/452. On the four-barred sigma, see Meiggs 1966, pp. 91–93; for nu and upsilon, M. Walbank, "Criteria for the Dating of Fifth-Century Attic Inscriptions," in Φόρος*: Tribute to Benjamin D. Meritt*, D. W. Bradeen and M. F. McGregor, eds., Locust Valley, N.Y. 1974, pp. 164–169. The annotations to *IG* I^3 45 (D. Lewis) suggest *ca.* 445. Cf. H. B. Mattingly ("Athenian Finance in the Peloponnesian War," *BCH* 92, 1968 [pp. 450–492], p. 469), who places the inscription late in the third quarter of the century.

75 For the text, F. Hiller von Gaertringen, *IG* I^2 44. Line 2, stoichos 12 preserves the tip of a descending diagonal stroke at lower right, a cut which by its position and slope is best restored as xi. I find no trace of the strokes reported for this stoichos in *IG* I^3 45, a horizontal and an ascending oblique. As edited there, line 2 reads: [τ]ὲν πόλιν [.] ΑΟ∠[. . .].

walls rendered the citadel again secure on three sides, the north, south, and east. The west, made fast a decade later by the Propylaia, was apparently still in ruins at mid-century. On the testimony of *IG* I^3 45, however, we may be confident that it too had a defensible wall at least for most of its length: the decree provides for but sixty days' work to complete the circuit.

The limited project decreed by *IG* I^3 45 and its express concern with surreptitious entry suggest that it sealed a minor opening, a hidden entrance perhaps, or a stretch where the natural rock had seemed barrier enough. It would, of course, have been meaningless to seal such access were the gateways to the citadel not already secure. That is, *IG* I^3 45 forms a *terminus ante quem* for the Propylon Stage 3.

Dinsmoor Jr.'s study favors a date for Stage 3 in the 460's, arguing that the alternatives, a date directly after the Persian Wars, or after mid-century, are both unlikely. He considers a date in the 440's implausible, in particular, because it leaves the Akropolis unfortified over several decades and locates the rebuilding of the Propylon at a time when plans for its successor, the Mnesiklean Propylaia, appear to have been already afoot.[76] *IG* I^3 45, however, encourages a different view of the problem. If the rebuilding of the gatehouse, Stage 3, and the restoration of a defensible circuit of the Akropolis go together, not a necessary equation but logical and straightforward, then Stage 3 ought to be the immediate forerunner of the decree.

A Periclean rebuilding of the Old Propylon may appear wasteful and ill planned, coming as it would within a decade of work on the Propylaia. We need recall, however, that the Stage 3 structure was thoroughly makeshift, a mix of reused marble blocks and new-cut poros. Quickly executed, never intended to stand for long, it secured the Akropolis in advance of the permanent, monumental rebuilding already then in planning.[77]

The arguments we have applied to dating Stage 3 of the Propylon and the upper courses of the North Wall are, of themselves, too skeletal and circumstantial to establish the 440's as more than a logical and plausible context for the two. I will have more to say on the problem in the concluding chapter of this study and will further the argument for a late date at that time. It is sufficient to present purposes, however, simply that the two finds admit of a dating within the general period suggested by other criteria on Stage III.

A final dating criterion is furnished by the irregular trapezoidal masonry of the Stage III bastion crown. We have observed that this wall precedes the laying of the substructures for the double anta of the Southwest Wing, having thus a *terminus post quem non* of *ca.* 435. The trapezoidal stonework of the wall appears, at the same time, unlikely to be far in advance of that date. As noted in previous discussion, the earliest attested parallels for irregular trapezoidal are late 5th century.[78]

As heterogeneous and diverse as are the criteria for dating Stage III, they constitute together a remarkably consistent body of evidence. The cyma-reversa moldings on the rectangular altar, although not open to narrow, ironclad dating, strongly indicate a placement for Stage III in the 440's. A date well into the 5th century is reinforced by the irregular trapezoidal stonework of the bastion crown, a style of masonry first paralleled in fortifications

[76] Dinsmooor, Jr. 1980, pp. 63–64.

[77] Kalpaxis 1986, pp. 105–106, a study that appeared while mine was essentially completed, defends a similar date for Stage 3 (*ca.* 450–440) but on different grounds. Kalpaxis notes a close relation between Stage 3 and the propylon of the Sanctuary of Poseidon at Sounion.

[78] See pp. 18–19 above.

built late in the Peloponnesian War, and is further compatible with the masonry of the naïskos, closely related to the upper courses of the North Akropolis Wall and the anta wall of Old Propylon Stage 3. Absolute limits for dating Stage III are given finally by the Peiraeus limestone block at the southwest corner of the naïskos (F 2) and the substructures of the Propylaia, establishing respectively a *terminus post* and *terminus ante quem* of 465–435.[79]

It remains to discuss the terracotta figurines from the poros repository, the foundation deposit for Stage III. The figurines belong to an Attic series believed to have died out toward the close of the Archaic period, more than a decade before the *terminus* for Stage III. Further research or new excavation may conceivably establish that this figurine type extends further into the 5th century than is commonly believed.[80] The Nike Sanctuary deposit aside, however, finds have been nearly all from Archaic contexts. It thus appears more probable that the Nike terracottas are survivals, finds from an Archaic stratum that was disturbed in the Stage III rebuilding. The foundation deposit for the Artemision on Delos offers a close analogy. While the deposit itself is Hellenistic, its contents are overwhelmingly from the Late Bronze Age, thought to have been unearthed from a complex of Mycenaean ruins directly beneath the temple.[81]

Should the terracottas indeed be survivals, their most likely source is the terracotta-laden stratum that underlay the Stage III altar.[82] It remains impossible to determine at what stage or stages of construction such finds may have come to light. Stratification for Stages I to III was extensively disturbed by the amphiprostyle-temple foundations, and the excavation record is limited for the strata that survived. We may single out, however, the one most likely eventuality: that the stratum with terracottas reached west as far as the corner footing

[79] There have been various dates attached to these remains in the past. Welter (1939, cols. 11–12) assigned the euthynteria of the naïskos to the late 6th century and considered its walls a post-Persian rebuilding, arguing from the different clamps used in the two. He viewed the gamma-T of the euthynteria as a variant of the Z-clamp, considered at that time an early clamp form. It is now clear, however, that Z-clamps continued well into the 5th century, and there are numerous projects that used Z and double-T clamps together, including the Classical sheathing of the bastion (Balanos 1956, p. 789). On the history of the Z-clamp, see more recently Dinsmoor, Jr. 1980, pp. 27–28.

As observed in note 19 above, p. 50, a rare form of claw chisel was used to carve the interior of the anathyrosis on several euthynteria and wall blocks of the naïskos. Tool marks from one distinctive claw with a wider second tooth are evident on euthynteria E 1 and anta A 1. The euthynteria shows no sign of having been reset: its tooling is consistent and of a piece, and its blocks have but one set of clamp cuttings. The thesis of separate phases for the euthynteria and walls of this structure is thus firmly ruled out.

Other authors have proposed an Archaic or post-Persian date for the naïskos without specific arguments: Dinsmoor 1950, p. 151 (after 479 B.C.); I. T. Hill, *Ancient City of Athens*, London 1953, p. 145 ("built, or perhaps rebuilt, shortly after the Persian Wars"); C. Tiberi, *Mnesicle*, Rome 1964, pp. 62–63 (after the Battle of Marathon, 490 B.C.); Bergquist 1967, p. 26 (mid-6th century); Boersma 1970, p. 178, no. 46 (late Archaic restored after 479, or first built after 479); Travlos 1971, p. 148 (built after the Battle of Marathon, restored after 479); Gruben 1976, p. 190 (after the Persian Wars).

A mid-5th-century date for the naïskos is anticipated by Bundgård 1974b, pp. 43–49, and 1976, p. 44.

[80] As suggested by Bundgård 1974b, p. 47: "mais il a été fabriqué . . . jusqu'au milieu du Ve siècle." Also Bundgård 1976, p. 45.

[81] R. Vallois, *L'architecture hellénique et hellénistique à Délos* I, Paris 1944, p. 14; Gallet de Santerre and Tréheux 1947–1948, pp. 251–252.

[82] See p. 31 above.

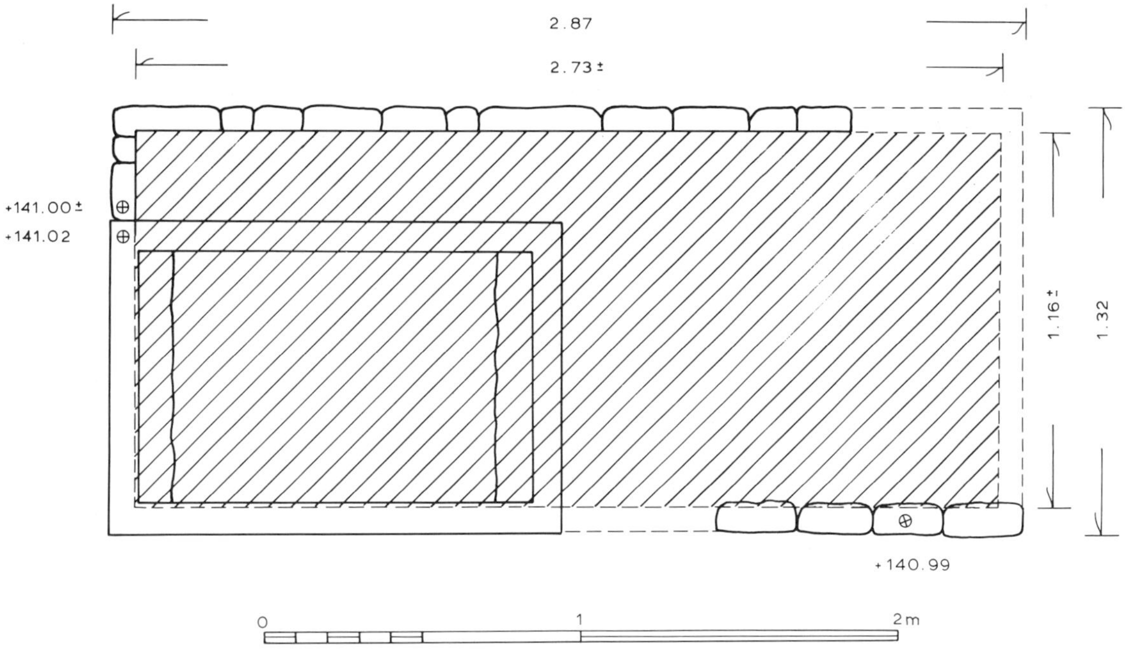

FIG. 14. Mud-brick extension of the rectangular altar

trenches for the now missing eastern end of the naïskos. The restored length of the naïskos, 3.65 m., places its eastern end 2.2 m. from the Stage III altar.

Conceivably, the decision to prepare a foundation deposit grew directly from the discovery of the terracottas. Confronted with these primitive, unfamiliar images, the workmen, we may imagine, were quick to enforce their reburial. An equally religious respect may have motivated the irregular beddings used elsewhere for Stage III. Prompted by an exegete or perhaps simply on their own, the workmen kept further trenching to a bare minimum.

STAGE IIIA

At some point within the life of Stage III the rectangular altar was enlarged in mud brick, roughly doubling its length and extending its width by half (Fig. 14). Part of the rubble socle and mud-brick face from this enlargement was uncovered by Welter along the east side of the altar, while a further stretch of socle was revealed by Balanos at the west.[83] The remains were removed in the work of restoration.

83 Welter 1923, pls. IV:3, V:4, 8, pp. 193–194 tentatively identifying the finds as a windscreen. Welter (1939, col. 11) furnishes the correct interpretation. Balanos makes no mention of these remains in his report, but they are sketched in pencil on a plan in the archives. The following labels and notations accompany the sketch. Referring to the socle: «ΠΕΤΡΕΣ» and «Β(αθμὸς) 1(.)22 ἀπὸ εὐθυντηρία». Alongside the socle: «εὑρέθη πμ 6:00 [word illegible] 4 Δεκεμβρίου [1936] θραυσμένος». To the inside of the socle: «ΧΩΜΑ». Compare the

As reconstructed from Welter's drawings, the socle for the extension was *ca.* 0.25 m. high and stood even with the base slab of the altar. It extended east from the northeast corner of the base slab for 0.35 m. and turned south for a preserved length of 1.85 m. A further stretch of socle on the west, 0.97 m. in length, preserved the southwest corner of the extension. These remains, encompassing opposite corners of the rebuilding, establish the length and width of the Stage IIIa altar as 2.88 × 1.13 m.

As recorded by Welter, the mud-brick face of the altar was set back *ca.* 0.07 m. from the socle and stood to a preserved height of 0.50 m. The core was of packed earth.[84]

---

the following altar enlargements: Pergamon, Demeter Sanctuary, Altar D, W. Dörpfeld, "Die Arbeiten zu Pergamon 1910–1911, I: Die Bauwerke," *AthMitt* 37, 1912 (pp. 233–276), p. 248, pl. 16. Kommos, Greek Sanctuary, Altar C, J. Shaw, "Excavations at Kommos (Crete) during 1977," *Hesperia* 47, 1978 (pp. 111–170), pp. 142–145, Altar H; *idem*, "Excavations at Kommos (Crete) during 1978," *Hesperia* 48, 1979 (pp. 145–173), pp. 162–164; *idem*, "Excavations at Kommos (Crete) during 1980," *Hesperia* 50, 1981 (pp. 211–251), pp. 225–226. Athens, Altar of the Twelve Gods, Thucydides 6.54.7.

84 I would thus understand the label ΧΩΜΑ on the archival plan cited in note 83 above, p. 67.

VII
THE SANCTUARY OF THE LATE 5TH CENTURY: STAGE IV

Stage IV saw the Nike Sanctuary enlarged and reworked from the ground up, reformed into one of the most splendid sanctuaries of the Akropolis. The lines of the bastion were redrawn in harmony with the Mnesiklean Propylaia, with the new level of the sanctuary brought close to that of the Southwest Wing, over a meter above the euthynteria of the Stage III naïskos (Frontispiece, Plan A). The naïskos gave way to a small Ionic temple of marble, richly adorned with sculpture. The mud-brick altar, Stage IIIa, was succeeded by a large, elaborately profiled marble altar. And last, the bastion was crowned on its three exposed sides by a finely sculptured parapet, a frieze of Nikai as votaries of Athena (Pls. 21, 22).

A series of exacting publications on the Classical bastion has left its stages far better known than earlier stages of the cult.[1] The description of Stage IV that follows draws foremost on this scholarship, with the addition of evidence from Balanos' drawings where appropriate. Most important, the drawings provide the first detailed record of the amphiprostyle-temple foundations (Pls. 7, 10–12, 14–17).

ASHLAR SHEATHING OF THE BASTION

The Stage IV bastion sheaths and overbuilds its Bronze Age predecessor, rendering the podium for the sanctuary larger, higher, and more regular in its lines (Fig. 15, Pls. 5, 7–9, 11, 14–17, Plan A).[2] The walls are formed of massive Peiraeus limestone ashlars backed by poros blocks.

The sheathing runs roughly parallel to the Mycenaean bastion on the south. It turns a right angle at the west, evening the acute southwest corner of its predecessor, and returns on the north in line with the Southwest Wing of the Propylaia. The south flank is built entirely of stretchers, the new face passing roughly a block width in front of the old face. The west, its line pulled forward with the widening of the southwest corner, has considerably greater depth, up to 3.5 m. at its northern end. Toward the base of the bastion on the west is a bipartite niche with a central pier, an ashlar copy of the Mycenaean niche directly behind (Frontispiece).[3]

The sheathing presses closest to the Bronze Age bastion on the north. The ashlar face clears the tip of one Cyclopean boulder at the northwest corner of the bastion by as little

[1] Ross, Schaubert, and Hansen 1839; Bohn 1882, pp. 29–31; Orlandos 1915, pp. 27–44; *idem* 1947–1948, pp. 1–38.

[2] Bohn 1882, pp. 29–31; Balanos 1956, pp. 789–795. Detailed photographs of the bastion sheathing before restoration, Picard n.d., pls. 32, 33.

[3] Bohn 1882, p. 30; Balanos 1956, pp. 789–793. Cf. Fig. 16, Pl. 8, and Pl. 13:a for the relation of the Mycenaean and Classical niches. The former was found sealed by a Stage IV rubble packing, and there were propitiatory remains at an adjacent cult site.

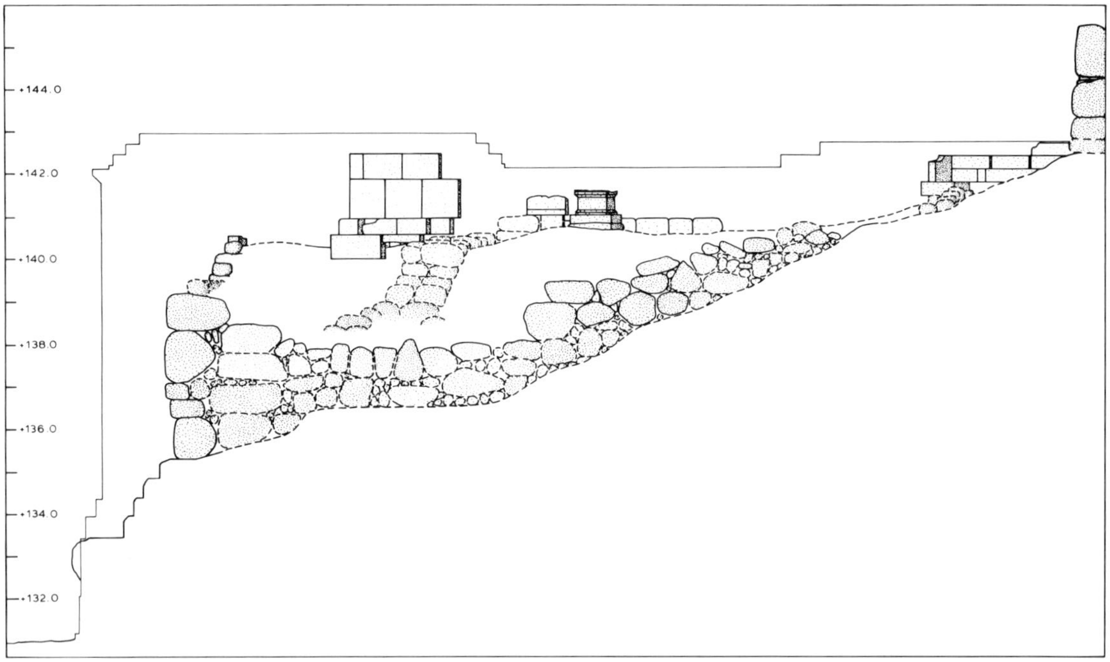

FIG. 15. The early Nike Sanctuary and bastion in elevation from the south

as 0.25 m. The ashlar courses at levels +138.09 and +137.65, courses 9 and 10 counted from the bastion crown, are obliquely jointed to fit around the boulder, while the salient tip of the boulder appears to have been capped by a thin polygonal slab, now missing (Fig. 16, Frontispiece, Pls. 14, 18).[4] There appear to have been other salient boulders in the lower stonework of the bastion on the north, for the lowest courses of the sheathing are set forward of and slightly oblique to the upper wall face.

The sheathing is crowned by a low molded course of Pentelic marble, a fascia with a deep cyma reversa below and thin crowning ovolo above (Pls. 13:a, 18).[5] At +142.13, this finishing course is nearly level with the middle step of the krepidoma of the Propylaia (+142.115).[6]

APPROACHES TO THE SANCTUARY

There were two approaches to the sanctuary, through the Southwest Wing of the Propylaia or up a stair built into the bastion on the north (Fig. 17). The former was the primary entrance: the Southwest Wing opens to the sanctuary in a broad, unsecured double portal suitable both to processions and to the easy conduct of sacrificial victims. The stair offered a narrower

[4] The polygonal block, if indeed set in, was never clamped in place. We may note, however, that the sides of the polygonal opening are prepared with anathyrosis. I have derived the levels of the bastion courses from Balanos' drawing, Plate 11.

[5] Ross, Schaubert, and Hansen 1839, pls. III, V; Shoe 1936, pl. XXXVI:2; Picard n.d., pl. 35:2.

[6] For the relative levels of the Nike Sanctuary and Propylaia, see Wrede 1932, p. 75, fig. 1.

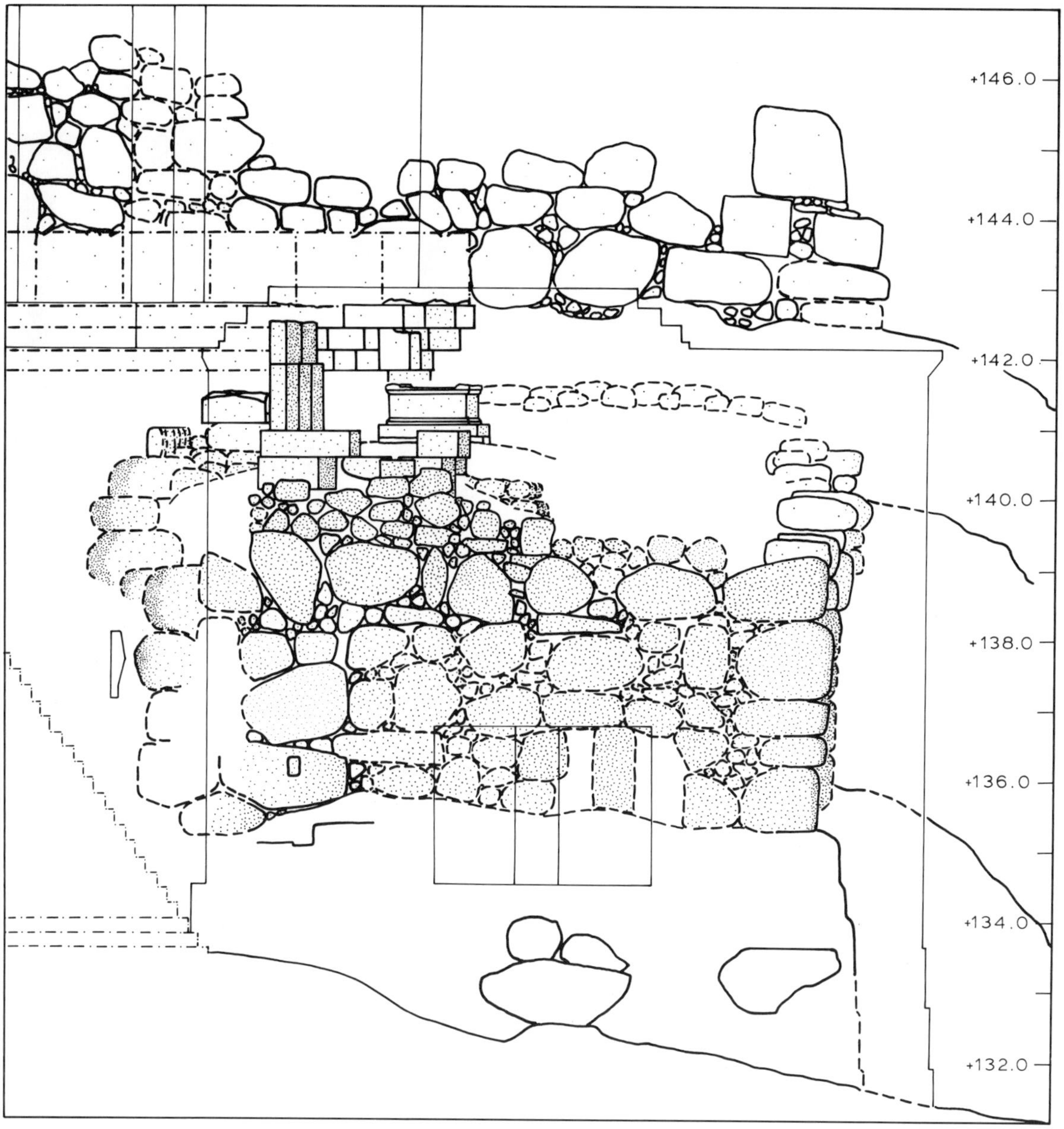

FIG. 16. The early Nike Sanctuary and bastion in elevation from the west

and steeper, though more direct ascent from the western Akropolis approach. Its lower flight, now largely destroyed, was built against the podium for the Southwest Wing (Pl. 18). A short flight of eight steps, five now preserved, rounded the gatepost at the western end of the podium, Pier W, to complete the ascent.[7]

[7] *Ibid.*, pl. 34:2. On the form of the stair, see Bohn 1880b, pp. 85–91; *idem* 1882, p. 30; Wrede 1932, pp. 88–90, figs. 1, 2, 4, Beil. XVI.

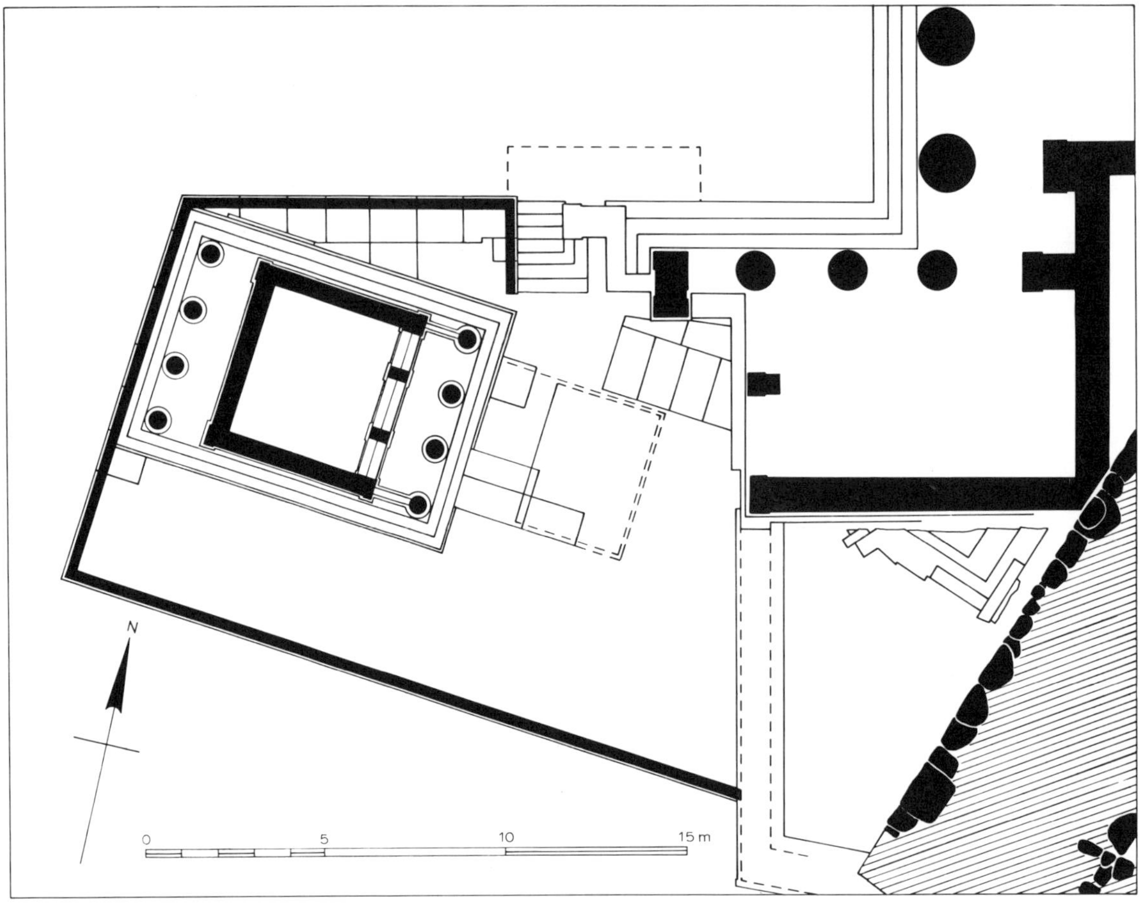

FIG. 17. The late 5th-century (Stage IV) Nike Sanctuary and southwest wing in plan

TEMPLE OF ATHENA NIKE

The well-known Temple of Athena Nike is of Pentelic marble, Ionic, tetrastyle amphiprostyle in plan, measuring 8.17 × 5.40 m. on the stylobate (Fig. 17; Pls. 18, 19:b).[8]

Its foundations, replaced by reinforced concrete in the 1930's, are carefully recorded in Balanos' drawings.[9] Save for a ring of Peiraeus limestone blocks in the first course (Pl. 14), the foundations were of poros throughout, laid four courses deep on the north (Pl. 17), four to five courses deep on the east (Pls. 7, 17), and five deep on the south (Pls. 7, 10, 12). These courses cut through extensive earlier remains. Broad stretches of the irregular trapezoidal

[8] For the Nike Temple: Ross, Schaubert, and Hansen 1839, pp. 10–11, pls. I, II, V–X; Orlandos 1915, pp. 27–44, pls. V, VI; Balanos 1956, pp. 776–807; Orlandos 1947–1948, pp. 1–38, pls. I, II. Scholarly overviews with bibliography: Travlos 1971, pp. 148–149; Boersma 1970, no. 47, p. 179. For detailed photographs, see Picard n.d., pls. 32–41 (taken before the 1930's rebuilding). Stylobate dimensions are from Dinsmoor 1950, p. 340.

[9] Balanos 1956, pp. 783–784; Welter 1939, cols. 13–14.

bastion crown (Stage III) were cleared along the northern and western limits of the sanctuary; the east face of the Mycenaean crosswall was partially dismantled; and the eastern end of the naïskos was razed, and the remainder of its walls cut down. The temple foundations bond with the bastion sheathing on the north and west, making clear that bastion and temple are of one plan.[10] The unity of the two projects is clear as well from the fact that on the west the bastion crown and the euthynteria of the temple, directly above, are fashioned from one block of stone.[11]

The plan of the Nike Temple preserves the essentials of Greek temple design in reduced and simplified form. Between its tetrastyle amphiprostyle porches is a small cella, clear width 4.15 m., clear depth 3.78 m.[12] Two piers *in antis* stand in place of a doorwall. There is no pronaos or opisthodomos.

The distinctive character of the Nike Temple is as evident in elevation as in plan, above all in the unusual proportions and rich ornament of the temple. Its column bases are of a type only soon before introduced into Attic building, profiled with a reeded torus over a scotia over a plain torus. They are unusual within this new Attic tradition, however, for the diminished height of the lower torus: it measures roughly a fifth the height of the full base, against the more usual third (Pl. 19:b).[13] The anta and pier bases and the exterior of the toichobate have this same profile, reeded torus over scotia over low plain torus.[14] The columns of the temple are relatively stocky, with a ratio of height to lower diameter of 7.82, among the heaviest proportions known from the Ionic order.[15] The capitals, like the bases, vary a recently coined Attic type.[16] Characteristic are the paired fillets along the bolsters, bulbous volute eyes, strongly emergent echinus with carved egg-and-dart, and an ovolo profile at the abacus (Pls. 19:a, 20:b).

The anta capital of the temple is formed of three dominant profiles, cavetto over cyma reversa over ovolo, the latter two moldings each underscored by an astragal.[17] The sequence is echoed on the piers; and the two upper elements, cavetto and cyma reversa, are carried fully around the cella as an epikranitis.[18] The epistyle too is richly ornamented, its exterior face divided into three fasciae and crowned by a low cavetto over an ovolo and astragal.[19] The stepped epistyle, traditional in Ionia, was then new to Attica, employed to that point only

[10] So Welter 1939, col. 13.

[11] Köster 1906, p. 141; Balanos 1956, p. 783; Welter 1923, p. 198; Picard n.d., pl. 35:2.

[12] For the dimensions of the cella, Orlandos 1915, p. 37.

[13] Picard n.d., pl. 35:1, 3. Profiles: Ross, Schaubert, and Hansen 1839, pl. VII; Shoe 1936, pp. 179–180, pl. LXXV:13.

[14] Picard n.d., pl. 35:1, 3. Profiles: Ross, Schaubert, and Hansen 1839, pl. X:2 (anta base), 4 (pier base); Shoe 1936, pl. LXVI:2 (anta and pier).

[15] Dinsmoor 1950, p. 186. The ratio of column height to lower diameter for the Ilissos Temple, 8.25; Propylaia, 9.89; Erechtheion north portico, 9.35; east portico, 9.52; west front, 9.05.

[16] Ross, Schaubert, and Hansen 1839, pls. VII–IX; Picard n.d., pls. 38:2, 39:2. For the definition and history of the type, Puchstein 1887, pp. 14–18; Martin 1944–1945, pp. 360–374; Shear 1963, pp. 380–382; Miles 1980, pp. 318–320.

[17] Ross, Schaubert, and Hansen 1839, pl. X; Shoe 1936, pl. XVI:1.

[18] Ross, Schaubert, and Hansen 1839, pl. X; Shoe 1936, pl. XXXIX:9.

[19] Ross, Schaubert, and Hansen 1839, pls. IX, X; Shoe 1936, pl. XII:4; Picard n.d., pls. 37:1, 2, 38:2.

in the interior of Athenian buildings.[20] The Nike Temple is the first to apply it to the exterior. Also unprecedented is the use of a cavetto to crown the ovolo on the epistyle.[21] A cavetto is used again to crown the broad ovolo of the sima.[22] By far, most of the moldings on the Nike Temple were left uncarved, the notable exceptions being the reeded upper torus of the base moldings and the echinus of the capitals. Traces of paint were noted by Ross on the epistyle, anta capitals, and coffers, and Orlandos records a painted band of lotus-and-palmette along the ovolo of the sima.[23]

As is characteristic of 5th-century architecture at Athens, the design of the Nike Temple is enlivened by a wealth of architectural refinements. The axis of the inner columns on the tetrastyle façades tips back 0.022 m. toward the cella; the flank walls taper and lean in, with a batter on the exterior of 0.022 m.; and the corner columns mirror the inclination of both the front and side, their axes tipping in on a diagonal, 0.031 m.[24] The antae of the Nike Temple, each aligned with a corner column, are vertical on their principle face, rather than inclined to the façade as usual.[25] Of note finally are the steps of the krepidoma. The treads tip forward slightly (*ca.* 0.003–0.004 m.), and the risers batter back.[26] The krepidoma has no horizontal curvature.

The building techniques employed in the Nike Temple are largely traditional, with a few notable exceptions. T-dowels, a relatively rare type, are used to secure the corners of the krepidoma and the successive courses of the antae. The eastern antae are secured in addition by bronze empolia, 0.045 m. square.[27] The latter fastening is ordinarily confined to column drums and is traditionally of wood.[28] Equally unusual are the wooden empolion-shaped dowels, 0.07 m. on a side, used to secure the base of the columns to the stylobate.[29]

The richly detailed, finely worked architecture of the Nike Temple has a fitting complement in its sculpture. The friezes, 0.45 m. high, depict scenes of battle on the north, south, and west and a divine gathering on the east (Pl. 20).[30] The pediments, interior height 0.555 m., bore small-scale statuary doweled to the geison with thin rods.[31] Only a few

[20] Propylaia: Bohn 1882, pl. XII. Ilissos Temple: Stuart and Revett, I, chap. 2, pl. VIII. Cf. the mid-5th-century Temple of Athena at Sounion whose plain epistyle is crowned by a fillet (A. K. Orlandos, «Σχετικὴ ἔκθεσις», ΑρχΕφ 1917 [pp. 181–186], p. 185, fig. θ, pl. 6).

[21] Ross, Schaubert, and Hansen 1839, pl. IX. An ovolo alone is the canonical epistyle crown in early Ionic. See Shoe 1936, pp. 170–171.

[22] Stevens 1908, p. 405, fig. 10; Shoe 1936, pl. XIX:7.

[23] Ross, Schaubert, and Hansen 1839, p. 11; Orlandos 1947–1948, pp. 32–33, pl. II. For the anta capitals, see now H. Büsing, "Zur Bemalung des Nike-Tempels," *AA* (*JdI* 105) 1990, pp. 71–76.

[24] Orlandos 1947–1948, pp. 16–17, 24–25.

[25] *Ibid.*, p. 18.

[26] *Ibid.*, pp. 10–11.

[27] Balanos 1956, p. 782, fig. 9; Orlandos 1947–1948, pp. 19–20, figs. 13–15.

[28] Martin 1965, pp. 291–294; Orlandos 1966–1968, II, pp. 113–115. For antae secured with bronze empolia, compare the Treasury of Cyrene at Delphi, J. Bousquet, *Topographie et architecture: Le Trésor de Cyrène* (*Fouilles de Delphes* II, vi), Paris 1952, pp. 41–42, pl. 16.

[29] Orlandos 1947–1948, p. 22, fig. 5.

[30] Blümel 1923; *idem* 1950–1951, pp. 135–165; Harrison 1970, pp. 317–323; *idem* 1972a, pp. 195–197; *idem* 1972b, pp. 353–378; Pemberton 1972, pp. 303–310; T. Hölscher, *Griechische Historienbilder des 5. und 4. Jahrhunderts v. Chr.*, Würzburg 1973, pp. 91–98; Ridgway 1981, pp. 89–93; Felten 1984, pp. 118–131.

[31] Despinis 1974, pp. 8–24.

fragments survive but sufficient to identify a Gigantomachy in the east pediment, a second battle, apparently an Amazonomachy, in the west. Preserved sima blocks from the peak and corners of the gable establish that there were bronze akroteria.[32]

The cella was secured by a set of three grilles, one across the central portal, pier to pier, and one to each side, from the piers to the antae. Two further grilles were mounted one on each side of the eastern portico, from the antae to the corner columns. The marble sills for these grilles were elaborately molded. The two that flank the portico have reeded torus over scotia over low plain torus, corresponding to the base moldings on the columns and antae. The three across the cella reproduce only the lower elements of the base moldings, scotia over low torus; the reeded torus is replaced by a low threshold of the same height.[33]

BASE FOR THE CULT STATUE

There remains little evidence for the setting of the cult statue in Stage IV. The four paving slabs of the cella were torn up in the construction of the Turkish crypt, set directly below, and no fragments of the base itself have been identified. Although I have made no systematic search for remains, I can report at least one promising fragment in the Akropolis Museum, the exterior corner of a relief with a winged, wind-blown figure depicted just at the angle. In a manner proper to sculptured bases, the figure projects beyond the corner, facing front but partly overlapping the side.[34]

STAGE IV ALTAR, SANCTUARY PAVING, AND BASTION FILL

Three blocks from the prothysis of the Stage IV altar lie against the lowest step of the krepidoma of the temple at the east. Their level is +142.345.[35] Little survives of the altar itself. As judged from its poros foundations, recorded by Bohn and Kawerau, and from the traces of its bedding on the preserved prothysis, it stood at a clear distance of 1.70 m. from the temple and measured *ca.* 3.9 m. across.[36]

[32] Boulter 1969, pp. 133–140. The cuttings on the akroterion bases are inappropriate for marble, thus excluding such statuary as once attributed by Linfert 1968, pp. 427–434.

[33] See further Ross, Schaubert, and Hansen 1839, p. 11; Orlandos 1915, pp. 29–30; *idem* 1947–1948, pp. 11–16; Büsing 1970, fig. 79.

[34] Athens, AcrM 6470. Found in 1960 between the Parthenon and Erechtheion. Preserved height 0.30 m. Figure height, estimated 0.50 m. Late 5th century. Brouskari 1974, p. 118; Goulaki 1981, pp. 55–58. Compare the corner figures on the base for the Nemesis at Rhamnous, frieze height 0.50 m.: Despinis 1971, pp. 66–71; V. Kallipolitis, «Ἡ βάση τοῦ ἀγάλματος τῆς Ῥαμνουσίας Νέμεσις», ΑρχΕφ 1978 (pp. 1–87), pls. 2:α, β, 26, 27 (NatM 212); pl. 18:α (NatM 4958); Petrakos 1986, pls. 113:4, 114:1, with new joins.

[35] Orlandos 1947–1948, p. 6, fig. 4.

[36] Early excavations on the bastion uncovered two slabs of the prothysis *in situ*, as reported by Julius 1876, pp. 217–218, pl. XII; see also Bötticher 1880. Fragments from several other slabs were freed from Turkish walls by Bohn and restored to place east of the temple (Bohn 1880a, p. 262; *idem* 1882, pp. 30–31, pl. XX; Kavvadias and Kawerau 1906, col. 137, pl. H′; Bundgård 1974a, p. 203). Balanos enters blocks from the altar foundations on the longitudinal cross-section (Pl. 11). Compare also the excavation photograph Welter

There remain paving slabs *in situ* at the northeast corner of the sanctuary. A further section of paving at the northwest corner was removed and reset by Balanos in the 1930's (Fig. 17). The paving slabs are Pentelic marble set on poros rails. Welter records that the rails and paving at the northeast rested on a fill formed entirely of Pentelic marble working chips, while according to Bohn there were seemingly identical fills in the eastern sanctuary.[37]

NIKE PARAPET

The exposed sides of the bastion, north, west, and south, and the west side of the northern stair were protected by a continuous marble parapet 1.05 m. in height, sculptured on the exterior (Pls. 21, 22). This monument, the well-known Nike Parapet, survives in several large slabs and a wealth of smaller fragments, nearly all in the Akropolis Museum.[38] The parapet depicts a similar scene on each of its three long sides, Athena Nike seated on a rock throne attended by winged Victories, some leading bulls in sacrifice to the goddess, others decking trophies variously with hoplite panoplies, Persian spoils, and tokens of naval victory.[39]

DATING OF THE SANCTUARY

Four forms of evidence bear on the chronology for Stage IV: the general history of the Attic building program for the period of the Peloponnesian Wars; the chronology of the Nike Sanctuary relative to the Propylaia as indicated by the plan and form of the Southwest Wing; the style and technique of the Nike Temple; and the style of the sculpture of the sanctuary, foremost the temple friezes and the Nike Parapet.

Attic Building during the Peloponnesian War

No less than two exigencies of the Peloponnesian War saw Athens suspend her sacred building program.[40] Inscriptions attest that work on the Erechtheion lapsed for several years, to be resumed abruptly in 409/408, presumably in the euphoria of Alkibiades' victories at Kyzikos and in the Hellespont.[41] It appears that work originally came to a halt in 413,

1939, col. 9, fig. 5. For the position and dimensions of the altar, Orlandos 1947–1948, p. 6, fig. 4; Travlos 1971, figs. 205, 206.

37 For a record of preserved paving slabs, Bohn 1882, pl. XX; Bundgård 1974a, pl. 203; Balanos 1956, pl. I. For the rails, Bohn 1880a, p. 264; Köster 1906, p. 141, note 35, fig. 4; Welter 1923, pl. V:7. Bastion fill: Welter 1923, p. 194, pl. V:7 (transverse cross-section); Bohn 1880a, p. 264.

38 Carpenter 1929; Brouskari 1974, pp. 156–163; Ridgway 1981, pp. 96–98, 103, with additional bibliography. Dr. Brouskari is currently working on a reconstruction of the parapet in cooperation with the Basel Antikenmuseum. The last comprehensive reconstruction was undertaken by Dinsmoor (1930, pp. 281–295). A few of the preserved sculptures and several figures now lost are reflected in a series of neo-Attic reliefs. See W. Fuchs, *Die Vorbilder der neuattischen Reliefs* (*JdI* Erganzungs-Hefte 20), Berlin 1959, pp. 6–20.

39 For the iconography of the parapet, see Stewart 1986, pp. 53–73; Simon 1988, pp. 69–73.

40 On the history of Attic building in this period, see Boersma 1970, pp. 82–96.

41 *IG* I^3 474–479; Paton 1927, pp. 452–454.

in the wake of the Spartan occupation of Dekeleia and the Sicilian disaster.[42] The hurried fortification of Sounion, Thorikos, and perhaps also Rhamnous in 412, undertaken to protect grain shipments from Euboia, attests Athens' priorities at this turn in the war.[43]

There is compelling, if less direct, evidence that work came to a halt at least once before, in the early years of the war. The indications are in part *ex silentio*, a conspicuous gap in the epigraphical and literary record on Athenian building from the final year of accounts for the Parthenon and Propylaia, 433/432, until 424, when plans were developed to shorten the city's defenses with a *diateichisma*.[44] Evidence for sacred, as opposed to military, construction resumes a few years later, beginning with a decree of 422/421 for construction of a bridge across one of the Rheitoi, two shallow salt-water ponds on the Sacred Way to Eleusis.[45]

That Attic building was indeed suspended at the outbreak of the Peloponnesian War is confirmed by the buildings themselves. Work on the Propylaia ended in 433/432, perhaps a few months from completion: there remain lifting bosses and several millimeters of working surface on the outside face of the walls of the structure and protective surfaces, as well, on the krepidoma and paving slabs.[46] The Temple of Nemesis at Rhamnous remains in a similar state, with columns left unfluted and protective surfaces on the krepidoma and walls, suggesting that the approaching war brought work to an abrupt halt.[47] Scholarship on the

[42] So Paton 1927, p. 453; Dinsmoor 1950, p. 188; Gruben 1976, p. 193, among others. It would appear that the complex of stoas at the Sanctuary of Artemis at Brauron was left unfinished at this time as well. See C. Bouras, Ἡ ἀναστήλωσις τῆς στοᾶς τῆς Βραυρῶνος, Athens 1967, pp. 149–159.

[43] Sounion: Thucydides 8.4; Mussche 1964, pp. 423–432. Thorikos: Xenophon, *Hell.* 1.2.1; Mussche 1961, pp. 176–205. Rhamnous: stretches of the wall are tentatively dated late 5th century by Winter 1971, p. 161, note 41; cf. Pouilloux 1954, pp. 67–92.

[44] Parthenon accounts, *IG* I^3 436–451 (447/446–433/432); Propylaia accounts, *IG* I^3 462–466 (437/436–433/432). The *diateichisma* may not have been built or even begun at this time. Aristophanes alludes to major plans for the project in *Equites* 817–818, performed in 424. No 5th-century remains, however, have come to light. See H. A. Thompson and R. Scranton, "Stoas and City Walls on the Pnyx," *Hesperia* 12, 1943, pp. 334–336.

[45] *IG* I^3 79. Further inscriptions follow in close succession: *IG* I^3 78 (*ca.* 422), construction of storehouses at the sanctuary of Demeter at Eleusis; *IG* II^2 1649–1650, introduction of the cult of Asklepios in 420; *IG* I^3 84 (418/417), construction of a temenos wall for the Neleion and for the interior precincts of Kodros, Neleus, and Basile. Cf. also *IG* I^3 472 (421/420–416/415), accounts for the cult statues of the Hephaisteion.

Courby (*Délos* XII, i, pp. 220–225) has proposed a date of 425–417 for the Temple of the Athenians on Delos, drawing partly on epigraphical, partly on literary sources. A 4th-century inventory with a seemingly comprehensive list of wreaths offered at earlier Delia allows Courby to locate the opening of the temple treasury in 417. If less than conclusive, Courby's argument is persuasive, in all, and is widely accepted. There is less agreement as to when work on the temple began. The purification of Delos in the winter of 426/425 and the foundation of the Delia the following spring appear less to provide a starting date than a *terminus post quem*. So Dinsmoor 1950, p. 184; Shear 1963, p. 407.

[46] Bohn 1882, pp. 5, 32–33; Kalpaxis 1986, pp. 127–133. Kalpaxis doubts that the war was the immediate reason that work was suspended. I would stress, however, that the expectation, not the actual outbreak of war, caused the halt. There is evidence that already in 434, the apparent date of the Kallias Decrees, the Athenians were making major decisions in the expectation that hostilities were imminent.

[47] So Dinsmoor 1950, p. 182; *idem*, "Rhamnountine Fantasies," *Hesperia* 30, 1961 (pp. 179–204), p. 179; A. Trevor Hodge and R. A. Tomlinson, "The Temple of Nemesis at Rhamnous," AJA 73, 1969 (pp. 185–192), p. 185; Knell 1979, p. 67, among others. Miles (1989, pp. 226–235) dates the Nemesis Temple *ca.* 430–420 and attributes the abandonment of work not to the approach of war but to insufficient funds. Miles convincingly

cult statue of Nemesis lends strong support to this view. Roman copies of the statue place the original at around the start of the war in the late 430's. Its sculptured base, however, is worked in a more developed, post-Pheidian style. The statue appears either to have been delayed half-finished or to have waited years for installation.[48]

Of note, finally, are signs of a delay in the building program of the Hephaisteion: the project was halted apparently at ceiling level.[49] As observed by Shoe, the hawk's beak moldings on the temple fall into two distinct groups of seemingly disparate date. The earlier moldings adorn the epikranitis of the peristyle, the lower epikranitis of the pronaos, and the horizontal geison. The more developed set come directly above, on the upper epikranitis of the pronaos, the ceiling beams of the peristyle, and the raking geison.[50] One study of the ceiling coffers gives fresh evidence of a break: the coffers carry two sets of masons' marks, the second set seemingly inscribed after the war.[51] As at Rhamnous, the sculptures of the Hephaisteion support the idea of a break. The friezes of the temple appear to be of roughly the same stage as the pediments of the Parthenon, from around the mid-430's.[52] The pickaback group of two maidens, long considered an akroterion for the temple, and the cult statues date from the resumption of work in the late 420's.[53]

---

rebuts Dinsmoor's widely accepted thesis on the Hephaisteion architect. Dinsmoor had used the thesis to bracket tightly the date of the Nemesis temple to 436–432. Because Dinsmoor's arguments are mistaken, however, does not mean that his general dates are wrong. I feel that Miles glosses over the discrepancy in the styles of the cult statue and base and that she overestimates the chronological reliability of temple moldings. The architectural proportions and moldings on the Temple of Nemesis (see Miles 1989, pp. 160–164, 170, 208, 227) are as appropriate to the later 430's as to the mid-420's.

48 So Despinis 1971, pp. 55–61. Despinis places the base in the later 420's. The distinction of statue and base is even clearer in research by Evelyn B. Harrison, who locates the base in the last decade of the 5th century. For the base, see Petrakos 1986, pp. 89–107. The disputed provenance of the akroterion fragment Athens, NatM 2348, discourages its use in reconstructing the history of the temple. For the attribution of NatM 2348 to Rhamnous, see S. Karouzou, "Ein Akroter klassischer Zeit," *AthMitt* 77, 1962, pp. 178–190; Delivorrias 1974, pp. 188–189.

49 On this established appellation for the temple, *Agora* XIV, pp. 140–142. In view of research by Evelyn B. Harrison (1977, pp. 137–178, 265–287, 411–428), it is important to note that, the cult statues excepted, the evidence here adduced for a break in work is valid irrespective of the identification.

50 Shoe 1936, pp. 108, 128. Shoe's observations are employed in reconstructing the chronology of the building first by C. H. Morgan, "Sculptures of the Hephaisteion," *Hesperia* 32, 1963 (pp. 91–108), pp. 101, 107.

51 Wyatt and Edmonson 1984, pp. 135–167. Judged against inscriptions, the letter forms of the first set of mason's marks are Late Archaic, perhaps no later than 480, impossibly early for the Hephaisteion. The lettering was never intended to be seen, however, and may not be canonical; in the end the authors associate the marks with the preparation of the ceiling on the ground *ca.* 455–445. The ceiling appears to have been first installed after the break, with the addition of the second set of marks at that time.

52 For the dating, Childs 1985, pp. 236–239; earlier voiced by Delivorrias 1974, p. 49, among others. For a review of scholarship on the dating of the Hephaisteion friezes, see Jose Dörig (*La frise est de l'Héphaisteion*, Mainz am Rhein 1985, pp. 74–79), who, however, argues for a longer break in work, with the friezes *ca.* 445. Cf. Bockelberg (1979, pp. 23–50), who locates the friezes *ca.* 425. On the chronology of the Hephaisteion, see Dinsmoor 1941, pp. 150–160.

53 For the pickaback group, Athens, Agora Mus. S 429, H. A. Thompson, "The Pedimental Sculpture of the Hephaisteion," *Hesperia* 18, 1949, pp. 235–236, 241–243, pls. 53, 54; and more recently Harrison 1982, p. 49 (dated around 420). The Hephaisteion project may have continued longer than commonly thought. Harrison informs me that she would now date the pickaback group as late as the early 4th century. Although the heavy

It remains unclear how long the Attic building program lay idle. The Bridge Decree of 422/421 provides a *terminus ante quem*. The epigraphical record, however, remains spotty, and we may well imagine the actual start to have been several years before. Scholars have often considered Demosthenes' Ambraciot victories of 426/425 as the earliest time when Athens' mood and fortunes appear suited to a revival. A pair of golden Nikai, the first of the war, were dedicated in that year, and the victories in Ambracia were commemorated on the Akropolis with a major *ex voto*.[54] Such evidence, however, is more suggestive than definitive, and breaks of both longer and shorter duration have been often proposed.[55] The date when Attic building resumed remains uncertain.

The Chronology of Stage IV relative to the Propylaia

Several aspects in the design of the Southwest Wing of the Propylaia establish that, while begun in advance of Stage IV, it was planned and executed with the firm expectation that

---

wear on the back of the piece has commonly been interpreted as weathering, some scholarship has preferred to restore the work not to the roof but to the pediments of the temple, Delivorrias 1974, pp. 33–40; H. A. Thompson, *The Athenian Agora: Guide to the Excavation and Museum*, 3rd ed., Athens 1976, pp. 195–196. The accounts for the cult statues, *IG* I^3 472, date from 421–415. The Stoa of Zeus Eleutherios in the Agora is the one building from this period that can be dated stratigraphically. Pottery from its fill and from the remains of shops beneath it belongs as late as the early 420's (*Agora* XIV, p. 100). The stoa thus appears to belong in the first wave of building after the break. Among minor projects, best dated is the square *abaton* in the northwest corner of the Agora with context pottery suggesting construction at about the same time, "in the years after 430": T. L. Shear, Jr., "The Athenian Agora: Excavations of 1972," *Hesperia* 42, 1973 (pp. 359–407), p. 364.

54 For the resumption of building in or after 425, see Furtwängler 1893, pp. 209–210. Golden Nikai, *IG* I^3 468; a second, undated inscription, *IG* I^3 467, records the dedication of two further Nikai. Wesley E. Thompson suggests a date for this second pair around 430 ("The Golden Nikai and the Coinage of Athens," *NC* 10, 1970 [pp. 1–6], p. 2); Harold B. Mattingly argues rather for a date after *IG* I^3 468, toward the end of the Archidamian War ("Athens and Eleusis: Some New Ideas," in *Φόρος: Tribute to Benjamin D. Meritt*, D. W. Bradeen and M. F. McGregor, eds., Locust Valley, N.Y. 1974, p. 95). As established by *IG* II^2 403, a statue of Athena Nike was dedicated from spoils of 426–425.

55 Boersma (1970, p. 85) places the resumption of Attic building around 425/424, after Athens' victory at Pylos. A date earlier in the Archidamian War is often suggested on the basis of *IG* I^3 132, a fragment preserving the opening lines of a building decree for a temple. Following a proposal by A. B. West (*apud* Paton 1927, pp. 647–648), scholars have equated Σμίκυθο[ς], the presiding officer of the decree, with the fragmentary ––θος, the presiding officer for *IG* I^3 66, thus dating the two decrees to the same day of the prytany Akamantis in 427/426. So Dinsmoor 1939, pp. 124–125; also H. B. Mattingly, "Periclean Imperialism," in *Ancient Society and Institutions: Studies Presented to Victor Ehrenberg on his 75th Birthday*, E. Badian, ed., New York 1967 (pp. 193–223), pp. 203–204, who, however, reassigns the two to 425/424. On a date *ca.* 425/424 for *IG* I^3 66, already Gomme 1956, pp. 329–332. That the two decrees had the same epistates is more tempting than certain. The name Smikythos is repeatedly attested in Attica through the 5th and 4th centuries (Kirchner 1901–1903, nos. 12772–12778, 12781–12784, 12787–12790, 12792–12797), and other common Attic names (e.g., [Βόη]θος, [Παραμύ]θος would equally fit *IG* I^3 66. David Lewis, editor for the third edition of *IG* I, leaves I^3 132 undated.

Too little survives of I^3 132 to determine the project. It is associated with the Erechtheion by L. D. Caskey (in Paton 1927, pp. 279–280); Dinsmoor took it to mark the start of work on the Nike Temple (1939, pp. 124–125), a theory he later dropped (1950, pp. 185–186, note 4); and Mattingly assigns it to the Hephaisteion (*loc. cit.*).

Miles (1989, pp. 227–235) points to a relative increase in building projects in Attica around the mid-420's, but she questions whether there was any absolute break after 432.

the bastion would soon be raised to the level of the Propylaia.[56] The treatment of the western face of the Southwest Wing as a portal attests this unmistakably (Fig. 17). This entryway, 4.91 m. across, was far too broad and too high above Stage III to have been intended as the landing for a stair. The Southwest Wing was to give access, not to the Nike Sanctuary then in use, but to one in planning.

The materials and technique of the foundations and substructures of the Propylaia make clear that plans to raise the bastion were firm already from the very start of the Propylaia project. Those parts of the substructures of the Propylaia that the builders intended to leave visible are faced entirely in marble. Thus the north and west sides of the podium for the Pinakotheke, fully exposed, are of marble throughout, while the south face of that podium and the north face of the podium for the Southwest Wing, opposite, are faced in marble above and poros below, the two stones meeting along a descending line that corresponds in level to the now missing grand stair. By contrast, the south and west sides of the Southwest Wing rest on coarsely worked foundations, not on a podium proper, and are of poros throughout.[57] They were built on the expectation that they would eventually be covered.

It is noteworthy that while the architect of the Propylaia, Mnesikles, anticipated a rise in the level of the Nike Bastion, he failed to provide for a number of aspects of the Stage IV Nike Sanctuary as actually built. The ashlar sheathing on the north face of the bastion, its line fixed by the inner face of the Southwest Wing, barely clears the stonework of its Mycenaean predecessor. As noted earlier, a Cyclopean boulder projects to a point within 0.25 m. of the Classical face at courses 9 and 10, and the spreading base of the Mycenaean bastion forces the lowest few courses of sheathing forward of the wall face at odd angles. There appears to have been no thought given to sheathing the bastion when the lines of the Propylaia were set.[58]

The form of Pier W and of the substructures to its east is equally significant. Pier W was designed to serve Stage III of the sanctuary, not IV. Founded at +139.09, roughly the level of the central stairway to the Propylaia, inclined slightly to the west, and dressed to be seen on all three faces, it is unmistakably a gatepost. It seemingly marked the foot of a northern stair to the Stage III sanctuary, an entrance installed, we may suppose, when the proper eastern entrance to the sanctuary was blocked by the podium for the Southwest Wing. When Stage IV raised the level of the sanctuary to +142.13, *ca.* 1.10 m. above Stage III on the north, the northern stair was redesigned in an "L". It rounds Pier W at +140.43, somewhat over a meter above the pier's original threshold.[59]

56 On the priority of the Southwest Wing over Stage IV of the bastion, see Wrede 1932, pp. 74–91; Bundgård 1957, pp. 177–182; cf. Schleif 1933, pp. 177–184.

57 On the foundations for the Southwest Wing, see Köster 1906, p. 139, fig. 4; Wrede 1932, p. 86.

58 So Bundgård 1957, p. 181.

59 See Dinsmoor 1950, p. 205; Bundgård 1957, pp. 177–178, 180–181. Elevations for Pier W: Wrede 1932, Beil. 16. Bohn (1882, p. 15) notes that a short stretch of the Stage III bastion crown opposite Pier W is abraded, apparently from foot traffic, confirmation that the Stage IV stair did indeed have a predecessor. For Pier W, see further Bohn 1880b, p. 86; Köster 1906, p. 146; Wrede 1932, pp. 74–91, figs. 1–4. Like Pier W, the poros substructure from Pier W to the double anta was also planned to accord with the Stage III level of the bastion. The blocks on its inner (western and southern) faces are carefully dressed and jointed from the level of the Stage III sanctuary up. See Wrede 1932, pp. 76–77, Beil. 15; cf. Schleif 1933, pp. 177–178.

The Propylaia ill accords with Stage IV in a final respect, the design of the krepidoma for the west side of the Southwest Wing. The western krepidoma of the wing, worked in marble only at the stylobate, appears to anticipate a level for the Nike Sanctuary either even with the floor of the Southwest Wing or at most one step down. The steps, like the substructures of the Propylaia, were consistently worked in marble where intended to be seen.

At some point after the poros substructure for the Southwest Wing had been completed and before the steps and superstructure were begun, stages of construction that may conceivably have been separated by months or even a year or more, the decision was made to build the Nike Sanctuary not even with or a step down from the Propylaia but two steps down (0.625 m.). Mnesikles modified the plan of the Southwest Wing accordingly: the western stylobate was pulled 0.295 m. back from its original line, and the outer edge of the poros foundations thus revealed was dressed to form a second step of the krepidoma.[60] The revision required, in turn, a redesign of the entablature of the wing. The shift at the stylobate pulled the southwest anta and central pier of the façade 0.20 m. behind the corresponding third column of the north façade. The western epistyle was recentered on the third column by halving its width: it is formed of one block 0.50 m. in width, in contrast to the epistyle and backer on the north, width 1.01 m. The western entablature resumes full width at frieze level. The frieze and frieze backer, combined width 0.87 m., overhang the interior face of the epistyle 0.37 m.[61]

The characteristics and anomalies of the Propylaia here reviewed provide several points of reference on the chronology for Stage IV. The open west face of the Southwest Wing and the rough poros courses of the podium below make clear that a major rebuilding of the bastion was anticipated already from the first years of the Propylaia project. How concrete and detailed those early plans were is less certain. The hastily fashioned poros step on the Southwest Wing's west krepidoma and the attendant shift of the west façade, while not conclusive evidence of themselves, strongly suggest that plans for the bastion were still fluid when the Propylaia was well under way.[62] Finally, the Propylaia substructures provide a *terminus post quem* for the start of actual construction on Stage IV. The podium for the Southwest Wing, aligned on the north rather with the Mycenaean than the Stage IV bastion, and Pier W, keyed to the level of Stage III, were surely begun in advance of work on Stage IV. That Pier W was built to serve the old sanctuary when plans to raise the bastion were already firm further suggests that the start of work on IV was not felt imminent. The evidence, in all, points to a date for Stage IV at or after the completion of the substructures for the Propylaia;

[60] Bundgård 1957, pp. 174–175, 178; cf. Wrede 1932, p. 90, figs. 3, 4.

[61] On the reconstruction of the western epistyle, Bohn 1882, p. 27, pl. XVI. For its dependence on the displacement of the stylobate below, Bundgård 1957, pp. 73–75, 174–175, fig. 42. As observed by Bundgård (p. 175), the outward batter of the southwest anta, long a puzzle in scholarship on the Southwest Wing, likely also results from the shifted stylobate. The batter has the effect of pulling the western entablature 0.05 m. back towards the axis of column three. A more recent study by Dinsmoor agrees that the displacement of the stylobate and the makeshift entablature of the wing are linked, but he traces the cause to a modification in the plan of both western wings: Dinsmoor, Jr. 1982, pp. 28–30.

[62] Cf. Bundgård 1957, p. 175.

the second or third year of the Propylaia project, *ca.* 435, may serve as a conservative *terminus ante quem non.*

Temple of Athena Nike: Architectural Dating Criteria

There are strong parallels between the Nike Temple and several other Attic buildings of Periclean and post-Periclean date: most important are the Propylaia (437–432), the Erechtheion (*ca.* 420–413, 409–406),[63] and the Temple on the Ilissos, a small temple on the outskirts of the city measured and drawn in the 18th century by Stuart and Revett but now largely destroyed. The Ilissos Temple remains difficult to date, but judged from pottery contemporary with its foundations and a few surviving blocks of the figured frieze, it appears to belong *ca.* 435–430.[64]

[63] Paton 1927, pp. 452–456; Dinsmoor 1950, p. 188. A beginning date *ca.* 420 is consistent with more recent scholarship on the *Erechtheus* of Euripides. On the strength of several new fragments, scholars have reexamined the play's context and likely date. At the close of the work, Athena commands Erechtheus' widow, Praxithea, to construct a walled shrine for the slain hero: πόσει δὲ τῶι σῶι σηλὸν ἐν μέσηι πόλει / τεῦξαι κελέυω περιβόλοισι λαΐνοις (C. Austin, "De nouveaux fragments de l'*Erechtheé* d'Euripide," *Recherches de papyrologie* 4, 1967, fr. 65). The lines refer apparently to the Erechtheion, then in planning. Calder has suggested that the construction of the Erechtheion was actually decreed in the year of the play, performed in the opinion of most scholars in 423 or 422 (W. M. Calder III, "The Date of Euripides' *Erectheus*," *GRBS* 10, 1969, pp. 147–156; cf. C. W. Clairmont, "Euripides' *Erechtheus* and the Erechtheion," *GRBS* 12, 1971, pp. 485–495; M. Treu, "Der Euripideische *Erechtheus* als Zeugnis seiner Zeit," *Chiron* 1, 1971, pp. 115–131). To correlate the play and the building so exactly pushes the evidence too hard. Very likely the Athenians had formed general plans to rebuild the temple for the old image of Athena already under Perikles. The lines of the *Erechtheus* suggest that the project had become topical and was firmly anticipated, but they are at base a *terminus ante*, not *ad quem.* So M. Vickers ("Persepolis, Vitruvius and the Erechtheum Caryatids: The Iconography of Medism and Servitude," *RA* 1985, pp. 3–28), who, however, favors an implausibly late date for the beginning of construction.

[64] Miles 1980, pp. 309–325. Scholarship over the last several decades has proposed a range of dates for the sculptured frieze. *Ca.* 450: Studniczka 1916, pp. 197–230. *Ca.* 445–440: Childs 1985, pp. 207–251. *Ca.* 440: Lippold 1950, p. 159; A. Delivorrias, "Eine klassische Kora-Statue vom Metroon am Ilissos," *AntP* 9, 1969, p. 10. *Ca.* 430–420: Dohrn 1957, p. 23; Picon 1978, pp. 67–73; A. Krug, "Der Fries des Tempels am Ilissos," *AntP* 18, 1979, pp. 1–20. Judged overall, the Ilissos frieze appears older than the frieze of the Nike Temple. Figures in the latter tend to be more freely posed in relation to the frieze plane, and drapery folds are more supple and linear. Attention has recently been drawn to a few renderings on the Ilissos frieze best paralleled on monuments after 430, specifically the three-dimensional pose of the seated figure on slab C, the clinging garment of the suppliant on slab E, and the free swing of drapery across the upper torso of the running figure on slab D. Evaluated against the wealth of stylistic evidence for an earlier date, these few "forward looking" details inspire little confidence. They appear to reflect stylistic advances made already in the years approaching 432. For the arc of drapery over the chest of the running figure, compare Brommer 1963, pls. 86 (West C, daughter of Kekrops), 48:1, 49 (East M, Aphrodite); *idem* 1979, pls. 114 (West C), 141 (East M); clinging garments, *idem* 1963, pl. 111 (West N, Iris), *idem* 1979, pl. 122. For the seated figure, compare equally developed examples of foreshortening from the Hephaisteion frieze, Bockelberg 1979, pls. 25 (East 18, fallen warrior), 44 (West 14, kneeling Lapith).

A closely written argument on a high date for the frieze treats the seated figure on slab C in detail (Childs 1985, pp. 230–236). Childs acknowledges that the pose is unparalleled in sculpture before the late 430's, and he suggests the possible influence of painting, where the mastery of foreshortening was more advanced than in sculpture. One comes away from this study with a richer understanding for how relatively isolated was the Ilissos frieze from the major stylistic currents of its day. This heterodoxy makes the influence of painting all the more plausible. Given the indications of the temple architecture, however, the recently analyzed context

The column bases and capitals of these four buildings form a close group, distinctively Attic in form. The base type, reeded torus over scotia over plain torus, is first known from the Propylaia and repeated in closely analogous form on the Ilissos Temple and the Erechtheion.[65] The Nike Temple bases are a minor variant, notable for their thin lower torus (Pl. 19:b).[66]

The Attic capital, distinguished by paired fillets along the bolsters, bulbous volute eyes, a strongly emergent echinus carved egg-and-dart and an ovolo-profiled abacus, is, like the column base, first attested on the Propylaia.[67] The Nike Temple capitals are close in proportions to this model, though at half-scale,[68] but they are perceptibly richer in design, with strongly emergent profiles and tautly spiraled volutes. The capitals of the Erechtheion are more elaborate still, with carved egg-and-dart on the abacus; an extra pair of fillets on the bolster; a guilloche above the echinus replacing the normal corner palmettes; and an elaborate necking, a carved lotus-and-palmette bordered by bead-and-reel.[69]

Since the first definition of the Attic capital type by Puchstein, scholars have seen a line of development from the capitals of the Propylaia to the Nike Temple to the Erechtheion.[70] The place of the Nike Temple capitals is clear in such details as the profile of the bolster, relatively flat on the Propylaia, more strongly concave on the Nike Temple, and still deeper and more complexly profiled on the Erechtheion. The rendering of the fillets is equally revealing. On the Propylaia capitals, the fillet at the lower edge of the bolster is flush with the palmette zone directly below. On the Nike capitals it projects forward of that zone, and on the Erechtheion it projects forward and is more strongly profiled. Finally, the place of the Nike capitals after the Propylaia is affirmed by their corner palmettes. The palmettes on the Nike capitals are of so-called flame design, a type apparently first coined for the floral akroteria of the Parthenon.[71] The petals, four to a palmette, follow a gentle double curve and are strongly three-dimensional, with a high, grooved rib, steep, concave sides, and pointed tips. The tips of the palmette extend partly over the carved echinus directly

---

pottery from the site, and the existence of late Periclean parallels for the most advanced features of its sculpture, a date *ca.* 435 appears, in all, the most plausible.

65 Shoe 1936, pp. 179–180, pls. LXVI:1 (Propylaia), LXVI:3, 4 (Erechtheion); Shear 1963, pl. 89:b (Propylaia, Erechtheion); Wesenberg 1981, p. 32, fig. 1 (Ilissos Temple, Propylaia, Erechtheion); Stuart and Revett, I, chap. 2, pl. VI (Ilissos Temple).

66 It has been argued that the Nike Temple is not a variant but a precursor of the developed Attic form. So Wesenberg 1981, pp. 31–42. I would second the opinion of Coulton (1977, pp. 101–104), who cautions against falsely regularizing the development of the type. Shear (1963, p. 380) suggests that the thin lower element on the Nike Temple may bring the base into proportion to the relatively stocky shafts of the columns.

67 Puchstein 1887, p. 14, fig. 10; Martin 1944–1945, pp. 361–374.

68 Dinsmoor 1950, p. 186; Shear 1963, p. 380. The Propylaia capitals are 0.533 m. in height (= 2 × 0.267 m.) and 1.660 m. in width (= 2 × 0.830 m.). Those on the Nike Temple measure 0.270 × 0.830 m.

69 Puchstein 1887, p. 24, fig. 16; Paton 1927, pl. XXII.

70 Puchstein 1887, pp. 14, 18–19; Furtwängler 1893, pp. 210–211; Shear 1963, pp. 380–383.

71 On the development of the palmette in the 5th century, see H. Möbius, *Ornamente der griechischen Grabstelen*, Berlin 1929, pp. 9–21; I. Kleemann, *Der Satrapen-Sarkophag aus Sidon* (*IstForsch* 20), Berlin 1958, pp. 80–85; Childs 1985, pp. 241–248. Parthenon akroteria: H. Gropengiesser, *Die pflanzlichen Akrotere klassischer Tempel*, Mainz am Rhein 1961, pp. 2–17, pls. I–X; I. S. Mark, "New Fragments of the Parthenon Akroteria," *Hesperia* 46, 1977 (pp. 141–144), pl. 56; E. Berger, "Antikenmuseum Basel—Sammlung Ludwig: Auszug aus dem Jahresbericht 1981," *AntK* 25, 1982 (pp. 162–168), p. 166, fig. 3.

below. The corner palmettes on the Propylaia capitals are of more traditional form. The petals bend in one direction only, six to a palmette, and their tips end above the echinus. As typical of older palmettes, the petals are relatively flat and have rounded tips.[72]

Less easily interpreted as a dating criterion, but still of major importance, are the close ties between the Nike Temple and the Temple on the Ilissos. The Ilissos Temple is the first attested amphiprostyle temple in Greek architecture.[73] Measuring 5.85 m. across the stylobate, with Ionic tetrastyle porches and no opisthodomos, it furnishes a direct precedent for the Nike Temple in scale and plan. The two temples differ measurably only in length. The Nike Temple does away with the pronaos and shortens the cella of its predecessor, resulting in a structure 4.52 m. shorter on the stylobate.[74]

The architectural detail on the Nike Temple and the Ilissos Temple is as closely related as their plans. We may note two usages for which the Ilissos Temple and Nike Temple are the first known examples: the repetition of the profile of the column bases on the base moldings of the cella, the exterior toichobate, the anta bases, and in the case of the Nike Temple the bases of the piers; and the coining of a new sequence of moldings, cavetto over cyma reversa over ovolo, applied to the capitals of the antae, and on the Nike Temple again to the piers.[75]

[72] The capitals of the Ilissos Temple, preserved in the drawings of Stuart and Revett (I, chap. 2, pls. VI, VII), seemingly date between the Propylaia and the Nike Temple. See Miles 1980, pp. 318–320. The profile of the bolsters and the placement of the fillets bear close comparison to the Nike examples, but the corner palmette is of older form, a hybrid between the traditional corner palmette of the Propylaia and the flame palmette of the Nike Temple. The petals are of traditional form, rounded at the tips, but are larger than those on the Propylaia capitals, four to a palmette, and lie in a double curve that brings them slightly over the echinus (Stuart and Revett, I, chap. 2, pl. VII). The study by Childs (1985, pp. 245–246) draws attention to the palmettes on the epikranitis of the Ilissos Temple (Stuart and Revett, I, chap. 2, pl. VIII), similar to the corner palmettes of the capitals in having S-curved petals of traditional rounded design. The palmettes on the epikranitis of the Temple of Nemesis at Rhamnous are of similar form (Society of Dilettanti, *Unedited Antiquities of Attica*, London 1817, chap. 6, pls. 5, 9). It appears that this palmette type was current for only a few years as a minor, more conventional variant on the flame design.

[73] W. Dörpfeld, "Zu den Bauwerken Athens," *AthMitt* 36, 1911 (pp. 39–72), p. 41; Shear 1963, pp. 389–390, note 111. The early Ionic Temple A on Paros, studied by Gottfried Gruben, is a noteworthy precedent. From the preserved eastern foundations the building is restored as hexastyle amphiprostyle: G. Gruben, "Der Bergtempel A vom Paros," *AA* 1982 (pp. 197–229), pp. 222–224. Compare the 6th-century Doric temple of Artemis Knakeatis at Tegea. The east end was tetrastyle prostyle with the full plan restored by Konstantinos A. Rhomaios as tetrastyle amphiprostyle: K. A. Rhomaios, «Τεγεατικὸν ἱερόν ᾿Αρτεμίδος Κνακεάτιδος», ΑρχΕφ 1952 (pp. 1–31), pp. 5–8. On prostyle plans in the 6th century, see B. A. Barletta, "An 'Ionian Sea' Style in Archaic Doric Architecture," *AJA* 94, 1990 (pp. 45–72), pp. 55–60.

[74] On the close relation between the two buildings, see Ross, Schaubert, and Hansen 1839, pp. 10–11; Studniczka 1916, pp. 198–201; Shear 1963, pp. 388–399; Miles 1980, pp. 318–322. The piers of the Nike Temple, among the earliest known in Greek architecture, have been considered a conflation of cella doorwall with distyle-in-antis pronaos columns; see Büsing 1970, pp. 73–75; J. J. Coulton, *Architectural Development of the Greek Stoa*, Oxford 1976, pp. 129–130. For the restoration of the Ilissos Temple pronaos with two columns in antis, see A. Barrett and M. Vickers, "Columns in Antis in the Temple on the Ilissus," *BSA* 70, 1975, pp. 11–16, ascribing to the temple a pair of column bases stored in the Roman Agora.

[75] Ilissos Temple base moldings: Stuart and Revett, I, chap. 2, pls. VI, VIII. The following early Ionic buildings may serve as contrast. Temple of Artemis at Ephesos: column bases are profiled torus over scotia; walls and antae have no base molding; all are set on a plinth (Hogarth 1908, pp. 257–258, 264–266). Siphnian

The Nike Temple has notable ties, finally, to the Erechtheion. The repetition of the profile of the column bases on the base moldings of the cella occurs also there, now in more embellished form. The base moldings on the north and south toichobate of the cella, on the eastern antae of the cella, and on the parapet for the Porch of the Maidens have the upper and lower tori both reeded, not the upper torus alone; the column bases of the north portico have a carved guilloche on the upper torus; and the antae on the north have a guilloche above and reeded torus below.[76] The anta capitals on the Erechtheion relate to the Nike and Ilissos Temples similarly.[77] The three have the same sequence of moldings: cavetto, cyma reversa, astragal, ovolo, and astragal. On the Erechtheion, however, the cyma reversa, ovolo, and astragals are carved. Among a range of other architectural usages that tie the two buildings is the rare superimposition of a cavetto molding on an ovolo. The Nike Temple introduces the pairing on the exterior crown of the epistyle, cavetto over ovolo over base astragal; the interior epistyle crown on the north porch of the Erechtheion repeats the sequence, this time with the ovolo and astragal carved.[78]

The Nike Temple and Erechtheion are further related in their use of refinements and building techniques. The inward lean of the columns of the Nike Temple occurs again on the Erechtheion, a refinement otherwise unknown to the Ionic order.[79] The eastern antae of the Erechtheion follow the example of the Nike Temple in having their principle face vertical, again unusual.[80] And the krepidomas of the Nike Temple and Erechtheion are closely related, the steps tipped slightly, the treads forward, the risers back, a rare refinement first attested on the Parthenon.[81] Among construction techniques shared by the Nike Temple and Erechtheion, one may note the use of T-dowels in the stylobate and antae[82] and the doweling of the column bases to the stylobate.[83] The latter is known in the 5th century only from these two buildings; the former is attested on the Temple of the Athenians on Delos as well.[84]

Treasury, Delphi: the base of the podia for the karyatids is molded cyma reversa over plain fillet; the wall and anta bases have a beaded astragal (Dinsmoor 1913, p. 12, fig. 2, p. 17, fig. 3). Anta capitals: Stuart and Revett, I, chap. 2, pl. VIII.

76 Paton 1927, pl. V (north wall); pls. VI, XXVI (south wall and Porch of the Maidens); pl. XVI (eastern anta); pls. XXII, XXIII (north porch).

77 *Ibid.*, pls. XVIII, XX:2, 3; XXIII, XXXVI:3, 5.

78 *Ibid.*, pls. XXII, XXX, no. 16; Shoe 1936, pl. XI:3.

79 Shoe 1936, p. 19 (columns of the east portico). Before study of the east portico of the Erechtheion, such inclination was thought to have occurred only in Doric: so J. Durm, *Baukunst der Griechen*, 3rd ed., Leipzig 1910, p. 298; C. Dugas, *Le sanctuaire d'Aléa Athéna à Tégée*, Paris 1924, p. 19, note 4.

80 Paton 1927, pp. 19, 30.

81 Parthenon, A. K. Orlandos, Ἡ ἀρχιτεκτονικὴ τοῦ Παρθενῶνος I, Athens 1976, pl. 26; Erechtheion, Paton 1927, p. 18.

82 Paton 1927, pp. 194–195.

83 *Ibid.*, p. 19, pls. II, XVIII:2.

84 For the practice of doweling columns to the stylobate in Late Classical and Hellenistic architecture, see Martin 1965, p. 294. T-dowels on the Temple of the Athenians on Delos, *Délos* XII, i, pp. 199–200, figs. 259–262. Erechtheion, Paton 1927, pp. 194–195. The T-dowel is first attested in the base of the Athena Parthenos, used in the corner blocks of the base: W. B. Dinsmoor, "The Repair of the Athena Parthenos: A Story of Five Dowels," *AJA* 38, 1934 (pp. 93–106), pp. 93–94, fig. 2. Compare the North Building on Delos, where it is used at the corners of the wall: F. Courby, *Le Portique d'Antigone ou du Nord-Est* (*Exploration archéologique de Délos* V), Paris 1912, pp. 57–58, figs. 78, 79; Nereid Monument at Xanthos, in the corner blocks of the basement and

For the most part, the similarities in architectural usage between the Nike Temple, Ilissos Temple, Propylaia, and Erechtheion serve more to indicate the general contemporaneity of the four than to aid in establishing narrow absolute dates.[85] We may note in summary the few architectural criteria that appear more diagnostic. Foremost is the apparent place of the Nike Temple capitals between those of the Propylaia and the Erechtheion. The link back to the Propylaia appears the stronger, from the strict correspondence of the two in proportions, scaled 2:1, and from the close adherence of the Nike Temple to the earlier capitals in overall design. The Erechtheion capitals, with their additional fillets, carved guilloche above the echinus, and lotus-and-palmette necking, seem substantially more distant.

Architectural refinements and technique provide further dating criteria. Of the three distinctive refinements on the Nike Temple, the slight incline of the treads and risers of the krepidoma, the vertical set of the antae, and the inward lean of the columns, the latter two are paralleled only on the Erechtheion, the first on the Parthenon and the Erechtheion. The use of an empolion-shaped dowel of the Nike Temple to fix the columns to the stylobate is again paralleled only on the Erechtheion, and the use of T-dowels in the krepidoma and antae is found on the Erechtheion and the Temple of the Athenians on Delos. There is some slight disparity in this evidence, with the form of the capitals suggesting a date closer to the Propylaia, building refinements and technique suggesting a date closer to the Erechtheion. We ought thus to be conservative in converting the evidence into absolute dates. Architectural criteria point to a date for the Nike Temple at earliest toward the close of the Propylaia project in the late 430's, at latest in the early years of the Erechtheion project, begun *ca.* 420.[86]

---

the temple walls: P. Coupel and P. Demargne, *Le Monument des Néréides: L'architecture* (*Fouilles de Xanthos* III), Paris 1969, p. 45 *et passim.* "Blind" dowels, a form transitional to T-dowels, have been noted in the western corner blocks of the Parthenon frieze: W. B. Dinsmoor, "New Evidence for the Parthenon Frieze," *AJA* 58, 1954 (pp. 144–145), p. 145. Compare the shallow cuttings in "T" form on the Knidian Treasury at Delphi, apparently for lead dowels, Dinsmoor 1913, p. 10, fig. 9.

[85] The problem of distinguishing mere variations in architectural form from stylistic development proper continues to cloud arguments on the Nike Temple. On the relative dating of the column bases see note 66 above, p. 83. Occasionally, the proportions of the column shafts on the Nike Temple have been taken to suggest a date *ca.* 450: so Studniczka 1916, p. 200, and more recently H. Lauter, *Zur gesellschaftlichen Stellung des bildenden Künstlers in der griechischen Klassik*, Erlangen 1974, p. 32. Evidence developed by Shear (1963, p. 379), however, relates the proportions to the scale of the order. Nike Temple, column height 4.05 m.; column height to lower diameter, 7.82. Stoa of the Athenians at Delphi (around 455 B.C.?), column height *ca.* 3.30 m.; column height to lower diameter, *ca.* 7.83. Two sets of columns (both third quarter of the 5th century B.C.) recovered from the post-Herulian fortifications in the Athenian Agora, first set, column height 5.87 m.; column height to lower diameter, 7.12; second set, column height 6.67 m.; column height to lower diameter, 7.81. For the Stoa of the Athenians, P. Amandry, *Topographie et architecture: La Colonne des Naxiens et la Portique des Athéniens* (*Fouilles de Delphes* II, viii), Paris 1953, p. 41, p. 83, fig. 6; J. Walsh, "The Date of the Athenian Stoa at Delphi," *AJA* 90, 1986, pp. 319–336; columns from the post-Herulian fortifications, H. A. Thompson, "Activities in the Athenian Agora: 1959," *Hesperia* 29, 1960 (pp. 327–368), pp. 351–356.

[86] Miles (1980, p. 323), following an oft-stated opinion that the marble working chips under the pavement of the Nike Sanctuary stem from the Propylaia project, argues that work on the bastion must have begun before the close of the earlier project. She divides the Nike project into two stages, the first (bastion sheathing and temple foundations) dating from *ca.* 434–432. Wesenberg's study (1981, pp. 47–51) considers the bastion project to have been interrupted as well. Reasoning from two unused, mispositioned clamp cuttings on the epistyle of the temple, Wesenberg argues that the cella was originally to have been fully open at the east; piers were added

The Sculpture of the Sanctuary: Stylistic Analysis

The progress of work on Stage IV may be gauged finally from the style of the Nike Temple frieze (Pl. 20) and the Nike Parapet (Pls. 21, 22). As long recognized, the frieze of the temple falls somewhere between the two major dated works of late 5th-century sculpture, the sculptures of the Parthenon, completed in 432, and the Erechtheion frieze, 409–406.[87] The criteria for this placement may be better addressed by stages as we proceed, beginning first with drapery style.[88]

Drapery on the Nike Temple frieze is more linear in conception than on the Parthenon. Drapery ridges tend to be longer and of more uniform width and are more widely and regularly spaced. Fabric tends to be thinner, occasionally clinging to the body, the beginning of the so-called damp-fold style;[89] and motion lines are more lively and sinuous.[90] These developments are carried further on the Erechtheion frieze. The linear design of the drapery, still confined largely to the ridges, is accented as well through narrow slot folds, a play of light against dark.[91] Florid, undulating ridge folds are more frequent, used not only in rendering motion but throughout the design,[92] and damp-fold drapery is more prevalent.[93]

Among undated works, the Nike Temple frieze appears to be related to the Erechtheion karyatids in particular. A number of peplophoroi on the east frieze of the Nike Temple are draped much the same as the karyatids, with the lower border of the kolpos curved strongly at the waist.[94] On both monuments the figures stand in a supple, rhythmic contrapposto, the

---

to the plan at the resumption of the project in the 420's, with the temple then already complete to the architrave. Neither argument convinces. Balanos' drawings show that the east side of the cella was supported by three courses of foundations laid of a piece with the remaining foundations for the temple (see Pls. 14–16; on this area of the plan, note 39 above [p. 10], pp. 25–27): the piers were seemingly planned from the start. The clamp cuttings appear to be simply a craftsman's error. As suggested by Orlandos (1915, p. 36), they were worked on the ground, then corrected in place. The working chips under the sanctuary paving are more likely from the Nike Temple itself than from the Propylaia, as discussed p. 138 below. It is important to note, however, that while there remains no concrete indication that work on Stage IV overlapped the Propylaia, neither does the architecture of the sanctuary exclude the possibility.

[87] So already Furtwängler 1893, pp. 220–222; in modern scholarship only Blümel has dissented from this opinion (1923, pp. 39, 41–42; 1950–1951, pp. 135–158). Blümel divides the slabs of the temple into two groups, one "Doric" (including b, c, e, and o), dating from the 440's, the other "Attic-Ionic" (a, f, l, m), dating from around 420 (1950–1951, pp. 142, 146, 154–155). The dates depend on the now long-refuted hypothesis that work on Stage IV of the Nike Sanctuary was interrupted by the Propylaia. A generation of scholarship on Attic sculpture has seen the distinction of "Doric" and "Attic-Ionic" fall away. One tends now to view the frieze as essentially unified in style, from the hand of a close-knit group of workmen: e.g., Lippold 1950, p. 194; Schlörb 1964, pp. 38–39; Despinis 1971, p. 169.

[88] The following are the major studies on the evolution of late 5th-century drapery: Dohrn 1957, pp. 15–32; R. Carpenter, *Greek Sculpture*, Chicago 1960, pp. 135–151; Hiller 1971; L. Alscher, *Griechische Plastik* II, ii, Berlin 1982, pp. 201–228; Harrison 1988, pp. 99–105.

[89] Blümel 1923, pls. I–III, VIII, slab a, East 1 and 3; pls. IV–VI, slab a, mounted figure second from right. Picard n.d., pls. 38:2 (first and third from left); 41:4.

[90] Blümel 1923, pls. I–III, slab b, East 4, 5; Picard n.d., pl. 38:2 (fourth and fifth figures from left).

[91] Boulter 1970, pls. 8 (AcrM 1238), 11 (AcrM 1071).

[92] *Ibid.*, pls. 1 (AcrM 2825), 5 (AcrM 284), 19 (AcrM 1073), 26 (AcrM 1074).

[93] *Ibid.*, pls. 11 (AcrM 1071), 14 (AcrM 1076), 29 b (AcrM 1291).

[94] Pl. 20:a, East 10, 12; Pl. 20:b, East 17, 19. For the karyatids, see H. Lauter, "Die Koren des Erechtheion," *AntP* 16, 1976, pp. 7–54, pls. 1–56.

arch of the kolpos seeming to form a pivot between the upper and lower body. However different the scale of the monuments, drapery style is also very close. On the karyatids as on the frieze, the weight leg is hidden behind the straight, deeply cut folds of the skirt, while the free leg, a step forward, is largely revealed by clinging drapery. On both, the folds of the overfall are widely spaced and curve freely over the torso. The pervasiveness and consistency of these stylistic ties suggest the two monuments were worked side by side, or at most a few years apart.[95]

Between the Parthenon sculptures and the Erechtheion frieze, the sole reference points for absolute dating are document reliefs, modest reliefs usually of standing or seated figures carved atop decrees. Four such works have bearing on the date of the frieze: (1) The relief that crowns the Bridge Decree, *IG* I^3 79 (422/421). It has four standing figures: Demeter, Kore, Demos (?), and Athena.[96] (2) The relief for a treaty between Athens and Argos, *IG* I^3 86 (417/416). It preserves the better part of two figures: Zeus, seated, and Hera, standing.[97] (3) The relief from a decree honoring the citizens of Neapolis in Thrace, *IG* I^3 101 (410/409). It preserves the figure of Athena at right.[98] And (4) the relief from an annual account of the Treasurers of Athena, *IG* I^3 375 (410/409). It shows Athena and Erechtheus(?) on opposite sides of the sacred olive tree.[99]

Within this group, the two reliefs from 410/409 stand farthest from the frieze, both notably more advanced in their handling of contrapposto, foreshortening, and drapery. The stances on the reliefs are more fluid than on the Nike Temple, closer to Polykleitan models. The poses of the figures shift subtly relative to the picture plane, the gentle rotation of the figure being supported on a broader, more thorough mastery of foreshortening. Drapery style is more evolved as well. On the Nike Temple frieze, drapery is arranged in ways that create a visual break at the waist of the figures, strengthening the opposition of the upper torso and legs in the stance. On the reliefs, drapery rather leads the eye through the waist, thus complementing the new, more Polykleitan pose. Finally, drapery folds are differently treated on the two. Drapery clings more on the reliefs, and where it hangs free, it increasingly tends to follow along significant body contours, outlining the form. Typically, such outlines are effected with ridge folds, but narrow, deeply shadowed furrows are used as well.

To the opposite side of the frieze from the reliefs of 410/409, and far closer in style, is the relief on the Bridge Decree of 422/421. The relief on the Bridge Decree shows the integration of Attic and Polykleitan tradition at an early, still tentative stage. The figures trail the free leg,

95 On the contemporaneity of the two, see Furtwängler 1893, p. 221; Dohrn 1957, pp. 56, 67; also Lauter (note 94 above, p. 87), p. 44.

96 Eleusis, Mus. 63, Binnebössel 1932, no. 5; H. Speier, "Zweifiguren-gruppen im fünften und vierten Jahrhundert vor Christus," *RömMitt* 47, 1932 (pp. 1–94), pls. 8:1, 2; 9:1; F. Eckstein, "Das Hekataion in der British School zu Athen," *AntP* 4, 1965 (pp. 27–36), p. 31, figs. 3–5; Lawton 1984, no. 6, pp. 111–116; Meyer 1989, no. A 5, p. 33.

97 Athens, AcrM 2431+2980+2981, O. Walter, "Zu attischen Reliefs," *JOAI* 18, 1915, Beib. col. 89, fig. 33; *idem* 1923, no. 2, pp. 1–3; Binnebössel 1932, no. 9; Lawton 1984, no. 8, pp. 118–121; Meyer 1989, no. A 8, p. 33.

98 Athens, EM 6598, J. Svoronos, *Das Athener Nationalmuseum*, Athens 1908, pl. 204; Binnebössel 1932, no. 15; Lawton 1984, no. 12, pp. 126–128; Meyer 1989, no. A 15, p. 34.

99 Paris, Louvre, Ma 831, Binnebössel 1932, no. 14; Speier (note 96 above) pl. 10:3; W.-H. Schuchhardt, *Epochen der griechischen Plastik*, Baden-Baden 1959, p. 85, fig. 68; Lawton 1984, no. 13, pp. 128–133; Meyer 1989, no. A 16, p. 34.

and there is a hint of reciprocal sway from the legs to the torso. The contrapposto, however, still holds closely to the vertical, and remains strictly frontal.[100] We may compare the figure of Demeter on the relief to East 10 on the Nike frieze (Pl. 20:a). A close typological descendant of the relief figure, East 10 stands with its hips rotated slightly and set more to the side, its upper body more strongly bent in compensation. Its dress reinforces the more strongly moved contrapposto. The lower edge of the kolpos is raised to the waist and strongly arched, thus coming, as on the Erechtheion, just at the division of the two major countermotions of the stance. The Nike frieze is more developed than the relief on the Bridge Decree in other respects as well. Garments on the frieze tend to cling more, more fully revealing the free leg of the peplophoroi, while in some few cases the drapery clings over the full body, the damp-fold style proper.[101] Of note, finally, are changes in the folds themselves. Ridge folds on the frieze tend to be thinner and more widely spaced than on the relief on the Bridge Decree and more artfully drawn.

Although perceptible, the stylistic distance between the relief on the Bridge Decree and the Nike Temple frieze consists more in myriad small departures and reworkings than in any large advance. The distance from the frieze to the reliefs of 410/409 is by contrast far more dramatic. That the frieze is in fact relatively closer to 422/421 than 410/409 is confirmed by the document relief for the Athens-Argos treaty of 417/416. Sinuous curves and flutters of drapery, applied only to figures in motion on the frieze, have developed into a mannerism on the treaty relief. The standing Hera on the relief has a fluttering, seemingly windswept veil, while Zeus' mantle bends in decorative waves around his hips. Such relative inconsistencies between drapery motive and narrative are hallmarks of the developed Rich Style. They look beyond the style of the Nike Temple to the Nike Parapet.

However valuable the indications from any one of the document reliefs here considered, their testimony is considerably the stronger for its internal consistency.[102] The two reliefs from 410/409 are in a style well beyond the frieze. The Rich Style characteristics on the relief from 417/416, though nearer the frieze, point beyond it as well. And last, the relief on the Bridge Decree from 422/421 appears a slight step earlier. On this evidence, the frieze belongs in the years around 420–418, early in the Peace of Nikias.[103]

[100] On the integration of Attic and Polykleitan stance, Dohrn 1957. The Velletri Athena (Harrison 1977, pp. 150–155, figs. 8–17) appears to stand at or near the start of the tradition. Polykleitan poses appear already on the Parthenon frieze: Brommer 1977, pls. 11 (West III, 4), 107 (North XLII, 133), 144 (South XXV, 61), 166 (East I, 1), 186 (East VII, 52). The poses on the frieze, however, have no immediate followers. As reintroduced into Attic sculpture a generation later, Polykleitan stance is more tentative, apparently influenced again from without.

The preserved figure of Athena from a document relief in Paris seemingly belongs between the Nike Temple frieze and the decree reliefs of 410/409 (Paris, Louvre, Ma 2414, M. Bieber, "Attische Reliefs in Cassel," *AthMitt* 35, 1910 [pp. 1–16], pl. 4; Beil. to p. 12; Meritt, Wade-Gery, and McGregor 1949, II, pl. 15). The relief was once thought to be from *IG* I^3 66 (Meritt, Wade-Gery, and McGregor 1949, II, p. 76), a decree passed likely in 427/6. More recent study rejects the attribution however (D. Bradeen and M. McGregor, *Studies in Fifth-Century Attic Epigraphy*, Norman, Okla. 1973, pp. 121–122), as indeed the figure style confirms. Lawton (1984, no. 77, pp. 244–245) and Meyer (1989, no. A 21, p. 44) both doubt the association.

[101] Blümel 1923, pls. I–III, VIII, slab a, East 1 and 3; Picard n.d., pl. 38:2 (first and third figures from left).

[102] The even progression in the style of the record reliefs five years by five years, decade by decade is perhaps the one most important validation of their worth as dating comparanda. See Lawton 1984, p. 84.

[103] Scholars in essential agreement with these dates include Lippold 1950, p. 194 (begun soon after 421); Dohrn 1957, p. 24 (soon after the relief on the Bridge Decree); Fuchs 1983, p. 442 (*ca.* 420). But compare Hiller

The close of work on Stage IV may be gauged from the style of the Nike Parapet, the most developed of the preserved sculptures from the sanctuary. The style of the parapet evolves gradually beginning on the north side and following around to the south, as characteristic of a monument carved over several years.[104] The most advanced sculptures, a group including notably the Sandalbinder (AcrM 973, Pl. 22:a), the seated Athena from the south parapet (AcrM 989 left, Pl. 22:b), and a well-preserved standing Nike (AcrM 7098 left), are close to but a stage earlier than the Erechtheion frieze.[105] Among the small circle of criteria that distinguish the two, of first importance is the greater value placed on negative, shadowed form in the later monument. Folds on the Erechtheion tend to be more deeply cut and more regularly and evenly shaped, thus setting up a play of dark against light. The parapet figure closest to the Erechtheion in this respect is the standing Nike, AcrM 7098 left. Her peplos falls between her legs in a series of thin, high-walled ridges carved with an eye as much to their spacing, the effect of the shadowed furrows between them, as to the ridges themselves. Such devices are noticeably more developed on the Erechtheion frieze. Narrow, slotlike folds are rendered throughout the drapery of AcrM 1071 right,[106] for example, in arcs around the breasts and at the kolpos, as well as in long folds between the legs. The Erechtheion frieze displays more developed forms of contrapposto as well. The standing figure AcrM 1245 rotates and sways in a contrapposto roughly comparable to the stance of Athena from the treasurers' account of 410/409, or the related figure of Athena on the decree honoring Neapolis from the same year.[107] Two other figures on the frieze, AcrM 1077 and AcrM 1074, have yet more developed poses. They sway strongly but with free leg advanced.[108] The latest carving on the parapet appears by contrast a step before the reliefs. Nowhere is contrapposto as rhythmically conceived or as strongly turned.[109] These comparisons, in all, point to the parapet having been already complete at the halt of work on the Erechtheion in 413.

The start of work on the parapet is best gauged from the chronology of the sanctuary as a whole. The frieze of the temple dates, as we have seen, *ca.* 420–418. Allowing for completion

---

1971, p. 50 (same stage as to the relief on the Bridge Decree); a portion of the frieze is dated to the 440's by Blümel, see note 87 above, p. 87.

[104] See Harrison 1982, p. 47, note 35; *eadem* 1988, pp. 103–105.

[105] Athens, AcrM 989 left, a corner slab, and AcrM 973 and 7098 are securely attributed to the south by their dowel holes. See Dinsmoor 1926, pp. 16–17, 18, 19. For Athens, AcrM 7098 left, Welter 1939, col. 21, figs. 10, 11; Brouskari 1974, fig. 334. Parapet dated before the Erechtheion: Carpenter 1929, p. 81; Dohrn 1957, pp. 24–25; C. Hofkes-Brukker, "Vermutete Werke des Paionios," *BABesch* 42, 1967 (pp. 10–71), pp. 36–37; Boulter 1970, p. 23. Others have judged the two to be roughly contemporary: A. Michaelis, "Die Zeit des Neubaus des Poliastempels in Athen," *AthMitt* 14, 1889 (pp. 349–366), pp. 364–366 (parapet after 411, following Athens' Hellespontine victories); Furtwängler 1893, p. 222; Lippold 1950, p. 194; Schlörb 1964, p. 39 (begun in 408); *idem*, "Nochmals zum Datum der Bauplastik des Asklepiostempels von Epidauros," in *Festschrift für G. Kleiner*, H. Keller and J. Kleiner, ed., Tübingen 1976, pp. 64–66 (the Erechtheion frieze is contemporary with the parapet but appears later due to theme); Fuchs 1983, pp. 443–446 (*ca.* 409–406). The realization that the style of the parapet evolved by degrees over several years of carving makes this split of opinion more understandable, without, however, resolving it. Harrison (1988, pp. 103–105) dates the north side of the parapet before 413, the west and the western corner of the south *ca.* 410–400, and the remainder of the south after 400. To my eyes, the Erechtheion frieze, while a good deal more developed than the north side of the parapet, is somewhat beyond the south side too.

[106] Boulter 1970, pl. 11.

[107] Athens, AcrM 1245, Boulter 1970, pl. 24:a; decree reliefs, notes 98 and 99 above, p. 88.

[108] Athens, AcrM 1077, Boulter 1970, pl. 5; Athens, AcrM 1074, *ibid.*, pl. 26.

[109] Compare, for example, Athens, AcrM 7098 left, cited in note 105 above; Athens, AcrM 999, Brouskari 1974, fig. 337 (with recent join).

of the pediments and akroteria, we may expect a beginning date for the parapet in or around 416. The fluttering drapery on the relief for the Athens-Argos treaty of 417/416 provides welcome confirmation.[110] It gives the earliest dated testimony for Rich Style mannerisms that appear already well developed on the parapet, and in fact on the earliest of the slabs.[111] The internal development of the parapet style north to south, an orderly if subtle advance, accords with this date as well. Begun *ca.* 416, completed in or soon before 413, it was the fruit of a short intense campaign of carving, perhaps some three years' work.

A key problem in the chronology of Stage IV remains to be discussed, the state of the project at the cessation of Attic building in 432. As earlier observed, the form of the Southwest Wing establishes the mid-430's as a *terminus ante quem non* for Stage IV.[112] The relief on the Bridge Decree furnishes a valuable second point of reference. We have found the Bridge Decree (422/421) to be a chronological reference point for both sculpture and architecture. Its crowning relief, and other, later decree reliefs, help to narrow the date of the Nike Temple friezes to *ca.* 420–418, while the text of the decree gives the first firm evidence of sacred building at Athens since work broke off in 432.

The resumption of sacred building at Athens late in the Archidamian War, whatever the immediate occasion and context, must surely have encompassed new work on the Akropolis, the wealthiest and most august of cult sites; the Akropolis was unlikely to have been idle while other sacred projects moved forward.[113] The testimony of the Bridge Decree is of special interest in this light. It suggests that the carving of the Nike Temple friezes followed the resumption of Attic building by at least a small interval: the relief on the Bridge Decree, a step earlier than the friezes, is a *terminus ante quem* for the resumption of building. This suggests that the Akropolis program first began as architectural construction and that work in sculpture resumed only later. When we consider the apparent span of the Nike project, by common estimate some three or four years in construction,[114] then the date of the relief on the Bridge

[110] For the relief, note 97 above, p. 88.

[111] Athens, AcrM 4, Nike erecting a tropaion, Carpenter 1929, pl. III; Athens, AcrM 977, Nike mounting a stair, *ibid.*, pl. I; Athens, AcrM 972, two Nikai leading a bull, *ibid.*, pls. V, VII. The slabs are from the north side of the parapet and from the short return bordering the stair: see Dinsmoor 1926, pp. 14, 17. It is above all the florid mannerisms of the early parapet style, drapery whipped and swirled far beyond the needs of narrative, that set it apart from the Nike Temple frieze. Scholars have tended to compare the frieze to the south side of the parapet (Furtwängler 1893, p. 222; Blümel 1923, pp. 22–24; *idem* 1950–1951, pp. 153–155), worked when the fever of the Rich Style had already cooled. There is an unmistakable distance between such figures as East 1 on the frieze and the Nike erecting a tropaion, Athens, AcrM 989 right, or East 3 and the Sandalbinder (East 1 and 3, Blümel 1923, pls. I–III, VIII; AcrM 989 right, Carpenter 1929, pl. XXV; Sandalbinder, Pl. 22:a). The parapet figures show a more developed stage of the damp fold style, with drapery more fully revealing the contour and surface of the figures. The parapet style is also notable for its greater decorative energy. The parapet is calmer on the south than on the north. Even on the south, however, drapery line flicks and dances appreciably more than on the frieze.

[112] Pp. 81–82.

[113] Compare the history of the Akropolis program in its first generation under Perikles, R. Meiggs, "The Political Implications of the Parthenon," *Parthenos and Parthenon* (*Greece and Rome* Supplement to vol. 10), Oxford 1963, pp. 36–45. The Hephaisteion, not covered by the oath, appears to have been begun a few years before the Parthenon: its cella was widened and interior columns added seemingly in imitation of the Akropolis project. See Dinsmoor 1941, pp. 154–156. I draw attention, however, to a study that places the beginning of the Hephaisteion after the Parthenon: Coulton 1984, I, pp. 40–44; II, pp. 368–369.

[114] Cf. Dinsmoor 1950, pp. 185–186, note 4 (427–424 B.C.); followed by Shear 1963, p. 388; Wesenberg 1981, p. 53 (437/436–433/432). Travlos (1971, pp. 148–149) argues for a slightly shorter schedule, 427–425/424.

Decree and friezes point to a starting date for the bastion project either first with the renewal of public building in the 420's or at very earliest in the late 430's, a construction season or two before the cessation of building in 432.[115]

[115] One does not know when in the Nike project the friezes were begun, but it is unlikely to have been before work on the temple itself, that is, toward the middle or end of the project. For the carving of the frieze blocks on the ground rather than in place, Harrison 1972b, p. 321.

VIII
ANCIENT SOURCES ON THE HISTORY OF THE SANCTUARY

The written sources on the history of the Nike Sanctuary fall into three groups: antiquarian references to the cult statue; sources on the history of Athens and the Akropolis in general; and inscriptions on the history and administration of the cult. The three tend rather to complement than to overlap one another. Sources on the cult statue bear foremost on the Archaic cult, general historical sources on the period 480–450, and inscriptions on the years of the Athenian Empire, from 450 to the end of the Peloponnesian War.

CULT STATUE OF ATHENA NIKE

The cult image of Athena Nike is referred to in literary sources three times: in a fragment of Heliodoros, an Athenian antiquarian of the 2nd century B.C.; and in two passages of Pausanias, writing in the later 2nd century after Christ. The statue is mentioned as well in a late 5th-century decree bearing on the cult, *IG* I³ 64A.

The fragment of Heliodoros survives in a lexicographic entry of Harpokration, which citation reads in full:

> Νίκη ᾿Αθηνᾶ· Λυκοῦργος ἐν τῷ Περὶ τῆς ἱερείας. ὅτι δὲ Νίκης ᾿Αθηνᾶς ξόανον ἄπτερον, ἔχον ἐν μὲν τῇ δεξιᾷ ῥόαν, ἐν δὲ τῇ εὐωνύμῳ κράνος, ἐτιμᾶτο παρ' ᾿Αθηναίοις, δεδήλωκεν ῾Ηλιόδωρος ὁ περιηγητὴς ἐν α' Περὶ ἀκροπόλεως.[1]
>
> Nike Athena: [cited by] Lykourgos in *Concerning the Priestess.* That the Athenians venerated a wingless *xoanon* of Nike Athena, a pomegranate in the right hand, a helmet in the left, is attested by the periegete Heliodoros in Book I of *Concerning the Akropolis.*

Pausanias refers to the statue only in passing, first in discussing a cult image of Enyalios at Sparta and again before a votive image of Nike at Olympia:

> 3.15.7. τοῦ ναοῦ δὲ ἀπαντικρὺ πέδας ἐστὶν ἔχων ᾿Ενυάλιος, ἄγαλμα ἀρχαῖον. γνώμη δὲ Λακεδαιμονίων τε ἐς τοῦτό ἐστιν ἄγαλμα καὶ ᾿Αθηναίων ἐς τὴν Ἄπτερον καλουμένην Νίκην, τῶν μὲν οὔποτε τὸν ᾿Ενυάλιον φεύγοντα οἰχήσεσθαί σφισιν ἐνεχόμενον ταῖς πέδαις, ᾿Αθηναίων δὲ τὴν Νίκην αὐτόθι ἀεὶ μενεῖν οὐκ ὄντων πτερῶν. τόνδε μέν ἐισιν αἱ πόλεις αὗται τὰ ξόανα <τὸν> τρόπον ἱδρυμέναι καὶ ἐπὶ δόξῃ τοιαύτῃ.
>
> Opposite this temple is an ancient image of Enyalios in fetters. The notion of the Lakedaimonians about this image is that, being held fast by the fetters, Enyalios will never run away from them; just as the Athenians have a notion about the Victory called Wingless, that she

[1] Harpokration, *Lexicon,* ed. W. Dindorf, Oxford 1853; Jacoby, *FGrHist* 373, F2. The text is repeated in *Souda, s.v.* Νίκη ᾿Αθηνᾶ.

will always stay where she is because she has no wings. That is why Athens and Sparta have set up these images after this fashion.[2]

5.26.6. παρὰ δὲ τὴν 'Αθηνᾶν πεποίηται Νίκη· ταύτην Μαντινεῖς ἀνέθεσαν, τὸν πόλεμον δὲ οὐ δηλοῦσιν ἐν τῷ ἐπιγράμματι· Κάλαμις δὲ οὐκ ἔχουσαν πτερὰ ποιῆσαι λέγεται ἀπομιμούμενος τὸ 'Αθήνησι τῆς 'Απτέρου καλουμένης ξόανον.

Beside the image of Athena is one of Victory, dedicated by the Mantineans, but the war is not mentioned in the inscription. Kalamis is said to have made it without wings, in imitation of the so-called wingless image at Athens.[3]

The last source on the statue, *IG* I^3 64A, is the most difficult to interpret, although potentially the most informative. The inscription, discussed in full below (pp. 108–110 below), outlines a late 5th-century public project in the Nike Sanctuary; the commission bears in some manner on τὸ ἀρχαῖον ἄγαλμα, "the ancient image", mentioned in the second to last sentence of the text. The sentence is fragmentary and difficult to reconstruct, problems best treated with the decree as a whole. We may here present a firm conclusion from that discussion: that the *archaion agalma* of the inscription and the *xoanon* of the written sources are one and the same.

The written sources refer to the goddess of the sanctuary by several different titles. Her proper title is Athena Nike, first attested on the inscribed Archaic altar of the cult and commonly used in official contexts through the 5th and 4th centuries and into the Hellenistic period.[4] Fifth-century texts of a less formal nature often call the goddess simply Nike,[5] and indeed this short form, seemingly colloquial at first, appears to have become increasingly accepted[6] and to have led even to the popular confusion of Athena Nike, a form of Athena, and Nike, the personification. This is implicit in the term *apteros*, "wingless", first attested in Heliodoros. The modifier is superfluous for an audience who understands the image as Athena: it would be exceptional for Athena to have wings.[7] It is for those who rather see her as the normally winged Nike. "Wingless", used simply as an adjective in Heliodoros, is for Pausanias the very title of the goddess: τῶν δὲ προπυλαίων ἐν δεξιᾷ Νίκης ἐστὶν 'Απτέρου ναός. "On the right of the Propylaia is a temple of Wingless Victory."[8] It appears that by Roman times the popular usage had fully supplanted the original cult title.

[2] Translation based on Frazer 1898, I, p. 157.

[3] Translation based on Frazer 1898, I, p. 279.

[4] Among the last inscriptions with the title Athena Nike: (1) *SEG* XXX 69, line 16 (*ca.* 304–302 B.C.); (2) *IG* II^2 677, line 4; *SEG* XXVII 2 (*ca.* 250 B.C.); (3) *IG* II^2 1006, line 14; *SEG* XXI 474 (122/121).

[5] E.g., *IG* I^3 64, line 36, ἐς τὸν νεὸν τε̃ς Νίκες. *SEG* XII 80, lines 4–6, ἣ πρώτη Νίκης ἀμφεπόλευσε νεών.

[6] Demosthenes, *Exordia* 54, καὶ γὰρ ἐθύσαμεν τῷ Διὶ τῷ σωτῆρι καὶ τῇ 'Αθηνᾷ καὶ τῇ Νίκῃ. I would count the reference to the goddess in the Themistokles Decree as another 4th-century instance, Meiggs and Lewis 1969, no. 23, lines 38–40, θύ]σαντας ἀρεστήριον τῶι Διὶ τῶι Παγκρατεῖ καὶ τῆι 'Αθηνᾶι καὶ τῆι Νίκηι καὶ τῶι Ποσειδῶνι τῶι 'Ασφα[λ]είωι. Compare, however, B. D. Meritt, "Greek Historical Studies" (*Lectures in Memory of Louise Taft Semple*, first series, 1961–1965), Princeton 1967, p. 125, who suggests that the καὶ between τῆι 'Αθηνᾶι and τῆι Νίκηι is a copying error.

[7] On winged Athena, L. Savignoni, "Minerva Vittoria," *Ausonia* 5, 1910, pp. 69–108; and more recently E. Berger, *Die Geburt der Athena im Ostgiebel des Parthenon*, Basel 1974, p. 20, in regard to the Pitcairn Nike.

[8] 1.22.4; cf. 3.15.7, τὴν Ἄπτερον καλουμένην Νίκην; 5.26.6, τῆς 'Απτέρου καλουμένης ξόανον.

To weigh Pausanias' testimony on the *xoanon*, one needs to know whether he actually saw the statue or whether he knew it secondhand, from Heliodoros perhaps or some other, unattested source. We may note that he cites the work not when on the Akropolis in Book 1 but in Lakonia and at Olympia, Books 3 and 5. The *xoanon* is not the only major statue that Pausanias treats out of place. To name one, he first cites the nearby Hekate Epipyrgidia by Alkamenes in his commentary on Aigina (2.30.2). Such omissions are nonetheless unusual and noteworthy, the more so for an author so strongly interested in statuary and cult.[9] When Pausanias does come to the statue of Nike in Books 3 and 5, there is no hint of firsthand knowledge. His comments are couched in the third person ("The Athenians have a notion," "Kalamis is said to have made") and deal rather with the history and origins of the statue than with its present state or appearance. To the degree that the passages draw on other than local lore, a source such as Heliodoros appears most likely.[10]

Pausanias' knowledge of the *xoanon* is important, first, with regard to its date. If the *apteros* Nike at Athens did in fact inspire the Olympia Nike by Kalamis, as Pausanias recounts, then the Athenian image must have been set up at latest within Kalamis' working career, that is, no later than *ca.* 430.[11] We may note, however, that even if the tradition is false (scholars have observed how thin its etiology[12]), it still is a guide for dating, provided that Pausanias knew the *xoanon* at first hand. Quite knowledgeable about sculpture,[13] Pausanias is unlikely to have passed along a tradition on the two works that their respective styles appeared to contradict. Given the suspicion that the periegete never in fact saw the statue at Athens, however, the oft-cited dating significance of the Olympia passage falls away.

Beyond Pausanias, there are two further bases to date the statue, both less often noted in earlier scholarship than the Olympia passage, but in the end of relatively greater importance:

[9] On Pausanias' strong interest in cult statuary, Frazer 1898, I, pp. xxv, xxxiii–xxxv; R. E. Wycherley, "Pausanias in the Agora of Athens," *GRBS* 2, 1959 (pp. 22–44), p. 24; Habicht 1985, p. 23. Pausanias takes careful note of such famed images as the Athena Parthenos and the ancient image of Athena Polias but also nearly every other attested Classical and pre-Classical cult statue in the city of Athens: Brauronian Artemis (1.23.7), Athena Hygieia (1.23.4), Dionysos Eleutherios (1.20.3), Hephaistos and Athena Hephaisteia (1.14.6), Apollo Patroos (1.3.4), the Mother of the Gods (1.3.5), Aphrodite Ourania (1.14.7), and Aphrodite in the Gardens (1.19.2).

[10] Compare the treatment of Donohue (1988, pp. 54–55), who also tends to doubt that Pausanias saw the *xoanon* itself. It appears that Pausanias consulted a number of relatively rare sources only after he had written Book I; so S. Settis, "Il ninfeo di Erode Attico a Olimpia e il problema della composizione della Periegesi di Pausanias," *AnnPisa* ser. 2, 37, 1968 (pp. 1–63), pp. 38–41. That Περὶ τῆς Ἀκροπόλεως was perhaps among these is suggested by Pausanias 1.37.1. The periegete there points out the tomb of one Heliodoros, apparently the antiquarian, but fails to mention, much less comment on, that scholar's Akropolis treatise, so conspicuous a forerunner to his own. The omission prompts Jacoby to suggest that Pausanias had then no firsthand contact with this major source (*FGrHist* IIIb, Commentary, p. 145).

[11] So Jeffery 1980, p. 1237; cf. Benndorf (1879, p. 21), who takes the Olympia statue as a literal copy of the Athenian and assigns both to Kalamis. Benndorf's arguments are now largely out of date, notably his attempt to date the *xoanon* by the Nike Temple, then considered Kimonian. Benndorf suggests that the statue was a thank offering for Kimon's victories on the Eurymedon and that its pomegranate is a symbol of Side. For the dates of Kalamis, see J. Dörig, "Kalamis-Studien," *JdI* 80, 1965, pp. 138–265.

[12] F. Studniczka, *Kalamis*, Leipzig 1907, p. 51; P. Orlandini, *Calamide: Le Fonti*, Bologna 1950, pp. 58–59.

[13] Frazer 1898, I, pp. lx–lxiii.

first, by its attributes, the pomegranate and helmet attested by Heliodoros; and second by the term *archaion agalma* in *IG* I^3 64A.

We may reasonably expect the objects carried by the statue to reflect central aspects of the cult, and indeed literary and epigraphical sources and the sculptural program of the Stage IV sanctuary all bear this out. Athena Nike was a goddess of martial victory and fertility above all.[14] The helmet and pomegranate capture the two spheres simply and directly.[15] Greek art begins to employ attributes in the Orientalizing period, above all in work based closely on Near Eastern models.[16] They become more common in the second half of the 7th century; it is then one begins to see vase depictions of Herakles in lion skin and Hermes with kerykeion.[17] Monumental sculpture, more type-bound than painting, gives clear evidence of attributes from the early 6th century, and we may note with interest that the pomegranate is among the first attributes known, common in Attic sculpture from around 580 on.[18] On this evidence the *xoanon* of Nike ought to date, at earliest, from the first quarter of the 6th century. There are pitfalls to this argument: the statue may have been reworked, with the attributes added later. This is the case for the ancient image of Athena Polias, reworked to hold a phiale.[19] If less than incontrovertible, however, the absence of attributes in sculpture

[14] Euripides, *Ion*, apparently written soon after the completion of Stage IV, is the one most important literary source. Athena Nike is there invoked twice, once by Kreusa praying to bear a child (lines 452–471) and again as a warrior goddess (1528–1529). Numerous sources attest the cult as a protector of martial victory. Sacrifice to secure victory in battle: Demosthenes, *Exordia* 54; Themistokles Decree, cited in note 6 above, p. 94; and *SEG* XXX, 69, lines 9–17 (end of the 4th century B.C.). Dedication of a thank offering for military victory: *IG* II^2 403, lines 6–12 (Archidamian War, 426–425); *IG* II^2 677, lines 4–6 (defeat of the Gauls, 277 B.C.). On *IG* II^2 403, see pp. 113–114 below.

Military victory is perhaps the single most important theme of the decorative program, denoted by Nikai raising tropaia on the parapet, by historical battles on the friezes of the temple, and by mythical battles in the temple pediments. Fertility appears by contrast a background theme. Note, for example, the undertone of sexuality in the representation of the seated Athena Nike on the south side of the parapet, her sheer, ungirt chiton slipping down from her left shoulder (Pl. 22:b). On the significance of the slipped chiton, see E. Harrison, "Two Pheidian Heads: Nike and Amazon," in *The Eye of Greece* (Festschrift Martin Robertson), D. Kurtz and B. Sparkes, eds., Cambridge 1982, pp. 86–87.

[15] On the pomegranate as a symbol of fertility, see Farnell 1896, I, pp. 216–217; M. Lugauer, *Untersuchungen zur Symbolik des Apfels in der Antike* (diss. University of Erlangen), Bamberg 1967, p. 86; F. Muthmann, *Der Granatapfel*, Bern 1982, pp. 64–65. The contexts in which Athena appears holding a helmet have been investigated by N. Kunisch, "Zur helmhaltenden Athena," *AthMitt* 89, 1974, pp. 85–104.

[16] See representations of the so-called Mistress of the Animals and male gods with similar attributes of power: *LIMC* II, pp. 624–625, nos. 14–18; Cretan shields, E. Kunze, *Kretische Bronzereliefs*, Stuttgart 1931, pls. 3, 5:2, 49; J. Boardman, *The Cretan Collection in Oxford*, Oxford 1961, pp. 134–139.

[17] K. Fittschen, *Untersuchungen zum Beginn der Sagendarstellungen bei den Griechen*, Berlin 1969, p. 118 (SB 22), Herakles with lion skin(?), Protocorinthian alabastron, Florence, Mus. Arch. 79252, third quarter of 7th century; pp. 139 (GP 25), 151 (SB 38), Herakles in lion skin, Hermes with kerykeion, Cycladic amphora, Athens, N.M. 354, late 7th century; pp. 169–170 (SB 69), Hermes with kerykeion, Chigi Vase, Protocorinthian, Rome, Villa Giulia, *ca.* 640. Herakles with lion skin: bronze sheet from the Heraion, Samos, Vathy, Arch. Mus. B 2518, P. Brize, "Samos und Stesichoros: Zu einem früharchaischen Bronzeblech," *AthMitt* 100, 1985, pp. 53–90, pl. 15.

[18] Richter 1968, no. 42, figs. 139–146 (Berlin Kore, Berlin, Staatl. Mus. 1800, reported to be from Keratea, *ca.* 580–570); no. 43, figs. 147–150 (Pomegranate Kore, AcrM 593, *ca.* 580–570); no. 59, figs. 198–200 (AcrM 677, *ca.* 560).

[19] See Kroll 1982, pp. 65–76.

before the 6th century and the prevalence of the pomegranate in Attic sculpture beginning around 580 remain valuable guides in placing the work.

That the statue is called *archaion* in *IG* I^3 64A is also potentially important for dating. *Archaion* may be read in that text in one of two ways. It is either conventional, in effect the title of the work, or may be there to distinguish the work from one or more others.[20] The latter usage is by far the more common, in inscriptions as in language in general, and we may note that it goes well with other evidence from the Nike Sanctuary. As discussed below (pp. 113–114), a Late Classical inscription attests a second statue of Athena Nike, a tithe from victories in the sixth and seventh years of the Peloponnesian War (426–425). It may well be this second statue, commissioned or newly dedicated, that prompted the term *archaion* for the cult statue proper.

As an adjective of *arche* (origin, beginning), *archaios* means at root "of or pertaining to origins", "original", "initial".[21] It came early to be applied above all to people, objects, or institutions of the distant past: founding fathers, antiquities, ancestral laws. A number of early statues are so designated. The Erechtheion accounts use the term *archaion agalma* for the cult statue of Athena Polias, an image dating apparently from the 8th or 7th century,[22] and the late 5th and 4th-century inventories for the Sanctuary of Artemis at Brauron refer to the legendary image of Artemis, the statue said to have been brought by Iphigeneia, as the *archaion hedos*.[23] More recent objects could also be termed *archaia*. A mid-5th-century inscription orders the setting up of a stele behind τõ νεὸ τõ ἀρχ[αίο, a reference to the Peisistratid Temple of Athena,[24] and the Bridge Decree of 422/421 applies the same phrase to the Peisistratid Telesterion.[25] The *archaion agalma* of the Nike Sanctuary could on this evidence be as late as the late 6th century. We have seen the early 6th century to be an upper limit for the statue on the basis of its attributes. The criteria together place the work in or around the middle Archaic period.

That we know Pausanias' usages and style far better than those of any other antiquarian source makes the question of whether he himself saw the cult statue especially important. Both Heliodoros and Pausanias call the image a *xoanon*. One knows from elsewhere in Pausanias' *Guide* that this author employed the term *xoanon* in an unusually narrow sense. He means by it either an early image made of wood or, on occasion, a later work that recalls such an image in technique and bearing.[26] The term is attested in Heliodoros only in the one fragment

[20] For a discussion of the two usages, see Paton 1927, pp. 465–476, on the *archaios naos* of the Erechtheion inscriptions.

[21] Cf. Polystratos, Περὶ ἀλόγου καταφρονήσεως, ed. C. Wilke, Leipzig 1905, col. XIVa, line 12; Clement of Rome 1.47.

[22] *IG* I^3 474, line 1 (409/408).

[23] *IG* I^3 403, line 13 (*ca.* 416–415). The case for tying the reference to the Tauric statue is reviewed by T. Linders, *Studies in the Treasure Records of Artemis Brauronia Found in Athens*, Stockholm 1972, p. 14.

[24] *IG* I^3 7, line 6 (*ca.* 450).

[25] *IG* I^3 79, line 8 (422/421).

[26] Pausanias distinguishes *xoana* from stone images in the following passages: 2.11.8, 2.37.2, 9.11.4; cf. 4.34.7, where the contrast is to bronze. The different woods used in *xoana* are enumerated in 8.17.2. The term *xoanon* is applied by this author to over sixty works, of which two are demonstrably of late date. One is an acrolithic image of Eileithyia clothed in real garments (7.23.5), a work by Damophon of Messene, active around the mid-2nd century B.C. and known for his interest in older style. The second, more briefly mentioned, is also

on Athena Nike, with no internal indication of its meaning. It is clear from several other authors, however, that Pausanias' usage was far from standard. Hesychios, a late antique lexicographer who draws heavily on Hellenistic sources, defines *xoana* as ἀγάλματα, εἴδωλα, ζῴδια, κυρίως δὲ τὰ ἐκ ξύλων ἐξεσμένα, ἢ λίθων (statues, images, statuettes, principally those carved from wood or stone).[27] Strabo applies the term to two chryselephantine works, the Zeus at Olympia (8.3.30) and the Hera at Argos (8.6.10), and to the marble Nemesis at Rhamnous (9.1.17). Finally, Lucian extends the term to works of bronze and silver (*Alexander* 18; *De Syria Dea* 39).[28] In the likelihood that Heliodoros is the one eyewitness to the *xoanon* of Nike, we need to weigh the term cautiously. It establishes neither the material nor the date of the work.

THE PERSIAN DESTRUCTION ON THE AKROPOLIS AND THE OATH OF PLATAIA

The inscribed Stage I altar and the several sources on the Archaic cult statue, if spare and scattered evidence, do at least all bear explicitly on the sanctuary and cult. The sources for the period of the Persian Wars are more expansive and varied but throughout addressed to broader events. Nowhere is the cult mentioned by name. I begin with the Persian Destruction of the Akropolis in 480 B.C.

As told by Herodotos (8.41, 51–53), Xerxes entered Athens and found only the Akropolis defended. The population had retreated before him, the men of fighting age to Salamis, where the fleet had been gathered, the women, children, and elderly variously to Troizen, Aigina, and Salamis. The Akropolis garrison was a motley crew, a few treasurers of the goddess and some workmen ranged behind a timber barricade, "the wooden walls", hastily constructed across the Akropolis gate. The Persians besieged the gate for several days without success but at last found entry by a steep, narrow ascent on the north. They slaughtered the garrison, plundered the temple of the goddess, and put the whole of the Akropolis to flames (8.53, τὸ ἱρὸν συλήσαντες ἐνέπρησαν πᾶσαν τὴν ἀκρόπολιν).[29]

Xerxes' navy was crushingly defeated at Salamis a few days later, and the king hastily retreated to Asia with most of his army. The following year Mardonios, his captain, reoccupied the city, again unopposed, and encamped for several weeks (Herodotos 9.3). As the Greeks moved to counterattack, Mardonios wasted now the whole of the city of Athens and withdrew to Boiotia:

> 9.13.2. ὑπεξεχώρεε ἐμπρήσας τε τὰς Ἀθήνας, καὶ εἴ κού τι ὀρθὸν ἦν τῶν τειχέων ἢ τῶν οἰκημάτων ἢ τῶν ἱρῶν, πάντα καταβαλὼν καὶ συγχώσας.

---

acrolithic, by the same sculptor (8.31.6). Pausanias also notes a *xoanon* of Hekate by Myron (2.30.2). For the term *xoanon* in Pausanias, Frazer 1898, I, pp. 69–70; Bennett 1917, pp. 8–21; Papadopoulos 1980, p. 3; Donohue 1988, pp. 140–148.

27 Hesychios, *Lexikon* II, ed. K. Latte, Copenhagen 1966, *s.v.* ξόανα.

28 Cf. *Etymologicum Magnum*, *s.v.* ξόανον: stone, ivory, or wood. Clement of Alexandria, *Protrepticus* 4.40 (Potter): wood or stone.

29 For the discovery of a stele from the shrine of Aglauros and its bearing on the topography of this account, see G. Dontas, "The True Aglaurion," *Hesperia* 52, 1983, pp. 48–63.

He fired Athens, threw down and demolished whatever of its fortifications, houses, or sanctuaries were still standing, and withdrew.

This second destruction is described again by Thucydides in recounting the Athenians' return to their city on the defeat of the Persians at Plataia:

1.89.3. καὶ τὴν πόλιν ἀνοικοδομεῖν παρεσκευάζοντο καὶ τὰ τείχη· τοῦ τε γὰρ περιβόλου βραχέα εἱστήκει καὶ οἰκίαι αἱ μὲν πολλαὶ ἐπεπτώκεσαν, ὀλίγαι δὲ περιῆσαν, ἐν αἷς αὐτοὶ ἐσκήνωσαν οἱ δυνατοὶ τῶν Περσῶν.

And they prepared to rebuild the city and the walls, for there was little left of the circuit, and most of the houses were in ruins; there survived only the few dwellings occupied by the Persian leaders themselves.

Thucydides' account appears almost a corrective to Herodotos: not everything was razed, but most. The earlier author's hyperbole aside, however, the two accounts agree closely.[30] Archaeology gives much the same picture. Excavations on the Akropolis, in the lower city, and elsewhere in Attica have shown both the thoroughness and severity of the sack and that some few walls survived.[31]

Diodoros of Sicily reports that, on the approach of Xerxes' armies across Thrace in the spring of 480, the Greek allies took counsel together on the Isthmos and swore an oath:

11.29.3. οὐ ποιήσομαι περὶ πλείονος τὸ ζῆν τῆς ἐλευθερίας, οὐδὲ καταλείψω τοὺς ἡγεμόνας οὔτε ζῶντας οὔτε ἀποθανόντας, ἀλλὰ τοὺς ἐν τῇ μάχῃ τελευτήσαντας τῶν συμμάχων πάντας θάψω, καὶ κρατήσας τῷ πολέμῳ τῶν βαρβάρων οὐδεμίαν τῶν ἀγωνισαμένων πόλεων ἀνάστατον ποιήσω, καὶ τῶν ἱερῶν τῶν ἐμπρησθέντων καὶ καταβληθέντων οὐδὲν ἀνοικοδομήσω, ἀλλ' ὑπόμνημα τοῖς ἐπιγινομένοις ἐάσω καὶ καταλείψω τῆς τῶν βαρβάρων ἀσεβείας.

I will not set life before liberty, nor will I desert my leaders alive or dead. I will bury all allied troops who die in the battle, and, if I defeat the barbarians in the war, I will not raze to the ground any of the cities that fought against them, and I will not rebuild any temple that has been burnt and destroyed, but I will let them be and leave them as a memorial of the sacrilege of the barbarians.[32]

The ancient tradition on the oath is among the most tangled and confusing of any from the Persian Wars. It is mentioned by neither Herodotos nor Thucydides, but first in the 4th century, and sources are by then of two minds. Theopompos of Chios draws attention to the oath as one of several events from the Persian Wars that 4th-century Athens was then

[30] On their relation, Gomme 1945, p. 257. Herodotos had, in fact, himself noted a standing wall several chapters earlier, 5.77.3, apparently in reference to the Akropolis North Wall.

[31] On the Persian Destruction, see Kavvadias and Kawerau 1906, cols. 23–32 *et passim*; H. A. Thompson, *The Tholos of Athens and Its Predecessors* (*Hesperia* Supplement 4), Princeton 1940, pp. 29–33; *Agora* XIV, p. 20; Noack 1927, p. 93. Survivals include several stretches of the Mycenaean circuit wall of the Akropolis; the ruins of the Old Temple of Athena, including a stretch of the peristyle with full entablature; and the Temple of Dionysos Eleutherios. For the Mycenaean circuit, see Iakovidis 1983, pp. 79–82; Old Temple of Athena, Paton 1927, pp. 447–452; Temple of Dionysos, E. Fiechter, *Das Dionysos-Theater in Athen*, Stuttgart 1935–1936, I, pp. 11–12; III, pp. 66–68; Kalligas 1965 (note 2 above, p. 42), p. 14; Boersma 1970, no. 55, p. 189.

[32] Trans. Meiggs 1972, p. 504.

falsifying and exploiting to political ends. As later cited by Theon, Theopompos (*Philippica*, Book 25) states that

> <ὁ> Ἑλληνικὸς ὅρκος καταψεύδεται, ὃν Ἀθηναῖοί φασιν ὀμόσαι τοὺς Ἕλληνας πρὸ τῆς μάχης τῆς ἐν Πλαταιαῖς πρὸς τοὺς βαρβάρους, καὶ αἱ πρὸς βασιλέα Δαρεῖον Ἀθηναίων <καὶ> Ἑλλήνων συνθῆκαι. ἔτι δὲ καὶ τὴν ἐν Μαραθῶνι μάχην οὐχ οἵαν ἅπαντες ὑμνοῦσι γεγενημένην, καὶ ὅσα ἄλλα, φησὶν, ἡ Ἀθηναίων πόλις ἀλαζονεύεται καὶ παρακρούεται τοὺς Ἕλληνας.
>
> The Hellenic oath which the Athenians say the Hellenes swore before the battle at Plataia is falsified as is the treaty of the Athenians and the Hellenes with King Darius. And furthermore, he says the battle at Marathon was not what everyone keeps repeating it was, and "all the other things that the city of the Athenians brags about and uses to dupe the Hellenes."[33]

Theopompos excepted, the earliest sources on the Oath of Plataea are all Attic, and as Theopompos indeed implies, the tradition of the oath is unusually fluid, reshaped from occasion to occasion. The tradition first appears to have come alive around the mid-4th century, perhaps prompted by its quotation in the *Inquiries* of Ephoros, completed *ca.* 340.[34] One can trace the trail no earlier. The *Panegyrikos* of Isokrates, composed *ca.* 380 B.C., recalls the Persian destruction of Greek sanctuaries and singles out the *Ionians* for an oath not to rebuild their temples (4.156), presumably a reference to the Persian sack of Greek cities in Asia Minor after the Ionian revolt of 499. The Ionian oath is attested nowhere else in ancient literature, and scholars have wondered whether Isokrates may simply be confused.[35] Confused or not, however, his silence is highly significant. There can have been at that time no living memory of the Athenians themselves having sworn such an oath.

The earliest extant text of the Oath of Plataia is in a speech by Lykourgos against Leokrates (*Leok.* 81) dating from *ca.* 330. The Lykourgan version has one provision unknown to Diodoros, "and I will tithe all the cities that have sided with the barbarians,"[36] but is otherwise close in phrasing, an apparent sign that both depend on Ephoros.

A stele from the Attic deme of Acharnai gives a third and final version of the oath.[37] Set up in the sanctuary of Ares and Athena Areia in or around the third quarter of the 4th century, it records the Plataian Oath together with the Ephebic Oath, sworn by Attic youths on coming of military age.[38] The stele is graphic evidence of how important was the Plataian Oath in the ideology of late 4th-century Athens, like the Ephebic Oath an exemplar of piety and nobility in war. Equally important, however, it shows how malleable was its tradition. Unlike the Ephebic Oath of the stele, closely in agreement with manuscript versions, the Plataian Oath is broadly reshaped. The texts of Diodoros and Lykourgos refer

33 Text and trans. based on Connor 1968, p. 78.

34 Ephoros was almost certainly Diodoros' source. See R. Drew, "Diodoros and His Sources," *AJP* 83, 1962, pp. 383–392.

35 See Meiggs 1972, p. 505.

36 Cf. Herodotos (7.132) who records a similar pledge before Thermopylai; Diodoros (11.3) locates this latter pledge on the Isthmos but says it was sworn some half-year before the Plataian Oath.

37 L. Robert, *Études epigraphiques et philologiques*, Paris 1938, pp. 302–316; Tod 1948, II, no. 204, pp. 303–307; G. Daux, "Serments amphictioniques et serment de Platées," in *Studies Presented to David M. Robinson* II, St. Louis 1953, pp. 775–782.

38 On the ephebeia, see Rhodes 1981, pp. 493–495.

to allies and Medizers collectively, never to individual cities. The stele records an oath ὃν ὤμοσαν Ἀθηναῖοι, "sworn by the Athenians," and continues καὶ νικ[ή]σας μαχόμενος τοὺς βαρβάρους δεκατεύσω τὴν Θηβαίων πόλιν, "and having fought and defeated the barbarians, I will tithe Thebes,"[39] and again καὶ οὐκ ἀναστήσω Ἀθήνας οὐδὲ Σπάρτην οὐδὲ Πλαταιὰς οὐδὲ τῶν ἄλλων πόλεων τῶν συμμαχεσαμένων οὐδεμίαν, "and I will not attack Athens, Sparta, or Plataia nor any one of the other allied cities." Beyond these differences in wording are yet more glaring discrepancies in the very composition of the oath. The fifth pledge of the literary version, to leave the destroyed sanctuaries of the Greeks as a memorial to impiety, is omitted from the stele, and several new lines are added at the end: a pledge that "I will not leave an allied city to starve in siege, nor will I cut it off from fresh water, be it friend or foe," and a concluding set of curses, both seemingly adapted from the age-old oath of the Amphiktyonic League.

Besides the literary and epigraphical evidence on the oath, there is a substantial body of archaeological and architectural evidence, above all from Athens and the Attic countryside. The excavation of the Athenian Agora in particular has clarified the nature and scope of public works at Athens in the decades after the Persian invasion. The rebuilding of the Agora began with a few essential civic structures in the 470's, notably the Bouleuterion and the Heliaia, and continued with new works in the 460's, the Stoa Poikile, the Tholos, and new walks and gardens.[40] Throughout this time the cult sites of the Agora lay in ruins: the temenos of the Twelve Gods and the altar of Aphrodite Ourania were first restored in the late 5th century, and the Agora's major civic cult of Apollo, first in the 4th century.[41] The years from 479 to mid-century show no rebuilding of cult sites whatsoever.[42]

Scholars early in this century nearly all judged the Oath of Plataia a fabrication, citing Isokrates, Theopompos, and the silence of 5th-century sources. The weight of archaeological evidence has gradually effected a shift, however, with now increasing voices for the alternative: that the oath was real; that the Athenians abrogated it in the middle years of the 5th century, leaving its tarnished memory to fade; and that it was discovered and publicized a century later by Ephoros. Theopompos charges Athens not with forging or fabricating events, at

39 Cf. Polybios 9.39, where Thebes is again mentioned alone.

40 *Agora* XIV, p. 20.

41 H. A. Thompson, "Buildings on the West Side of the Agora," *Hesperia* 6, 1937 (pp. 1–224), pp. 222–223; Crosby 1949, p. 98; *Agora* XIV, pp. 133–134 (Altar of the Twelve Gods), pp. 136–137 (Apollo Patroos); T. L. Shear, Jr., "The Athenian Agora: Excavations of 1980–1982," *Hesperia* 53, 1984 (pp. 1–57), pp. 24–40 (Altar of Aphrodite Ourania).

42 Scholars skeptical of the oath have countered this evidence with two building projects attested in literary sources: the Temple of Athena at Plataia, built from spoils of the Battle of Plataia (Plutarch, *Arist.* 20.3), and the telesterion at Phlya, restored by Themistokles (Plutarch, *Them.* 1.3). Neither carries serious weight against the archaeological evidence. The passage on the Temple of Athena has been thought a variant on a story better recorded by Pausanias (9.4.1): the dedication of the sanctuary of Athena Areia from spoils of the Battle of Marathon. To judge from the artists employed, Pheidias for the cult statue, Polygnotos for a set of murals, the project may conceivably date from after Athens' renunciation of the oath. For Polygnotos' murals in the Pinakotheke at Athens, presumably late work by the artist, Pausanias 1.22.6. Numerous scholars have located the temple in the second quarter of the 5th century. So W. Gauer, *Weihgeschenke aus den Perserkriegen* (*IstMitt* Beiheft 2), Tübingen 1968, pp. 98–100. But cf. G. Becatti, *Problemi Fidiaci*, Milan 1951, p. 175 (after 450). It has been suggested that the telesterion at Phlya, as a private sanctuary, did not come under the oath; so Meiggs 1972, p. 506.

least not explicitly, but with falsifying them to her own ends.[43] "The battle of Marathon was not what everyone keeps repeating it was," he accuses. The "falsification" of the Oath of Plataia appears of the same cloth. The stele from Acharnai indeed shows this exactly, a document edited and recast for Athenian ends, even to the omission of the long-renounced temple clause.

Given the archaeological record, the mere realization that the written sources on the oath admit of its authenticity is important. It is the more noteworthy that two scholars have carried the argument further. Peter Siewert has shown that the language and phrasing of the oath have their closest parallel in oaths of the Late Archaic period.[44] Such phrasing is foreign to 4th-century fabrication, which often researched the historical context of a document but had little ear for style. And second, Russell Meiggs has made clear how incongruous the oath would be as a forgery.[45] It was viewed with pride in 4th-century Athens, a testament to the city's resolve and valor. Yet all could see that the temple clause had been broken. The oath has the gray tones of an authentic tradition, not the glow of a propaganda piece. The observations of these two scholars weight the scales yet farther toward the genuineness of this tradition.[46]

The first written evidence for the major rebuilding of shrines at Athens comes in the middle years of the 5th century, beginning with the Parthenon (447–432).[47] To uphold the oath, one has also to confront the issue of its abrogation. So uncomplimentary an action as abrogation is unlikely to have been widely remembered, at least in local sources. There does appear to be one relevant document however, the so-called Congress Decree, quoted in Plutarch's *Life of Pericles* (17.1). The decree records Athens' plan to meet with delegates of the Greek states and deliberate:

[43] See especially Connor 1968, pp. 79–89.

[44] Siewert 1972, pp. 17–45, 109–110. Siewert is judging the oath overall, not specifically the temple clause, whose authenticity he doubts.

[45] Meiggs 1972, p. 505.

[46] The following scholarship has taken the oath as genuine: A. Raubitschek, "The Covenant of Plataea," *TAPA* 91, 1960, pp. 178–183; N. G. L. Hammond, *Classical Age of Greece*, New York 1975, p. 95; M. Ostwald, *Autonomia*, Chico, Cal. 1982, pp. 18–21, with special reference to the treatment of Thebes. Against: see reviews of P. Siewert, *Der Eid von Plataiai*, Munich 1972, L. Robert, *REG* 86, 1973, pp. 91–92; A. Dreizehnter, *Gnomon* 47, 1975, pp. 379–383; and N. D. Robertson, "The True Nature of the Delian League (II)," *AJAH* 4, 1979 (pp. 110–133), pp. 117–119.

[47] Note that there have been frequent attempts, some very well argued, to date other Attic temples before the Parthenon. Most important is the Hephaisteion, thought to have been begun in the 450's. Excavations in the foundations of the Hephaisteion make clear that it is the first temple on the site, and some have reasoned that it does not transgress the oath. It is unclear whether the cult itself existed in 480. On the date of the Hephaisteion, see Dinsmoor 1941, pp. 150–160; Wyatt and Edmondson 1984, pp. 159-161. Compare Coulton 1984, I, pp. 40–44, II, pp. 368–369. Coulton sets the start of work after 447. The Older Parthenon, commonly dated to the 480's, is placed by some in the 460's, e.g., Carpenter (1970) and Bundgård (1976, pp. 14–22, 54–83). Cf. the reviews of W. B. Dinsmoor Jr., *AJA* 75, 1971, pp. 339–340, and H. A. Thompson, *AJA* 82, 1978, pp. 256–258. On a pre-Persian date for the "Kimonian Telesterion" at Eleusis, see T. L. Shear, Jr., "The Demolished Temple at Eleusis," in *Studies in Athenian Architecture, Sculpture, and Topography Presented to Homer A. Thompson* (*Hesperia* Supplement 20), Princeton 1982, pp. 128–140. W. B. Dinsmoor, Jr. (1971, pp. 37–51) argued a date after 450 for the Temple of Athena at Sounion.

... περὶ τῶν Ἑλληνικῶν ἱερῶν, ἃ κατέπρησαν οἱ βάρβαροι, καὶ τῶν θυσιῶν ἃς ὀφείλουσιν ὑπὲρ τῆς Ἑλλάδος εὐξάμενοι τοῖς θεοῖς ὅτε πρὸς τοὺς βαρβάρους ἐμάχοντο, καὶ τῆς θαλάττης, ὅπως πλέωσι πάντες ἀδεῶς καὶ τὴν εἰρήνην ἄγωσιν.

... on the problem of the Greek temples which the barbarians had burnt, the sacrifices which they still owed on behalf of Greece in fulfilment of the vows made to the gods when they fought the barbarians, and the sea, that all should sail in security and maintain the peace.[48]

The congress never did take place. Plutarch says that "Sparta was beginning to be bothered by the growing power of Athens" (ἀρχομένων δὲ Λακεδαιμονίων ἄχθεσθαι τῇ αὐξήσει τῶν Ἀθηναίων) and refused to join. Sparta and Athens were strong allies in the aftermath of Salamis and Plataia. They first came to part ways in the Third Messenian War (464–459), a split that widened when Kimon, Sparta's ally at Athens, was ostracized in 461, and Perikles rose to power in his place. Following Plutarch, a few scholars have been inclined to see the Congress Decree as one of the first initiatives of the new democratic regime.[49] The text of the decree itself, however, above all its reference to the "problem of the Greek temples burnt by the barbarians," rather indicates a date close to the inauguration of the Periclean building program in the early 440's.[50] Peace with Persia, just concluded or possibly renewed at mid-century, gave adequate pretext for abrogating the Plataian Oath.[51] The Congress

48 Translation based on Meiggs 1972, p. 153.

49 A. Schmidt, *Das Perikleische Zeitalter* I, Jena 1877, p. 47; U. von Wilamowitz-Moellendorff, *Aristoteles und Athen*, Berlin 1893, II, p. 340, note 15. The view, rare in traditional scholarship, was revived by Walsh 1981, pp. 31–63.

50 So H. T. Wade-Gery, "The Question of Tribute in 449/8 B.C.," *Hesperia* 14, 1945 (pp. 212–229), pp. 222–224; cf. Gomme 1945, pp. 366–367; Meritt, Wade-Gery, and McGregor 1950, III, pp. 279–281; Meiggs 1972, pp. 512–515. Robin Seager has argued that the Congress Decree is a fabrication, its text laced with 4th-century usages and ideology ("The Congress Decree: Some Doubts and a Hypothesis," *Historia* 18, 1969, pp. 129–141; also A. Bosworth, "The Congress Decree: Another Hypothesis," *Historia* 20, 1971, pp. 600–616). Meiggs's treatment (1972, pp. 512–513) by no means rejects this argument out of hand. That scholar is concerned to point out, however, as indeed we have seen at first hand with the Oath of Plataia, that ancient tradition rarely transmits such texts *verbatim*. The anachronisms of the Congress Decree, as equally the Themistokles and Arthmios Decrees, do not of themselves establish forgery. It is difficult to imagine someone fabricating the tradition of the congress. The initiative was neither a success nor in any dramatic sense a failure; it never got underway. Who then gained from the fiction? On this, see Meiggs 1974, p. 514; G. Griffith, "A Note on Plutarch *Pericles* 17," *Historia* 27, 1978, pp. 218–219; B. MacDonald, "The Authenticity of the Congress Decree," *Historia* 31, 1982, pp. 120–123.

51 On the Peace of Kallias, see Wade-Gery 1940, pp. 121–156 (= 1958, pp. 201–232); Meiggs 1972, pp. 129–151. Two scholars have argued that there was a negotiated peace with Persia already in the 460's: Walsh 1981, pp. 31–63; and E. Badian, "The Peace of Callias," *JHS* 107, 1987, pp. 1–39. Badian argues that an initial peace was negotiated by Kimon with Xerxes *ca.* 463, and that, long lapsed, it was revived with Artaxerxes at mid-century. It is unclear whether this scholar considers the Congress Decree authentic. Note, at any rate, that the context of the decree given by Plutarch, ignored in the traditional mid-5th-century dating of the decree, is equally incompatible with Badian's chronology. If the decree is an initiative of the 460's, as Plutarch implies, it ought by Badian's scenario to have been the work of Kimon, not Perikles. The issues, however, are complex, while the date of the Congress Decree is nowhere key to our argument. In advance of the further scholarship that will surely come on these issues, I have held to the traditional chronology.

Decree attests the hope for a broad endorsement of that abrogation. When the congress fell through, Athens proceeded on her own.[52]

IG I[3] 35: THE NIKE TEMPLE DECREE

The inscription is from the obverse of an opisthographic stele found in 1897 on the north slope of the Akropolis.[53] The upper edge of the stone is dressed to receive a crowning block, apparently a relief, now missing.[54] The text reads:

[– – – – – – – – – – ἐπρυτάνευε] *on the upper stone*
[ἔδοχσεν τε͂ι βολε͂ι καὶ το͂]ι̣ [δέ]μ̣ο̣[ι· . . .]
[. . . 7 . . . ἐπεστάτε, Γλ]α̣ῦ̣χος εἶπε· [τε͂ι]
[᾿Αθεναίαι τε͂ι Νί]κ̣ει *h*ιέρεαν *h*ὲ ἂγ[κλ]-
[ερομένε λάχε]ι ἐχς ᾿Αθεναίον *h*απα[σο͂]-
[ν καθίστα]σθαι καὶ τὸ *h*ιερὸν θυρο͂σα-
ι καθ᾿ ὅ τι ἂν Καλλικράτες χσυγγράφσ-
ει· ἀπομισθο͂σαι δὲ τὰς πολετὰς ἐπὶ τ-
ε͂ς Λεοντίδος πρυτανείας. φέρεν δὲ τ-
ὲν *h*ιέρεαν πεντέκοντα δραχμὰς καὶ
τὰ σκέλε καὶ τὰ δέρματα φέρεν το͂ν δε-
μοσίον· νεὸν δὲ οἰκοδομε͂σαι καθ᾿ ὅ τι
ἂν Καλλικράτες χσυγγράφσει καὶ βο-
μὸν λίθινον.
*h*εστιαῖος εἶπε· τρε͂ς ἄνδρας *h*ελέσθ-
αι ἐγ βολε͂ς· τούτος δὲ μετ[ὰ] Καλλικρά-
[το]ς χσυγγράφσαντας ἐπ[ιδεῖχσαι τε͂]-
[ι βολ]ε͂ι καθ᾿ ὅ τι ἀπομ[ισθοθέσεται . .]
[. . . 6 . . .]ει το σ – – – – – – – – – – – – – – – – –
– –[55]

[Prytany of – – – – – – – – – –] [. . . . .] [Resolved by the Boule and the demos, ... 10 . . . . presided, Gl]aukos so moved: that a priestess of [Athena

[52] On the abrogation of the oath and the Attic building program, first Bates 1901, pp. 319–326; revived by Dinsmoor 1941, pp. 156–158.

[53] EM 8116, Kavvadias 1897, cols. 173–194.

[54] So *IG* I[2] 24 (F. Hiller von Gaertringen); Schlaifer 1940, pp. 257–259; Boegehold 1969, pp. 175–180; *IG* I[3] 35 (B. D. Meritt and M. McGregor). Cf. Dinsmoor (1923, pp. 319–320), who argued that the text continued considerably above the joint, the preserved lines being rather an amendment to a main decree above; so also Meritt 1941, pp. 307–315; Meritt and Wade-Gery 1962, pp. 109–111.

[55] Text based on *IG* I[3] 35. It is likely but not certain that Leontis was in the prytany at passage of the decree. See Boegehold 1969, p. 179. For line 2, Tod 1946, I, no. 40, p. 79. Line 3, Φαλ]α̣ι̣κός is a possible alternative to Γλ]α̣ῦ̣χος; see Meiggs and Lewis 1969, no. 44, p. 108; Boegehold 1969, pp. 179–180. For lines 4–6, see Meritt and Wade-Gery 1962, p. 110.

> Ni]ke be established, to be [chosen by lot] from among all Athenian women, and that doors be built to close the sanctuary, the specifications to be set by Kallikrates. The *poletai* shall let the contract in the prytany of Leontis. Give the priestess a salary of fifty drachmas and the legs and hides of public victims. And build a temple, the specifications to be set by Kallikrates, and an altar of worked stone.
> Hestiaios so moved. Three men are to be chosen from the Boule. They are to draw up specifications with Kallikrates and [to present them to the Boule], with the work to be let accordingly [– – – –].

Like the other documents of this chapter, the Nike Temple Decree is here interpreted in its own right, independent of its possible relation to the architecture of the Nike Bastion. I return to the architectural context of the decree, specifically whether the temple commissioned in lines 12–13 is the Stage III naïskos or the amphiprostyle temple, in Chapter 9.

IG I³ 35 appears to date to the mid-5th century, as indicated by its letter forms and as supported as well by the attested career of Kallikrates, the architect for the project. The mason used developed Attic letters, including rounded beta, developed rho, and phi with extended vertical, with a single exception, the older three-barred sigma. Dated inscriptions from 454/453 B.C. attest phi with extended vertical, and from 453/452 rounded beta and developed rho. The last dated inscription with three-barred sigma is 447/446.[56] The few extant sources on Kallikrates fit well with these dates. Plutarch states that he was contractor for the Middle Wall, built soon after 450, and that he served jointly with Iktinos as architect of the Parthenon, begun in 447.[57] Finally, an inscription, its letter forms roughly contemporary with those of the Nike Temple Decree, entrusts Kallikrates with design of a short stretch of Akropolis fortifications.[58]

The Nike Temple Decree gives twofold evidence: its enactments are explicit testimony of intended changes in the cult and also implicit evidence on the state of the sanctuary at the time the decree was passed. The latter, the more elusive, requires particular attention. The phrase τὸ *h*ιερὸν θυρõσαι, "to fit the sanctuary with doors," is appropriate to, and in normal usage only to, a sanctuary that was then open. If the sanctuary already had doors, semantic logic requires that the relation of new and old be made clear: for example, "to repair the doors," "to replace the doors," "to make a second doorway," etc.[59] By the same token, the phrase νεὸν δὲ οἰκοδομε͂σαι . . . καὶ βομὸν λίθινον, "to build a

[56] Phi with projecting vertical, *IG* I³ 259; rounded beta and developed rho, *IG* I³ 260; three-barred sigma, *IG* I³ 265. See Meiggs 1966, pp. 91–98.

[57] Plutarch, *Per.* 13.5. On the date of the Middle Wall, see Gomme 1945, pp. 312–313; Meiggs 1972, p. 188. For the chronology of the Parthenon project, see Dinsmoor 1921, pp. 233–247; Burford 1963, pp. 23–35.

[58] *IG* I³ 45. For the text, p. 64 above; the inscription belongs by letter forms *ca.* 450–445; see note 74 above, p. 64.

[59] Compare a decree concerning a 4th-century repair of the Sanctuary of Asklepios, *IG* II² 1046, lines 14–18: καὶ διὰ τοῦτο παρα|καλεῖ τὴν βουλὴν ἐπιχωρῆσαι ἑατῶι κατασκευάσαντι ἐκ τῶν|ἰδίων θυρõσαι τὸ ἀρχαῖον πρόπυλον, στεγάσαι δὲ καὶ τοῦ|προπύλου τὸ ὀπίσωι μέρος καὶ τὸν ναὸν τὸν ἀπέναντι τῆ[ς]|εἰσόδου χάριν τοῦ τὴν ἀρχαίαν ἀποδοθῆναι τῶι ἱερῷ τάξιν.

temple and altar of worked stone," addresses a sanctuary with no altar of worked stone (there may perhaps have been a simple altar of rubble or mud brick) and no temple.[60] It appears that the Nike cult was then of rudimentary form, a modest altar in an unwalled shrine.

With the existing state of the bastion in mind, the thrust of the Nike Temple Decree becomes far more clear. No mere reworking or renewal, it appears to raise the cult from the ground. The sanctuary is to be fenced in and is to have a temple and a new-built altar. And the cult, served by some other official, the priestess of Athena Polias perhaps, is henceforth to have a priesthood of its own.[61]

[60] A number of epigraphers have taken *lithinos* to mean "marble" in Attic inscriptions, not the broader "worked stone". Note, however, that the ancients differentiated stones not by geological category, limestone versus marble, but by the location of the quarry: *lithos Pentelikos*, *lithos Hymettios*, *Eleusinaikos*, *Aiginaios*, etc. See R. E. Wycherley, "Penteletheh," *BSA* 68, 1973, pp. 349–353; *idem*, "Poros: Notes on Greek Building-Stones," Φόρος: *Tribute to Benjamin D. Meritt*, D. W. Bradeen and M. F. McGregor, eds., Locust Valley, N.Y. 1974, pp. 179–187; *idem*, *The Stones of Athens*, Princeton 1978, pp. 267–279. Cf. the specifications for the arsenal of Philo, *IG* II² 1668: the document is titled [σ]υνγραφαὶ τῆς σκευοθήκης τῆς λιθίνης, with the building stones then differentiated within. The walls and columns are of Peiraeus limestone (᾽Ακτίτου λίθου); the column capitals and the lintels of the doors of Pentelic (λίθου Πεντελη̈κοῦ); the thresholds of Hymettian (λίθου ῾Υμηττίου); and the door jambs of Pentelic or Hymettian (λίθου Πεντελη̈κοῦ ἢ ῾Υμηττίου).

As noted by Bundgård (1974b, p. 47, note 5), the phrase ἀναγράψαι ἐν στήληι λιθίνηι, common at the close of Attic inscriptions, orders that the text be inscribed on stone as distinct from the rarer bronze or less permanent whitened board.

On the condition of the sanctuary at passage of the decree compare Kavvadias 1897, col. 181, ᾽Εκ ταύτης δηλ. μανθάνομεν ὅτι τὸ ἱερὸν τῆς Νίκης ἐν τοῖς χρόνοις καθ᾽ οὓς ἐξεδόθη τὸ ψήφισμα τοῦτο ἐν κακῇ διετέλει καταστάσει. ῾Η μὲν εἴσοδος αὐτοῦ ἐστερεῖτο θυρωμάτων, ὁ δὲ βωμὸς δὲν ἦτο λίθινος· θα ἦτο, ὡς φαίνεται, πρόχειρόν τι κατασκεύασμα ἐκ πλίνθων ἢ ἐκ κοινῶν ἀκατεργάστων λιθαρίων καὶ χώματος. Dittenberger (*Syll.*³, no. 63, p. 77) comments, "Fuit igitur iam ante medium saeculum quintum in occidentali et meridionali arcis angulo delubrum Minervae Victoriae, sed simplicissimum, sine templo, sine porta, ara ex terra aut caespitibus modo composita, sine sacerdote." He adds on *lithinos* (p. 78), "Adiectivum indicat fuisse quidem iam antea aram, sed non lapideam." Hicks and Hill 1901, no. 37, p. 61: "At the time when the decree was passed, there existed only a primitive shrine, or probably even a mere altar of ashes, dedicated to the worship of Athena Nike." Prott and Ziehen 1896–1906, II, i, no. 11, p. 49: "Ceterum hoc testimonio nihil dubii relinquitur, quin iam ante templum aedificatum fanum ᾽Αθηναίας Νίκης fuerit quamvis parvum et modestum—carebat enim ara lapidea nec foribus claudebatur."

The phrasing of the decree may be partially or wholly dependent on historical and legislative issues now lost to us. For example, several architects may have competed for the project, with the phrase νεὸν δὲ οἰκοδομε͂σαι καθ᾽ ὅ τι ἂν Καλλικράτες χσυγγράφσει acknowledging the winner. The phrase would then tell nothing about the presence or absence of any previous structure. With regard to λίθινος, perhaps several materials were being considered for the altar, with stone the final choice. I think both my examples are strained, but they may show that semantic inference of this type can, at best, strongly indicate, not prove.

[61] The inscription is an important document on the democratization of religion in 5th-century Athens. Traditional aristocratic priesthoods were confined to a single clan; see Feaver 1957, pp. 123–159; Garland 1984, pp. 77–80. For the restoration *hè* ἂγ [κλερομένε λάχε]ι (lines 4–5), compare the epitaph of Myrrhine, the first priestess of Athena Nike, discussed pp. 111–113 below. A few scholars have argued that the decree rather reorganizes an existing priesthood than creates one anew: Schlaifer 1940, p. 259; B. Jordan, *Servants of the Gods* (*Hypomnemata* 55), Göttingen 1979, pp. 32–33; Garland 1984, pp. 90–91. The ancients tended to reorganize religious practices by adding to them or setting up parallel procedures, not by suspending the old. I

Of final note is how closely the project is to be supervised. A time limit is set for letting the contracts, and as moved by Hestiaios, the Boule is to collaborate with Kallikrates on the design. The former provision appears intended to speed the project,[62] and that may well be the aim of the latter as well. The one known parallel to the amendment of Hestiaios is an amendment to an Athenian decree of 446/445 concerning Chalkis, *IG* I^3 40, lines 64–69, the appointment of three members of the Boule to work with a seer in sacrificing victims. The Chalkis decree makes clear that time was of the essence. The sacrifices are to be made ὁς τάχιστα, and the board is to see that there is no delay.[63]

IG I^3 36: DECREE ON THE SALARY OF THE PRIESTESS

The inscription is carved on the reverse of the Nike Temple Decree.

a. 424/423

ἔδοχσεν τε̃ι βολε̃ι καὶ το̃ι δέ-
μοι· Αἰγεὶς ἐπρυτάνευε, Νεοκ-
λείδες ἐγραμμάτευε, ῾Αγνόδε-
μος ἐπεστάτε, Καλλίας εἶπε· τ-
ε̃ι *h*ιερέαι τε̃ς ᾿Αθενάας τε̃ς Νί-
κες *v* πεντήκοντα δραχμὰς τὰ-
ς γεγραμμένας ἐν τῆι στήλ[ηι]
ἀποδιδόναι τὸς κωλακρ[έτας],
οἳ ἂν κωλακρετῶσι το̃ Θ̣[αργηλ]-
[ιῶ]νος μηνός, τῆι ἱερ[έαι τῆς ᾿Α]-
θην]αίας τῆς Νίκη[ς . . . . 8 . . . .]
— — — — — — — — — — — — — — — —[64]

know of no parallel for so changing a priesthood. Be that as it may, the view strains the natural sense of lines 4–6 of the Nike decree and tortures the epitaph of Myrrhine.

62 The designated tribe, Leontis, either was then in the prytany or, if the decree was passed in the ninth prytany, may have been the final, tenth tribe; see Meritt 1941, p. 311. The time provided to let the contracts is at most some ten weeks. Compare the timetable for the repair of the Akropolis walls, *IG* I^3 45 (p. 64 above), to be let so that work could be completed within sixty days.

63 The boards appear to function essentially as subcommittees, created in part to act in place of, in part to prepare the work of the parent body. It is notable that just two such boards are attested, and within at most a few years of each other. They are in each case set up in an amendment, not in the main body of the decree, which only underlines the marginal status of the procedure. They appear to have been an innovation that never took hold. On the Nike board as intended to speed the project, Bundgård 1976, p. 169. Hiller considers that it may have been to amend or alter the work (*IG* I^2 24, p. 14); Mattingly (1982, p. 385) that it may be at least partly due to the size and complexity of the undertaking.

64 Text based on *IG* I^3 36. The text is inscribed in two hands: lines 1–6 ending at the blank space are in Attic script and are rigorously stoichedon; the remainder is in Ionic, on a shifted letter grid. The blank space has the traces of a pi and carved directly over, an alpha, both *in rasura.* Compare, however, Meiggs and Lewis 1969, no. 71, p. 204 where the traces are read as 𐅄, the numerical symbol for fifty.

> Resolved by the Boule and the demos, the tribe of Aigeis held the prytany, Neokleides was secretary, Hagnodemos presided, Kallias so moved: the *kolakretai* in office in the month of Thargelion shall pay the priestess of Athena Nike the fifty drachmas inscribed on the stele. . . .[65]

The decree is dated by its secretary, Neokleides, also secretary for *IG* I³ 75, a treaty between Athens and Haliai; *IG* I³ 36 and 75 are thus from the same prytany, the same year. The latter text has been shown to belong in the fall or winter of 424/423 on historical grounds.[66]

IG I³ 36 is in the nature of a rider to the Nike Temple Decree, long delayed.[67] The enactment itself is clear, that the priestess be paid her designated salary by certain officials at a certain time, but too little is known of the context of the decree to be certain of its purpose. Some have thought that it reaffirms or strengthens the earlier decree, with the idea that the priestess' salary was not being paid or was paid irregularly.[68] Alternatively it may modify the earlier decree, changing the officials by whom she is paid, the time of year, or both.

IG I³ 64A: DECREE ON A PROJECT FOR THE NIKE SANCTUARY

The inscription is from the obverse of an opisthographic stele found in 1921 built into a stair at the base of the North Akropolis Wall.[69] Broken above, below, and at right. The line width is uncertain. A few passages of the text appear most easily restored with a line width of thirty-seven letter spaces, and I have followed earlier editors in adopting this width. The text can be dated by its lettering roughly 440–415.[70]

[. . . 7 . . .] ̣ εια[. . . . . 25 . . . . τ]-
[ὸν δε͂μ]ον διαχ[ειροτονε͂σαι . . . . 15 . . . .]
[. . .] ἒ ἐλέφαντο[ς . .]ν̣ ε̣ [. . . . . 18 . . . .]
[. . .] δόχσει ταῦτα ἔναι καθό[τι ἂν . . . . . 11 . . . . .]
[. . .]αι τε͂ι θεο͂ι καὶ ᾿Αθεναίο[ν. . . . 10 . . . . τὸν δ]-
ὲ [βο]λόμενον γράφσαντα ἀποδ[εῖχσαι . . . 8 . . .]
δ̣[έ]κα ἑμερο͂ν ἐπειδὰν δόχσει [. . . 6 . . μὲ ἒλαττο]-
ν ἒ πεχ[υ]αῖον. γραφόντον δὲ ἀπ[αγγέλαντες πρὸς]
τ[ὸ]ς ἐπ[ι]στάτας· ἑ δὲ βολὲ μὲ α[. . . . . . 15 . . . .]
[. .]νκ[. .]θει̣ [. . . 6 . . .]τοπ̣ [.]τ[. . . . . . 15 . . . .]

[65] For the repetition of the dative, see B. Keil, *Anonymus Argentinensis*, Strassburg 1902, p. 319.

[66] Meritt and Davidson 1935, pp. 65–71; A. B. West, "Prosopographical Notes on the Treaty between Athens and Haliai," *AJP* 56, 1935, pp. 72–76; Wade-Gery 1940, pp. 127–132 (= 1958, pp. 207–211). The evidence has been cautiously reviewed by D. M. Lewis, *Sparta and Persia*, Leiden 1977, pp. 76–77.

[67] On such riders, Meritt and Wade-Gery 1963, p. 69, in reference to *IG* I³ 71, lines 54–58 (425/424).

[68] Tod 1946, I, p. 178; Meiggs and Lewis 1969, p. 204.

[69] Pogorelski and Hiller von Gaertringen 1922, pp. 187–192; Pogorelski 1923, pp. 314–317; Dinsmoor 1923, pp. 318–321.

[70] Meiggs 1972, p. 501. Cf. F. Hiller von Gaertringen, *IG* I² 88/89, where the inscription is grouped with decrees from 421–404; D. M. Lewis, *IG* I³ 64, *ca.* 430–420. My text is reworked from *IG* I³ 64.

[. .]νο[. ᾿Α]θ̣εναί[ον] καὶ τõν χσυμ[μάχον . . . . 9 . . . .]
[. . .]ο[. . . .]ερ̣[. . 5 . .]ο ἀρχιτέ[κτο . . . . . 12 . . . . .]
[.]εισ[. . . 7 . . .]ες ἐν τε̃ι πρότ[ει . . . . . 13 . . . . .]
[. . . . 10 . . . . τ]ον δρυφακτο[ν. . . . . . 15 . . . . . .]
.[. . . . 11 . . . .]ν̣ φσέφισμ[α. . . . . . . 16 . . . . . .]
ζέσθο [καὶ κατε]ργασάσθο [ὁς κάλλιστα. περὶ δὲ τ]-
[õ] μισθõ αὐτõι *h*ε βολὲ *h*ε νέ[α μετά τε τõν ἐπιστα]-
τõν καὶ τõ ἀρχιτέκτονος [προβόλευμα ἐχσενεγ]-
κέτο ἐς τὸν δε̃μον. τούτον [δὲ . . . . . 13 . . . . . ἐπ]-
ιμελόσθον *h*οι ἐπιστάται [. . . . . . 16 . . . . . .]
[.]α[.] τὸ ἀρχαῖον ἄγαλμα ἐπ[. . . . . . 15 . . . . . . Νί]-
κες *h*ος κάλλιστα ἀργύρι̣[ον . . . . . . 15 . . . . . .]
ο τε̃ς θεõ *h*όθενπερ ἐς το[. . . . . . . 18 . . . .]

vacat

This decree is tied to the Nike Sanctuary by the restoration Νί]κες in lines 21–22 and by the mention of the Nike Temple (τὸν νεὸν τε̃ς Νίκες) in line 36 of the reverse, I³ 64B. The surviving text is too fragmentary to recover *verbatim*, but one may follow the general sense at least. Lines 2–5 call for the demos to vote on the materials to be used in a project, whether ivory or one or more alternatives now lost. Lines 5–9 arrange an open contest for the design. Drawings must be not less than a foot across and must be submitted within ten days with prior notification of the board of supervisors. The text then becomes more difficult to recover. Lines 9–11 appear to treat the judging of the contest. The Boule is to consult the Athenians and the allies and only then is to proceed. Line 12 mentions an architect and line 14 a grille or barrier. Lines 15–19 provide for the execution of the project. It is to be made to the finest standards in accord with the vote, and the Boule of the following year is to consult with the supervisors and the architect and to submit a proposal on funding to the Ekklesia. Next comes the mention of an ancient image (line 21), an intriguing fragment whose restoration is perhaps the most debated of any in the inscription. Early editors restored the text from the Erechtheion accounts, believing the image to be the ancient cult statue of Athena Polias. Lines 19–21 were made to read:

τούτον [δὲ χσυμπάντον συνεπ]-
[ι]μελόσθον *h*οι ἐπιστάται [τõ νεὸ τõ ἐμ πόλει ἐν]
[*h*õι] τὸ ἀρχαῖον ἄγαλμα.[71]

The board of supervisors for the temple on the Akropolis that houses the ancient image is to join in overseeing all this.

Soon after this restoration was published, the stone was cleaned of some last remaining mortar and a new letter was revealed: the second checker of line 21 is an alpha, not, as had been restored, an omikron. The third edition of the *IG* has reworked the text to fit the new reading:

[71] Pogorelski 1923, p. 316; Hiller von Gaertringen *loc. cit.*

τούτον [δὲ . . . . . . 13 . . . . . ἐπ]-
ιμελόσθον *hοι* ἐπιστάται [τõ ἀρχαίο νεὸ ἐν *hοι*]-
[κ]α[ί] τὸ ἀρχαῖον ἄγαλμα.

These . . . are to be seen to by the board of supervisors for the ancient temple in which is also the ancient image.

The restoration, though not impossible, is strained by the intrusive *kai* of line 21, with a resulting title for the Erechtheion without parallel either in the Erechtheion accounts or in any other document on that building. *IG* I^3 skirts the question of this highly important passage.

The inscription refers three times to the supervisors of the Nike project. The first two times (lines 9 and 17–18), they are called simply *hoi epistatai* without further qualification. To restore a full title at the third mention is to distinguish the final *epistatai* as a separate board: the design of the project and matters of payment are to be supervised by one board, with part or all of the work to be then overseen by the board for the Erechtheion. A board of supervisors was normally answerable to the Demos directly, or to the Boule acting in its stead.[72] To involve others from a wholly different project is without parallel in the history of public building at Athens and is patently illogical. The alternative is to refer line 21 not to the image of Athena Polias but to the *xoanon* of Athena Nike.[73] We have seen that there was a cult image in the sanctuary already in the second quarter of the 6th century, the image on the Stage I cult-statue base, and have found that the sources on the famed *xoanon* of Athena Nike are consistent with a statue of this early date. This statue, saved from the Persian Sack, could well have been termed *archaion* in a document of the later 5th century.

When one equates the *archaion agalma* with the *xoanon* of Athena Nike, lines 19–22 fall readily into place. Restored before as one long clause, the lines appear now to encompass three: the main clause [ἐπ]ιμελόσθον *hοι* ἐπιστάται; a subordinate clause introduced by *hό*πος, to be restored at the start of the lacuna on line 20; and a genitive absolute, beginning the sentence at line 19. The subordinate clause had τὸ ἀρχαῖον ἄγαλμα as its subject, directly preceded by the verb, with part of its third person singular passive ending preserved in the late-recorded alpha of line 21. The lacuna on line 21 ought then to be a participial phrase beginning with ἐπί. It may help now to take the sentence in order, without however trying to fill all of its still considerable gaps. The sentence begins along the lines of, "Once these things are done" or "agreed", that is, with a retrospective statement bearing on the previous provisions of the decree. It continues, "the board of supervisors is to see to it that the ancient statue is . . . in the . . . of Nike as beautifully as possible." The decree then concludes with a provision on funding.

It remains to relate the decree to the architecture of the sanctuary, on which see pp. 138–140 below.

IG I^3 64B: ACCOUNT OF EXPENDITURES FOR THE NIKE TEMPLE

IG I^3 64B is a building account on the reverse of the stele for *IG* I^3 64A. The line width depends on the line width of the obverse and is thus probable but not certain.

[72] P. J. Rhodes, *The Athenian Boule*, Oxford 1972, pp. 124–127.
[73] So Paton 1927, p. 454, note 1.

The carving is a different hand than *IG* I^3 64A but appears generally comparable in date, *ca.* 440–415.[74]

\- -
[..............31..............]'Αθ[ενα.] Στοιχ. 37?
[.............28............. ἐ]π̣ὶ τὸ α[. . .]
[.............28.............] χρυσὸς ἐ[ον]-
[έθε ....20......... τ]ὰ καλύμμα[τα]
[............26............] χρυσίο τιμ[έ .]
[.........18......... προσεδέ]εσεν ἐς ἐπισ[κε]-
[υὲν ....21.........] τιμὲ τούτο [. . . .]
[..........20.......... προ]σεδέεσεν χρ[υσιο]
[..........20.......... χσ]ύλον ὀνε͂ς ἐς τὲ[ν . .]
[..........21..........]ΔΔΔΔⱵⱵⱵⱵII· ὀνε[. . .]
[........17........ μι]σθομάτον το͂ν ἄλλο[ν . .]
[.........18.........ΧΧ𐅅ΗΗΗ𐅄ΔⱵⱵⱵⱵIII[. . . .]
[........17........] ἐς τὸν νεὸν τε͂ς Νίκες [. . .]
[........16........] ΔΔΔⱵⱵIIIC.
vacat

The account records expenditures "for the Nike Temple" (line 36). There is mention of gold (lines 26, 28), coffer covers (line 27), and wood (line 32); an account of supplementary purchases "for repairs" (lines 29–30) and apparently also for gold (line 31); a sum for "other contracts" (lines 34–35); and a concluding total (lines 36–37). Lines 33, 35, and 37 preserve the remains of numbers, all missing their initial digits. The middle figure, the best preserved, was at least 2,864 drachmas, 3 obols, and may have been considerably more. The final number appears to have been the sum total for the account.

EPITAPH FOR THE PRIESTESS OF ATHENA NIKE

The epitaph is on a low stele (H. 0.98 m.), found near the modern Athenian suburb of Zographou at the western foot of Mt. Hymettos.[75]

Καλλιμάχο θυγ|ατρὸς τηλαυγὲ|ς μνῆμα <τόδ' ἐστίν>,
ἣ πρώτη | Νίκης ἀμφεπόλ|ευσε νεών.
εὐλο|γίαι δ' ὄνομ' ἔσχ|ε συνέμπορον, ὡ|ς ἀπὸ θείας
Μυρ|ρίν<η ἐ>κλήθη συ|ντυχίας ἐτύμω|ς:
πρώτε 'Αθηναί|ας Νίκες ἕδος ἀ|μφεπόλευσεν
ἐ|κ πάντων κλήρω|ι Μυρρίνη εὐτυ|χίαι.[76]

[74] On the difference in hands and their general contemporaneity, see Pogorelski and Hiller von Gaertringen 1922, p. 192; Dinsmoor 1923, p. 320. My text is based on *IG* I^3 64.

[75] EM 13,132; *SEG* XII 80; Papademetriou 1951, pp. 146–153.

[76] For τόδ' ἐστίν, see line 1, see Kakridis 1952–1953, pp. 143–145. The addition evens the meter, with the whole thus formed of three elegaic couplets. For the correction, line 4, Lewis 1955, p. 1.

This distinguished grave is for Kallimachos' daughter,
Who first tended the temple of Nike.
Her name was a companion of her repute, called
Myrrhine truly by the luck of the gods.
She first kept the shrine of Athena Nike,
Fair-fated Myrrhine, picked by lot among all.

This epitaph greatly furthers our knowledge of the priesthood of Athena Nike, otherwise attested for the period only by the Nike Temple Decree. It gives the name of the first priestess, Myrrhine, the name of her father, Kallimachos,[77] the manner of her selection, by sortition from among all (physically qualified) Athenian women,[78] and some idea of her age and length of time in office. The epitaph dates from the later 5th or early 4th century on epigraphical criteria, most importantly, the lettering and the confusion of the Ionic and Attic alphabets.[79] The decade 425–415 may serve as a firm upper limit, with the weight of epigraphical opinion rather pointing toward a date around 400 B.C.[80]

The epitaph establishes that, at very least, Myrrhine was in office around twenty-five years. If appointed as a maiden, a common practice,[81] she would have been around forty or forty-five years of age at the earliest likely date of her marker in 425 B.C. If she lived to the turn of the century, she would have been a stately sixty or sixty-five.[82] That the latter date may in fact be correct has found support in a close rereading of Aristophanes *Lysistrata*, performed in 411. As argued by David M. Lewis, Lysistrata, leader of the women's revolt, and her supporter Myrrhine parody respectively the priestess of Athena Polias and the Priestess of Athena Nike.[83] The association explains the strong religious overtones of the play and both characters' unexpected familiarity with their Akropolis setting.

77 Possibly the Kallimachos known to have been archon in 446/445 (Diodoros 12.7)

78 Taken as the basis for restoring *IG* I³ 35, lines 4–5: *hὲ* ἂγ̣ [κλερομένε λάχε]ι. See Meritt and Wade-Gery 1962, p. 110.

79 The Atticisms come toward the close of the text: epsilon rather than eta in πρώτε and Nίκες, line 5; and the apparent uncertainty over eta in line 4, as inscribed: Μυρρίνε ἠκλήθη. On vestiges of Attic in Ionic texts, L. Threatte, *The Grammar of Attic Inscriptions*, I, *Phonology*, Berlin 1980, pp. 49–51.

80 Papademetriou 1951, p. 146 (late 5th or early 4th century); Kakridis 1952–1953, p. 143 (around 400); Lewis 1955, p. 1 (could be as early as 420, but appears *ca.* 400). Clairmont (1979, pp. 103–110) has pointed to seemingly identical lettering on the epitaph of Myrrhine and the well-known lekythos of Myrrhine, NatM 4485, and proposed that both are from the same grave. The lekythos was found under Syntagma Square, apparently from a cemetery just outside the ancient city wall. The stele is from the countryside some 3 km. distant. Clairmont suggests that the latter may have been carried from the city in reuse. The stele, however, is intact and in excellent condition, with no trace of mortar or recutting. It appears to have lain in the soil undisturbed since antiquity. Even if the lettering on the two monuments is in fact by the same hand, as Clairmont suggests, this does not of itself join the two memorials. Nor is the shared name Myrrhine, relatively common in Attica, a noteworthy tie. The two monuments are best kept apart. One study accepts that one memorial was set up in Zographou, the other at the city walls, but continues to maintain with Clairmont that both are for the same person: Rahn 1986, pp. 195–207. I question Rahn's thesis that the figure of Myrrhine depicted on the lekythos bears attributes of the priesthood. Her bracelet and diadem are simple badges of her wealth, inappropriate for mourning *per se* but right for her journey to the underworld.

81 On the appointment of youths to the priesthood, see Garland 1984, p. 85.

82 Compare the priestess of Hera at Argos who served $56\frac{1}{2}$ years (Thucydides 2.2.1; 4.133). Also note 84 below, p. 113 on Lysimache.

83 Lewis 1955, pp. 2–12.

The priestess of Athena Polias was in fact named Lysimache in the late 5th century, not Lysistrata.[84] Aristophanes may have altered the name for a theatrical purpose, now obscure, or perhaps because Lysimache had recently died, so as not to defame her.[85] That Myrrhine is called by name makes clear that she, at least, was still living.

IG II² 403: REPAIR OF A STATUE OF ATHENA NIKE

IG II² 403 is formed of two joining fragments, the second badly split and battered. Of its 33 preserved lines of text, the first 2 and final 14 are beyond restoration. I give lines 3–19:

[.........21.........]ς· τῶν [προέδ]-
[ρων ἐπεψήφιζε ....8....]ς ἐκ Κε[ρ]αμέ[ω]-
[ν.......15.......]ς [Λα]κιάδης [εἶ]πε[ν]·
[περὶ ὧν οἱ ἡιρη]μένοι ὑπὸ τοῦ δήμ[ο]υ λ[έ]-
[γουσιν ἐπὶ τὴν] ἐπισκευὴν τοῦ ἀγά[λ]μα-
[τος τῆς Ἀθηνᾶ]ς τῆς Νίκης ἣν ἀνέ[θ]εσαν
[Ἀθηναῖοι ἀπὸ] Ἀμπρακιωτῶν κα[ὶ τῆ]ς ἐν
[Ὄλπαις στρατ]ιᾶς καὶ τῶν ἐπαν[αστ]άντ-
[ων τῶι δήμωι τ]ῶι Κερκυραίων [καὶ ἀπ'] Ἀν-
[ακτοριῶν, δεδ]όχθαι: τῆι βο[υλῆι] :·:
[...προσ]αγ[αγ]εῖν αὐτοὺς εἰς [τὸν δῆ]μον
[....8....]ε[ἰ]ς τὴν πρώτην ἐκκ[λησί]αν [κ]-
[αὶ χρηματί]σαι, γνώμην δὲ ξυμ[βάλ]λεσ[θ]-
[αι τῆς βουλ]ῆς εἰς τὸν δῆμον [ὅτι δ]οκε[ὶ]
[τῆι βουλῆι π]ερί τε τῆς θυσία[ς τῆ]ι θε[ῶι]
[θῦσαι τὴν ἱέρε]ιαν τῆς Ἀθηνᾶς τὸ ἀρε[σ]-
[τήριον ὑπὲρ τοῦ δ]ήμου.[86]

Of the presiding board, . . . of the deme of Kerameis called the vote. . . . son of Lakiades so moved. Concerning the report of the committee of the demos on the restoration of the statue of Athena Nike dedicated by the Athenians from the spoils of the Ambraciots and the army in Olpai, the insurrectionists at Korkyra, and the Anaktorians: the Boule counsels that the people call the committee before it . . . in the first Ekklesia and deliberate the matter. And add the Boule's resolution to the demos on the sacrifice to the goddess, that the priestess of Athena should make the propitiatory offering on the people's behalf.

The inscription appears to date from the period of Lykourgan reforms, *ca.* 338–326, a time of widespread renewal and rebuilding at Athens.[87] The official attention given the repair and the heightened concern about propitiating the gods suggest a statue of more than ordinary importance. Lykourgos undertook to replace or restore a number of works

[84] Pliny, *HN* 34.76, Demetrius Lysimachen quae sacerdos Minervae fuit LXIIII annis.

[85] On the stemma of the priesthood of Athena Polias, see Lewis 1955, pp. 1–12. Lewis argues that Lysimache in fact lived into the early 4th century.

[86] Text, J. Kirchner, *IG* II² 403.

[87] F. W. Mitchel, "Lykourgan Athens," *Lectures in Memory of Louise Taft Semple*, 2nd ser., 1966–1970 (*University of Cincinnati Classical Studies* 2), Norman, Okla. 1973, p. 205. Cf. Sokolowski 1962, no. 35, pp. 68–69.

of precious metal, including several Golden Nikai and the gold and silver *pompeia* of the goddess.[88] The Nike may have been of comparable value.

At repair, the statue was around a century old. The spoils from which it is made are from the sixth and seventh years of the Archidamian War: the victory over the Ambraciots and the recovery of Olpai took place in the winter of 426/425 (Thucydides 3.108, 111); the defeat of the revolutionaries on Korkyra and the occupation of Anaktorion in summer 425 (Thucydides 4.46, 49). There is record of two Golden Nikai dedicated in 426/425, also in apparent celebration of war victories.[89] The Athena Nike may have been dedicated as early as the following year, or like some other memorials of the period, first in the closing years of the Archidamian War or in the Peace of Nikias.[90]

On the view that *IG* II^2 403 refers not to an image of Athena Nike but to the cult image itself, see p. 123 below.

88 Account of expenditures for the Golden Nikai and gold processional vessels, *IG* II^2 1493+1494+ 1495 (334/333), F. W. Mitchel, "Demades of Paeania and *IG* II^2 1493, 1494, 1495," *TAPA* 93, 1962, pp. 213–229; *idem*, "*IG* II^2 1493: Corrigenda," *AJA* 70, 1966, p. 66. Decree honoring Lykourgos, *IG* II^2 457 (307/306), [Plutarch], *Vitae 10 orat.* 852B; Pausanias 1.29.16.

89 *IG* I^3 468.

90 Compare the Nike of Paionios at Olympia, whose inscription states it to be from war spoils, undoubtedly spoils of the Archidamian War (cf. Pausanias 5.26.1). Judged by style, it was first executed *ca.* 420. See T. Hölscher, "Die Nike der Messenier und Naupaktier in Olympia," *JdI* 89, 1974, pp. 70–111; Meiggs and Lewis 1969, no. 74, pp. 223–224.

IX

THE NIKE TEMPLE DECREE AND THE ARCHITECTURAL STAGES OF THE NIKE SANCTUARY

Having discussed in turn the physical and written evidence on the history of the Nike cult, it remains to bring these two bodies of evidence together. Previous scholarship has never attempted a comprehensive correlation of texts and material evidence, but one problem at least has been repeatedly addressed: the place of the Nike Temple Decree in the history of the Nike cult. Over generations of study there has grown up the firm opinion that the temple commissioned in the Nike Temple Decree is the amphiprostyle Nike Temple, our Stage IV. We have devoted this chapter to a review of this lengthy history of scholarship and to a reconsideration of the problem in light of our findings on the sanctuary.

The weight of modern opinion that associates the Nike Temple Decree with the amphiprostyle temple may be seen to rest on two largely independent lines of scholarship: first, the debate concerning the relative dates and histories of the Nike Bastion and the Propylaia, issues first raised in the 1870's with the demolition of a massive Frankish tower that overbuilt the Southwest Wing and that had largely hindered investigation of the site; and second, scholarship on the Nike Temple Decree, discovered in 1897. It is sufficient to note two early studies in the first category, an article of 1876 by Leopold Julius on the plan of the Southwest Wing[1] and Furtwängler's treatment of the date of the Nike Temple in *Meisterwerke*.[2]

Concerned to explain the acanonical plan of the Southwest Wing, newly revealed with the removal of the Frankish tower, Julius formulated a theory that would be oft-repeated in discussion of the site. He argued that the Southwest Wing had been originally designed on the dimensions of the Pinakotheke but that construction was halted and the lines of the wing were redrawn in deference to ongoing work on the Nike Sanctuary.[3] It was Furtwängler who laid the foundations for the modern chronology of the Akropolis building program, establishing the place of the Nike Sanctuary after the Propylaia and before the Erechtheion. He suggested a date for the Nike Temple after 426 B.C. While Furtwängler rejected the argument that the Nike project itself could have forced a change in the Propylaia, he nonetheless seized on Julius' thesis, reworking it as a conflict not about projects *per se* but about the very conduct and ideology of the building program: the radical plans of Perikles, champion of the Propylaia, against the conservatives, guardians of the Nike cult.[4]

The discovery of the Nike Temple Decree in 1897 suddenly added an epigraphical dimension to the bastion problem. Kavvadias was attentive to the letter forms of the decree and placed it *ca.* 450. He ignored Furwängler's dating of the temple, however: in his view

[1] Julius 1876, pp. 216–228.
[2] Furtwängler 1893, pp. 207–222.
[3] Julius 1876, pp. 216–228.
[4] Furtwängler 1893, pp. 209–210; Furtwängler 1898, I, pp. 380–390.

the decree and the Nike Temple followed one another in close succession. Others, however, were soon to face the problem of the decree more squarely, notably Alfred A. Körte, who in a short study of 1910 set out what was to become the established understanding of the problem.[5] Convinced of Furtwängler's date for the Nike Temple, and thus confronted with a delay of some twenty-five years from the Nike Temple Decree to the actual execution of the project, he proposed to extend the idea of conflict in the building program back to the 440's. He read the Nike Temple Decree as a stalled initiative of the conservatives, its progress checked by Periclean plans for the Propylaia; the project was at last pushed through after construction of the Southwest Wing, as the conservatives regained their political stature late in the Archidamian War. Körte thought to find dramatic confirmation in a new restoration of the mover of the Nike Temple Decree, [Hipponi]kos. He identified Hipponikos as Hipponikos son of Kallias, a nephew of Kimon, and proposed that the Kallias who moved the Decree on the Salary of the Priestess, *IG* I^3 36, was Hipponikos' son. The house of Kallias was thereby seen to have had a strong family tie to the cult, the son having attended to the long-unfinished plans of his father.[6]

Körte's thesis stood at the forefront of bastion scholarship for close to half a century, reworked and embellished but in essentials unchanged. We may single out two prominent contributions. In 1916 Studniczka proposed that plans for the stalled Nike Temple had been used instead for the Ilissos Temple, thus the closely related plans and near identical elevations of the two temples.[7] This thesis was then completed by Dinsmoor, who suggested that the plan of the Nike Temple, modeled on the plan of the Ilissos Temple minus the pronaos and with a shorter cella, had resulted from the encroachment on the territory of the Nike Sanctuary by the Southwest Wing.[8] New epigraphical and historical research also lent strength to Körte's theory, notably work on *IG* I^3 36 by Meritt and Davidson in 1936 and a study on the Peace of Kallias by Wade-Gery in 1940. The accepted date for *IG* I^3 36, *ca.* 424/423, was fixed by Meritt and Davidson in research on an Athenian treaty with Halieis, *IG* I^3 75, enacted under the same secretary as *IG* I^3 36, that is, during the same prytany.[9] At some point in the same administrative year belongs a decree in honor of Herakleides of Klazomenai, *IG* II^2 8, a decree which in turn dates a treaty between Athens and Persia, an apparent renewal of the Peace of Kallias. It was for Wade-Gery to integrate these findings with the history of the Nike Sanctuary.[10] The Kallias whose son Körte restored as mover of the Nike Temple Decree was the leader of an Athenian embassy to Susa in 450 or 449, the man for whom the so-called Peace of Kallias is named. The identification of the Kallias of *IG* I^3 36 (424/423) as son of Hipponikos, grandson of Kallias, thus appeared to be reinforced by the parallel relations of *IG* I^3 35 and 36 to peace with Persia. "It [*IG* I^3 36] is doubtless consequent on the news of the Treaty, being a renewal of 24 [*IG* I^3 35] which itself was doubtless consequent on the news of the Treaty with Artaxerxes."[11]

5 Körte 1910, pp. 623–627.
6 *Ibid.*, pp. 626–627.
7 Studniczka 1916, p. 230.
8 Dinsmoor 1950, p. 186.
9 Meritt and Davidson 1935, pp. 65–71.
10 Wade-Gery 1940, pp. 121–156 (= 1958, pp. 201–232).
11 Wade-Gery 1940, p. 130 (= 1958, p. 209).

The evidence for Körte's thesis, part architectural, part epigraphical, had by Wade-Gery's day been so widened and reworked that it was difficult to comprehend in its entirety. In fact, a close look at the history of the problem shows that, as the thesis was being elaborated from one side, it was already unraveling from the other. Consider first the architectural arguments for the thesis. Julius' view that the Southwest Wing had been curtailed in mid-construction was prompted first by the anomalous plan of the wing, the awkward meeting of its north façade, an exact mirror of the Pinakotheke, and the south wall, positioned not at the outer corner of the north façade but one column in (Fig. 17). He and other early scholars were convinced that Mnesikles would never have planned the wing that way unconstrained, and they proceeded to isolate architectural details that seemingly substantiated the idea that the project was abruptly altered. Julius noted that the southwest anta of the Southwest Wing was inclined forward, implying a now-missing column or door post to the west.[12] The wing appeared to have been partly built as if it were to have the same depth as the Pinakotheke but had been abruptly shortened. The poros first step of the krepidoma of the Southwest Wing on the west appeared to reinforce this view. Julius thought that it was originally the covered underpinning for the stylobate, recut to form an exposed step at the shortening of the wing.[13] Bohn's excavations of 1880 put these theories to rest. The foundations for the Southwest Wing were seen to turn a corner just beneath the southwest anta. There was no major revision from foundations to upper structure.[14]

Although the specifics of Julius' thesis had been refuted, the idea that the plan of the Southwest Wing had been radically altered was reaffirmed by a succession of later scholars, each time on new evidence. Wolters was the first to reopen the question, noting that a restoration of the northern stair to the bastion in eight even steps brought the stair landing, not even with, but a half riser (*ca.* 0.10 m.) above the Nike Sanctuary paving.[15] Wolters saw this as confirming a planning change. He reasoned that the Nike Bastion must have been started before the Southwest Wing, with its sheathing originally built one course (0.30 m.) higher than presently preserved, perfect in level for a flight of nine steps; at the construction of the Propylaia, the bastion was lowered a course, with the match of stair and bastion coursing thus destroyed.

Wolters' views on the stair were a matter of debate for several decades. In 1911 Dörpfeld revived the idea of an eight-step stair, noting that the eighth step would come 0.10 m. above the level of the sanctuary paving, just to the level of the Nike Temple euthynteria. He suggested that the sanctuary paving and the bastion crown were originally intended to be at the level of the temple euthynteria, but that they were lowered 0.10 m. to accord with the level of the Southwest Wing. The northern stair was left with its landing a half-step above the sanctuary paving, and 0.10 m. of the Nike Temple euthynteria were left exposed.[16]

[12] Julius 1876, pp. 219–220. Julius considers the anta to have been originally a door post; cf. Bötticher 1864, pp. 41–72. Dörpfeld (1885, pp. 42–45) argues that it was planned as an anta from the start, meant to align with the end column of a western colonnade.

[13] 1876, p. 223.

[14] Bohn 1880a, p. 267.

[15] Wolters 1890, pp. 92–101.

[16] W. Dörpfeld, "Zu den Bauwerken Athens," *AthMitt* 36, 1911 (pp. 39–72), pp. 55–60.

Dörpfeld's theory was then revised by Welter in 1923.[17] Welter noted that the western euthynteria of the Nike Temple was worked in one piece with the bastion crown. To lower the level of the sanctuary, one would have to cut these crown-euthynteria blocks down. Yet as Welter observed, the blocks do not look recut. The contact band of anathyrosis along the top of the blocks has the same width as at the sides; one would have expected the band at the top to be thinner if it were cut down. And also the complex molding along the edge of the crown, a cyma reversa crowned by a fascia and thin ovolo, appears fully original and unaltered. Welter accepted that the level of the sanctuary was lowered 0.10 m., but he located the change before rather than after the laying of the combined western euthynteria and bastion crown. He reasoned that the bastion project had been halted with only the eastern euthynteria of the temple in place.

The long-standing problem of the stair was finally resolved by Wrede in a detailed study of 1932.[18] Wrede observed how illogical it would have been to lay the euthynteria on the east side of the temple before laying it on the west. One would expect the builders to start at the fixed line of the western bastion face and to work eastward. Left to explain the form of the stair, Wrede argued compellingly that like the euthynteria, it too had been built unaltered. He restored a stair of eight steps, the top step with full height on the exterior and half-height on the interior, as appropriate to a sill.

Wrede's study calmed rather than ended scholarship on the putative curtailment of the Southwest Wing.[19] It is important, however, for refuting the last of the proposed technical and archaeological evidence on the problem. If there was a change in plan, it left no trace in either the substructures of the Southwest Wing or the walls and paving of the bastion.

As the archaeological side of Körte's thesis was giving way, the epigraphical too was coming under renewed scrutiny. In 1924 Dinsmoor reexamined the Nike Temple Decree and saw the restoration *H*ιππ[όνικος to be in error. Körte had recorded three complete letters and the remains of a fourth: kappa, omikron, and sigma at the end; and the lower tip of a vertical stroke before them, iota as he restored it, alternatively tau, upsilon, or phi. Dinsmoor observed the corner of a fifth letter, the diagonal stroke of an alpha or gamma. The traces fit not Hipponikos, but Γλ]ạῦ̣κος.[20]

The seeming connection between the Peace of Kallias and the Nike cult, stressed by Wade-Gery, rests in large part on Körte's restoration. Wade-Gery knew of Dinsmoor's reading, then in print for several years, and steers clear of the older restoration, but he shapes his thesis as if nothing had really changed. The rebuilding of Attic sanctuaries in the 440's and 430's is tied to the Peace of Kallias, in the sense that it depends on the abrogation of the Oath of Plataia, and the abrogation in turn on reconciliation with Persia. Any more pointed tie between the Nike Temple Decree and the Peace requires other evidence. The identification of Hipponikos son of Kallias as the mover of the decree had seemed to be

17 Welter 1923, pp. 196–201.

18 Wrede 1932, pp. 74–91.

19 A detailed attempt to refute Wrede and reassert the priority of the Southwest Wing came the following year, see Schleif 1933, pp. 177–184. Cf. Schweitzer 1950, pp. 116–125, who returns to the position that the Southwest Wing was curtailed in mid-project.

20 Dinsmoor 1941, p. 159, note 337; first reported by Tod 1933, I, no. 40, p. 79.

just such evidence; with the restoration undone, the tie dissolves. Lost too is a compelling reason to identify the Kallias of the rider, *IG* I^3 36, as Hipponikos' son. Even if this later Kallias were descended from the major architect of the mid-century treaty with Persia, the fact that Kallias, grandson of Kallias, moved a bill in the same administrative year that the Peace was renewed means little of itself. The special tie of the sanctuary to the house of Kallias and to peace with Persia both appear on examination to be illusory.

To lay Körte's theory to rest is not to solve the problem of the Southwest Wing. If the irregular meeting of the north and west façades of the wing, the anomalous southwest anta, and the poros step did not in fact arise in a curtailment of the project, how then are they to be explained? Scholarship in the field of Greek architecture generally, and research on the Propylaia in particular, have tended away from arguments on style and form alone toward greater awareness of the interaction of form, function, and context. That the Propylaia might never have been intended to be symmetrical, unthinkable to Dörpfeld or Bohn, is now well accepted. One has come to appreciate better the range of functions encompassed in the various parts of the Propylaia and the challenge of drawing them into an architectural unity. The Pinakotheke and Southwest Wing, distinct in purpose and history, are made to appear a balanced pair through the false façade of the latter. Recent research on the nature of architectural planning in antiquity further clarifies the anomalies of the Southwest Wing. We earlier found that the poros step and southwest anta of the wing do in fact attest a minor planning change. As discussed in Chapter 7,[21] the west façade of the wing was shifted *ca.* 0.30 m. eastward at the stylobate. The western foundations thus exposed were recut to form a step between the wing and the planned level of the Nike Sanctuary two steps below. One is now less inclined to see this as a sign of conflict between the two projects than as a function of traditional, craftsmanly design practices. The architect appears to have worked without detailed plans and elevations, reworking the design in mid-project as problems emerged.[22]

Finally, the theory, developed first by Dinsmoor,[23] that the plans for the Nike Temple were themselves abridged in mid-project, can also be seen to be mistaken. The uncovering of the Stage III sanctuary makes clear the true starting point in planning Stage IV: the monumental Stage IV altar had to overlie its Stage III predecessor.[24] It is sited as far to the east as possible under this constraint, with its west front passing directly over the westernmost (southwest) corner of the rectangular altar. The Stage IV Nike Temple had then to be accommodated to the area of the bastion west of the altar with its dimensions tightly restricted. The temple plan responds not to any encroachment by the Southwest Wing but to the very limits of the cult site itself. Nor is a putative first plan of the Nike Temple ever likely to have been used for the Ilissos Temple. Studniczka broached that theory on the assumption that the Ilissos Temple and the Nike Temple Decree were contemporary. Research by Miles, however, points to a

21 P. 81 above.

22 Bundgård 1957, pp. 66–75; Coulton 1978, pp. 51–73; *idem*, "Incomplete Preliminary Planning in Greek Architecture: Some New Evidence," in *Le Dessin d'architecture dans les sociètès antiques*, Leiden 1985, pp. 103–121; cf. W. B. Dinsmoor, Jr., "Preliminary Planning of the Propylaia by Mnesicles," in *Le Dessin d'architecture*, pp. 135–147.

23 1950, p. 186.

24 On the positioning of the altar of a sanctuary through successive stages of cult, see Burkert 1985, pp. 87–88.

date for the Ilissos Temple in the 430's.[25] The very underpinnings for Studniczka's theory have thus come into question.

That the seeming evidence for conflict or delay in the execution of Stage IV has gradually proved false does not of itself exclude the traditional reading of the Nike Temple Decree. It does, however, strongly encourage the exploration of alternatives. One such alternative was suggested in 1961 by Mattingly. This scholar argues that the Nike Temple Decree and the Nike Temple are in fact contemporary, not both from the 440's as thought by Kavvadias, but both from the 420's.[26] The three-barred sigma of the decree, commonly thought to establish a mid-5th-century date, is considered by Mattingly rather to be a loose dating criterion, insufficient to outweigh the logic of the later placement.

Mattingly's challenge quickly led epigraphers to reexamine the dating value of 5th-century letter forms in general and the three-barred sigma in particular. In 1965 Meiggs tabulated the forms of the letters in some 65 inscriptions securely dated between 460 and 430 B.C. The three-barred sigma is last attested in 446. The corpus of dated inscriptions from 445 to 431, some 50 texts, all use the later four-barred form.[27] The dating value of the three-barred sigma thus stands confirmed. Beyond this evidence, there is yet a further problem with Mattingly's thesis. The second provision of the Nike Temple Decree, τὸ *h*ιερὸν θυρō̃σαι, appears inappropriate to Stage IV. *Hieron* appears to refer to the sanctuary as a whole, "to fit the temenos with doors."[28] Stage IV, however, was an open sanctuary; neither the north bastion stair nor the western portal of the Southwest Wing were barred. *Hieron* might alternatively mean "temple": "to fit the temple with doors". When cited six lines later in the decree, however, the temple is termed a *neōs* not a *hieron*, and the Stage IV temple was in any event closed by grilles (*phragmata*) not doors (*thurai*).[29] Mattingly's thesis unravels on inspection.[30]

If the Nike Temple Decree in fact belongs *ca.* 450–445, as its letter forms indicate, there remains the possibility that it pertains not to Stage IV but to the preceding Stage III. As observed by Bundgård, the provisions of the decree and the Stage III remains are in close agreement. The naïskos was apparently open and unsecured. Its anta and wall blocks preserve no trace of a door wall or grille. If access to the temple was restricted (and with the cult statue installed it would have to be), then the sanctuary itself must have been closed. The restored plan of Stage III, Figure 13, postulates just such an enclosure footed on the irregular

[25] Miles 1980, pp. 316–322. On the dating of the Ilissos Temple, see note 64 above, pp. 82–83.

[26] Mattingly 1961, pp. 169–171. For elaboration on the thesis, *idem* 1965, pp. 273–281; *idem* 1982, pp. 381–385.

[27] Meiggs 1966, pp. 86–98.

[28] So Kavvadias 1897, col. 178; *Syll.*³ I, no. 63, p. 77; Prott and Ziehen 1896–1906, II, no. 11, p. 49, and others.

[29] On the meaning of *phragma*, p. 139 below.

[30] Note that the incompatibility of Stage IV and the decree bears also on Körte's thesis. There, however, the hypothesized delay of the project and its ultimate accommodation to the Southwest Wing make a discrepancy from commission to execution understandable. Meiggs and Lewis (1969, p. 111) offer another way around the problem. The first-mentioned project in the decree, τὸ *h*ιερὸν θυρō̃σαι, refers in their view to work to be begun immediately, at the Stage III level; νεὸν δὲ οἰκοδομε̃σαι, to work planned for some time in the future. The matter is reconciled in both cases by assuming a delay from the commission of Stage IV to its execution.

trapezoidal Stage III crown.[31] The phrase "to fit the sanctuary with doors" thus applies to Stage III simply and naturally. The fifth provision of the decree, to build a *neōs* and *bomos lithinos*, appears equally suited to this stage. I have referred to the Stage III temple throughout as a naïskos, the term traditionally given in current scholarship to very small temples. This diminutive, however, is first attested in the Hellenistic period and remains rare.[32] Even the small, one-room Stage III temple was in proper 5th-century usage a *naos*.[33] Finally, the *bomos lithinos* of the inscription goes well with the main altar of the Stage III sanctuary, worked of Aiginetan poros.[34] On only one point do the inscription and the Stage III remains appear at odds. The inscription provides for a single altar in the sanctuary, and Stage III appears to have had two, the main rectangular altar and the square altar to its north. I identified the second block as an altar primarily for its reuse of the inscribed Stage I altar block as underpinning. We may reason, thus, that as successor to the altar of Patrokles, the square altar was under private aegis and not covered by the decree.

As earlier discussed, the Nike Temple Decree is both explicit evidence for a planned renewal of the Nike Sanctuary and implicit evidence on the state of the sanctuary at the time the decree was passed. Epigraphers have consistently interpreted the simple, unqualified provision νεὸν δὲ οἰκοδομε̄σαι to mean that there was then no temple in the sanctuary, and taken βομὸν λίθινον to imply an existing altar of another material, perhaps mud brick or ash. The picture is of a spare, open-air sanctuary suddenly fenced round and reworked in more imposing form. Notwithstanding the date and nature of this renewal, early editors viewed it apart from the Oath of Plataia, whose historicity they doubted. We have reviewed the considerable archaeological evidence that now supports the oath, however, and noted the shift of scholarly opinion in its favor. If we indeed uphold the oath as genuine, then the rebuilding of the Nike Sanctuary *ex nihilo* takes on new significance. It was Wade-Gery who first associated the Nike Temple Decree with the Peace of Kallias. The loss of Hipponikos as mover of the decree loosens that tie, as we have seen, but as one project in the general revival of sacred building at mid-century, all of it dependent on the abrogation of the oath; the equation, if general, still holds. The tie of the Nike Temple Decree to Stage III is yet clearer in this light. Not only do the date and terms of the decree fit the Stage III remains, but the apparent form of the sanctuary at the passage of the decree and the preceding state of the bastion, Stage II, agree closely as well. The Nike Sanctuary survived the Persian Sack as an irregular earthen mound with a simple altar likely of mud brick or ash. The decree implies an unfenced, open-air shrine with an altar built of material other than cut stone.

The Nike Temple Decree and Stage IV are by contrast an awkward match. We have seen the implausibility of downdating the inscription to coincide with Stage IV. At the same time, research has shown the established explanation for a delay between the two, the seeming conflict between the Propylaia and Nike projects, to be unfounded. One is left with an

[31] Several scholars have restored a temenos wall on the Stage III crown, including Welter, Wrede, and Stevens. See note 45 above, p. 56.

[32] Taranto, bilingual dedication to Artemis, *SEG* 30, 1980, no. 1220 (late 2nd century to early 1st century B.C.); Strabo 14.1.14; Josephus, *Antiquitates Judaicae* 8.226.

[33] Cf. Herodotos 2.63, on the Egyptian ritual at Papremis: τὸ δὲ ἄγαλμα ἐὸν ἐν νηῷ μικρῷ ξυλίνῳ καταχεχρυσωμένῳ προεκκομίζουσι τῇ προτεραίῃ ἐς ἄλλο οἴκημα ἱρόν.

[34] On the meaning of *lithinos*, note 60 above, p. 106.

unexplained quarter-century gap between commission and execution. We have further seen that the terms of the decree ill accord with the sanctuary as built: the decree provides for a closed temenos, and Stage IV is open. The language of the decree is equally telling. We have seen that the inscription implies a sanctuary that then had no *neōs* or *bomos lithinos*. The mud-brick expansion, Stage IIIa, meets the latter requirement, but the naïskos is plainly at odds with the former. If the naïskos was standing, intact or even in ruins, when the decree was passed, we would expect the term *neōs* to be qualified in some manner: "to build a new temple", "to build a temple of Pentelic marble". In the absence of any positive evidence that plans for the bastion were delayed, or any significant inconsistency between the decree and Stage III, a tie to Stage IV appears strained and unwarranted. The decree accords simply and economically with the Stage III sanctuary and with that stage alone.

X
THE ARCHITECTURAL HISTORY OF THE SANCTUARY: CONCLUSIONS

In this final chapter we summarize our most important findings on the archaeology and history of the sanctuary and give a general account of the development of the cult site from the 6th through the 5th centuries.

THE CULT STATUE OF ATHENA NIKE

Our study has revealed that two joining blocks, long known, served originally as part of the base for the cult statue of the Nike Sanctuary. The blocks preserve the plinth cutting for the cult statue virtually intact and substantially further our knowledge of that image. The form of the plinth establishes that the statue was of marble and was seated. The tooling of the base suggests a date around 600–560 B.C.

Heliodoros and Pausanias know of a cult statue of Athena Nike highly venerated in their day. Both call the statue a *xoanon* and note that it is *apteros*, "wingless", unlike normal images of Nike. According to Heliodoros, the statue held a pomegranate in the right hand, a helmet in the left.

The new evidence on the cult statue of Athena Nike generated by our study leads to a basic question: is the statue known to Pausanias and Heliodoros the same as the statue that stood on the newly identified Archaic base? Did the Archaic statue survive the Persian Wars?

Some scholars have equated the *xoanon* of Pausanias and Heliodoros with a statue of Athena Nike attested by an inscription, a statue dedicated as a tithe from victories in the sixth and seventh years of the Archidamian War, 426–425.[1] They suggest that this image was made expressly to serve as a cult image in the amphiprostyle Nike Temple, our Stage IV. Having come to a closer understanding of the stages and chronology of the Nike Sanctuary, we are now in a position to rule this view out, or at least to show it to be highly implausible. Especially relevant is the mid-5th-century date of the Stage III naïskos. This small temple, referred to as a *neōs* in the Nike Temple Decree, was aligned with and centered on the Stage III altar. Its primary purpose was surely to house a cult image. It points to the existence of such an image on the bastion after the Persian Wars and before the amphiprostyle temple.

A second piece of evidence comes from a reexamination of *IG* I³ 64A, a decree concerning a late 5th-century project in the Nike Sanctuary. The decree, dated *ca.* 440–415, makes reference to an *archaion agalma*, an "ancient image". To judge from other occurrences of the word *archaion* in 5th-century inscriptions, the statue of I³ 64A ought to date to the Archaic period or earlier. Editors of the inscription have identified the statue as the cult statue of

[1] For the *xoanon*, pp. 93–98 above; *IG* II² 403, pp. 113–114 above. The two are associated first by Furtwängler 1893, p. 211. Dohrn 1957, p. 21; Travlos 1971, p. 149; and Jeffery 1980, pp. 1237–1238.

Athena Polias, termed *archaion* in the Erechtheion accounts, and indeed the oldest and most venerable image of the city. In a close review of the text, we found this established reading to lead to an awkward restoration of the *archaion agalma* clause, lines 19–21, and to strain the sense of the text as a whole.[2] The knowledge that there was a cult statue in the Nike Sanctuary in the Archaic period encourages a different reading: that the *archaion agalma* of the inscription is the cult image of Athena Nike herself.

Before we attempt the direct association of the Archaic cult image of Nike and the *xoanon* mentioned by Heliodoros and Pausanias, we need to consider how well the respective evidence on the two accords. Heliodoros states that the *xoanon* held a pomegranate in the right hand, a helmet in the left. Would these attributes be appropriate to the apparent date of the Stage I base, 600–560? Attributes first become common in Attic sculpture in the early 6th century, and the pomegranate is among the first attested. The two attributes of the statue, one in each hand, give it a relatively complex iconography for this early period, but again there are good parallels. Compare, for example, a statue of Delian Apollo by Tektaios and Angelion (a bow in his right hand, the Charites in his left).[3]

In one respect only are the written sources and the Stage I base potentially at odds. The term *xoanon*, roughly synonymous with "statue" in Heliodoros and other late authors, is used by Pausanias in a narrow and antiquarian sense. He applies it exclusively to statuary carved of wood; the Stage I base held a marble work. We have seen, however, this contradiction to be more apparent than real. That Pausanias relates only others' views about the *xoanon*, without a single firsthand observation, and that he mentions the statue first in Book 3, not when actually at the Nike Bastion in Book 1, suggest that he knew the work at second hand. He appears to have adopted the term *xoanon* unquestioned from his source, perhaps Heliodoros himself.

The body of evidence on the cult statue of Athena Nike, archaeological, epigraphical, and literary, gains strength above all from its internal consistency. A number of sources could of themselves be differently interpreted. Brought together, however, their voice is compelling: the *xoanon* of Athena Nike dates from the foundation of the Stage I sanctuary. Saved from the Persian Sack, it was returned to the bastion in Stage III, installed on a new base in the naïskos.[4] The purpose of the naïskos now becomes clear. It would be a meager shelter for a

[2] Pp. 109–110 above.

[3] Plutarch, *De mus.* 14; cf. Pausanias 2.32.5. Note that Hellenistic reflections show the statue's attributes reversed. The bow is in the left, the canonical hand for this weapon, and the Graces in the right. See *LIMC* II, *s.v.* Apollon, no. 390c–e. Compare also the self-portrait of Theodoros of Samos, a file in the right hand, a miniature quadriga in the left (Pliny, *HN* 34.83). Among extant statuary, note the three-bodied monster from the pediment of the so-called H-Architecture on the Akropolis: Wiegand 1904, pl. IV; Brouskari 1974, fig. 55.

[4] The decision to unseat and transport a marble statue, even a small one, speaks for a planned, orderly evacuation of the city. The transport of the work would have required several men and, most likely, hoisting equipment. Herodotos and the Themistokles Decree, the two main sources on the Athenian evacuation, differ significantly on chronology. The Themistokles Decree places the order to evacuate in the weeks before Thermopylai (Meiggs and Lewis 1969, p. 52), while Herodotos puts it within days of Xerxes' entry into Athens (8.41). The removal of the *xoanon* of Nike would be possible in either case but would be all the more likely with greater warning.

The so-called Endoios Athena, AcrM 625, appears to be another marble work that survived the Persian Wars. It dates from the late 6th century but was found on the north slope of the Akropolis beneath the newly fashioned cult statue. As the provisional shelter for an already existing image, however, its modest form is appropriate and sufficient. Finally, the image was moved from the Stage III sanctuary to the cella of the amphiprostyle temple.

Heliodoros is the one extant Hellenistic source on the statue. On his authority it was still on the bastion in the 2nd century B.C. Conceivably, it was removed by Sulla, among the scores of works he stripped from the city in 84 B.C.[5] We have come to doubt, at any rate, that it was still accessible on the Nike Bastion in Pausanias' day.[6]

Our findings, as they clarify the history of the cult statue, also give new evidence on its appearance. The fragment of Heliodoros has long attested "a wingless *xoanon* holding a pomegranate in the right hand, a helmet in the left." The Stage I base now sharpens this picture considerably: the image was a seated work of marble, under lifesize, dating from *ca.* 580–560 B.C. (cf. Fig. 3).

STAGE I: THE ARCHAIC SANCTUARY

The present study has drawn attention to two previously unrecognized survivals from the Archaic sanctuary: two joining blocks from the base for the cult statue; and an early rebuilding of the bastion crown, the survival from an extensive reterracing of the site. It has also pointed to a stratum from this period, figurines and Archaic black-figured pottery unearthed in the reinstallation of the Stage III altar. These finds considerably broaden the evidence on the early cult, hitherto attested only, if significantly, by an inscribed block from the Archaic altar.

The Archaic sanctuary was unearthed part *in situ* (the stonework along the bastion crown and the early stratum) and part reused (the statue base and the block from the altar). I found the figurines and pottery from the stratum to point to a date between 610 and 480 B.C. The rubble bastion crown dates from around 800–560, judged from its technique; the statue base belongs *ca.* 600–560 by its masonry; and the inscribed altar block, 580–530 by letter forms. These datings span in common the years 580–560, and I have argued the likelihood that the finds are indeed from a single major phase of the cult, our Stage I.

Given how rarely Greek cult statuary was set in the open, and that the *xoanon* of the Nike Sanctuary is known to have been later housed indoors, successively in the Stage III naïskos and the amphiprostyle temple, we may expect that it was set in a temple already in Stage I. A review of the "floating temples" from the Akropolis, building remains unconnected

Erechtheion, not in the Persian debris. Weathered from centuries of exposure, it is commonly thought to have stood on the Akropolis in the Classical period. On AcrM 625, Schrader 1939, no. 60, pp. 109–111; Brouskari 1974, pp. 71–72. On the identification of the statue as the Athena by Endoios seen by Pausanias, G. Dickens, *Catalogue of the Akropolis Museum* I, Cambridge 1912, p. 162.

[5] On Sulla's looting of Athens, see W. S. Ferguson, *Hellenistic Athens*, London 1911, p. 55. Art work carried to Rome, Lucian, *Zeuxis* 3; shields from the Stoa of Zeus, Pausanias 10.21.6; columns from the Olympieion, Pliny, *HN* 36.45; Library of Apellikon, Plutarch, *Sulla* 26.1.

[6] An alternative to the removal or destruction of the statue is that it was actually in the Nike Temple at Pausanias' visit but that for some reason the periegete was not allowed up to the site. We earlier noted that the nearby triple-bodied Hekate was also omitted from Book 1; it appears in the section on Aigina (2.30.2). The Hekate appears to survive in Roman copies, some dating from as late as the second century after Christ (E. B. Harrison, *Archaic and Archaistic Sculpture* [*The Athenian Agora* XI], Princeton 1965, pp. 94–95).

to foundations, yields two structures, known collectively as the A-architecture, appropriate to the Stage I bastion in date and scale.

From its discovery, the inscribed Stage I altar has been taken to mark a major stage in the development of the cult.[7] That the altar carried the name of the goddess, "Altar of Athena Nike", rather suggests that worship of the goddess at that site, or perhaps in that manner, was new and unfamiliar. Perhaps the cult was newly founded or the title of the deity had been altered, as might happen in a major cult reorganization. That Stage I marked just such a turning point is, in fact, dramatically confirmed by this study. Stage I transformed the bastion from a Dark Age ruin to a finished sanctuary. The bastion was reterraced to an even level, a temple and altar were constructed, and a cult image was installed.

The scattered written sources on the early cult history of the Akropolis record only one event from the general period of Stage I: the reorganization of the Panathenaic festival in 566 B.C. A succession of scholars has tried to tie this event to the bastion. Welter suggests that Athena Nike was a patroness of agonistic competition in general and of the Panathenaic Games in particular, citing 4th-century vases that show Nike sacrificing a bull at the conclusion of a torch race, possibly the Lampas of the Panathenaia, and on the testimony of a decree on the Lesser Panathenaia that prescribes the sacrifice to Athena Nike of one of the finest cows of the Panathenaic hecatomb.[8] Raubitschek takes Welter a step further, locating the statue of Panathenaic Athena on the bastion.[9]

A full review of the evidence on the cult casts serious doubt on these views. The attributes of the *xoanon* of Athena Nike, the helmet and pomegranate, show the goddess' primary interests to be military victory and fertility. The martial interests of the cult are strongly affirmed in the decorative program, the battles on the friezes and the pediments of the temple, and the *tropaia* on the parapet. Nowhere is there an allusion to athletics. Literary and epigraphical sources tell the same story: there are prayers to the goddess as protector of fertility, prayers before battle, and dedications of military spoils, but no mention of games.[10] The evidence cited on the Panathenaia pales by comparison. The Nike leading a bull on the vases appears to be merely an artistic motif, borrowed from the Nike Parapet but not intended to allude specifically to the Nike cult. Earlier vases show Nike restraining a bull at a choregic victory, surely without reference to the bastion.[11] We may note that some of the 4th-century vases omit Nike and show instead Eros or one of the torch runners leading the bull. Nike appears to be simply a personification of the torch victory. The assumed significance of the Panathenaic inscription appears equally open to question. The inscription

[7] First by Welter 1939, cols. 12, 14.

[8] *Ibid.*, cols. 11–12; *IG* II² 334, lines 20–21: [θυόντων ταὐ]ύτας τὰς βοῦς ἁπάσας ἐπὶ τῶι βωμῶι τῆς [᾽Αθηνᾶς τῶι με]γάλωι, μίαν δὲ ἐπὶ τῶι τῆς Νίκης προκρί[ναντες ἐκ τῶν] καλλιστευουσῶν βοῶν, καὶ θύσαντες τῆ[ι ᾽Αθηνᾶι τῆι] Πολιάδι καὶ τῆι ᾽Αθηνᾶι τῆι Νίκηι ἁπασῶ[ν τῶν βοῶν. . . . For the vases, see H. Schoppa, "Beiträge zur attischen Vasenmalerei nach Meidias," *AA* 1935, cols. 33–50; H. Metzger, *Les Représentations dans la céramique attique du IVᵉ siècle*, Paris 1951, pp. 351–357.

[9] Raubitschek 1949, pp. 359–364.

[10] Prayer before battle: Euripides, *Ion* 1528–1529; Demosthenes, *Exordia* 54; Themistokles Decree, Meiggs and Lewis 1969, no. 23, lines 38–40; *SEG* XXX 69, lines 9–17. Thank offering for military victory: *IG* II² 403, lines 6–12; *IG* II² 677, lines 4–6. Fertility: Euripides, *Ion* 452–471.

[11] Bologna, Mus. Civ. 286, *ARV*² 1158, E. Pfuhl, *Malerei und Zeichnung der Griechen*, Munich 1923, III, fig. 562; cf. *ARV*² 1123, no. 4.

prescribes a secondary sacrifice not only to Athena Nike but to Athena Hygieia,[12] yet no one has seen the games as central to this third cult. Moreover, it is doubtful that the Panathenaic sacrifice to Nike was of great antiquity. The two altars of the Stage III sanctuary are too small for so major a sacrifice as a cow. It is conceivable, of course, that the Panathenaic sacrifice to Nike was more modest in Stages I–III and was first expanded in IV. Be that as it may, all other sources, artistic, literary, and epigraphical, so consistently point to other cult interests on the bastion that such Panathenaic offerings, if they do indeed go back to the earliest cult, can only have been one among a range of rituals in the sanctuary.

However isolated the Panathenaic reforms of 566 in written testimony on the Akropolis, the Akropolis ruins themselves show that this general period, the second quarter of the 6th century, was one of intense and widespread activity on the citadel. The second quarter of the 6th century saw the Akropolis grow from a relatively modest, little-trafficked site to a major cult center. The first stone temple of Athena dates from these years, preserved in the so-called H-architecture and Lion Pediments, and there are several smaller structures of roughly comparable date, the Red, Herakles, and Olive Tree Pediments. The ancient approach to the Akropolis was replaced by a monumental ramp, and a long line of major dedications begins, such costly votives as the Rambearer and the Pomegranate Kore.

The reforms of 566 must surely have had a major place in this transformation, but they can hardly account for it all. A relative backwater in the early and mid-7th century, Athens had raised herself to a major trading city by the mid-6th. With this rising prosperity she undertook to expand and reorganize her cults and festivals on a broad scale.[13] We can now see the cult of Athena Nike to be an important instance, roughly contemporary to the reorganization of the Panathenaia but by all evidence independent of it.

The cult title Athena Nike appears to be original to the bastion. The title is known from a few other sites, Erythrai, Delos, and Megara, but the testimony is spare and relatively late, with none of the cults seeming to be of major scale.[14] Unlike other established titles of Athena formed with an adjectival or predicate epithet (e.g., Athena Polias, Athena Nikephoros, Athena Promachos), the title on the bastion joins Athena with a second deity, Nike, a personification and minor spirit (*daimon*) known to have been worshiped independently elsewhere.[15] Such fused titles are usually thought to arise from the annexation or assimilation of a preexisting local cult by a major god: so, for example, Ares Enyalios, the fusion of an Olympian with a pre-Greek deity; Artemis Hekate, Olympian and Eastern deity; and Poseidon Erechtheus, Olympian and hero.[16] We may expect the joining of an Olympian

[12] *IG* II^2 334, line 9.

[13] On the social and political history of Attic building in the 6th century, see E. Kluwe, "Peisistratos und die Akropolis von Athen," *Wissenschaftliche Zeitschrift der Friedrich-Schiller-Universität, Jena, Gesellschafts- und sprachwissenschaftliche Reihe* 14, 1965, pp. 9–15; Boersma 1970, pp. 11–18; F. Kolb, "Die Bau-, Religions- und Kulturpolitik der Peisistratiden," *JdI* 92, 1977, pp. 99–138; Rhodes 1981, pp. 184–186. Shapiro 1989 deserves special mention for its integration of archaeological, iconographic, historical, and economic evidence in the interpretation of cult.

[14] Temenos of Athena Nike, Erythrai, *Syll.*^{3} III, no. 1014, line 29 (3rd century B.C.); dedication to Athena Nike on Rhodes, *IG* XII, 20; sanctuary at Megara, Pausanias 1.42.4.

[15] Hamdorf 1964, pp. 58–59.

[16] Nilsson 1967, p. 388.

and a personification to be the same: such titles as Artemis Eukleia, Athena Hygieia, and Athena Nike appear to reflect the preexisting worship of the lesser deity alone.[17]

The bastion excavations offer no concrete evidence for a pre-Stage I phase of the Nike cult. Given the *prima facie* expectation that there was such a stage, however, it may be useful to review the body of indirect evidence on the question. We have noted that at some point before Stage I the Bronze Age bastion suffered a major collapse.[18] If the cult of Nike antedated that destruction, then its pre-collapse remains would of course be all or largely lost. One extreme case would be if the bastion collapsed in the 6th century, immediately before Stage I. All the pre-Stage I cult would then be lost. Let us consider, however, the case of an earlier collapse: there would then have been a stretch of time for pre-Stage I remains to accumulate. The Stage I crown raised the ground level of the bastion around a meter on the west, ideal protection for these putative remains. If the remains encompassed dressed stone, or even substantial rubble, we would expect this to have been noted in the excavation record. By contrast, stratigraphy, pottery, and small finds were routinely ignored. We are left to conclude that a pre-Stage I cult, assuming that it did exist and that its record was not entirely obliterated by a 6th-century bastion collapse, will have been modest at best. If we conjecture an early cult at all, we should think of a very simple cult practiced on the ruins of the bastion in the open air.

STAGE II: THE POST-PERSIAN SANCTUARY

I have argued that Stage I closed in a massive destruction: its temple, the base for the cult statue, and the altar were leveled, and several stretches of bastion stonework were thrown down. Stage II marks the aftermath of that destruction, the cult site as a stony, rutted mound of earth. Having established that Stage I is Archaic and Stage III, mid-5th century, we may safely correlate the destruction between the two with the Persian destruction of Athens in 480 and 479.

The end date for Stage II is established, first, by the fact that the foundations for Stage III were cut to fit on the Stage II ground (pp. 37–39), making clear that Stage III directly succeeds Stage II, and second, by the association of Stage III with the Nike Temple Decree (pp. 115–122), passed in the early 440's. From 479 to roughly mid-century the Nike Sanctuary was left unterraced and unrebuilt.

The contention that the Plataian Oath contained a provision binding the Greeks not to rebuild the sanctuaries destroyed by the Persians and that this so-called temple clause was renounced by the Athenians at mid-century goes well with the evidence of Stages II and III and with the Nike Temple Decree. The Nike Temple Decree implies by its wording that when

[17] On the independent worship of personifications in early cult, see Hamdorf 1964, pp. 69–70; Burkert 1985, pp. 184–186. Hamdorf's study is notable for its careful balance of archaeological and literary evidence. Earlier scholarship, based more exclusively on texts, has argued that personifications were worshiped first as epithets and only later, in the late 5th or 4th century, on their own. So, for example, Nilsson 1952, pp. 31–40.

For Athena Nike as a fusion of Athena with Nike, Sikes 1895, pp. 280–283; Daly 1953, pp. 1124–1128. Early studies more commonly suggest that the personification of Nike follows, rather than precedes, the joint title Athena Nike. So first J. E. Harrison, *Mythology and Monuments of Ancient Athens*, London 1890, p. 366.

[18] P. 16 above.

it was passed in the early 440's, the Nike Sanctuary was without a *neōs*, "temple", or *bomos lithinos*, "altar of worked stone", that is, of poros or marble. This is just what the temple clause would lead us to expect. Stage II had no temple: the sanctuaries were not to be rebuilt. The temple clause, however, did not require that the Greeks abandon their ruined sanctuaries altogether. Festivals and thank offerings must surely have continued. That the Nike Temple Decree commissions an altar specifically of worked stone, *bomos lithinos*, while calling for a *neōs*, unqualified, seemingly stems from this fact: *lithinos* distinguishes the altar commissioned from the makeshift altar, perhaps of ash or mud brick, that then existed on the site.[19]

The picture of Stage II that emerges is of a cult in conformity not only with the spirit but with the very letter of the Oath of Plataia. There is evidence at most for a simple altar. The remaining bastion stayed in ruins. Earlier discussion of the Archaic cult statue showed it to have survived the Persian Sack.[20] Given the lack of a temple and the state of the sanctuary in general, we should expect the statue to have been kept somewhere else at this time, housed perhaps by the priestess of Athena or one of the Praxiergidai.[21]

STAGE III: THE SANCTUARY OF THE NIKE TEMPLE DECREE

Three elements of the Stage III sanctuary have long been seen to be contemporary: the naïskos, the rectangular altar to its east, and the square altar to the northeast. They are closely related in level and are distinctive for their Aiginetan poros stone and unusual tooling. In reconstructing the ground level of the Stage II sanctuary, I have been able to confirm this tie stratigraphically. The smaller underpinnings of the naïskos and the base slab for the rectangular altar, exceptional for their oblique and irregularly contoured resting surfaces, are seen to have been bedded directly on the Stage II ground; the square altar, partly bedded on the rubble crown of the bastion, was at Stage II level as well.

My study confirms the association of two other remains with Stage III: the poros repository and the irregular trapezoidal bastion crown. The repository, judged contemporary with the naïskos already by Welter,[22] is seen to have been founded on a level with the underpinnings of the naïskos foundations, both directly on the Stage II ground, while the irregular trapezoidal wall, first tied to Stage III by Bundgård,[23] is seen to be seated on Stage I remains, its relation to the succeeding building phase, Stage III, thus confirmed.

Close examination of the Stage III remains has led to a number of discoveries, most importantly concerning the naïskos and the mud-brick extension of the rectangular altar, Stage IIIa. Traces of floor plaster on the south euthynteria of the naïskos establish the exterior width of the structure, 2.47 m., and two newly discovered anta blocks give a close estimate of the length of the building, *ca.* 3.65 m. The reconstruction most often assumed in scholarship,

[19] So Kavvadias 1897, col. 181; *Syll.*³ I, no. 63, p. 87; Hicks and Hill 1901, no. 37, p. 61; Prott and Ziehen 1896–1906, II, 1, no. 11, p. 49.

[20] Pp. 123–124 above.

[21] Cult images kept in the homes of priests: bronze Zeus by Hageladas at Ithome, Pausanias 4.33.2; bronze Zeus and Herakles at Aigion, 7.24.4; cf. the tending of public cult in the home, Karneios at Sparta, 3.13.3; Sophokles' reception of Asklepios at Athens, *Etymologicum Magnum*, *s.v.* Δεξίων.

[22] 1939, col. 12.

[23] Bundgård 1974b, p. 43.

a simple Π-shaped cella fully open at the east, is here confirmed. The form of the Stage IIIa altar is clarified by a field drawing in the Balanos archives. The combined evidence of the drawing and published plans by Welter establish the dimensions of the enlarged altar as 2.87 × 1.32 m. at its base.[24]

The present study generates several new dating criteria for Stage III. The cyma-reversa moldings on the rectangular altar and the distinctive masonry of the naïskos both point to a date toward the middle of the 5th century. The moldings are of a profile first attested at Athens in the Periclean period, on the toichobate of the Temple of Poseidon at Sounion, and on the sills for the grilles on the pronaos and opisthodomos of the Parthenon. The masonry has its closest parallel on two Akropolis projects also apparently of mid-5th-century date, the upper freestanding courses of the North Akropolis Wall and the Old Propylon Stage 3. A date well into the 5th century is further supported by the trapezoidal stonework of the bastion crown, first paralleled in fortifications built late in the Peloponnesian War. Firm limits are established, finally, by the Peiraeus limestone block underpinning the northwest corner of the naïskos (F 2), shown by its dimensions and batter to have been quarried for the South Akropolis Wall, and by the substructures for the double anta and Pier W of the Southwest Wing, accommodated to the trapezoidal bastion crown. These provide respectively a *terminus post* and *terminus ante quem* of 465–435.

In Chapter IX we discussed whether to associate the Nike Temple Decree with Stage III or Stage IV. Traditional scholarship has paired the decree with Stage IV and has thus been faced with a quarter-century gap between the commission of the Nike project and its execution. This long delay, it is argued, was part of a larger conflict over the conduct of the Akropolis building program. In this view, the rebuilding of the Nike Sanctuary was championed by Kallias, son of Hipponikos, and other conservatives of the city. The radical faction of Perikles opposed the project in favor of a bold rebuilding of the gateway to the Akropolis, the building that came to be called the Propylaia. According to the thesis, the conservatives held their ground, and although the Nike project remained blocked, the conservatives succeeded in having the plans for the Southwest Wing of the Propylaia redrawn to better accommodate the anticipated form of the Nike Sanctuary. The Nike project was finally pushed through in the later 420's. Chapter IX reviews the history of scholarship on this long-debated thesis and argues that it be abandoned in favor of the simpler, more straightforward association of the Nike Temple Decree and Stage III.

KALLIKRATES AND STAGE III

Among all else, the Nike Temple Decree is a major source of information on the architect Kallikrates, there commissioned to design the doorway and temple of the Nike Sanctuary (lines 7–8, 12–13, καθ' ὅ τι ἂν Καλλικράτες χσυγγράφσει). Kallikrates is mentioned elsewhere in ancient sources three times. He is cited twice by Plutarch, as coarchitect of the Parthenon with Iktinos (*Per.* 13.4, τὸν μὲν γὰρ ἑκατόμπεδον Παρθενῶνα Καλλικράτης εἰργάζετο καὶ 'Ικτῖνος) and as contractor for the Middle Wall (*Per.* 16.5, τὸ δὲ μακρὸν τεῖχος, περὶ οἷ Σωκράτης ἀκοῦσαί φησιν αὐτὸς εἰσηγουμένου γνώμην Περικλέους,

[24] Welter 1939, col. 11.

ἠργολάβησε Καλλικράτης).[25] And third, a building decree, *IG* I³ 45, calls on him to design a minor addition to the Akropolis walls (lines 6–7, ταῦτα δὲ χσυνγρά̣φσαι] μὲν Καλλικρά[τ]ε). The projects appear all to have been close in date: the Nike Temple Decree and *IG* I³ 45 belong *ca.* 450–445; the Middle Wall dates from the mid-440's; and the Parthenon, from 447–438.[26]

The assumed connection of the Nike Temple Decree to the amphiprostyle temple has served as a starting point in nearly all research on Kallikrates' *oeuvre* and career. The similar amphiprostyle plan and detail of the Ilissos Temple has led several scholars to suggest that the latter temple too is by this architect,[27] while Studniczka argued that the actual *syngraphe* for the suspended Nike Temple was used for its near twin.[28] Kallikrates' authorship of the two temples has been argued more recently by Ione Shear, who attributes two further buildings to the architect, the Temple of the Athenians on Delos and the Erechtheion.[29] Carpenter reworked and expanded the list, omitting the Erechtheion and adding the Hephaisteion, the Temple of Ares, the Temple of Poseidon at Sounion, the Temple of Nemesis at Rhamnous, and, conspicuous in his argument, a putative Kimonian stage of the Older Parthenon.[30] Others have tried to reason from the Nike Temple to Kallikrates' role in the Parthenon. A study by Martin associates the architect with the Ionic elements of the Parthenon: the Ionic columns of the western cella and the Parthenon frieze.[31]

The association of the Nike Temple Decree with Stage III, rather than IV, entirely undermines this scholarship. The idea that Kallikrates was a master of the Ionic style, a natural inference from the Stage IV temple, now falls away, and with it the attribution of the Parthenon on Doric-Ionic lines. The attribution of the Ilissos Temple is likewise undone. The common hand behind the Nike and Ilissos Temples, the Erechtheion, and/or the Hephaisteion is still there to argue, but the concrete tie to Kallikrates is gone.

What we find to be the two extant works of Kallikrates, the Parthenon and the naïskos, could not be more dissimilar. The more important point to stress is that Stage III fits well with much of the other evidence on the architect. We have seen Stage III to be contemporary with Kallikrates' other attested works, all from the early years of the Periclean building program, and while the Middle Wall is on a wholly different scale, his work on the Akropolis Walls is roughly comparable, a project of some sixty days (*IG* I³ 45, lines 10–14). We earlier noted

25 Only Plutarch associates Kallikrates with the Parthenon. Strabo (9.395, 396) and Pausanias (8.41.9) name Iktinos alone as architect, while Vitruvius (7, *praef.* 12) pairs Iktinos with Karpion.

26 Middle Wall: Plato, *Gorgias* 455e; Gomme 1945, pp. 312–313 (perhaps 444–442 B.C.). Parthenon: Dinsmoor 1921, pp. 233–247; Burford 1963, pp. 23–35; Meiggs and Lewis 1969, no. 59, pp. 162–165. The architecture of the temple was essentially complete at the dedication of the cult statue in 438/437. Work continued on the sculpture to 432.

27 First W. R. Lethaby, *Greek Buildings*, London 1908, p. 154.

28 Studniczka 1916, p. 230.

29 Shear 1963, pp. 375–424.

30 Carpenter 1970, pp. 21–68, 83–109. Four of Carpenter's additions, the Hephaisteion, the Temple of Ares, the Temple of Poseidon, and the Temple of Nemesis, had earlier been grouped together by Dinsmoor (1950, pp. 181–183) as work of the "Theseum architect". For Kallikrates as author of a Kimonian stage of the Parthenon, also Bundgård 1976, pp. 49, 61–70. A more recent study combines Shear's attributions with the works of the "Theseum architect" and adds the Temple of Athena at Sounion (Giuliano 1982, pp. 325–332).

31 Martin 1976, pp. 427–442. Compare B. Wesenberg ("Wer erbaute den Parthenon?" *AthMitt* 97, 1982, pp. 99–125), who argues that the Parthenon entire is the work of Kallikrates and assigns the Older Parthenon to Iktinos.

that the naïskos is closely related to the upper courses of the North Akropolis Wall in stone and technique, leading us to wonder if the two projects might be by one architect. The upper North Wall, an extensive undertaking, cannot be the stopgap project described in I^3 45. In tying the architect of the naïskos to work elsewhere on the walls of the Akropolis, however, the inscription does give the further attribution of the upper North Wall greater plausibility. Kallikrates may well have been in charge of several Akropolis projects of relatively unassuming nature.[32]

STAGE III AND THE PERICLEAN BUILDING PROGRAM

The evidence here assembled on the condition of the Nike Bastion in the Early Classical period, Stage II, and the tie of the Nike Temple Decree to the succeeding Stage III combine to make the 5th-century history of the Nike Bastion among the clearest and best documented of any on the Akropolis. The evidence fully accords with the historicity of the Plataian Oath and attests indeed how strictly its temple clause was construed. From 479 to mid-century the bastion remained unterraced and unrebuilt, with at most a simple altar.

Scholarship on the Oath of Plataia has often read the temple clause less literally. Notably Dinsmoor, and more recently Meiggs, both strong partisans of the oath, have been content to date the naïskos to the Themistoklean or Kimonian period.[33] That we have found the naïskos to date rather from the mid-5th century makes no less important these scholars' understanding of the temple clause. The significance of the Oath of Plataia for the history of the Nike cult and for the history of post-Persian building at Athens in general needs to be reexamined.

The perceived adherence of a temple project to the Plataian Oath ought reasonably to have depended less on the scope and elaborateness of the rebuilding than on its spatial and functional relation to the surviving cult. The sanctuaries (*hiera*) were to remain as symbols and reminders, never to be rebuilt. Our findings on Stage III sharpen this issue, but in truth the evidence has been there from the start. However seemingly minor the Stage III sanctuary, it entirely overbuilt its predecessor and, in reterracing the bastion, covered all trace of the Persian Sack. It accords with and respects the temple clause in no way. The absence of dating criteria notwithstanding, partisans of the Oath might have suspected a mid-5th-century date from the start.

Scholarship firmly supports the idea of major construction on the Akropolis in the period of the Plataian Oath, notably on the Akropolis circuit wall and the Northwest Building.[34]

[32] A study by McCredie (1979, pp. 69–73) explores whether Kallikrates may have been more a practical engineer than an innovative designer: thus the choice of Kallikrates as architect of the Middle Wall and the walls of the Akropolis. In contrast Bundgård (1976, pp. 49–50) associates Kallikrates with several more distinguished projects, notably Stage 2 of the Old Propylon and the Older Parthenon. Dinsmoor, Jr.'s more recent study of the Old Propylon (1980) has significantly clarified the relation of this building to the Older Parthenon. One sees Bundgård to have conflated Propylon Stages 2 and 3, dating respectively *ca.* 485 and 450 B.C. It is specifically the steps of the gatehouse (Stage 2) that bear comparison to the Older Parthenon, and these are a full generation earlier than Kallikrates.

[33] Dinsmoor 1950, p. 151; Meiggs 1972, p. 498. Cf. Paton 1927, p. 448, note 4.

[34] On the date of the South Wall, note 52 above, p. 59; Northwest Building, p. 63 above.

The Northwest Building was a new project, not covered by the temple clause, while it is unclear if the citadel walls were themselves considered sacred; the work, at any rate, left the individual sanctuaries, the temples and altars of the citadel, entirely untouched. More controversial have been suggestions that the sanctuaries themselves were rebuilt. Early in this century Dörpfeld argued that the western cella of the Old Temple of Athena was restored and reroofed, and Holland argued a post-Persian stage of the Erechtheion.[35] Opinion was against the Oath of Plataia when these scholars worked, and they raise the issue of transgression at most in passing. The problem, however, has now to be squarely faced.

There is unequivocal evidence for the restoration of at least one pre-Persian building on the Akropolis, the Old Propylon, hastily and provisionally reerected closely on the lines of its predecessor. The evidence for the Old Temple of Athena and the pre-Erechtheion is not nearly so substantial, but Dörpfeld's and Holland's arguments are consistent and, in all, convincing. Dörpfeld notes the plentiful remains of the peristyle of the Old Temple reused in the North Akropolis Wall and found loose in the Persian debris: column drums; capitals; epistyle, frieze, and geison blocks; and pedimental sculpture. In contrast, little was found of the cella, and that nearly all from later contexts. The pattern suggests that the peristyle was razed and the cella repaired and kept in use.[36] The evidence for Holland's pre-Erechtheion is equally circumstantial, though also strongly suggestive. This modest structure, formed partly of reused blocks, appears to have coexisted briefly with the Erechtheion, left in place as the later project rose directly around it. Several of its blocks were found *in situ* under the western foundations of the Erechtheion, and there are further, indirect traces of the structure on the Erechtheion foundations opposite at the east.[37]

Although the evidence for a provisional rebuilding of the Akropolis is clear, the dating of these works is far less so. We earlier argued a mid-5th-century date for the Old Propylon Stage 3, noting its relation to the naïskos in masonry technique and arguing the likelihood that it narrowly preceded the resecuring of the Akropolis circuit decreed in *IG* I³ 45.[38] There is no equivalent evidence on the repair of the Old Temple of Athena or the pre-Erechtheion,[39] but the chronology of the Nike Bastion now strengthens the possibility that they too are late.

[35] W. Dörpfeld, "Der alte Athena-Tempel auf der Akropolis, V," *AthMitt* 22, 1897 (pp. 159–178), p. 166; *idem* 1919, pp. 9–25; Holland 1924, pp. 1–23.

[36] Dörpfeld 1919, p. 10.

[37] Holland 1924, pp. 10, 16–23.

[38] P. 65 above.

[39] The pre-Erechtheion appears to be referred to in an inscription concerning the Praxiergidai, *IG* I³ 7, lines 20–21, but there can be no certainty. See D. M. Lewis, "Notes on Attic Inscriptions," *BSA* 49, 1954, pp. 17–50. The lettering combines old and new Attic forms, the earlier phi with circumscribed vertical, with four-barred sigma, and rounded beta and rho. The date is at or close to 450. It was Dörpfeld's view (1919, pp. 10–11) that the cella of the Old Temple was restored and its peristyle immured in the North Wall soon after the Persian Sack. The blocks of the peristyle are not simply reused material but a carefully built memorial. They may conceivably date from well before the restoration of the cella. The uncertain date of the North Wall compounds the problem. Most would agree with Dörpfeld's Themistoklean date, but the evidence is minimal. Others have preferred a date after 450: A. Tschira, "Die unfertigen Säulentrommeln auf der Akropolis von Athen," *JdI* 55, 1940, pp. 242–261; *idem*, "Eine Tastung in der Cella des Parthenon," *AA* (*JdI* 80) 1965, cols. 401–428; Bundgård 1976, pp. 121–133.

When Athens set out to rebuild her shrines at mid-century, she was intent not simply on restoring them to use but on rebuilding them in truly an unrivaled form, of the finest materials and to the highest standard. There were capital and sufficient craftsmen for two or more concurrent building projects, at least to the outbreak of the Peloponnesian War. The Parthenon dates to the same years as the Hephaisteion and the Temple of Poseidon at Sounion, the latter two often thought to have followed one on the other; and the Propylaia overlaps the Ilissos Temple and the Temple of Nemesis at Rhamnous. There must certainly have been debate about the order of the projects and about what to do for the cults whose major rebuilding would have to wait. The greater number of cult sites appear to have been left simply in ruins, among them the cults of the Agora. There were, however, a number of circumstances that required special attention. A few shrines had extant cult statuary, the sanctuaries of Athena Polias and Athena Nike prominent among them. The *xoanon* of Nike, kept elsewhere under the oath, was provisionally returned to place in the Stage III naïskos, and it is reasonable to see the pre-Erechtheion as a similar case, built at mid-century to house the ancient image of Athena Polias. We have noted that *IG* I^3 45 attests a heightened concern with security at this time. The need to control access to the citadel appears natural at a time when cult statuary and, one may imagine, other *hiera* were being restored to place. It is logical, as we have seen, to place the rebuilding of the Akropolis gate, the Old Propylon Stage 3, soon before *IG* I^3 45, as part and parcel of the same concerns. Finally, the restoration of the Old Temple of Athena appears equally suitable to this period, perhaps marking the return of the treasury and temple stores of Athena to the Polias sanctuary.

Seen against the Parthenon and Hephaisteion, these interim measures are almost painfully makeshift and slight. We have noted that the Old Propylon Stage 3 combines reused marble and Aktite poros. Pigmented stucco hid the difference of materials and must have given the structure a certain flair, but the expediency is unmistakable. The pre-Erechtheion has much the same character, its preserved blocks also pieced and reused.[40] And finally Stage III of the Nike Sanctuary, if of new-quarried stone, is equally modest in design. The projects together appear a measured solution to what must surely have been a key problem at mid-century, the need to revive and restore not just a few chosen sanctuaries but truly the whole of Attic cult and ritual.

STAGE IV: THE FINAL REBUILDING

Unlike the early remains from the bastion, the sanctuary of the late 5th-century, Stage IV, has been extensively examined in previous scholarship. My description of the Stage IV bastion and amphiprostyle temple has largely drawn on this earlier work, with the occasional addition of evidence from Balanos' drawings and the benefit of one new find. Balanos' drawings provide the first detailed record of the amphiprostyle-temple foundations, documenting their depth, method of construction, and relation to the Stage III remains and confirming that they were indeed built of a piece with the bastion sheathing. The new find, the corner of

[40] Holland 1924, p. 12.

a relief preserving a winged, wind-blown female figure, appears from its scale, technique, iconography, and date to be from the Stage IV base for the cult statue of Athena Nike.[41]

STAGE IV WITHOUT THE NIKE TEMPLE DECREE

However valuable a review of the Stage IV architecture itself, of equal or greater importance is a reinvestigation of the written evidence from the period. The confirmation that the Nike Temple Decree, *IG* I^3 35, pertains to Stage III, not IV, clarifies the history of the late 5th-century cult no less than the history of Stage III. Gone is the delay between the commission of Stage IV and its execution; in the absence of contrary evidence, one should imagine Stage IV to have been built directly at its decree. Gone as well is the religious conflict between the conservative faction of Thucydides son of Melesias, champion of the Nike Sanctuary, and the building program of the democrats under Perikles.

THE DECREE ON THE SALARY OF THE PRIESTESS: A NEW INTERPRETATION

The reinterpretation of the Nike Temple Decree raises anew the question of the decree on its reverse, *IG* I^3 36, the provision on the salary of the priestess. We earlier noted that while the legislation itself is clear, that the priestess be paid by the kolakretai in office in the month of Thargelion, there is no hint of why this was being legislated. Scholars have reconstructed the intent of the decree according to their views on the history of Stage IV. The widely held view that the rider enforces the terms of the Nike Temple Decree, that the priestess's salary was not being paid or was paid irregularly, grew up from the idea that the Nike Sanctuary itself had been delayed.[42] Having seen that in fact there is no evidence of a delay, we now need to view the rider in a different light. If it did not enforce the provisions of the earlier decree, the one salient alternative is that it altered those provisions.

We have found the Nike cult to have been not thwarted and opposed but consistently strengthened over the second half of the 5th century, first in Stage III with the appointment of a priestess, then more dramatically in Stage IV with the costly enlargement of the sanctuary. A cult change in this period would be most readily intelligible if it too enhanced the cult. How could the brief legislation of *IG* I^3 36 have enhanced the cult? No one can be certain, of course, but let me broach what seems to me the most likely possibility. Remember that before the enactment of the Nike Temple Decree at mid-century the Nike cult had no priestess of its own. It was presumably under the care of the priesthood of some adjacent or related cult, the priestess of Athena Polias perhaps. It may be that the rider shifts the payment of the Nike priestess from the festival calendar of the cult that was previously in charge to the Nike cult's own festival calendar. There are no written sources on the festivals of Athena Nike, neither how many there were nor when they took place, but it is worth noting that the month

[41] P. 75 above.
[42] See *IG* I^2 24, p. 14.

specified in the decree, Thargelion, mid- to late spring, would be an appropriate time for the major festival of a goddess of fertility and war. It stands early in the campaigning season, a symbolic call to arms, and is equally a time of flowering and new growth.[43]

The Decree on the Salary of the Priestess and the Date of Stage IV

If the provision on the salary of the priestess (*IG* I^3 36) is a new measure, no mere enforcement of *IG* I^3 35, then the chronological relation of the decree to Stage IV needs to be rethought. Dinsmoor placed it at the close of Stage IV, apparently reasoning that the priesthood would have been of concern, above all, when the sanctuary was about to reopen.[44] Dinsmoor combined the firm date of *IG* I^3 36, 424/423, with several further sources to arrive at a three-year span for the Stage IV project: 427–424.[45]

The Nike Temple friezes are perhaps the single greatest obstacle to Dinsmoor's dating. We have noted that the female figures on the east frieze of the Nike Temple appear closely contemporary to the karyatids on the Erechtheion. Their absolute date can be gauged against the relief on the Bridge Decree (422/421) and further decree reliefs of 417/416 and 410/409. The friezes of the temple appear to belong *ca.* 420–418.

Dinsmoor's dates might be salvageable, perhaps, if it could be shown that the architecture and sculpture of the sanctuary were worked in two separate campaigns with, say, the frieze slabs set in blank and carved later. Minor recuttings have been observed, however, on the frieze figures, which strongly suggests that the figural friezes were carved on the ground. They were finished before they were installed and had to be recut slightly as they were actually set on the building.[46] Dinsmoor's dates appear a step too high.

Expansion of the Cult of Athena Nike

The Nike Temple Decree documents the growing status of the Nike cult at mid-century (Stage III): henceforth it is to have its own priestess. It is reasonable to look for evidence of further cult changes in the far more ambitious Stage IV rebuilding. We earlier proposed that the rider to the Nike Temple Decree, *IG* I^3 36, moved the payment of the priestess to coincide with the festival calendar of Athena Nike. Is there any other evidence that in fact the cult was changed or enlarged at around this time? We can point first to the monumental

43 Compare the Roman Maytime festival of *rosaliae signorum*, the parading of standards decked with wreaths and roses, A. S. Hoey, "Rosaliae Signorum," *Harvard Theological Review* 30, 1937, pp. 15–35.

44 Dinsmoor 1939, pp. 124–125.

45 *Loc. cit.* Few have endorsed Dinsmoor's major thesis, that the orientation of a temple is determined by the position of the rising sun on the major festival of the god in the year that work began. Whatever the validity of the theory, no such calculation could have been made for the Nike Temple, because the rising sun was blocked by the Pelasgian wall to its east, as Dinsmoor indeed admits. Dinsmoor cites three inscriptions in addition to *IG* I^3 36: an account for Golden Nikai, *IG* I^3 468; a 4th-century decree on the repair of a statue, *IG* II^2 403; and a building decree, *IG* I^3 132. He takes I^3 132 to mark the start of work on the Nike Sanctuary. The inscription, however, has no concrete tie to Athena Nike, and no firm date. The inscription on the Golden Nikai is equally uncertain evidence. There is no indication that the Golden Nikai were dedications on the bastion. That they were commissioned together with Panathenaic *pompeia* in the 4th century (*IG* II^2 1493+1494+1495) suggests a connection to Athena Polias. The statue repaired in *IG* II^2 403 may have been dedicated in 424, as Dinsmoor suggests, but again there is no direct evidence.

46 Harrison 1970, p. 321.

dimensions of the Stage IV altar. By its size it was intended for the sacrifice of major victims, cows and bulls. In fact, the Nike Parapet as much as celebrates these sacrifices: several slabs show Nike leading a bull to the altar.[47] By contrast, the Stage III rectangular altar is far more modest. It accommodated smaller offerings, perhaps sheep or goats. It appears that by Stage IV the ritual of Athena Nike had become more lavish and imposing.

Between Stages III and IV comes Stage IIIa, the mud-brick expansion of the rectangular altar. The Stage IIIa altar is not so large as the Stage IV altar, around two-thirds the length and a third the width, but its purpose, without question, was to prepare Stage III for major victims. It marks the specific point at which the ritual of the cult was expanded.

The Decree on the Salary of the Priestess, The Stage IIIA Altar, and the Start of Work on Stage IV

Art historical criteria suggest that the friezes of the Nike Temple were carved several years after the decree on the salary of the priestess, *IG* I^3 36. The friezes belong *ca.* 420–418, the decree is dated 424/423. If the decree bears a chronological relation to the building project, it fits best at the start, not, as Dinsmoor assumed, at the end of work.[48]

In the Nike Temple Decree, changes in the Nike cult and a rebuilding of the Nike Sanctuary were enacted together. Specifically, the appointment of a priestess was enacted at the same time as the (modest Stage III) temple, altar, and sanctuary doors. Having seen that the cult was substantially expanded after Stage III and, having explored the possible role of *IG* I^3 36 in that expansion, that this payment to the priestess was henceforth to coincide with the goddess' (new?) festival calendar, we are now in a position to posit a similar pattern for Stage IV: that the late 5th-century expansion of the ritual of Athena Nike was enacted by the Athenians at or around the time that they enacted the architectural rebuilding of the cult site. Enlarged setting, enlarged cult: the two enacted together.

No trace of the decree that enacted the Stage IV rebuilding has ever been securely identified.[49] Notwithstanding, it is tempting to think that *IG* I^3 36, given its likely intent, may have formed part of that larger enactment. *IG* I^3 36 would have been decreed and published separately from the other legislation because it formed in essence an amendment or rider to an earlier enactment, specifically the Nike Temple Decree: thus its inscription on the reverse of that then thirty-year-old decree.

We have seen that the sacrificial ritual of the Nike Sanctuary was expanded from Stage III to Stage IV. We have further seen that Stage IIIa, the mud-brick enlargement

[47] Plate 21:a; Carpenter 1929, pls. V, XVII, XXX right. Compare a 4th-century decree stipulating the sacrifice of a cow to Athena Nike in the Panathenaia, cited note 8 above, p. 126. The offering of a cow to the goddess is attested also in *SEG* XXX 69, line 16 (*ca.* 304–302), and *IG* II^2 1006, lines 14–15 (122/121).

[48] The bastion project was near completion when the temple friezes were set in. The temple still needed to be roofed and its details carved, but the major work of the project was already behind. If the project was decreed in 424/423, then construction spanned some five or six years. The pace of work may appear too slow, judged against the Propylaia. That far larger structure was completed in five years (*IG* I^3 462–466; Meiggs and Lewis 1969, no. 60, pp. 165–166). The pace of building at Athens, however, slowed measurably with the outbreak of the Peloponnesian War. The two campaigns of the Erechtheion, *ca.* 420–413 and 409–406, together total some ten years.

[49] For *IG* I^3 132, a fragment of a building degree occasionally associated with the Nike Temple, see note 55 above, p. 79.

of the Stage III altar, ought logically to mark the point at which these sacrifices began. There is no stratigraphic evidence to date Stage IIIa, no pottery was recovered from its core, for example, but its most logical placement, though not the only possible placement, would be contemporary with the start of work on Stage IV.

A building project at a religious site was not allowed to halt or interrupt the core ritual at that site. The religious functions of the sanctuary had to continue. One imagines that in most cases construction and core ritual were relatively easy to reconcile. The sanctuary altar would have been roped off from construction, and while, say, the temple was in progress and unusable, basic ritual would have continued at the altar in proper and appropriate form. The Stage III naïskos was indeed unusable while the Stage IV temple was being built. The east end of the naïskos was destroyed and its walls cut down in laying the Stage IV temple foundations. The Stage III altar, however, is unlikely to have been similarly incapacitated, at least not in the early stages of the project. Though rather inconvenient to the builders, the area of the altar is likely to have remained largely untouched at Stage III level as the bastion was sheathed and raised, the Stage IV temple foundations were laid, and the temple was built.

The Stage IIIa altar is the clearest extant evidence that the ritual of the Nike Sanctuary was expanded not after the Stage IV sanctuary was completed but before. If the Stage IV architectural project was decreed at the same time that the ritual of the Nike cult was expanded, then the Stage IIIa altar had a very simple function: this temporary construction of rubble and mud brick was built to accommodate the expanded ritual of Stage IV in advance of the completion of the Stage IV altar.

The stratigraphy of the sanctuary offers some support for this view. The bastion paving east of the Stage IV altar rests on a fill formed entirely of Pentelic marble working chips, a uniform stratum from the Stage III ground level up. If the chips are from the Nike Sanctuary,[50] then they show that the Stage III ground level was maintained at least until Stage IV work in marble (the bastion crown and the steps and upper work of the temple) was well underway. The Stage IV altar rendered the Stage IIIa altar unusable: the dictates of cult suggest that the eastern area of the Stage IIIa sanctuary was first filled when work began on the new altar of the cult.

IG I³ 64 AND STAGE IV

We have seen that the friezes of the Nike Temple are the best available guide for the chronology of Stage IV. Carved *ca.* 420–418, they are a *terminus post quem* for the setting of the

[50] On the provenience of the marble chips, see note 86 above, p. 86. We may compare the results of recent excavations at Kalapodi: R. Felsch, H. J. Kienast, and H. Schuler, "Apollon und Artemis oder Artemis und Apollon: Bericht von den Grabungen im neu entdeckten Heiligtum bei Kalapodi, 1973–77," *AA* (*JdI* 95) 1980, pp. 38–118, esp. p. 87. The earlier cult at Kalapodi remained accessible and in use through the laying of the Classical temple foundations. After being briefly moved for construction of the temple adyton, the cult was refounded and continued at the higher level.

If the Propylaia and Nike projects overlapped, the chips beneath the paving might conceivably be from the neighboring project. The interval of some eight years between the two, however, effectively precludes the possibility.

temple geison and the construction of the roof. *IG* I³ 64B, a building account that lists coffer lids and a total "for the Nike Temple," thus ought to date from around 418.

It is open to question whether *IG* I³ 64B and the decree on its obverse, 64A, pertain to the same project. This seems likely *prima facie*, however, and finds general support in the texts themselves. Both concern an architectural project: the decree twice mentions an *architekton*; the account lists expenses for the Nike Temple. And both concern precious materials: the decree provides a choice between ivory and one or more other materials; the account records purchases of gold.

My earlier discussion of the decree left open the meaning of *dryphakto[s]* in line 14. A *phragma* is a defensive work or barrier, and early scholars came naturally to think of the one prominent barrier of the Stage IV sanctuary, the Nike Parapet.[51] The other stem of the compound, *drys* (tree), weighs against this, however, pointing to a work of carpentry, not of marble carving.[52] Besides the parapet, there is only one other attested barrier in the Stage IV sanctuary, the grilles of the temple, and these are in fact a promising alternative. Temple grilles were routinely of wood, and the term *phragma*, its associated verb *phrassein*, and related variants were commonly applied to such latticework.[53] A workman installing the wooden grilles for the west wall of the Erechtheion is referred to as διαφάρχσαντι τὰ μετακιόνια.[54] And the accounts of the Temple of Asklepios at Epidauros employ the noun φάρχματα and the phrase φάρξιν τοῦ ναοῦ.[55]

If the Nike project decree in fact refers to the grilles of the temple, this can hardly have been its main subject. The elaborateness of the project, the choice of precious materials, the competition, and consultation with the allies are inappropriate to simple latticework. Temple grilles might rather protect a commission of this order, and in fact the grille-closed cella of the amphiprostyle temple was the one secure area of the Stage IV sanctuary. That the decree progresses directly from the *dryphakto[s]* (line 14) to the execution of the project (lines 15–16) supports the same idea: to carry out the project, the cella had first to be secure.

The *editio princeps* of the decree considered the project to be a statue.[56] That the text twice mentions an architect, however, and calls on contestants to submit a drawing (lines 6–8, γράφσαντα. . .[μὲ ἔλαττο]ν ἒ πεχ[υ] αῖον) points rather to an architectural project, or a project with at least a major architectural component.[57] Might something costly have been built into or within the cella? One thinks first of the Stage IV base for the cult statue. A gilded or chryselephantine base, however, would have overpowered the marble image, and what is more, I have already associated a fragment of Pentelic marble with the base, the corner figure of a sculptured frieze.[58] If not the base, a promising alternative is the ceiling of the cella.

[51] The association with the Nike Parapet is mentioned but rejected by Hiller von Gaertringen, *IG* I² 88, p. 47.

[52] Schol. Aristophanes, *Vesp.* 386, τὰ ταυλώματα τοῦ δικαστηρίου διὰ τὸ ἐκ ξύλων καὶ σανίδων τῶν ἐκ δρυὸς εἶναι κατεσκευασμένα. *Suidas*, *s.v.* Δρύφακτοι. ξύλινοι θώρακες, τὰ διαφράγματα, ἢ τὰ περιτειχίσματα, ἢ κιγκλίδες. For the *dryphaktoi* of the law courts, Aristophanes, *Eq.* 675, *Vesp.* 380.

[53] Ebert 1910, pp. 58–60; Orlandos and Travlos 1986, pp. 262–263.

[54] *IG* I³ 475, lines 256–257; Paton 1927, p. 370.

[55] *IG* IV² 102, lines 75–76, 253.

[56] Pogorelski and Hiller von Gaertringen 1922, pp. 189–190.

[57] So later editions, Pogorelski 1923, p. 314; *IG* I² 88, p. 47 (Hiller von Gaertringen).

[58] See p. 68 above.

The account on the reverse mentions coffer lids (*kalymmata*), and it was indeed not unusual for coffering to be preciously worked.[59] Such gilding tended to be restrained, confined to the central ornament of the coffer and perhaps a few details.[60] By contrast, the elaborate provisions on design and decision-making in the Nike project decree suggest something more, an interior of unusual richness.

STAGE IV AND ATTIC BUILDING DURING THE PELOPONNESIAN WAR

The findings of this study on Stage IV, as they revise and clarify the history of the bastion, cast a new and different light on the place of the sanctuary in the broader history of sacred building in Periclean and post-Periclean Athens. The findings are partly negative. The disassociation of the Nike Temple Decree from Stage IV undermines the sole remaining evidence for friction or conflict between the Nike Sanctuary and the Propylaia. The last several decades of research have seen no evidence of significant change in the plan of the Southwest Wing; the wing appears to have been built essentially as first designed. And the proper restoration of the mover of the Nike Temple Decree, Glaukos not Hipponikos, has thoroughly undermined other well-established theories, that the cult was the narrow favorite of the aristocratic faction at Athens and that its interests were bound to peace with Persia. This direction of research as a whole can now be laid to rest.

In its place comes a different view of the conduct and progress of building on the Akropolis. The first two projects of the program, the Parthenon and Propylaia, have long been seen to have been closely coordinated. The architecture of the Parthenon was completed in 438/437, the Propylaia begun the following year, 437/436, with workers seemingly shifted from one project directly to the next.[61] The chronology that I have put forth for the Nike Sanctuary points to an analogous coordination of the later projects of the Akropolis program. I have argued from *IG* I^3 36 that Stage IV of the Nike Sanctuary was begun *ca.* 424/423; building accounts locate the completion of the Erechtheion *ca.* 407/406. When exactly the first project left off and the second began is difficult to gauge. Especially noteworthy is the close stylistic relation between the east frieze of the Nike Temple and the Erechtheion karyatids. The two appear to have been carved side by side, or at most a few years apart. The frieze comes toward the close of work on the Nike Temple, the karyatids, toward the start of the Erechtheion. Judged from these two sets of sculptures, at least, the projects appear to come one right after the next, or even to partly overlap. The contiguity of the two projects is

59 Orlandos 1966–1968, I, pp. 125–126.

60 Compare the ceilings of the Erechtheion, Paton 1927, p. 409. Temple of Asklepios on Delos, *IG* XI 161A, lines 72–73: τοῦ νεὼ τοῦ ᾿Ασκληπιοῦ τῆς ὀροφῆς τὰ κρίνα λευκώσαντι κα[ὶ] τὰς κάλχας χρυσώσαντι; cf. Temple of Asklepios at Epidauros, *IG* IV^2 102, lines 82–83, Κλεινίας εἵλετο κυμάτια καὶ ἀστραγάλους καὶ κάλχας καὶ ἀστέρας χρυσῶσαι. Lines 26–29 of *IG* I^3 64B, among the more ambiguous of that inscription, now fall more easily into place. The *kalymmata* are not a purchase themselves but part of the entry on gold. *Exempli gratia*: χρυσὸς ἐ[ον]- |[έθε ἐς τὰς κάλχας(?) ....**9**.... ἐπὶ τ]ὰ καλύμμα[τα], |[σταθμόν ....**19**.........] χρυσίο τιμ[έ.] | [.........**18**.........]. For ἐπὶ τὰ καλύμματα, already *IG* I^3 64 (Lewis).

61 For the Parthenon and Propylaia accounts, see note 44 above, p. 77.

further indicated by their architecture. In his major study of 1947–1948, Orlandos notes how close are the Nike Temple and Erechtheion in building techniques and use of refinements, linked by such rare features as the fastening of the columns to the stylobate with an empolion-shaped dowel, the use of T-dowels in the krepidoma and antae, the vertically set antae, and the inward lean of the columns. "Le lecteur doit avoir remarqué à plusieurs reprises que les constructeurs du temple de Niké et ceux de l'Erechthéion ont fait usage des mêmes procédés techniques."[62] The number and distinctiveness of these technical parallels are more than one would expect of two buildings that were merely from the same general tradition; they seem a second indication that the two projects were coordinated. The explanation for this coordination remains unclear. It is likely to have been financial, at least in part. If so, however, it had the further advantage of making full, uninterrupted use of a highly skilled body of craftsmen. These workmen, schooled to the highest level of their respective crafts, would have soon drifted to other employ, perhaps even to wholly different lines of work. They were not easily replaced.

That the Periclean building program, however controversial when proposed, was in fact carried out without visible opposition puts not only the Nike Sanctuary but the very conduct of public building at Athens in a new light. We do not know the reason that the program was halted in 432, but it does not appear to have been political. The oft-suggested reason that it was economic, a fear of depleting the war chest, seems right. The reasons to resume work *ca.* 424/423 are more problematic. They may have turned, at least in part, on the mood and expectations of the city, the growing sentiment for peace in the final, stalemated years of the Archidamian War. The posited tie between the Nike Sanctuary and peace with Persia appears all the more interesting in this light. We have seen that the conclusion, or renewal, of peace with Persia at mid-century had more a general than a specific bearing on the sanctuary. The formal end of the Persian Wars set the stage for the building program as a whole, not the Nike project in particular. The case may be similar in 424/423. A renewal of the peace may have fostered a climate in which public building again seemed justified and desirable.

To attempt to clarify the architecture and archaeology of the Nike Sanctuary is not of itself to write a new cult history of the site. The architectural stages of the cult form something of a backbone: without an accurate chronology, without an accurate sequence of stages, the broader, more interpretive stuff of cult history would be too subjective to stand. Whoever takes up a full study of the cult will want to look afresh at the sculptures of the Nike Temple and Nike Parapet, both complex expressions of the character and interests of the goddess. Recently identified fragments of these sculptures, many still unpublished, promise new insight into a range of questions, from the poses and iconographies of individual figures to the form of the sanctuary program as a whole. Important research remains. Is there new light to be shed on the nature of Athena as Nike, the special aspect of the goddess on the bastion? What is the place of the cult in the development of a distinctive Periclean and post-Periclean approach to religion? The present study casts no light directly onto these, and indeed onto many other essential questions about the cult. If it succeeds in setting a new stage for such research, however, that of itself will be a gain.

62 Orlandos 1947–1948, p. 38.

APPENDIX A

AN EXCERPT FROM THE NOTES OF NIKOLAOS BALANOS ON THE EXCAVATION OF THE NIKE BASTION

ARCHAEOLOGICAL SOCIETY OF ATHENS, BALANOS ARCHIVES

The notes are on numbered sheets of scrap paper. The following conventions are used for the transcription: () to insert the termination of words abbreviated in the text; < > to correct the orthography of the text; [] to indicate that a word should be deleted. Balanos uses three dots (. . .) to indicate a missing dimension or inventory number.

Page 8

8 ᾿Ιαν.

Μετὰ τὴν ἀφαίρεσιν τοῦ πρώτου ἀναβαθμοῦ τοῦ κρηπιδώματος (8 ᾿Ιανουαρ. 1936) ἐπὶ τῶν τοιχωμάτων τῶν συμπληρούντων τὸν δόμον τοῦτον παρετηρήθη ὅτι εἰς τὸ πρὸς ἀνατολὰς τμῆμα τοῦ βορρείου τοίχου δύο λίθοι πλάτους ὁ πρῶτος 0,325 καὶ ὁ δεύτερος ... ἦσαν καθέτως τοποθετημένοι καὶ λοξὰ πρὸς τὴν διεύθυνσιν τοῦ βορ. κρηπιδώματος—μετὰ τὴν ἀφαίρεσιν τ<ῶν> ἐκ πωρίων σεσαθρωμένων λίθων τοῦ ἐσωτερικοῦ τοῦ κρηπιδώματος παρετηρήθη ὅτι ὁ δεύτερος κάθετος λίθος ἦτο ἐκ τῆς αὐτῆς φύσεως ὑλικοῦ ὡς ὅλοι οἱ ἐσωτερικοὶ λίθοι τοῦ κτίσματος ἐνῶ ὁ

Page 9

8–9 ᾿Ιανουαρ.

πρῶτος ἦτο ἐκ στερεωτέρου λίθου καὶ οὗτινος αἱ δύο πλευραὶ ἦσαν τελείως κατεργασμέναι μὲ ἀναθυρώσεις εἰς τὰ πλευρά.

Γενικοὶ καθαρμοὶ τοῦ μέρους τούτου ἀπέδειξαν ὅτι εὑρισκόμεθα πρὸ τοῦ βορρείου τοίχου τοῦ ἀρχαιοτέρου Ναοῦ τῆς ᾿Αθηνᾶς Νίκης, κατασκευασμένου ἐκ δύο λίθων· ὧν ὁ πρώτος ὕψους ... ὁ δεύτερος ὕψους ... (οὗτος εἶχεν ἀποκοπεῖ κατὰ τὸ ὕψος αὐτοῦ ὅπως ἡ ἄνω αὐτοῦ ἐπιφάνεια εὑρίσκεται εἰς τὸ ὕψος τοῦ 2ου ἀναβαθμοῦ). ῾Ο τοίχος οὗτος ἔχει νῦν ὕψος 1,635 καὶ ἑδράζεται εἰς εὐθυντηρίαν πλάτους ... καὶ ὕψους. ...

Page 10

10 ᾿Ιανουαρίου

ὑπὸ τὸν λίθον τῆς εὐθυντηρίας [του] καὶ τὸ δάπεδον τοῦ Ναοῦ τούτου εὑρέθη μικρ<ὸ>ς λάκος (ὀπὴ) περιέχουσα ἀρχαῖα εἰδώλια εἰς διάφορα μεγέθη (0,04–0,10) καὶ θραύσματα δοχείων καὶ δύο πολὺ μικρὰ κόκκαλα. ῞Ομοιοι λίθοι τῶν τοῦ βορ. τοίχου τοῦ ἀρχαιοτέρου Ναοῦ εὑρέθησαν δύο πρὸς συμπλήρωσιν τῆς στρώσεως τοῦ 2ου ἀναβαθμοῦ καὶ εἰς τὸ ὕψος τοῦ ὁποίου κατεργάσθη ἡ ἄνω ἐπιφάνεια καὶ τρίτος ἐντοιχισ. ἐις τὴν παρειὰν τοῦ κεκλι. τοίχου τοῦ θόλον (καθέτως). ὁ εἰς τὸ σημεῖον "γ" λίθος φαίνεται ὅτι εἶχε κυμάτιον κατὰ τὴν βάσιν.

Page 11

11 Ἰαν.

Ἀνασκαφέντος δὲ τοῦ ἐ<κ> [τὰ] τοῦ Ναοῦ χώρου εὑρέθη
α) ὀγκόλιθος διαστάσεων ... κείμενος ἐπὶ χώματος
β) Νέον ὑπόβαθρον τῆς Δυτ. προσόψ. τῶν Προπυλαίων
γ) ἄλλο καλὸν βάθρον ἔχον περίπου τὴν διεύθυνσιν τοῦ μεσημβρ. τοίχου τοῦ ἀρχαιοτέρου Ναοῦ.
Ἀπεφασίσθη δὲ ἀπὸ κοινοῦ μὲ τὸν κ. Οἰκον(όμον) καὶ Χιλ (B. H. Hill) νὰ ἐγκαταλειφθῇ ἡ περαιτέρω ἀνασκαφὴ πρὸ τοῦ Ναοῦ καὶ νὰ ἐπιδιωχθῇ ἡ ἀνακαίνισις τοῦ Δυτ. τοίχου. Ὁπότε κατασκευαζομένου τούτου ἐκ νέου θὰ εἶναι δυνατὸν νὰ ὑποθεμελιωθῇ ὁ ἀρχαιότερος Ναὸς ὡς καὶ ἡ ΒΑ γωνία τοῦ νεωτέρου χωρὶς νὰ κατεδαφισθῶσι.

Page 12
κατὰ τὴν κατεδάφισιν τῶν τουρκικῆς κατασκευῆς ἐπενδύσεων τῆς δεξαμενῆς, ἐξωτερικῶς δὲ μετὰ τὴν κατεδάφισιν τοῦ πρὸς δυσμᾶς 3. δόμου τῆς θεμελιώσεως τοῦ Ναοῦ τῆς ἑδραζομένης ἐπὶ τοῦ ἀρχαιοτέρου τούτου τείχους τοῦ περιβόλου τοῦ ἀρχαιοτέρου Ναΐσκου—κατὰ τὴν 25 Ἰανουαρ. 1936.

Page 13
ἀφαιρεθέντος τοῦ ἐπὶ τῆς ὀπῆς ταύτης πωρίνου λίθου (ἐκ τῶν τοῦ ὑποβάθρου τοῦ νεωτέρου Ναοῦ) εὑρέθη ὅτι ἡ ὀπὴ (περὶ ἧς ὁ λόγος ἀνωτέρω) ἦτο τετράγωνος ὀπὴ λαξευμένη ἐντὸς δύο παρακειμένων λίθων ... ὅρα σχέδ. καὶ φωτογρ. Κατὰ τὸν κ. Οἰκον(όμον) τοῦτο ἦτο "ἡρῶον"—Εἰς τὰ πέριξ χώματα εὑρέθησαν διάφορα μικρὰ τεμάχια ἀγγείων καὶ εἰδώλια—Ἡ ὀπὴ αὕτη θὰ εἶχε κάλυμμα λίθινον ὅπερ θὰ ἀντικατεστάθη κατὰ τὴν ἀνοικοδόμησιν τοῦ Νεωτ. Ναοῦ διὰ λίθου πωρίνου πάχους περὶ τὰ....

Page 14
Τὰς 15 Ἰανουαρ. ἤρξατο ἡ κατεδάφισις τοῦ Δυτ. τοίχου ἀφαιρεθείσης τῆς μαρμαρίνης κορωνίδος ἥτις ἀπετέλει καὶ τὴν πρὸς δυσμᾶς εὐθυντηρίαν τοῦ Ναοῦ—Ἐκ τῶν τεμαχίων τῆς κορωνίδος ταύτης δύο μόνον τεμάχια τὰ ὑπ' ἀρ. ... εὑρέθησαν ἐν καλῇ καταστάσει. Αἱ δύο γωνίαι τελείως κατεστραμμέναι πρέπει νὰ ἀντικατασταθῶσι ὡς καὶ ἓν διάμεσον τεμάχιον.
Παρατηρητέον ἡ διπλοῖ γόμφοι τῶν μαρμάρων τούτων—φωτογρ.

Page 15
Ἀπὸ τῆς 15 Ἰανουαρ. 1935 ἤρξατο ἡ ἀφαίρεσις τῆς κορωνίδος τοῦ Δυτ. τοίχου τῆς ἀποτελούσης καὶ τὴν εὐθυντηρίαν τοῦ Ναοῦ πρὸς τὸ μέρος τοῦτον.—Οἱ λίθοι οὗτοι συνεδέοντο ἀναμεταξύ των διὰ |—| μολυβδομένων ὡς καὶ μετὰ τῆς πρώτης σειρᾶς τῶν ἐκ Πειραιῶς λίθων διὰ καθέτων γόμφων—Ἡ πρώτη σειρὰ τῶν λίθων τούτων εἶναι τοποθετημένη δρομικῶς.

Page 16

25 Ἰανουαρίου

Ὄπισθεν τοῦ δόμου 4. (τοῦ μβατικοῦ) δὲν ἀνευρέθη ἡ πρόσοψις τοῦ Πελασγικοῦ τείχους ὡς ἀνεμένετο, ἀλλὰ μία στρῶσις ἐξ ὀγκολίθων ὁμοίων πρὸς τοὺς ἄλλους, τοὺς εὐθραύστους, τοῦ νεωτέρου ναοῦ.

εἰς τὸ βάθος τοῦ τετάρτου δόμου εὑρέθη τὸ πρόσωπον ἐκ μικρῶν λίθων ἀρχαιοτέρου τοίχου, ὅρα φωτογρ., ὅστις ἀποτελεῖ ὡς φαίνεται συνέχειαν τῶν ἐκ τῶν ἔσωθεν ἀναφαινομένων ὀγκολίθων.

Translation:
Editor's additions are in brackets, [ ]. More lengthy clarifications are in the notes.

Page 8

8 January

After the removal of the first step of the krepidoma (8 January 1936), it was observed that, among the blocks which completed that course, there were two blocks at the east section of the north wall, the first 0.325 in breadth and the second . . . : these blocks were laid upright on an oblique to the direction of the northern krepidoma. After the removal of heavily damaged poros blocks to the inside of the krepidoma, it was observed that the second upright block was of the same material as all the inner blocks of the structure [the Nike Temple], while the

Page 9

9 January

first was of harder stone and its two sides were completely worked with anathyrosis.[1]

General cleaning of this section showed that we are located in front of the north wall of the earlier Temple of Athena Nike [the naïskos]. The north wall is constructed of two blocks, of which the first is . . . in height, the second . . . in height. (The second was cut down so that its upper surface is at the height of the second step.) This wall [the north wall of the naïskos] has a preserved height of 1.635 and is seated on a euthynteria, width . . . , height. . . .

Page 10

10 January

Under the euthynteria course and the floor of this temple [naïskos] there was found a small pit (hole) containing ancient idols of different sizes (0.04–0.10) and fragments of pots and two very small bones. Blocks similar to those of the north wall of the earlier temple [naïskos] were found: two were found at the level of the second step, completing that course. Their upper surfaces were worked down to the height of the second step.[2] A third block was found immured (upright) in the wall of the barrel vault of the tholos.[3] The block at "C" appears to have had a molding along the base.[4]

Page 11

11 January

Excavating the area outside the [Nike] Temple there were found:
(1) a boulder of dimensions . . . lying on earth;
(2) a new foundation for the west face of the Propylaia;

[1] Balanos appears to be referring to blocks W5 and W6 of the north wall of the naïskos. Both blocks are of Aiginetan poros. The side walls of the naiskos are worked smooth with a claw chisel, an unusual technique. At this early point in the unearthing of this structure, its tooling may well have resembled anathyrosis.

[2] Balanos appears to be referring to naïskos blocks A1 and W8.

[3] Apparently refers to block W7.

[4] Apparently refers to block A2.

(3) another fine base with approximately the orientation of the south wall of the earlier temple [the naïskos].[5]

It was decided in common with Mr. Oikonomos and Mr. Hill that further excavation in front of the [Nike] Temple be abandoned and that we go ahead with the restoration of the west wall [of the bastion]. When this is rebuilt it will be possible to construct a foundation for the earlier temple [naïskos] and for the northeast corner of the later temple [Nike Temple] without removing [these two].

Page 12

In the demolition of the Turkish face of the wall of the cistern, and, on the exterior, after the demolition of the third course of the foundations of the [Nike] Temple on the west, that is to say, those foundations seated on that earlier wall of the peribolos of the earlier naïskos. . . .[6] [This is work done] on the 25th of January 1936.

Page 13

After removal of the poros block from on top of the hole—the poros block was part of the foundation of the later temple [Nike Temple]—it was discovered that the hole (described earlier) was a quadrangular hole chiseled into two adjacent blocks (see the plan and photograph).[7] According to Mr. Oikonomos this was a "heroon". In the surrounding earth were found various small fragments of vessels and idols. The hole itself would have had a stone covering which would have been replaced by a poros block ca. . . . in width during the rebuilding of the later temple [Nike Temple].[8]

Page 14

On the 15th of January the marble [bastion] crown, which also comprises the euthynteria of the [Nike] Temple on the west, was removed and the dismantling of the west [bastion] wall was begun. Of the pieces of the [bastion] crown, only two (with the numbers . . .) were found in good condition. The two corners are completely destroyed and must be replaced, as was also one fragment that lay between them. Note the double clamps of these marbles (photograph).[9]

Page 15

Starting on the 15th of January, 1936, the crown of the west wall [of the bastion] was removed. This wall also comprises the euthynteria of the [Nike] Temple in that region. These blocks were fastened together by |—| (clamps) leaded like the vertical dowels on the courses of Peiraeus limestone from course two down. The first course of these [Peiraeus] blocks were stretchers.

[5] Apparently a reference to the square altar northeast of the naïskos. Balanos means north wall of the naïskos, not south.

[6] The earlier peribolos of the naïskos apparently refers to the first (Stage I) rebuilding of the Mycenaean bastion.

[7] There were no plans or photographs appended to the field notes, nor were there applicable plans or photographs elsewhere in the archives.

[8] See Balanos' drawing of course 2 of the Nike Temple foundation, Plate 15. This shows a block partly overlying the repository, apparently the block to which the text refers.

[9] No photograph was attached to the field notes, nor was there an applicable photograph elsewhere in the archives.

Page 16

25 January

Behind course 4 [of the west face of the bastion sheathing] (formed of headers) we found, not the face of the Pelasgian Wall as we expected, but a course of large blocks [backers] similar to the other, badly shattered blocks of the later temple. Behind [this full] fourth course was the face of an older wall of small stones, see photograph,[10] which constitutes, it appears, a continuation of the boulders visible to the inside.

[10] No photograph was attached to the field notes. The photograph Balanos refers to may possibly be *AA* (*JdI* 54) 1939, cols. 3–4, fig. 2 (= Pl. 4).

APPENDIX B

THE DRAWINGS FROM THE BALANOS ARCHIVES, PLATES 7–17 TRANSCRIPTION OF LABELS AND COMMENTARY

All measurements are in meters. D. = depth; H. = height; L. = length; W. = width. Decimal points omitted from the original are supplied in parentheses.

PLATE 7. SELECTED ELEVATIONS RELATIVE TO THE EUTHYNTERIA OF THE AMPHIPROSTYLE TEMPLE.

NATURAL ROCK (labeled ΦΥΣΙΚΟΣ ΒΡΑΧΟΣ): inside northwest corner of the Mycenaean bastion, −6.63; rock outcropping beneath Classical niches, −8.212 (figure crossed out with −8.244 in pencil).

MYCENAEAN BASTION: west face, boulder at far left, −3.06; north face at northwest corner, −3.18; north face 2.3 m. from corner, −3.18; 3.3 m. from corner, −2.72. Crosswall: boulder 1.2 m. outside south euthynteria of the naïskos, −2.82; boulder southeast of south euthynteria, −2.82; boulder midway between north and south euthynterias, −2.75; boulder 0.8 m. outside north euthynteria, −2.72.

NAISKOS: underpinning at southwest corner (F 2), −1.674; underpinning at west (F 3), −1.674. Euthynteria: at south (E 2), −1.305; at west (E 3), −1.305. North wall, course 1 (W 2), −0.363.

REPOSITORY: east margin, −1.64; collar at southwest, −1.545; upper cavity, −1.64; lowest cavity, −1.839.

SQUARE ALTAR: at center, −0.718.

BASTION SHEATHING: west face at left, course 15, −6.86; course 16, −7.31; course 17, −7.755(?); course 18, −8.21. At niches, course 13, −5.947. Toward northwest corner, course 6, −2.72. On north, course 13, −5.947; course 14, −6.397; course 15, −6.86; course 16, −7.31.

AMPHIPROSTYLE TEMPLE: foundations, course 5, −2.37. Krepidoma, step 1, +0.255; step 2, +0.51; stylobate, +0.78. Toichobate, +0.997.

ELEVATIONS ABOVE SEA LEVEL.

NATURAL ROCK: outcropping beneath Classical niches, 133.969.

BASTION CROSSWALL: inside north euthynteria of naïskos, 140.545.

NAISKOS: underpinning at west (F 3), 140.643 [error: correct figure is +140.55]. Euthynteria at west (E 3), 140.918; on north (E 5), 140.916. North wall, course 1 (W 3), 141.862; course 2 (W 6), 142.469.

REPOSITORY: collar at northwest, 140.673.

SQUARE ALTAR: northwest corner, 141.480.

BASTION SHEATHING: west face at left, course 17, 134.441; course 18, 133.976. Toward northwest corner, course 6, 139.489. North face, course 16, 134.914.

AMPHIPROSTYLE TEMPLE: euthynteria, northeast corner, 142.213; krepidoma, step 1, 142.467.

SELECTED DIMENSIONS.

BASTION CROSSWALL: W. 1.45 inside north euthynteria of naïskos.

NAISKOS: clear width, south euthynteria to north wall, 1.775.

COMMENTS. Plate 7 records the bastion with considerable Mycenaean stonework already removed. (Compare Plate 10 where more of the Stage 1 crown is in place, and Plates 16, 17 with further stonework of the Mycenaean crosswall; the excavation photograph, Plate 3:b, documents the crosswall as first uncovered.) The crosswall is recorded at +140.545 inside the north euthynteria of the naïskos. The relative levels recorded to either side are over a meter lower however: −2.82 to −2.72 (= +139.39 to +139.49). The relative levels appear to have been taken after one or more courses of the crosswall had been removed.

The drawing gives a mistaken record of the stonework at a number of points. The Cyclopean boulder on the west face of the bastion at the northwest corner is shown above rather than below the lighter stonework directly to its south. Compare Plate 10, which records the proper relation between the two. Directly east of the boulder are two badly disintegrated blocks from foundation course 3 of the amphiprostyle temple (see Pl. 16, cf. Pl. 17). The boulder is shown partly covering these foundation blocks; like the lighter stonework of the façade, however, the course 3 foundations were in fact above the Cyclopean bastion. Course 3 is at +140.87. Plate 10 records the boulder at *ca.* +139.55.

Absolute and relative elevations on this plan were taken independently and, as shown by the levels on the crosswall, at different times. The exactingly measured cross-sections of the bastion, Plates 11 and 13:a, let one gauge their respective accuracies: Plate 7 gives the relative level of course 18 of the bastion sheathing as −8.21; it gives the absolute level as +133.976 (+ 142.213 [euthynteria] − 133.976 = 8.237). The measured distance from the euthynteria to course 18 is 8.174 m. (= 8.137 m. [courses 1–18] + 0.447 m. [crown + euthynteria] − 0.41 m. [course 18]). At distances of less than three meters the discrepancies are correspondingly less, e.g., the relative level of course 6 of the sheathing is given as −2.75, the absolute level as +139.489 (+142.213 − 139.489 = 2.724). The measured distance, euthynteria to course 6, is 2.722 m. (Pls. 11, 13:a).

PLATE 8. ELEVATIONS FROM SEA LEVEL.

NATURAL ROCK: at northwest corner of Classical sheathing, 133.523.

MYCENAEAN BASTION: bedding for pier in niche, 135.464; top of pier, 136.694. Southwest corner of bastion, 139.171.

BASTION SHEATHING: course 14 on north, 135.822; behind eastern niche, 135.804.

SELECTED DIMENSIONS.

MYCENAEAN BASTION: W. of northern niche, 1(.)28.

BASTION SHEATHING: full W. on west, 10.43; W. from northwest corner to northern niche, 3.37; W. from southwest corner to southern niche, 3.92; W. across niches, 3.14. Northern niche, W. at front, 1.185; at rear, 1.175; D. 1.236. Southern niche, W. 1.338;

D. (.)66. Pier, W. (.)617; D. (.)407; pier to back wall of niche, (.)218. Pier and southern niche combined, W. 1.963.

COMMENTS. On the rendering of the Mycenaean niches in this drawing, pp. 13–14 above.

PLATE 9. SELECTED ELEVATIONS FROM SEA LEVEL.

MYCENAEAN BASTION: at west, 139.179; at east, 139.558.

BASTION SHEATHING: course 1, 141.764.

AMPHIPROSTYLE TEMPLE: euthynteria, 142.214; krepidoma, step 1, 142.469; step 2, 142.724; stylobate, 142.994; column base, 143.211; toichobate, 143.211.

SELECTED DIMENSIONS.

BASTION SHEATHING: course 18, H. .485(?); course 19, H. .455; course 20, H. .455; course 21, H. (.)44; course 22, H. (.)44; course 23, H. (.)44; course 24, H. (.)70.

COMMENTS. The record of Cyclopean stonework in this drawing is approximate at best. The boulder at far right marked "139.558" is entered 0.7 m. too far to the west. Measurements on site place it 9.1 m. from the southwest corner of the bastion, not *ca.* 8.4 m. Other boulders in the drawing correspond only generally to the visible remains. Note that the general plan, Balanos 1956, pl. I, gives a different but no more accurate record of the southern crown.

PLATE 10. SELECTED DIMENSIONS.

MYCENAEAN BASTION: top course of boulders (behind sheathing courses 6 and 7), from left, L. 1(.)40, H. (.)85; L. 1(.)00, H. (.)90; L. 1(.)10, H. (.)80; L. 1(.)50, H. (.)80; southwest corner, top down, L. 1.50, H. (.)85; L. 1.40, H. 1(.)20; L. 1(.)40; H. (.)40; L. 1(.)00, H. (.)40; L. 1.15, H. (.)95.

COMMENTS. Plate 10 is a working drawing, like many in the archives. The draftsman has left calculations along the margin, and there are queries and instructions from Balanos at upper left and below.

PLATE 11. LABELS. Centered below: ΤΟΜΗ ΚΑΤΑ ΤΗΝ Ε–Ζ. Natural rock at lower left: ΛΑΞΕΥΜΑΤΑ ΦΥΣΙΚΟΥ ΒΡΑΧΟΥ (two times). Mycenaean bastion, west face: ΠΕΛΑΣΓΙΚΟΝ ΤΕΙΧΟΣ. Sheathing, up west face: ΕΞΩΤΕΡΙΚΟΝ ΠΕΡΙΒΛΗΜΑ ΠΥΡΓΟΥ. Amphiprostyle temple, east euthynteria: ΕΥΘΥΝΤΗΡΙΑ; foundation course 1 at east, ΠΕΙΡΑΙΩΣ. Between amphiprostyle temple and altar, ΑΝΑΤΟΛΗ.

DIMENSIONS.

MYCENAEAN BASTION: H. from bastion fill (below F 4) to euthynteria of amphiprostyle temple, 2.26.

NAISKOS: naïskos euthynteria to euthynteria of amphiprostyle temple, 1.295.

BASTION SHEATHING: bastion crown (including temple euthynteria), H. (.)447; course 1, (.)446; course 2, (.)445; course 3, (.)456; course 4, (.)463; course 5, (.)465; course 6, (.)461; course 7, (.)455; course 8, (.)456; course 9, (.)443; course 10, (.)46; course 11, (.)46; course 12, (.)46; course 13, (.)451; course 14, (.)451; course 15, (.)457; course 16, (.)458; course 17, (.)455; course 18, (.)41; course 19, (.)46. From top of course 1 to foot of course 18, 8.137.

STAGE III ALTAR: base slab, W. (.)97, H. (.)30; body of altar, H. (.)505. H. from base slab to euthynteria of amphiprostyle temple, 1.195.

STAGE IV ALTAR: underpinning, western block, L. (.)26; eastern block, L. (.)74, H. (.)41. H. from underpinning to euthynteria of amphiprostyle temple, (.)28.

AMPHIPROSTYLE TEMPLE: L. on euthynteria, 9.527; L. on stylobate, 8.119. H. from top of frieze to stylobate, 4.975. Frieze, H. (.)45; epistyle, H. (.)473; column, H. 4.05. Stylobate, H. (.)27; steps 1, 2, H. (.)255; tread, (.)316. Projection of euthynteria from step 1, (.0)72; projection of bastion crown from euthynteria, (.)1054.

COMMENTS. The drawing appears to be a composite of several sections. The natural rock, the lower courses of the Mycenaean bastion, and the west euthynteria of the naïskos are cut on a line *ca.* 9.0 m. behind the south face of the Classical bastion. The repository is on a line 0.25–0.4 m. to the south, 8.6–8.75 m. behind the south bastion face. The altar, shown in elevation, is from a point no more than 6.5 m. behind the south bastion face. Compare Plate 8, where a section line E–Z is entered *ca.* 9.0 m. behind the south bastion face.

The underpinning for the naïskos at the northwest (F 4) is shown resting on a level stony stratum of bastion fill. This is contradicted by Plate 3:b, which shows F 4 cutting *ca.* 0.15 m. into an uneven stony stratum. The level of the stratum in the drawing, +139.95 (= +142.213 − 2.26), approximates the level of the cement floor in the modern crypt. The drawing omits block F 6, the easternmost block of underpinning on the north side of the naïskos and misrecords the base slab of the rectangular altar: the resting surface of the base slab, shown as level, in fact rises *ca.* 0.12 m. to the east.

PLATE 12. LABELS. *NAISKOS:* south euthynteria, ΒΑΣΙΣ ΝΑΙΣΚΟΥ; north euthynteria and underpinning, ΒΑΣΙΣ ΝΑΙΣΚΟΥ; north wall, ΑΡΧΑΙΟΤΕΡΟΣ ΤΟΙΧΟΣ ΝΑΙΣΚΟΥ. *REPOSITORY:* ΑΡΧΑΙΟΤΕΡΟΣ ΒΟΘΡΟΣ Η ΒΩΜΟΣ. *AMPHIPROSTYLE TEMPLE:* Foundations, courses 1, 2: Αος ΔΟΜΟΣ ΕΣΩΤΕΡΙΚ. ΛΙΘΩΝ; Βος ΔΟΜΟΣ ΕΣΩΤΕΡΙΚΩΝ ΛΙΘΩΝ. Euthynteria, north and south: ΕΥΘΥΝΤΗΡΙΑ. Outside south euthynteria: ΜΕΣΗΒΡ. ΔΥΤΙΚΗ ΓΩΝΙΑ ΕΥΘΥΝΤΗΡΙΑΣ. Krepidoma, north and south, first, second, and third steps: Ι ΑΝΑΒΑΘΜΟΣ, ΙΙ ΑΝΑΒΑΘΜΟΣ, ΙΙΙ ΑΝΑΒΑΘΜΟΣ. Anta, north and south: ΟΡΘΟΣΤΑΤΗΣ. Anta at base: ΣΠΕΙΡΑ. *TURKISH PERIOD.* Crypt entryway, south wall: ΤΟΙΧΟΠΟΙΪΑ ΤΟΥΡΚΙΚΗΣ ΕΠΟΧΗΣ, ΕΙΣΟΔΟΥ. Doorpost of crypt: ΜΑΡΜΑΡΟΝ ΘΥΡΑΣ. Line of crypt vault: ΤΟΞΟΝ ΤΟΥΡΚΙΚΟΥ ΘΟΛΟΥ. Rubble at south edge of bastion: ΤΟΙΧΟΠΟΙΪΑ ΤΟΥΡΚΙΚΗΣ ΕΠΟΧΗΣ.

SELECTED DIMENSIONS.

NAISKOS: underpinning at south (F 1), H. (.)237; euthynteria, north and south, H. (.)369; south euthynteria, W. (.)40 [error: correct figure, 0.47 m.]. North wall, course 1: H. (.)942, W. (.)312; course 2, H. (.)60. W. of naïskos, inner edge of south euthynteria to north wall, 1.775; line of south wall to inner face of north wall, 1.84. H. from south euthynteria to upper edge of amphiprostyle-temple foundations, course 2, (.)42.

REPOSITORY: W. 1.0645; H. at north, (.)31, at south, (.)325; collar at north, H. (.0)95. Collar at north to upper edge of naïskos euthynteria, (.)24.

AMPHIPROSTYLE TEMPLE: W. across euthynteria, 6.80; W. across stylobate, 5.392. Toichobate, H. (.)217. Stylobate, H. (.)27; steps 1, 2, H. (.)255; W. of tread, (.)316. Euthynteria, full height, (.)2835; projection from bottom step, (.0)72. Foundations, course 1, H. (.)60; course 2, (.)58; course 3, (.)45; course 4, (.)46; course 5, (.)45.

COMMENTS. This section cuts *ca.* 7.2 m. behind the west face of the Classical bastion. The stratum of stones beneath the repository is incorrectly shown as rising up under the north euthynteria of the naïskos. Compare Plate 3:b and note 8 above, p. 39.

PLATE 13:a. LABELS. Centered below: ΤΟΜΗ ΚΑΤΑ ΤΗΝ Γ–Δ, with Γ–Δ corrected in ink to Κ–Λ. Along face of sheathing: ΕΞΩΤΕΡΙΚΟΝ ΠΕΡΙΒΛΗΜΑ ΠΥΡΓΟΥ. Stepped cuttings in rock: ΛΑΞΕΥΜΑΤΑ ΦΥΣΙΚΟΥ ΒΡΑΧΟΥ. Along rear wall of Classical niche: ΠΕΡΙΒΛΗΜΑ ΚΟΓΧΗΣ. Along face of Mycenaean bastion: ΠΕΛΑΣΓΙΚΟΝ ΤΕΙΧΟΣ. Along upper surface of bastion: ΔΑΠΕΔΟΝ ΤΣΙΜΕΝΤΟΥ; ΤΣΙΜΕΝΤΟΥ corrected in pen to ΝΑΙΣΚΟΥ and finally crossed out in pencil.

SELECTED DIMENSIONS.

MYCENAEAN BASTION: niche, H. 1.23; supporting pier, W. (.)37; from pier to niche back wall, (.)35. From roof of niche to top of Mycenaean bastion, 3.24. From top of bastion to euthynteria of amphiprostyle temple, 2.26.

BASTION SHEATHING: crown and courses 1–17, heights as given for Plate 11. Course 18, H. (.)495; course 19, H. (.)455; course 20, (.)455. From crown to foot of course 11, 5.499; from foot of course 11 to foot of course 16, 2.266. Set back of niche pier from face of bastion, (.0)8; from front face of pier to back wall of niche, (.)407.

AMPHIPROSTYLE TEMPLE: column base, H. (.)217. Heights of steps as given in Plate 11.

COMMENTS. The section is 4.65 m. behind the south face of the bastion. See Plate 8, where the cut is labeled I–K. The plan gives the distance from the amphiprostyle-temple euthynteria to the foot of course 11 as 5.499 m. Calculated from the heights of the individual courses the distance is 5.457 m. Similarly, the distance from the foot of course 11 to the foot of course 16 is given as 2.266 m. Course by course it comes to 2.277 m.

PLATE 13:b. LABELS. Centered beneath drawing: ΤΟΜΗ ΚΑΤΑ ΜΗΚΟΣ. Along stylobate of temple: ΔΑΠΕΔΟΝ ΝΑΟΥ.

DIMENSIONS.

CRYPT: H. from floor to lower entryway, (.)60; H. of entryway threshold, (.)20. H. from threshold to crypt vault, 1.20. H. from vault to stylobate of amphiprostyle temple, (.)40. H. of step in entryway, (.)25.

AMPHIPROSTYLE TEMPLE: stylobate, H. (.)27; steps 1, 2, H. (.)255; projection of euthynteria above paving, (.)10.

COMMENTS. Compare this section with the latitudinal section, Plate 12. The latter draws the lower entryway of the crypt on a level with course 2 of the eastern foundations for the amphiprostyle temple, that is, at +141.33. Plate 13:b records the same part of the crypt at

+141.19. The plan of the crypt entryway, Plate 14, draws the lower entryway as *ca.* 0.87 m. in length. Plate 13:b records the length as *ca.* 1.20 m.

PLATE 14. LABELS. *AMPHIPROSTYLE-TEMPLE FOUNDATIONS:* the two easternmost blocks on the north and south sides and the four blocks between on the east are labeled ΠΕΙΡΑΙΩΣ.

SELECTED DIMENSIONS.

BASTION SHEATHING: blocks on west face of bastion, from south, L. 1.235, W. (.)69; L. 1.25, W. (.)67; L. 1.88, W. (.)67; L. 1.226, W. (.)71; L. 1(.)20, W. (.)67; L. 1.82. L. of blocks on north face of bastion: from west (.)911; (.)615; (.)625; (.)615; (.)615; (.)60; (.)614; (.)617; (.)614; (.)62; (.)612; (.)619.

AMPHIPROSTYLE-TEMPLE FOUNDATIONS: course 1, H. (.)448 (at west). L. of blocks along south side of foundations: from west, 1(.)33; (.)58; (.)69; (.)72; (.)67; (.)70; (.)58; (.)55; 1(.)35; 1(.)64. W. of blocks across foundations 1.0 m. from west bastion face: from south, (.)73; (.)63; (.)58; (.)63; (.)58; (.)52; (.)50; (.)50; (.)53; (.)53; 2.4 m. from west face: from south, 1(.)26; (.)61; (.)60; (.)48; (.)54; (.)56; (.)58; (.)58; (.)52; across east end of foundations: from south: (.)995; 1(.)22; 1.15; (.)60; 2.05; 1.025. Setback of euthynteria from east side of foundations, (.)18; from south side, (.0)6.

COMMENTS. There are four cuttings for T-dowels: at the northwest corner of the sheathing; at the northeast and southeast corners of the temple foundations; and in the block adjoining the northeast corner on the south. Dimensions of "T" cuttings: in sheathing at northwest, across "T", (.)10, L. (.)10; foundations at northeast, across "T", (.)12, L. (.)10; block adjoining at south, across "T", (.)12, L. (.)10; foundations at southeast, across "T", (.0)8, L. (.)10. The six blocks of foundations between the north wall of the naïskos and the crypt entryway are a repair laid by Ross in 1835. See note 39 above, p. 10.

PLATE 15. SELECTED DIMENSIONS.

BASTION SHEATHING: course 2, H. (.)445; blocks of west face, W. 1(.)30; L. from south, (.)613; .613; (.)61; (.)615; (.)613; (.)595; (.)615; (.)613; (.)613; 1(.)875 (3 blocks); (.)84; L. of blocks on north face: from west, 1(.)835; 1(.)23; 1(.)23; 1(.)225; 1(.)225; 1(.)223.

AMPHIPROSTYLE-TEMPLE FOUNDATIONS: L. of blocks along south side of foundations: from west, 1(.)30; (.)73; (.)64; (.)69; (.)68; (.)63 m.; (.)69; (.)53; (.)52; (.)52; 1(.)28; along south side of foundations 2.3 m. in: from east, 1(.)39; (.)68; (.)68; (.)67. W. of blocks across foundations 2.2 m. from west face of bastion: from south, (.)77; (.)67; (.)70; (.)64; (.)66; (.)68; (.)73; (.)67; (.)46; 7.2 m. from west face: from south, 1(.)30; (.)63; 1(.)40; (over naïskos) (.)51; (.)50; (.)56; (.)60; (naïskos north wall) (.)312. Course 2 projects beyond temple euthynteria (.)135 on east, (.)145 on south.

COMMENTS. The six blocks of foundations covering the eastern area of the naïskos are a repair laid by Ross in 1835. See note 39 above, p. 10.

PLATE 16. SELECTED DIMENSIONS.

BASTION SHEATHING: course 3, H. (.)456; blocks on west face: W. (.)67; L. from south, 1(.)26?; 1(.)225; 1(.)84; 1(.)27?; 1(.)203; 1.80; L. of blocks on north face: from west, (.)918; (.)61; (.)615; (.)615; (.)615; (.)615; (.)612; (.)622; (.)614; (.)609; (.)606; (.)618; (.)612.

AMPHIPROSTYLE-TEMPLE FOUNDATIONS: L. of blocks down south side 1.0 m. in: from west, 1.20; (.)53; (.)54; (.)58; (.)58; (.)64; (.)72; (.)60; (.)60; (.)64; (.)65; (.)74; (.)76.; 1.8 m. in: from west, 1(.)36; 1(.)30; 1(.)24; 1(.)28; 1(.)20; 1(.)32; 1(.)20. W. of blocks across foundations 1.2 m. from west face of bastion: from south, .71; (.)65; (.)67; (.)58; (.)55; (.)56; (.)60; (.)58; (.)52; (.)50; 9.0 m. from west face: from south, 1(.)40; (.)50; (.)68; (.)63. Projection of course 3 beyond euthynteria of temple on south, (.0)6; on east, 1.0 m. from the southeast corner, (.0)8; on east, 1.8 m. from southeast corner, (.)21.

PLATE 17. LABELS. Inside west bastion face at left: ΧΑΛΑΣΜΕΝΕΣ, crossed out in pencil. Foundations overlapping Mycenaean crosswall from the east: 3ου ΔΟΜΟΥ. On one of the boulders of the Mycenaean crosswall in cursive: ἄνω ἐπιφάνεια Πελασγικοῦ τείχου.

SELECTED DIMENSIONS.

BASTION SHEATHING: course 4, H. (.)463; blocks on west face: W. 1(.)28; L. from south, (3 blocks) 1(.)815; (3 blocks) 1(.)825; (3 blocks) 1(.)825; (.)845; L. of blocks on north face: from west, 1(.)84; 1(.)23; 1(.)227; 1(.)23; 1(.)225; 1(.)22; (.)90.

AMPHIPROSTYLE-TEMPLE FOUNDATIONS: L. of blocks along south side 0.3 m. in: from east, 1(.)43; 1(.)33; 1(.)34; 1(.)34; 1(.)34; 1.6 m. in: from east, (.)69; (.)43; (.)65; (.)66; (.)67; (.)66; (.)68; (.)58; (.)58; (.)70; (.)70; 1(.)40. W. of blocks across foundations 2.0 m. from west face of bastion: from south, (.)60; (.)66; (.)66; (.)61; (.)60; (.)57; (.)60; (.)60; (.)62; (.)44; 6.5 m. from west face: from south, (.)67; 1(.)33; 8.4 m. from west face: from south, (.)70; 1(.)38; (.)69; (.)70; (.)57; (.)60.

COMMENTS. The drawing records two ashlar courses to the east of the Mycenaean crosswall: a row of five headers and two stretchers shown as if projecting from beneath. The two stretchers are not, however, from course 5 but from course 3: note the adjacent labels "3ου ΔΟΜΟΥ" and the record of the blocks in Plate 16. The headers are presumably from course 4, but are shown as though they overlapped the crosswall; their resting surface is in fact *ca.* 0.50 m. below the crown of that wall.

INDEX

PLATES

a. Naïskos and repository (base for the cult statue) from the southwest

b. Naïskos and repository (base for the cult statue) from the east

a. Repository (base for the cult statue) from the east

b. Repository with deposit of figurines from the southeast

a. Excavation photograph of the naïskos and repository from the east

b. Excavation photograph of the naïskos from the southwest

PLATE 4

Excavation photograph of the bastion from the southwest

PLATE 5

Rectangular altar and base slab from the northwest

a. Inscribed block from the Stage I altar

b. Exposed inner face of the bastion on the north

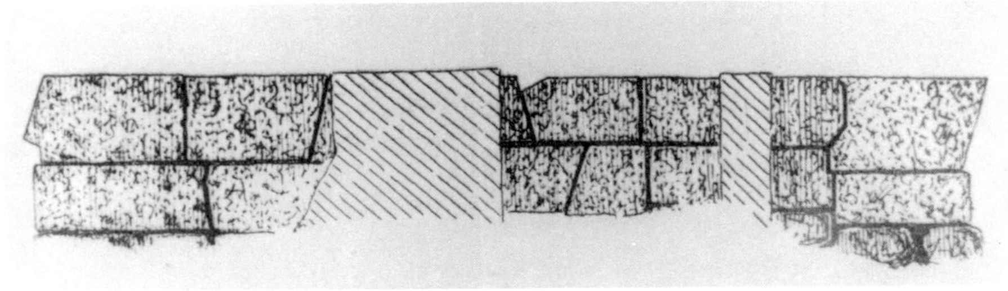

c. Irregular trapezoidal crown of the bastion, in elevation from the north

Balanos Archives: Detail from a general plan of the bastion

PLATE 8

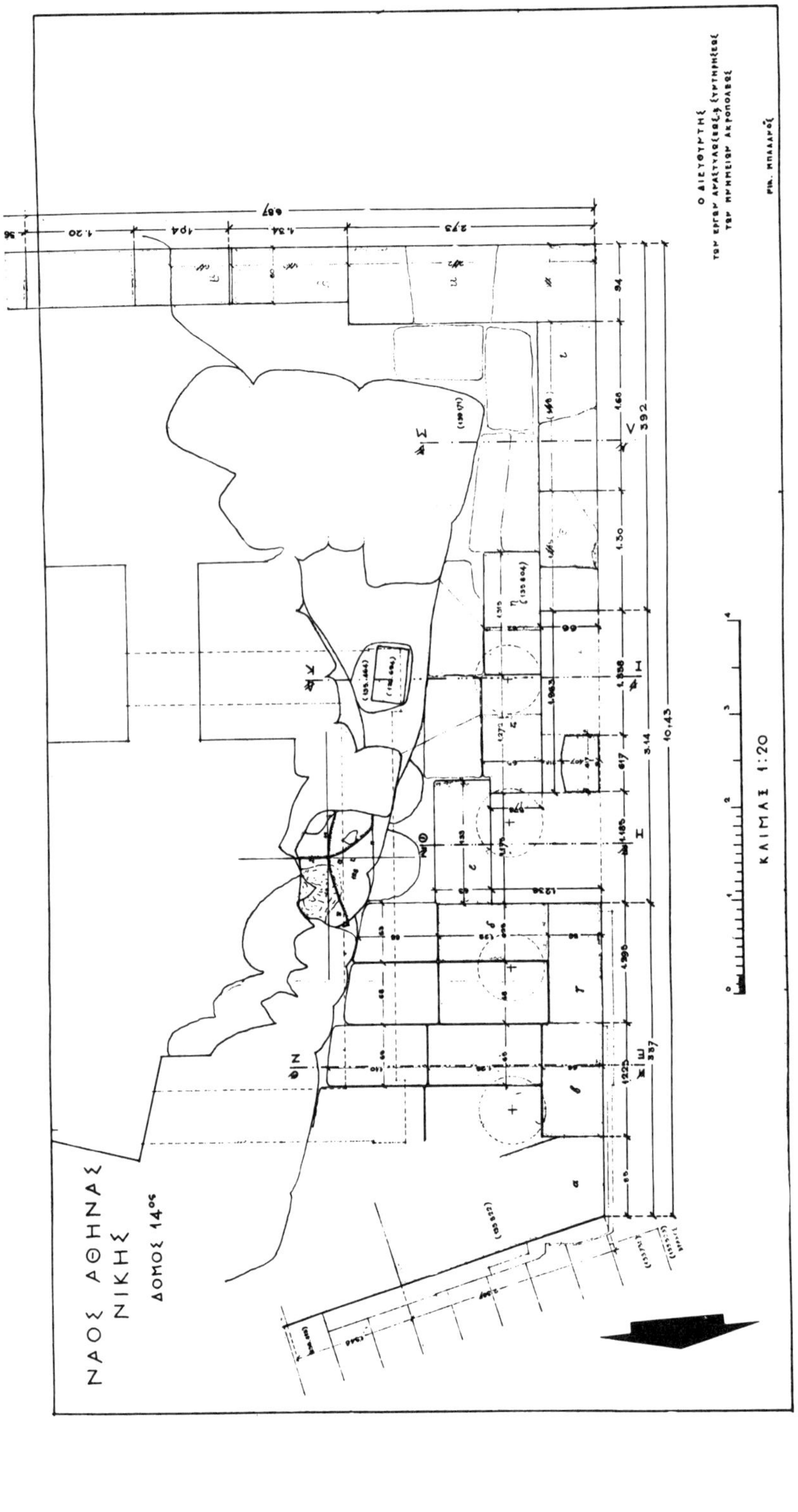

Balanos Archives: Plan of the western bastion at course 14 of the ashlar sheathing

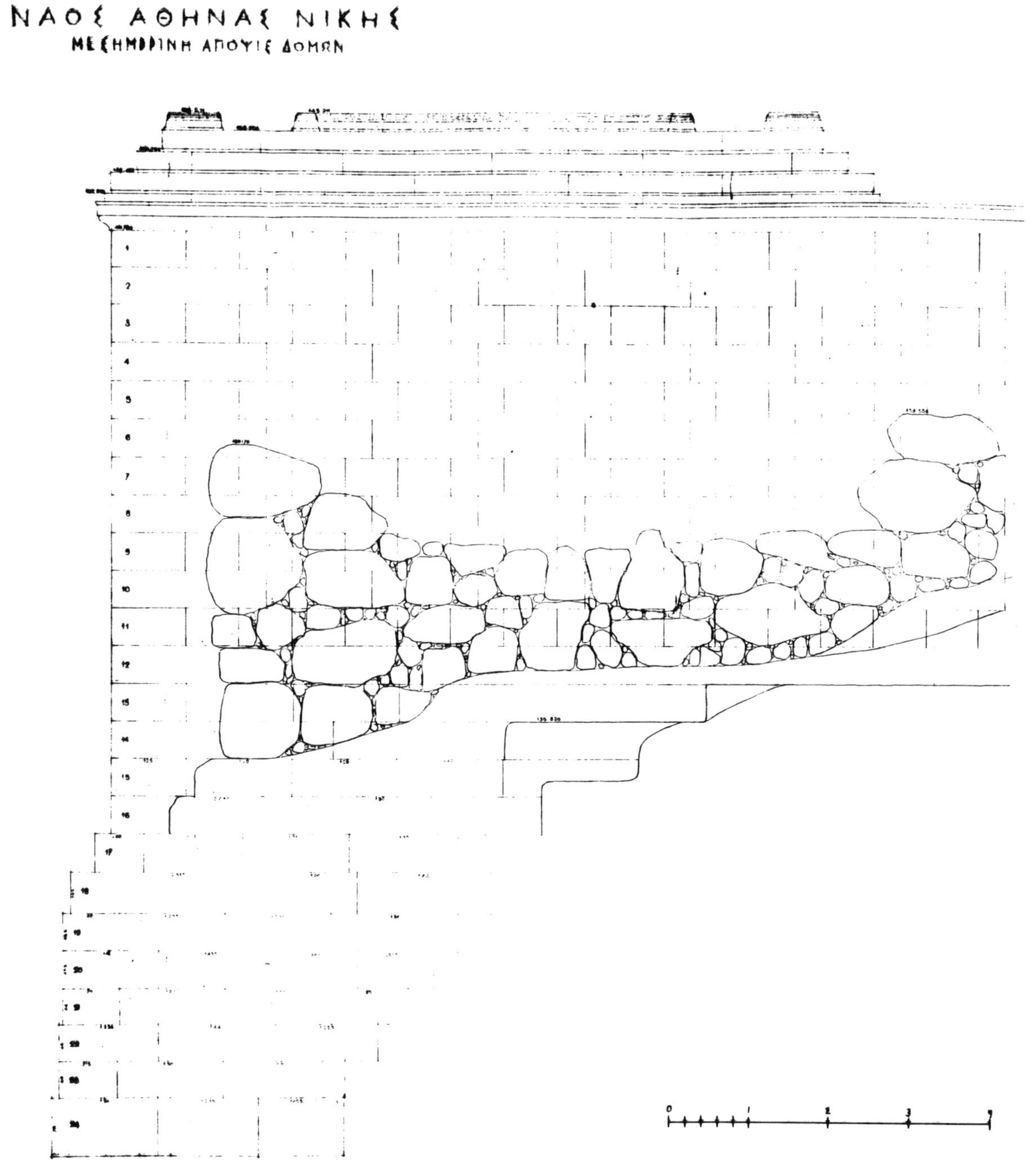

Balanos Archives: Elevation of the bastion from the south, with Mycenaean and Classical remains superimposed

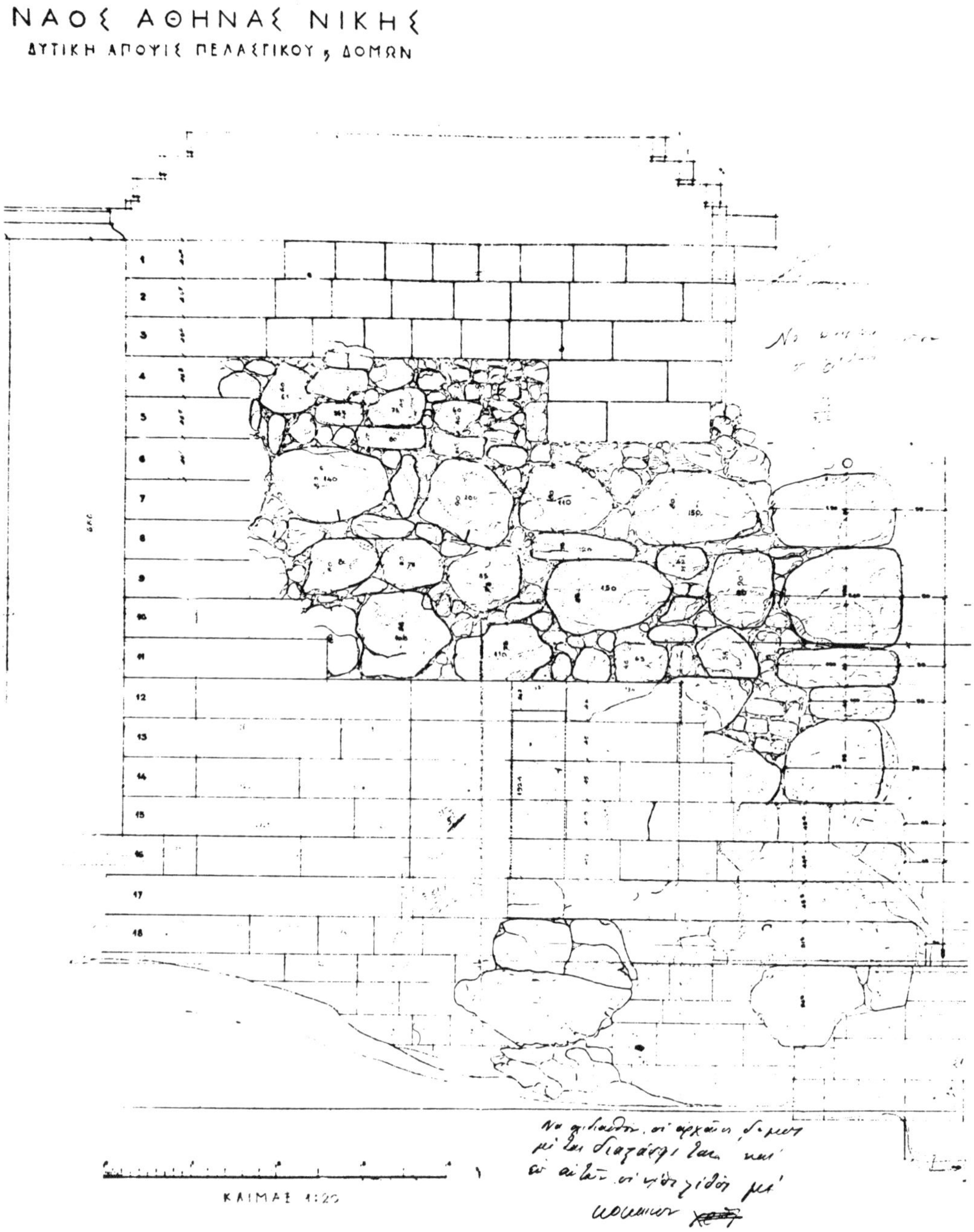

Balanos Archives: Elevation of the bastion from the west with the sheathing partly dismantled

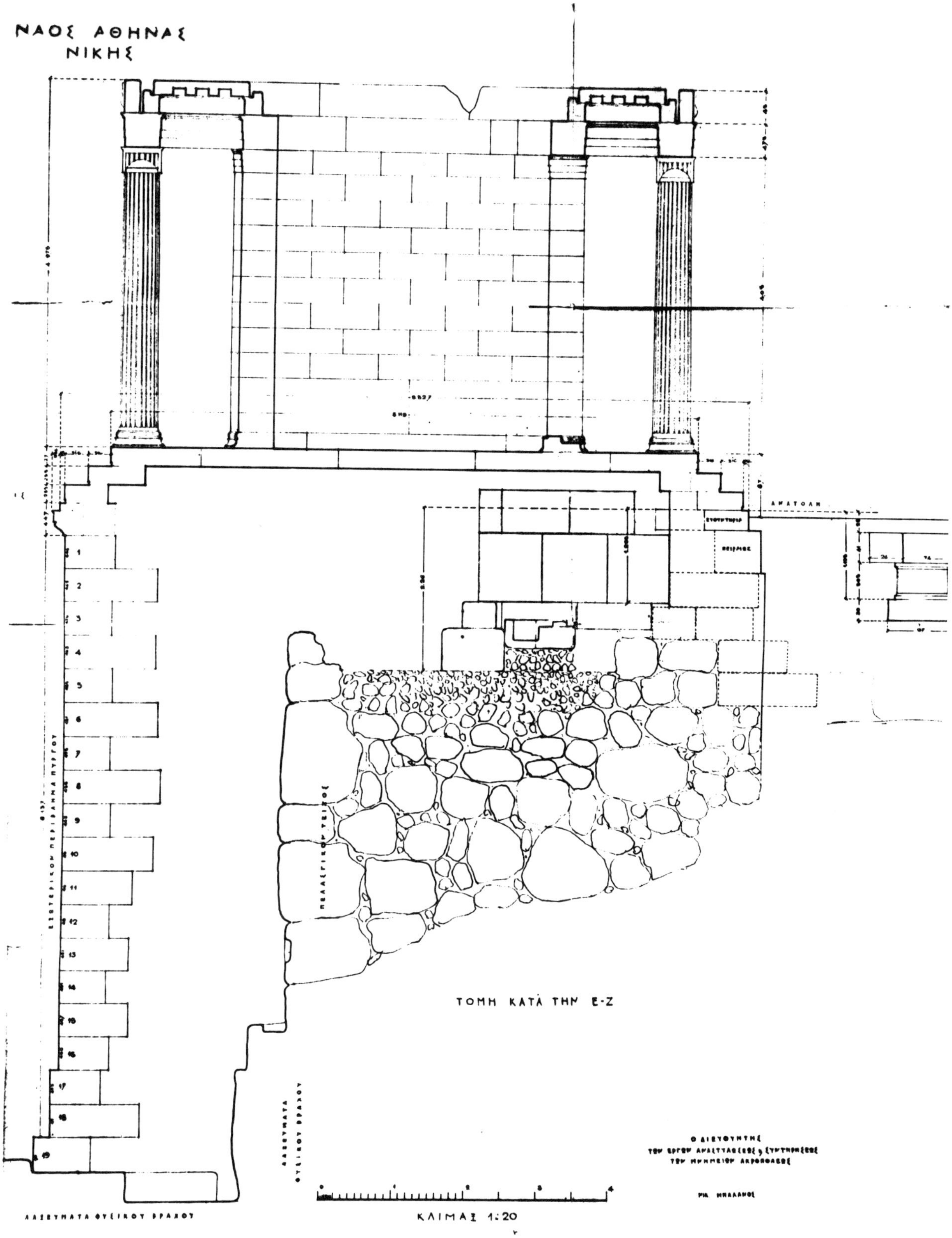

Balanos Archives: Longitudinal section of the bastion from the south

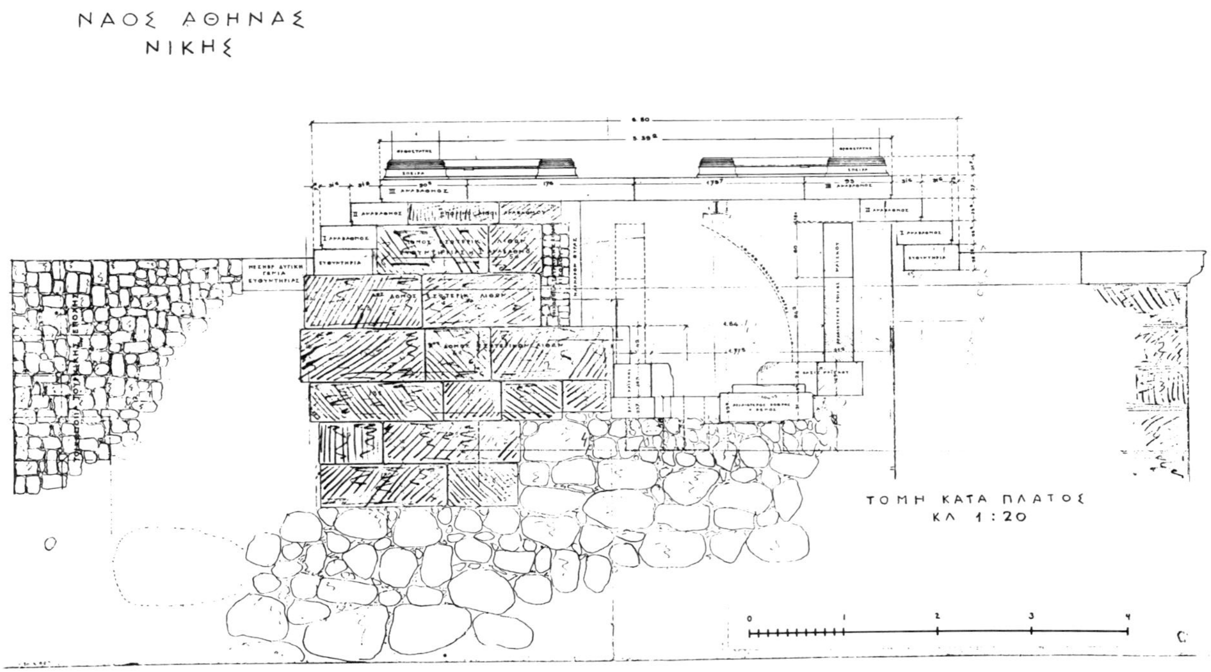

Balanos Archives: Transverse section of the bastion from the east

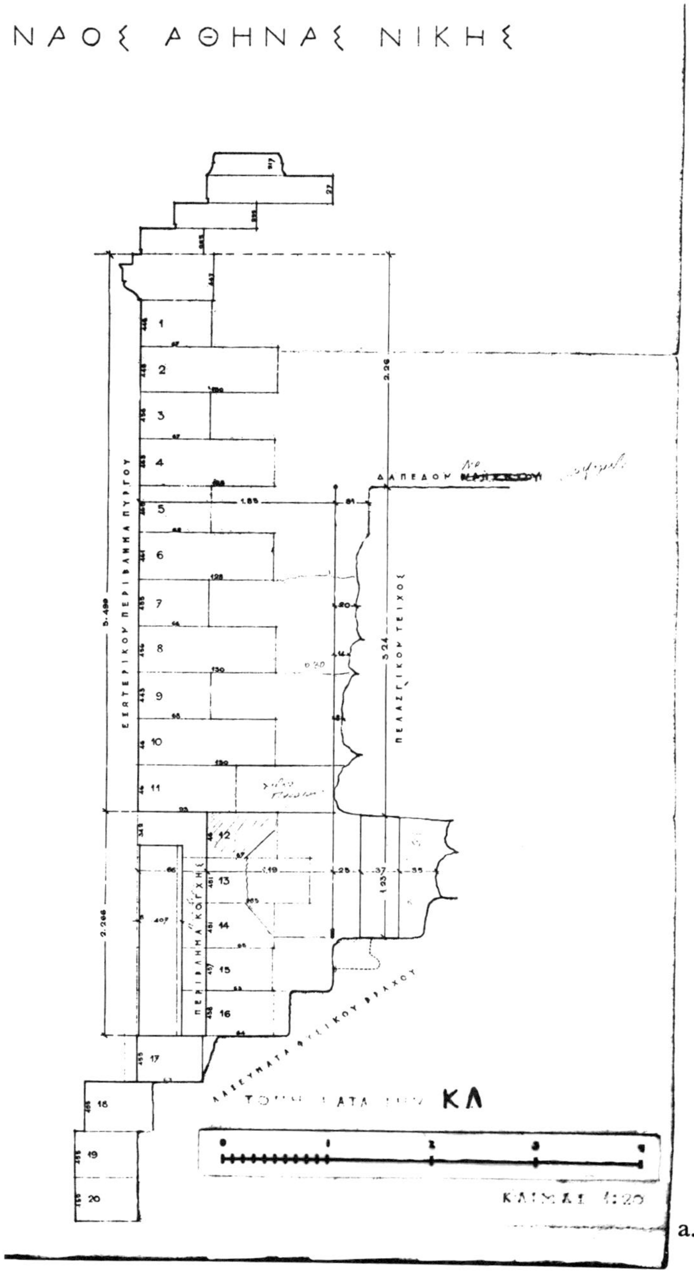

a. Balanos Archives: Longitudinal section of the western bastion showing the Mycenaean and Classical niches

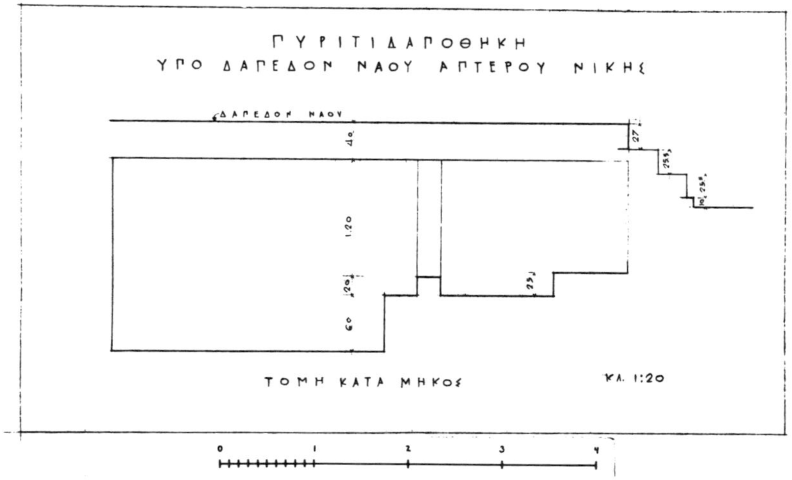

b. Balanos Archives: Longitudinal section of the Turkish crypt

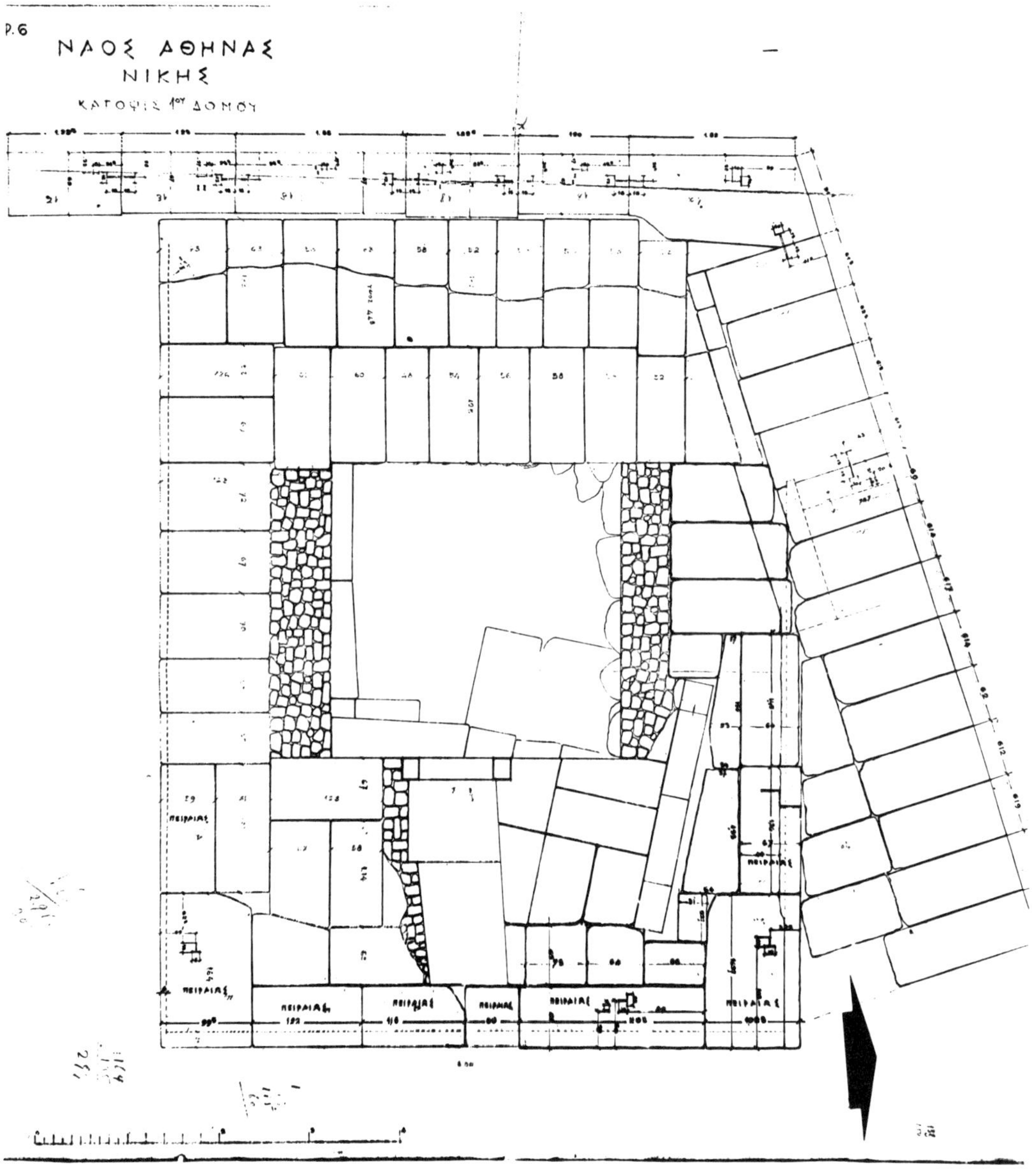

Balanos Archives: Course 1 of the foundations for the Nike Temple

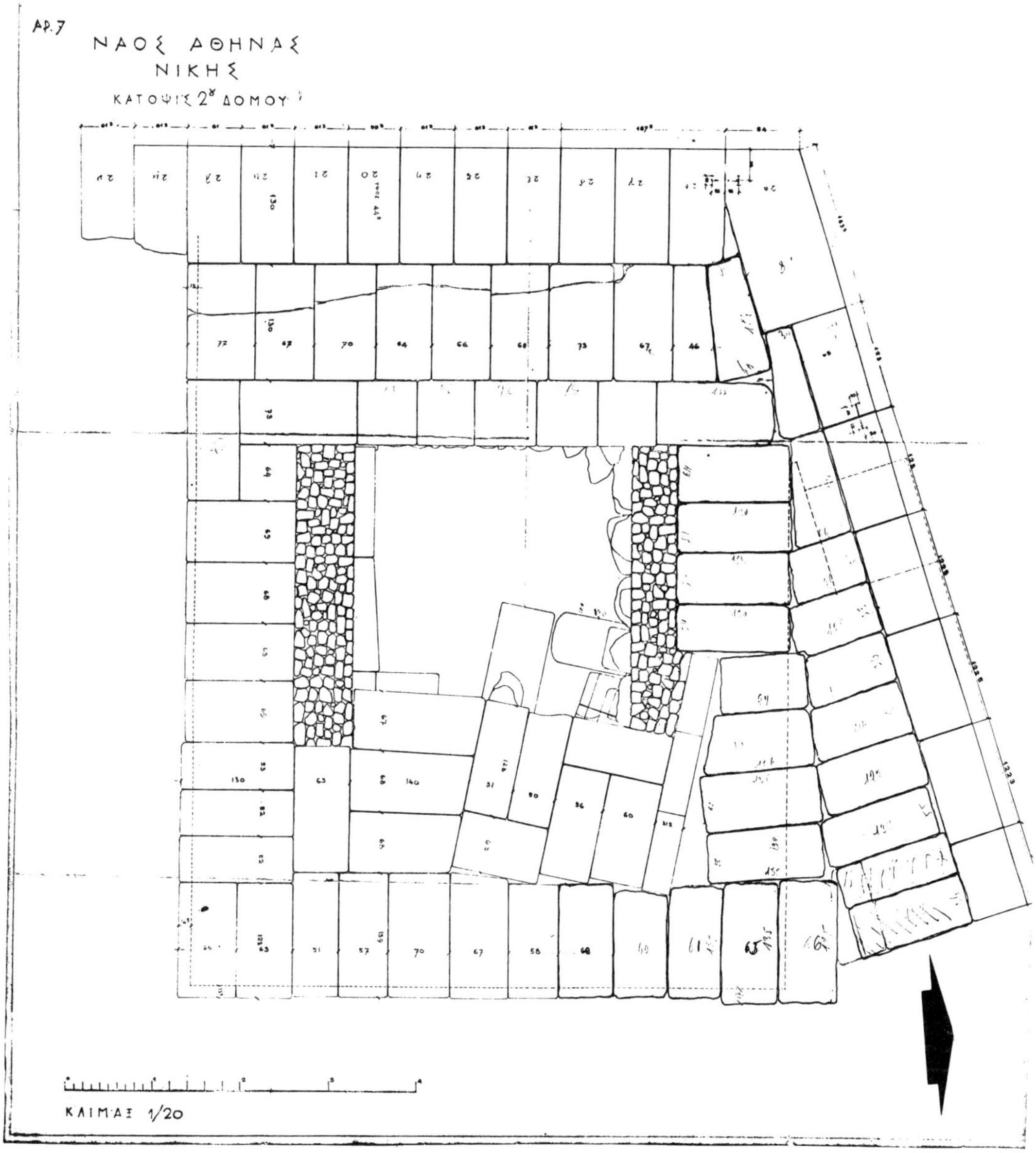

Balanos Archives: Course 2 of the foundations for the Nike Temple

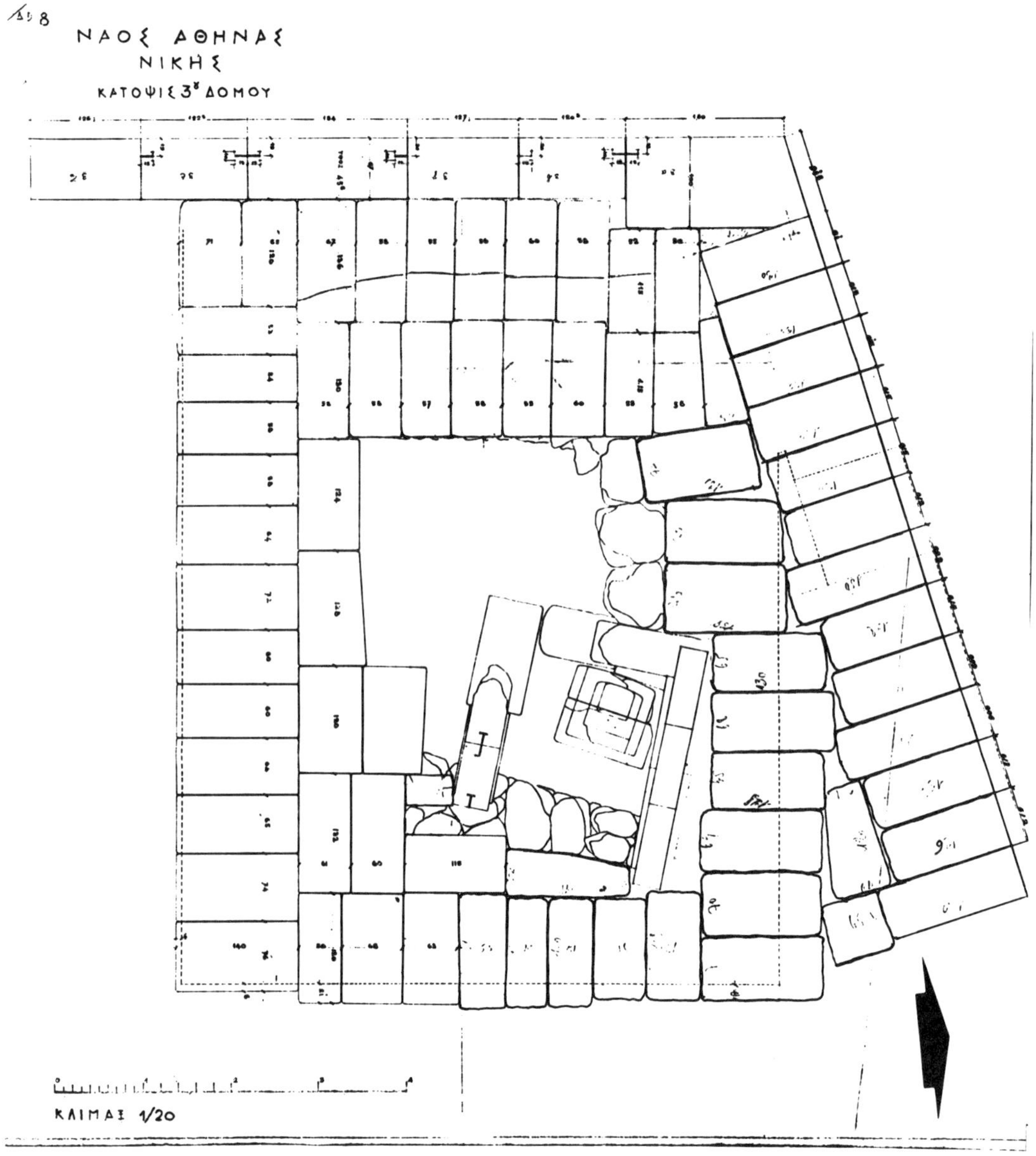

Balanos Archives: Course 3 of the Foundations for the Nike Temple

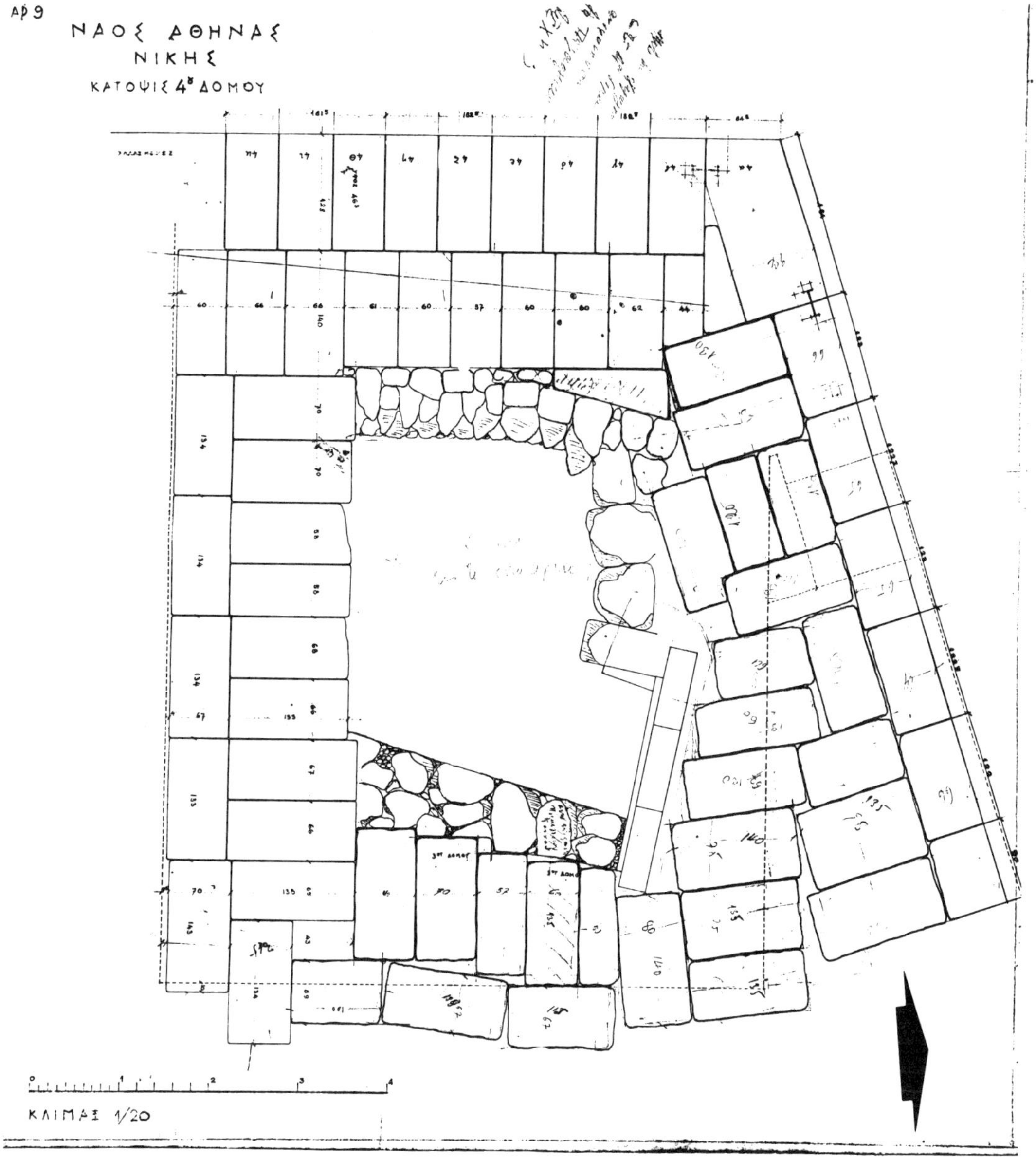

Balanos Archives: Course 4 of the foundations for the Nike Temple

Nike Bastion seen from the Pinakotheke

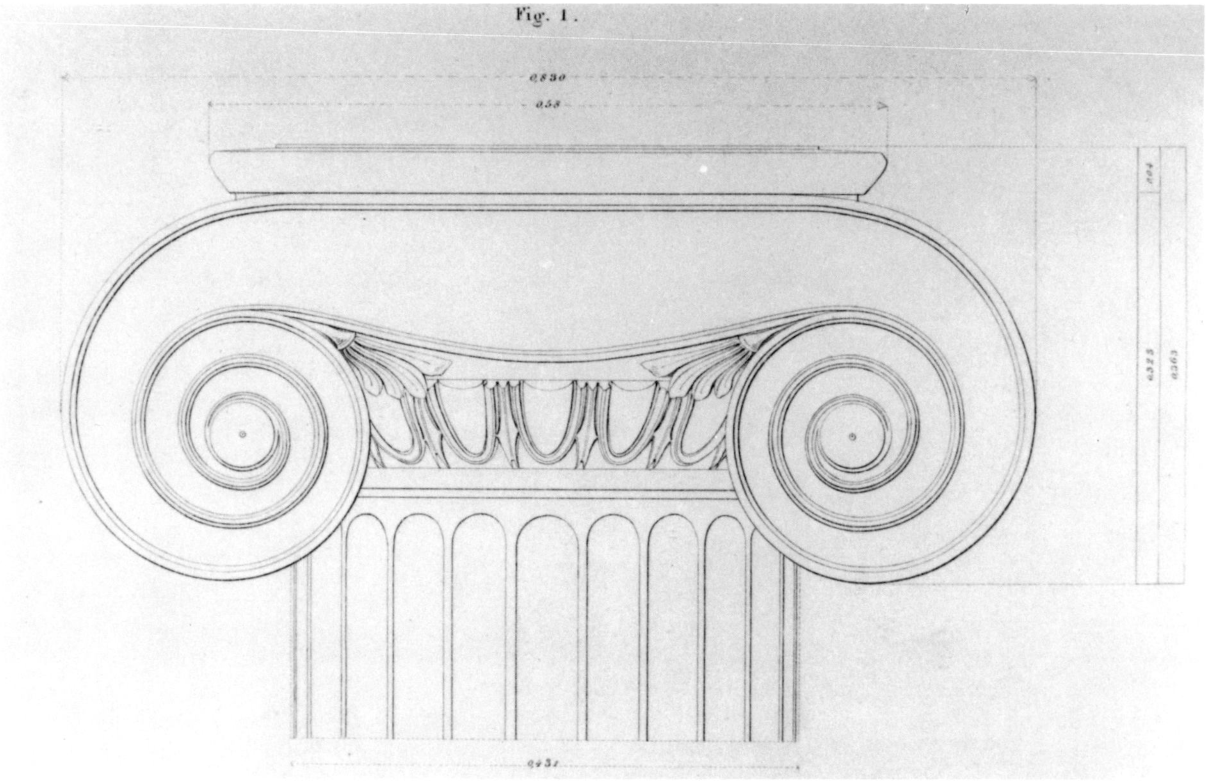

a. Ionic capital of the Nike Temple. Front view

b. Temple of Athena Nike. Detail of the northeast corner

a. East Frieze of the Nike Temple, Figures 8–14

b. Ionic capital and entablature of Nike Temple, including East Frieze Figures 17–24

a. Nike Parapet. Nikai conducting a bull to sacrifice, AcrM 972

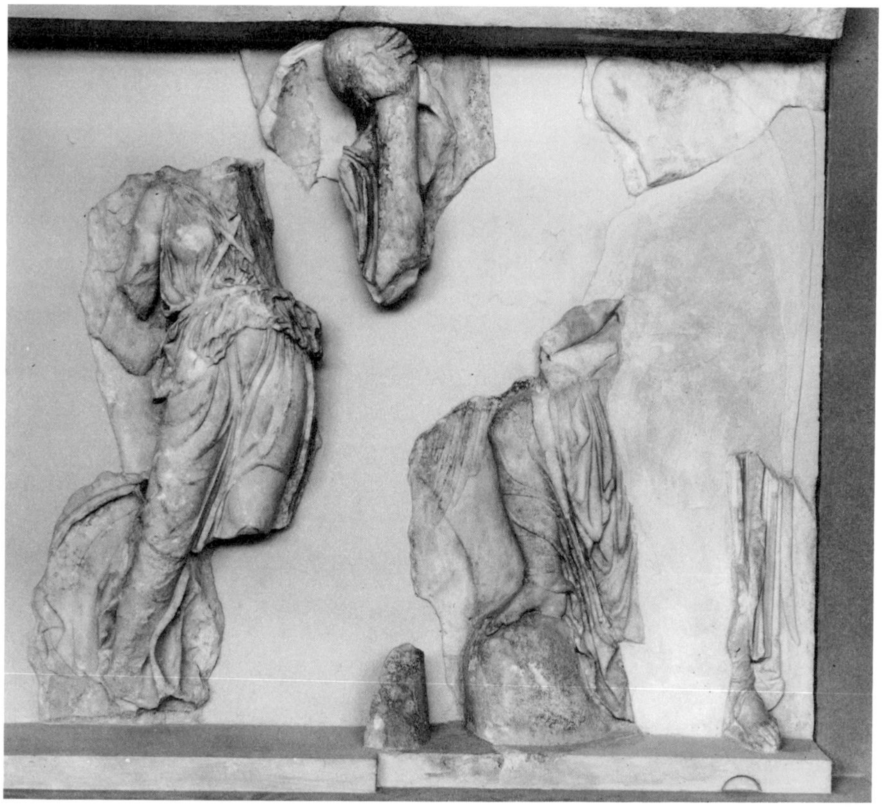

b. Nike Parapet. Fragments of Nikai erecting tropaia, AcrM 994

a. Nike Parapet. Nike adjusting her sandal, AcrM 973

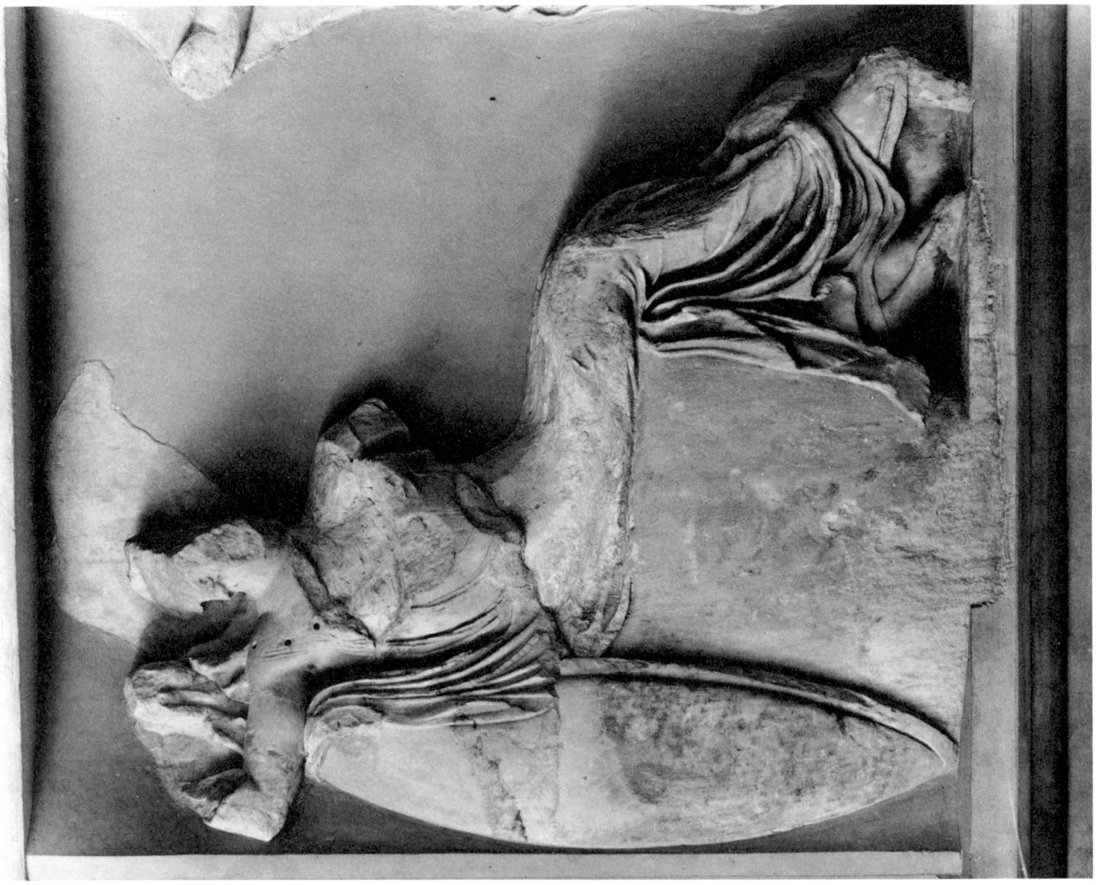

b. Nike Parapet. Athena Nike on a rock throne, AcrM 989

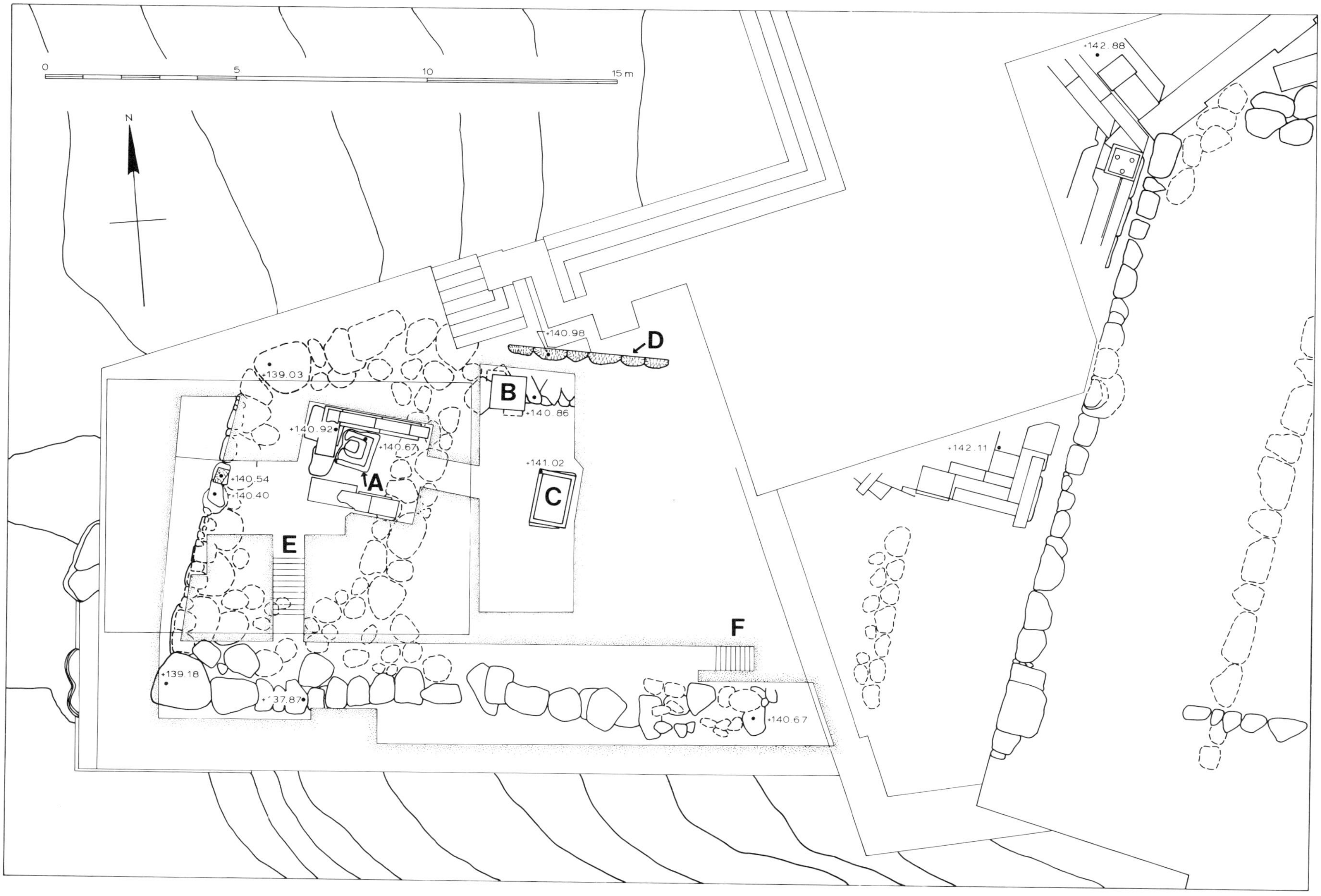

Actual-state plan of the early Nike Bastion and surroundings. (A) Poros repository, (B) Square Altar, (C) Rectangular Altar, (D) Irregular Trapezoidal Wall, (E) Modern Southeast Stairway, (F) Modern South Stairway